AWAKENING
BHARAT MATA

AWAKENING
BHARAT MATA

THE POLITICAL BELIEFS OF
THE INDIAN RIGHT

SWAPAN DASGUPTA

PENGUIN
VIKING

An imprint of Penguin Random House

VIKING

USA | Canada | UK | Ireland | Australia
New Zealand | India | South Africa | China | Singapore

Viking is part of the Penguin Random House group of companies
whose addresses can be found at global.penguinrandomhouse.com

Published by Penguin Random House India Pvt. Ltd
4th Floor, Capital Tower 1, MG Road,
Gurugram 122 002, Haryana, India

First published in Viking by Penguin Random House India 2019

10 9 8 7 6 5 4 3 2

ISBN 9780670091690

Typeset in Sabon by Manipal Digital Systems, Manipal
Printed at Replika Press Pvt. Ltd, India

www.penguin.co.in

This is a legitimate digitally printed version of the book and therefore might not
have certain extra finishing on the cover.

To my beloved Dadu
who lived his nationalism

Bande Mataram

Translated by Sri Aurobindo

Mother, I bow to thee!
Rich with thy hurrying streams,
Bright with thy orchard gleams,
Cool with thy winds of delight,
Dark fields waving, Mother of might,
Mother free.
Glory of moonlight dreams
Over thy branches and lordly streams, -
Clad in thy blossoming trees,
Mother, giver of ease,
Laughing low and sweet!
Mother, I kiss thy feet,
Speaker sweet and low!
Mother, to thee I bow.
Who hath said thou art weak in thy lands,
When the swords flash out in twice seventy million hands
And seventy million voices roar
Thy dreadful name from shore to shore?
With many strengths who art mighty and stored,
To thee I call, Mother and Lord!
Thou who savest, arise and save!
To her I cry who ever her foemen drave
Back from plain and sea
And shook herself free.

Thou art wisdom, thou art law,
Thou our heart, our soul, our breath,
Thou the love divine, the awe
In our hearts that conquers death.
Thine the strength that nerves the arm,
Thine the beauty, thine the charm.
Every image made divine
In our temples is but thine.

Thou art Durga, Lady and Queen,
With her hands that strike and her swords of sheen,
Thou art Lakshmi lotus-throned,
And the Muse a hundred-toned.
Pure and perfect without peer,
Mother, lend thine ear.
Rich with thy hurrying streams,
Bright with thy orchard gleams, Dark of hue, O candid-fair
In thy soul, with jewelled hair
And thy glorious smile divine,
Loveliest of all earthly lands,
Showering wealth from well-stored hands!
Mother, mother mine!
Mother sweet, I bow to thee,
Mother great and free!
I bow to thee, Mother,
richly-watered, richly-fruited,
cool with the winds of the south,
dark with the crops of the harvests,
the Mother!
Her nights rejoicing in the glory of the moonlight,
her lands clothed beautifully with her trees in flowering bloom,
sweet of laughter, sweet of speech,
the Mother, giver of boons, giver of bliss!

Terrible with the clamorous shout of seventy million throats,
and the sharpness of swords raised in twice seventy million
hands,
who sayeth to thee, Mother, that thou art weak?
Holder of multitudinous strength,
I bow to her who saves,
to her who drives from her the armies of her foemen,
the Mother!

Thou art knowledge, thou art conduct,
thou our heart, thou our soul,
for thou art the life in our body.
In the arm thou art might, O Mother,
in the heart, O Mother, thou art love and faith,
it is thy image we raise in every temple.

For thou art Durga holding her ten weapons of war,
Kamala at play in the lotuses
and Speech, the goddess, giver of all lore,
to thee I bow!
I bow to thee, goddess of wealth,
pure and peerless,
richly-watered, richly-fruited,
the Mother!
I bow to thee, Mother,
dark-hued, candid,
sweetly smiling, jewelled and adorned,
the holder of wealth, the lady of plenty,
the Mother!

Contents

Part II: History

Part III: Fault Lines

Preface

In 1991, *The Economist* report on India's general election was curiously entitled 'The winner came second'. The reference was to the Bharatiya Janata Party (BJP) which emerged as the main opposition to the Congress after a spirited campaign that centred on the demand to build a temple at the birthplace of Lord Ram—the central figure of the Hindu epic Ramayana—on the site of a sixteenth-century mosque in the town of Ayodhya. It was the Ayodhya campaign that set the terms of a political discourse that has persisted in one form or another till today.

Ostensibly, the demand was for a grand temple to be built on a site where an ancient Hindu temple had apparently once been demolished by invaders. In reality, the temple movement was a metaphor for larger questions on Indian nationhood, questions that had only been partially resolved after Independence in 1947. It is not that these issues hadn't been addressed earlier, during the struggle for freedom from British rule. The Ayodhya movement, invoking the historicity and sacredness of Lord Ram, rekindled some of those debates and, more importantly, gave them a popular connect.

The 1991 general election, preceded by a spectacular mobilization in northern and western India, was Hindu nationalism—hitherto considered a relatively marginal phenomenon in Indian politics—coming of age. On 6 December 1992, the disputed Babri Masjid was razed to the ground by a huge gathering that perceived the shrine as a symbol of 'national humiliation' and 'shame'. It was one of the defining moments of post-Independence India.

The emergence of the BJP was much more than an ordinary electoral phenomenon: it forced Indians to choose between two contrasting views of nationhood. On one hand, there were those who saw modern India in terms of secular republicanism, while on the other, those who sought to blend technological modernity with the country's Hindu inheritance. The BJP's rise, and the debates that accompanied the phenomenon, anticipated many of the concerns that find reflection today in the United States and Europe.

The rise of Hindu nationalism was also a profound intellectual challenge to the loose left-liberal consensus that had prevailed in India since Jawaharlal Nehru became prime minister in 1947. In 2014, after Narendra Modi won for the BJP a majority on its own, the challenge became sharper as large sections of the old establishment lost their pre-eminence and positions of authority. Consequently, there were accusations that the face of India was being changed unrecognizably by an assertive Hindutva movement.

Since the Ayodhya movement began, both the idea of Hindutva and the political character of the BJP have been scrutinized by scholars, usually with scepticism and even outright hostility. Consequently, there has been an inclination to view India's right-wing politics as either a variant of fascism or merely a collection of sectarian prejudices. The centres of intellectual power—notably academia and the media—have been particularly hostile to the BJP and those identified with it, an opposition that varies between condescension and shrill disavowal.

The inspiration for the right in India has come from multiple and, often, contradictory sources. The proprietorship of Hindutva does not, for instance, belong to Veer Savarkar, although his contribution is seminal. The Rashtriya Swayamsevak Sangh (RSS) too deserves serious attention, not merely for the influence it exercises on the BJP leadership, but for its approach to the larger question of national regeneration. Equally important is the influence of individuals such as Bankimchandra Chattopadhyay, Swami Vivekananda and Sri Aurobindo, not to mention the Arya Samaj movement.

This collection is an attempt to showcase the phenomenon of Hindu nationalism from a sympathetic position. I believe it is important to understand the phenomenon not only from the perspective of its critics but also in terms of how it perceives itself. There has, for example, been an accusation that Hindu nationalism is singularly detached from the freedom struggle. I have tried to show that many of the concerns that drive the Indian right are located in the country's nationalist culture, particularly at a time when it wasn't politically incorrect to use the expression Hindu. Equally, the smug contention that the impulses driving the BJP are based on the rantings of provincial pamphleteers and outlandish conspiracy theories has been contested. The Ayodhya movement in particular went far beyond the rabble-rousing speeches of sadhus and sadhvis and put the 'political' Hindu in focus. It also touched on India's reading of its own history, a revisionism that had its roots in pre-Marxist historiography.

In the course of the introductory essay and the collection of readings that accompany it, I have attempted to locate some of the ideas, attitudes and beliefs that define the Indian right. I have also sought to identify the nature of Indian conservatism and identify its similarities and differences with political thought in the West. The emphasis hasn't always been on the Modi appeal—which also incorporates issues of governance that are shaped more by pragmatic and managerial concerns than by ideology—but on the themes that motivate and drive the BJP core.

This book is not about Hindu nationalism in power, but as a social and political movement. I hope it will encourage a more informed understanding of a phenomenon that will remain relevant in Indian life far beyond victories and defeats in elections.

Swapan Dasgupta
New Delhi, March 2019

1

The Political Context

Till the turn of the century, the counting of votes in an Indian general election was a prolonged three-day affair. Since the electronic voting machines (EVM) were introduced nationally, the tense wait for an outcome has been reduced to barely three or four hours.

On the morning of 16 May 2014, it was clear to most Indians that the United Progressive Alliance (UPA) headed by the Congress that had governed the country since May 2004 was staring at certain defeat. In constituency after constituency there were reports of listless Congress campaigns and a mood of demoralization among supporters of a party that had governed India for the most part since Independence in 1947.

The dejection in the ranks of the Congress owed to two factors. First, over the past eighteen months or so, the UPA government had been relentlessly hammered on account of corruption scandals. Whether it was the allotment of leases for coal mining, the mismanagement of the Commonwealth Games in Delhi or the auction of spectrum for the telecommunications industry, the government had been dogged by grave charges of pilferage and cronyism. The government was further shaken by a movement against corruption led by Anna Hazare, a venerable Gandhian from Maharashtra. Prime Minister Manmohan Singh was a respected economist who, as finance minister in the government headed by P.V. Narasimha Rao, had boldly departed from the decrepit licence-permit-quota raj and ushered a period of high economic growth. But he was also viewed as an ineffective and weak leader, unable to resist pressures from venal coalition partners and manage conflicting pulls within his own Congress party.

Secondly, the Congress had always banked on a member of the Nehru–Gandhi family to both keep the fractious organization together and secure votes. Ever since Indira Gandhi transformed it into an appendage of her family in 1969, the principle of dynastic loyalty had come to define the party that had led the freedom struggle against British rule.

For the 2014 election, the Congress pinned its hopes on Rahul Gandhi, the son of Rajiv and Sonia Gandhi and the grandson of Indira Gandhi. Although Rahul had entered Parliament in 2004, winning his father's old parliamentary seat of Amethi in Uttar Pradesh, his involvement in politics was never wholehearted. In a country where political leadership involved a daily commitment, no holidays and unending engagement with party workers at all levels, Rahul's aloofness was interpreted to mean that he lacked either commitment or had no fire in his belly. He was also seen to be riddled with a sense of entitlement, perhaps a natural consequence of having lived in a durbar-like environment in New Delhi's Lutyens zone all his life.

To cap it all, Rahul was unable to shake off the tag that he was both slow and clueless about the complexities of India. At the start of the general election campaign, Rahul gave an interview to Arnab Goswami, the pugnacious anchor of the English-language channel Times Now. The interview was an unqualified disaster with Rahul parroting set phrases and seeming totally out of sorts. It would not be an exaggeration to suggest that after the interview, Rahul became a laughing stock, at least to India's middle classes that often set the terms of the political debate. The extent of demoralization this interview had on an already dispirited Congress was incalculable. While individual leaders fought doggedly to hold on to their turf, the party, as a whole, faced voters rudderless and leaderless. The election increasingly became 'plebiscitory' in character 'goading people to make a choice between two brands of leadership: Narendra Modi as a successful chief minister of "a model state" on the one hand and Rahul Gandhi as a leader who had yet to establish his political and administrative credentials'.[1]

By 11 a.m., that hot Friday morning in May, it was all over. That the Congress and its coalition partners had been routed was clear. The only remaining question was whether the challenger, the Gujarat chief minister Narendra Modi, the prime ministerial candidate of the Bharatiya Janata Party (BJP) and the National Democratic Alliance (NDA), would muster a clear majority. The fear among the BJP's supporters and the hope of its opponents was that a clear mandate would somehow elude Modi, leaving the field open for another messy bout of coalition building, an exercise that invariably exposed the dark underbelly of Indian politics.

In 2014, the Indian electorate gave a decisive verdict, more emphatic than even the most optimistic of Modi's supporters ever expected: the NDA coasted to a clear victory. More important, however, was the BJP's ability to win a majority on its own. For the first time since Rajiv Gandhi swept the board in the general election of 1984, no party had crossed the 272 mark in the Lok Sabha. There would be a coalition government, since the BJP had fought under the NDA umbrella, but a coalition that would not have to experience the pulls and pressures of blackmail and sectional demands—a recurrent feature of the past twenty-five years.

With the benefit of hindsight, political analysts attributed the BJP's victory to a 'Modi wave' that had engulfed northern, central and western India. The BJP maximized its tally in the states where it was traditionally strong, winning 190 of the 225 Lok Sabha seats in the Hindi-speaking states. In addition, 92 of the 318 seats it picked up from the rest of the country gave it the incremental tally to get past the majority mark. In the past, the best performance of the BJP had been 181 seats in the 1999 elections when it was led by Atal Bihari Vajpayee. In 2014, it secured 101 more seats, a truly impressive feat for which the credit went entirely to Modi.

That Modi exercised a huge charismatic appeal which translated into votes isn't in any doubt. Basing their findings on post-poll surveys, Pradeep Chibber and Rahul Verma have concluded that the BJP 'built an unprecedented social coalition of upper castes, with many OBCs [Other Backward Classes], Scheduled Castes and Scheduled Tribes voting for it as well . . . [The] party successfully capitalised on an ideological divide present in Indian society drawing support from both social conservatives and the economic right.'[2] This social coalition, of course, had the BJP's traditional following as its core, but just as the BJP had hoped when it anointed him the party's prime ministerial candidate in September 2013, it was given a huge booster dose by Modi.

There were sharply divergent perceptions of Modi in the electorate. He was seen by some as a Hindu *Hridaysamrat*, the modern-day Shivaji, an image that was bolstered by the feeling that he stood by the Hindus of Gujarat in the aftermath of the 2002 communal riots; to others he was the chaiwala's (tea seller's) son made good, a man who would be India's first backward caste prime minister; and finally, to others he was the great modernizer, a deft administrator who was not only committed to rapid economic growth but was also personally incorruptible.

It is rare for all the ingredients of a successful social coalition to be encapsulated in the personality of an individual. To this was added his ethical virtues: an austere lifestyle, total detachment from all family ties, and a reputation for total incorruptibility. Modi managed this heady cocktail. His formidable communication skills, a well-managed and imaginative publicity campaign, and a team of motivated volunteers and functionaries also helped in converting support into euphoria. It was not merely BJP and

Rashtriya Swayamsevak Sangh (RSS) volunteers that were out contacting voters, organizing meetings, and manning the polling booths. The Modi campaign benefitted immeasurably from the organized participation of the Hindu religious sects and their countless devotees and volunteers driven by a single-minded dedication to meaningful and positive change.

Yet, the harsh truth is that the scale of the victory was unanticipated. Future historians examining contemporary media reports will be struck by the overall scepticism of the analysts, particularly those writing in English, at Modi's prospects. It was confidently reported by a large section of the media[3] that there was no evidence of any wave and that even contiguous constituencies were indicating divergent trends—with caste being the governing factor—suggesting the absence of any overriding theme.

The scepticism was even more marked in quasi-academic assessments. The belief that the BJP was principally a party of the upper castes and traders still held sway. That Modi was himself from a backward caste was severely discounted, as was the BJP's impressive track record of mobilizing the rural middle castes during the Ayodhya movement. Finally, it was held that Modi's ability to influence voters in non-Hindi-speaking states, particularly south of the Vindhyas, was extremely limited. Even when it seemed that the Modi campaign was acquiring momentum, a large body of punditry believed that the BJP would find it extremely difficult to cross 220 Lok Sabha seats. It was suggested that in the messy business of crafting a post-election coalition, the smaller parties would be able to pressure the BJP into selecting a less 'polarizing' leader than Modi.[4]

Among the principal reasons why the prospects of a Modi victory were discounted was the consistent hostility of India's intellectual elite to saffron politics. In the initial decades after Independence when the Bharatiya Jana Sangh (the precursor of the BJP) was a fringe player in a Congress-dominated polity, the wariness was often aesthetic. The novelist Paul Scott captured this

disdain through the patrician Lady Lily Chatterjee's description
of Hindu nationalism:

> . . . Hindu did not mean Congress. No, no. Please be aware
> of the distinction . . . Hindu meant Hindu Mahasabha. Hindu
> nationalism. Hindu narrowness. It meant rich banias with
> little education, landowners who spoke worse English than the
> youngest English sub-divisional officer his eager but halting
> Hindi. It meant sitting without shoes and with your feet curled
> up on the chair, eating only horrible vegetarian dishes and
> drinking disgusting fruit juice.[5]

After Independence, many of these attitudes were transferred
to the durbar of India's first prime minister, Jawaharlal Nehru.
In a candid account of the Nehru years, Australian diplomat
Walter Crocker echoed the cosmopolitan disavowal of the
non-westernized politician in the Congress: 'Most of Nehru's
ministers, like most of the party caucus, were provincial
mediocrities, untravelled, ill-educated, narrow-minded; not
a few were lazy; some were cow worshippers and devotees of
ayurvedic medicine and astrology; some were dishonest.'[6]

Based on his interactions, Crocker listed 'Hinduism'—along
with maharajas, Portugal, moneylenders, certain American
ways, and whites in Africa—among Nehru's pet prejudices.[7] So
intense was Nehru's distaste for what he used to call the 'RSS
mentality' that he even subordinated the challenge posed by the
communist parties to the more pressing battle against 'Hindu
right-wing communalism'.[8]

The dismissive distaste of all politics that encapsulated the
Hindu ethos became more and more marked as the stranglehold
of the Congress began to weaken after 1967. In an essay published
that year, after the Jana Sangh emerged as a force in north India
in the wake of the pro-Hindi and anti-cow-slaughter agitations,
the writer Nirad C. Chaudhuri observed that 'the alienation
between the new intelligentsia and the traditional Hindu middle

class is virtually complete' with the traditionalists viewing the 'Westernised type of Indian only as a renegade or usurper'.[9] The cosmopolitan elite's incomprehension of the impulses that motivated the social conservatives—who combined an outward show of modernity with discomfort with the intellectual and social mores of westernization—became even more marked after the Ayodhya movement for a temple to be built at the birthplace of the Hindu god Ram acquired a mass dimension.

During the Jayaprakash Narayan–led movement (1973–75) against Indira Gandhi's government and the patchy struggle against the Emergency (1975–77), a host of non-Congress parties, including Lohia-ite socialists, Gandhians, free-market liberals, and even a section of the communist movement, were willing to rub shoulders with the 'Hindu right'. This was partly because those associated with the RSS and the Jana Sangh provided a ready pool of disciplined volunteers. However, after the collapse of the Janata Party government over the dual membership issue—the right of Janata Party members to be simultaneously associated with the RSS—the tendency to treat the Hindu right as political untouchables became quite pronounced. Even the nominal leadership of the genial Vajpayee—once described as the 'right man in the wrong party'—didn't make the newly formed BJP any more respectable. 'I don't know,' confessed communist member of Parliament (MP) Somnath Chatterjee whose father, incidentally, was a stalwart of the Hindu Mahasabha, 'what attracts people to the BJP.'[10] Chatterjee was echoing the bewilderment of Indians who saw themselves as modern, rational and open-minded to this antediluvian phenomenon.

In political terms, the Ayodhya movement and particularly L.K. Advani's rath yatra in 1990 from the Somnath temple in Gujarat was a watershed. From being a relatively small and well-knit political party with a disproportionate urban presence, the BJP was catapulted into the status of a mass party. Despite the fear that the electoral arithmetic was loaded against a party that dared to fight without alliances, the BJP emerged as the principal opposition to the Congress, winning 121 Lok Sabha seats and securing a majority in the Uttar Pradesh Legislative Assembly, in the 1991 general election. Its national tally may well have been nearer the 150-seat mark had the sympathy generated by Rajiv Gandhi's tragic assassination just prior to the later phases of voting not given the Congress performance a boost.

The 1991 election was significant in two respects.

First, the election witnessed the decimation of the Congress in the two crucial Hindi-speaking states of Uttar Pradesh and Bihar. Its combined tally fell from 131 of the 136 seats in 1984 to just six in 1991. It was a defeat from which the party has not recovered to date. Consequently, while the Congress could conceivably hope to remain the principal party by virtue of its clout in Maharashtra and the southern states (minus Tamil Nadu that had been yielded to the Dravidian parties in 1971), its chances of re-emerging as the dominant party, capable of winning a majority on its own, were permanently dashed.

Secondly, the 1991 election established the BJP as the alternative pole of Indian politics. Earlier, the tussle for the anti-Congress space had involved an uneasy coalition of the Hindu right, the fractured socialist parties inspired by Ram Manohar Lohia, the communist parties, and regional forces—mainly breakaways from the Congress. After 1991, the politics of anti-Congressism came to be unsettled by a new polarization involving the BJP and those viscerally opposed to it. While the BJP invoked nationalism, its opponents called for the unity of 'secular forces'. This binary became a defining feature of Indian politics after the BJP overtook the Congress in the Lok Sabha in the general election of 1996. Of the six general elections from 1996, the BJP has emerged as the largest party in four (1996, 1998, 1999, and 2014) and the Congress in two (2004 and 2009).

The growing political prominence of the BJP did not, however, lead to the emergence of an alternative intellectual ecosystem. During the freedom struggle, there was a strong nationalist tradition linked to Lokmanya Tilak and, subsequently, the

Hindu Mahasabha and Vinayak Damodar Savarkar. However, this variant of Hindu nationalism suffered a grievous blow following its association with the assassination of Mahatma Gandhi in 1948. The nucleus of the tradition—with significant modifications—was kept alive by individuals in the RSS and political stalwarts such as Shyama Prasad Mookerjee. However, confronted with the heady modernist vision proffered by Nehru, its impact was marginal. From Independence till the beginning of the 1990s, it was the broad Nehruvian consensus—based on the three pillars of secularism, socialism and non-alignment—that dominated political discourse. There were occasional challenges from both the right—apart from the Hindu right it included C. Rajagopalachari and the Swatantra Party—and the left. But these were mere ripples on the surface that left the hegemonic status of the consensus broadly intact. There was also a significant ideological cross-fertilization between the Congress and the left, especially those associated with the pro-Moscow Communist Party of India (CPI).

It is astonishing that the sheer scale of the 'Modi wave' remained undetected till the morning of 16 May 2014. This wasn't because the voters were uncharacteristically silent—as they were during the 1977 general election that turned out to be a referendum on Indira Gandhi's Emergency. Despite the scorching summer heat, Modi drew huge crowds at all his public meetings. More important, the BJP campaign was energetic and enthusiastic, features that were lacking in the Congress approach. Yet, a section of analysts chose to be in denial because they had already made up their mind that a Modi-led government was both unacceptable and detrimental to the country.[11]

At the heart of the apprehension was Modi's conduct during the Gujarat riots of March 2002 that followed the arson attack on a railway carriage carrying Hindu activists from the temple town of Ayodhya. In a letter to *The Guardian* on 10 April 2014, coinciding with the initial rounds of voting, a clutch of prominent public figures with strong India links including Salman Rushdie, Anish Kapoor, John McDonnell, Helena Kennedy, Deepa Mehta and Homi Bhabha wrote:

> Without questioning the validity of India's democratic election process, it is crucial to remember the role played by the Modi government in the horrifying events that took place in Gujarat in 2002. The Muslim minority were overwhelmingly the victims of pillage, murder and terror, resulting in the deaths of more than 2,000 men, women and children . . . Modi himself repeatedly refuses to accept any responsibility or to render an apology. Such a failure of moral character and political ethics on the part of Modi is incompatible with India's secular Constitution, which, in advance of many constitutions across the world, is founded on pluralist principles and seeks fair and full representation for minorities. Were he to be elected prime minister, it would bode ill for India's future as a country that cherishes the ideals of inclusion and protection for all its peoples and communities.[12]

In an unusual step, *The Economist* recommended that Indians should vote for the Congress because of Modi's lack of contrition over the riots that took place under his charge:

> If Mr Modi were to explain his role in the violence and show genuine remorse, we would consider backing him, but he never has; it would be wrong for a man who has thrived on division to become prime minister of a country as fissile as India. We do not find the prospect of a government led by Congress under Mr Gandhi an inspiring one. But we have to recommend it to Indians as the less disturbing option. If Congress wins, which is unlikely, it must strive to renew itself and to reform India . . . If, more probably, victory goes to the BJP, its coalition partners should hold out for a prime minister other than Mr Modi.[13]

This anyone-but-Modi approach saw his opponents even pin their hopes on L.K. Advani emerging as the consensual choice in the event the BJP and its allies fell short of an outright majority. In earlier elections, Advani had been pilloried by people of similar persuasion for being the architect of the Hindu mobilization that led to the demolition of the disputed sixteenth-century Mughal shrine in Ayodhya on 6 December 1992.

In the final phase of the campaign, the Congress and other opponents of Modi shifted their focus from bread-and-butter governance issues to a deliberation on the 'idea of India'. In an interview to *The Hindu* published on 26 April 2014, Rahul Gandhi asserted:

> We are now faced with a contest between two competing ideas of India. The Congress' idea of India is about inclusion, decentralisation, empowering people, and building partnerships for economic growth. The Opposition's idea seeks to divide the country on communal lines, capture resources for a select few, and centralise decision-making by putting all power into the hands of one individual. Our opponents want an India in which there is no place for the poor, no place for those with a different religion or ideology. This is a dangerous idea. It has been the proud legacy of the Congress party to fight and defeat this idea since the birth of our nation.[14]

The Congress president has reverted to the theme subsequently, as have those positing the virtues of 'Constitutional morality' and 'Constitutional patriotism' over attempts to attach Hindutva to nationhood. Delineating what would become the ideological battle over the entire period between the 2014 and 2019 general elections, a group of intellectuals (including, among others, Girish Karnad, Indira Jaisingh, Mahesh Bhatt, Romila Thapar, Nayantara Sahgal, and Githa Hariharan) disturbed by Modi's emphatic victory convened a conference on the 'Idea of India' in July 2014. The theme of the conference echoed the concerns voiced by the Congress during the general election and subsequently:

> Central to our idea of India is the affirmation of its diversity. The India we are part of belongs equally to all persons who make it its own—no matter what their religious faith (or the lack of it), their gender, caste, class, language, physical abilities, and sexual orientation. The bedrock of the Indian republic is the promise that all its citizens can find space in which to practise their beliefs and cultures, and live freely, confident they will be equally protected by the law of the land.
>
> This inclusive idea of India was stressed by Dr Ambedkar as the essential democratic idea of fraternity. This larger idea of fraternity or social solidarity also leads to the idea of the good state as one which defends the oppressed and disadvantaged, and ensures their access to basic rights necessary for a life with dignity.
>
> Unfortunately, not everyone shares this idea of India. There is another idea of India, an idea of majoritarian domination, which is alien to the social and political philosophy on which this country was built and consolidated.
>
> This is what this other idea of India leads to. Riots, polarisation. The pulling back of the state from public expenditure on health, education, and nutrition in favour of large subsidies to the private sector, weakening of labour and environmental protections, and the theft of natural resources in the name of development. And to enable all of this, a curbing of freedom so people can be told what to think, read, write, say, paint.[15]

It is significant that in addition to the defence of the Constitution, the opponents of Modi sought to twin the culture wars with a battle to maintain the primacy of the state in the economic life of the country. In short, the targets included not merely the Hindu right but the pro-market right as well. The entire Nehruvian consensus was sought to be resurrected as the alternative to the forces that had nurtured the spectacular rise of Modi.

The belief that the advent of a BJP-led government would inevitably lead to a wholesale transformation of India, including the disfigurement of the Constitution and the subversion of existing institutions, is a key feature of the 'liberal' narrative. Under the Modi dispensation, when the BJP commands an absolute majority in the Lok Sabha and controls more state governments than ever before, the attacks against right-wing subversion have become sharper and to the point where the term 'fascism' is bandied about generously. Shrill charges of transforming the very nature of the Republic were also made against the Vajpayee government, particularly when he appointed an innocuous committee of notables to suggest which aspects of the Constitution could do with a relook. However, since the first NDA government was a coalition where no party had a clear majority, the voices of shrill indignation did not always carry the same political weight. The only possible exceptions were the outrage over the gruesome murder of Christian missionary Graham Staines and his young sons in a remote corner of Orissa in 1999 and the Gujarat riots of 2002.

Under Modi, however, the anger has become visceral—fuelled, no doubt, by the growing popularity of social media, a convenient platform that revels in instant indignation. The sporadic incidents of anti-beef vigilantism by extremist Hindu groups, including the lynching of some Muslims suspected of either possessing or trading in beef, contributed to a grand show of solidarity by the anti-Modi intellectuals. The charges of growing intolerance and shrinking space for dissent—triggered by the murder of two 'rationalist' writers in Maharashtra—led to as many as forty writers and artistes returning awards that had been given to them at various times by governments past and present.[16]

The 'award wapsi' movement of 2015 and the 'Not in My Name' protests of 2017 were largely confined to the liberal

intelligentsia and activists associated with NGOs who felt
threatened by government restrictions on foreign funding. But
although their direct political impact within India was nominal,
the protests had a visible impact on the projection of both Modi
and his government overseas.

Modi's relationship with the English language media, and
particularly the foreign media, had always been awkward. After
the revolt of the intellectuals, the relationship became positively
hostile. The tendency to compare Modi with the likes of President
Erdoğan of Turkey, Prime Minister Viktor Orbán of Hungary, and
even President Vladimir Putin of Russia became more pronounced.
At a time when the Modi government was active in projecting
its transformational role in the economy and wooing foreign
investments, the wave of adverse publicity was a significant irritant.

The sharply divergent personalities of Vajpayee and Modi
also contributed to the quantum of polarization. Vajpayee was
a fixture of parliamentary politics since he first entered the Lok
Sabha in 1957. An accomplished orator who had a way with
words, he commanded a very high measure of personal respect
that cut across the political divide. He had served as minister of
external affairs in the short-lived Janata Party government of
Morarji Desai (1977–79) and his tenure had been marked by
continuity rather than radical change. He was in every respect
a Delhi insider with whom the existing establishment was
comfortable. During the Ayodhya agitation, Vajpayee had never
made any secret of his misgivings over the BJP taking up cudgels
for a movement that often obliterated the divide between political
and religious mobilization. It was often felt that his commitment
to the BJP that emerged after the electoral debacle of 1984 was
based more on corporate loyalty than ideological convergence.
His idea of the BJP was more in the nature of a broad anti-
Congress church than a party wedded to ideological certitudes.
Indeed, Vajpayee never thought of the political movement he
was associated with as right-wing. Writing in 1973, he described
the Jana Sangh a 'centrist party' that 'has been subjected to

attacks from both the extreme right as well as the extreme Left'. Protagonists of complete freedom in the economic sphere have assailed it being worse than communists. On the other hand, in the eyes of the so-called progressives, the Jana Sangh has been a reactionary party and a defender of vested interests.[17]

In May 1979, at the height of the crisis over dual membership, Vajpayee appeared only too willing to retreat from the more distinctive facets of the Jana Sangh: 'We have left the politics of Jana Sangh far behind. We should forget these things now and . . . participate . . . in only the nationalist stream of the Janata Party based upon the four principles of nationalism, democracy, religious equality and social equality.'[18]

Nor was this a heretical assertion. When the BJP was formed in 1980, it saw itself as a wholesome version of the Janata Party whose members also had the right to maintain their associations with the socio-cultural programmes of the RSS. It sought to distance itself from the perception that it was either the political extension counter of the RSS or a rigidly ideological party. In a move that was uneasily accepted, it put 'Gandhian socialism' among its defining principles. In a revealing interview to *Panchjanya* in late 1980, L.K. Advani was clear that 'in India, a party based on ideology can at the most come to power in a small area. It cannot win the confidence of the entire country— neither the Communist Party nor the Jana Sangh in its original form'.[19]

Prior to the 1996 general election when the BJP felt it had a strong chance of unseating the Congress government led by P.V. Narasimha Rao, Advani unilaterally announced that Vajpayee would be the party's prime ministerial candidate. His decision was centred on the calculation that the BJP had reached the limits of Hindu nationalist consolidation and that to win it must secure a large chunk of incremental votes, not to mention regional allies. In his view, only Vajpayee, among BJP leaders, had the necessary cross-party appeal to add to the assured Hindu nationalist support.

It was a shrewd move. Although the Vajpayee-led government lasted for a mere thirteen days in the face of a huge 'secular' gang-up in 1996, the BJP's positioning and Vajpayee's leadership saw many regional parties, including the Biju Janata Dal in Odisha, the Trinamool Congress in West Bengal and the All India Anna Dravida Munnetra Kazhagam (AIADMK) in Tamil Nadu, forge alliances with the BJP subsequently. By the time the United Front government collapsed in 1998, Vajpayee had become the obvious prime minister-in-waiting.

From 1996 till he lost the general election in 2004 and gently faded out of public life, Vajpayee sought to dispel the impression that the BJP only stood for an aggressive advocacy of India's Hindu identity. In tune with the concerns of the pro-market right, he persisted with the liberalization programme initiated by the Narasimha Rao government and haltingly continued by the shaky United Front governments of H.D. Deve Gowda and I.K. Gujral. Most notable was his programme of privatization of non-strategic public sector units, particularly hotels and even a bakery. A separate department of disinvestment was established and entrusted to ministers with definite private sector bias.

In political terms, privatization—as opposed to piecemeal divestment of the government's shareholding—was a huge shift. It directly assaulted the Nehruvian understanding, confined not merely to the Congress and the communist parties, that the state must occupy the 'commanding heights' of the economy. Unlike earlier governments, Vajpayee's administration focused principally on upgrading India's creaking infrastructure and promoting private sector investment, both foreign and domestic. In a big shift to the right, the focus on welfare programmes, although never abandoned, was significantly diluted. It is interesting that this shift, while obviously raising the hackles of the Congress and the left, also offended a significant section of the RSS fraternity. The Swadeshi Jagran Manch, ostensibly promoting the interests of medium and small businesses and the Bharatiya Mazdoor Sangh, a large trade union body linked to the RSS, were particularly vitriolic in their attacks on the government for apparently 'selling out' to multinationals.[20]

More than anything else, this opposition from within the parivar (family) clearly indicated that the divide between the pro-market right and the Hindu right—apparent in the very different appeals of the Swatantra Party and the Jana Sangh in the 1960s—was very much alive. Unlike the Swatantra Party which was never shy of its clear identification with business interests, the consensus within the BJP–RSS ecosystem was against any over-reliance on the market. This approach was summed up by Vajpayee in 1973:

> On economic issues, the Jana Sangh approach right from the outset has been based on pragmatic considerations and not on dogma. It rejected both complete nationalisation as well as free enterprise and favoured a middle course. It advocated nationalisation of defence industries but in respect of other industries suggested an approach which under overall state regulation, 'encouraged private enterprise to expand in the interests of consumers and producers alike'. The three-pronged approach—growth in production, equity in distribution, and restraint in consumption—commended by the Jana Sangh in 1951, is as valid today as it was then.[21]

In taking stands on economic issues, the BJP was traditionally guided by its core support base of traders, small and medium business, and the salaried middle classes. It always sought a balance between the interests of all the groups and often ended up being extremely tentative. It was suspicious of an over-intrusive state and favoured low taxes, but it favoured state protection against foreign multinationals and a welfare cushion. It was never enthused by the so-called neo-liberal agenda associated with Margaret Thatcher.

What really defined the BJP was its commitment to robust nationalism and a belief in a strong India. This is also what linked Vajpayee to his party. Among the first major acts of the Vajpayee government was the nuclear tests in May 1998 that offended the West but endeared the prime minister to his support base. For India's right, national security was always the big priority, as was an aggressive, no-nonsense stand against Pakistan. Vajpayee's bid to forge a peace settlement with Pakistan in February 1999 was hesitantly lauded, despite his Minar-e-Pakistan speech which amounted to formally repudiating the commitment to an Akhand Bharat (undivided India) and undoing Partition—an article of faith for the early Jana Sangh. However, when that initiative failed, India's right nationalists enthusiastically supported the government's tough response to Pakistan's military incursions in the Kargil sector of Jammu and Kashmir. Likewise, there was absolutely no hesitation in the movement's enthusiasm over the military mobilization that followed the terrorist attack on Parliament House on 13 December 2001. Although the mobilization didn't lead to another armed conflict with Pakistan, it, along with the enactment of tough anti-terror legislation, established the BJP's credentials as a party unequivocally committed to maintaining national security at all costs and despite all international pressures. This approach distinguished the Indian right from its political competitors.

The second feature that distinguished the Vajpayee government from regimes in the past was its positions on education and culture. These were subjects that, much more than the economy, obsessed the RSS. They were also of paramount interest to a BJP that defined Indian nationhood in terms of cultural nationalism.

Vajpayee appointed Murli Manohar Joshi, a former president of the party and a physicist who had trained under the redoubtable Meghnad Saha, as minister of human resources development, an umbrella ministry whose responsibilities extended to education. Joshi attached a great deal of importance to winning the 'ideological' war against the Nehruvians and

Marxists. On assuming charge, he is said to have remarked 'It's our turn now,' implying that he would quite proactively seek to tackle the distortions that had crept into education.[22]

The crusade against distortions in the teaching of history was a major concern of Joshi. He believed that it was the overwhelming Marxist influence in the history departments, an influence that filtered down to school textbooks, that was responsible for both distorting the past and undermining contemporary nationhood:

> No country would or should allow the distortion of its history. The fragmentation of Indian society has taken place because the Leftist historians have been saying that India is not a nation. Since the new facts demolish their theories, they are scared. Their entire edifice of calling themselves eminent historians . . . the sheen of that eminence is completely over . . . These historians all along have been adopting a Goebbelsian technique that if you keep repeating a lie thousand times it will become the truth.[23]

Always forthright with his views, Joshi effected a drastic overhaul of the Indian Council of Historical Research and commissioned alternative textbooks for schools. His robust approach didn't break the stranglehold of the left, for the simple reason that there was no alternative body of right historians in waiting. Reworking India's history remained an 'unfinished agenda'.[24] However, Joshi did succeed in raking up controversy after controversy, and became a hate figure of the left.

In hindsight, much of what Joshi did as human resource development (HRD) minister was symbolic. The battles involving him and the opposition were over the singing of the Saraswati Vandana at the inauguration of a conference of state education ministers and over his insistence on 'value education' as an integral part of the curriculum. The other battles were over appointments which, despite divisions on partisan lines, weren't always indicative of any deep-rooted ideological schism. Joshi successfully flagged the RSS–BJP concerns over ideological bias but couldn't really unsettle it. If he had another five years as HRD minister, the story may have been different. However, the NDA lost the 2004 election and had to wait another ten years to have another shy at ideological reorientation.

The Vajpayee government's defeat in 2004 came as a huge surprise, not least to the Congress. In hindsight, the failure to secure either a majority or for the BJP to retain its status as the largest party in the Lok Sabha was attributed to the unpopularity of its two southern allies—the Telugu Desam Party (TDP) in Andhra Pradesh and the AIADMK led by Jayalalithaa in Tamil Nadu. But the NDA also fared poorly in Bihar, West Bengal, and the all-important state of Uttar Pradesh. The defeats there were attributed to a spectacular measure of Muslim consolidation, said to be a reaction to the horror stories that emerged from the Gujarat riots of 2002. Finally, it was held that the India Shining campaign had completely misread the mood of the electorate by overpitching the sense of quiet confidence in the achievements of the Vajpayee government.

Within RSS-BJP circles, however, the diagnosis was very different. It was held that the karyakartas, the volunteers who worked tirelessly for the 'cause', were thoroughly demotivated after five years in power. Their disappointment stemmed from the Vajpayee government's inability to implement any of the 'distinctive' facets of the BJP programme, apart from India becoming a nuclear power. The clumsy attempt by the BJP campaign to reach out to Muslim voters backfired totally. The shrill 'anti-communal' propaganda around the Gujarat riots ensured that Muslims completely disregarded the BJP appeal and consolidated their votes at the constituency level in favour of a candidate most likely to defeat the NDA nominee. At the same time, the targeted overtures to Muslims put off those voters whose faith in the BJP was centred on its Hindu appeal. Post-facto anecdotal evidence, especially from the urban constituencies where the BJP lost heavily, referred to significant abstentions from its otherwise committed voters.

Not everyone in the BJP, however, drew the same conclusions from the defeat. Former deputy prime minister L.K. Advani who had been consistently cast as a hardliner during the tenure of the Vajpayee government—an image that was seriously at odds with his personality—felt that the BJP must make a concerted bid to remove the belief that it was anti-Muslim. Invited to Pakistan in June 2005 by the government in Islamabad, he sought to use the visit to link Hindu–Muslim amity with India–Pakistan friendship. His description of Muhammad Ali Jinnah as 'secular' may have had some basis in history but it triggered a huge storm in India. The RSS–BJP fraternity was horrified. Long accustomed to viewing Jinnah as the architect of Partition and the foremost proponent of the two-nation theory, the saffron camp felt he had gone too far in trying to effect an image makeover. Advani, however, was unrepentant and was totally bewildered by the grass-roots revolt and calls for his immediate removal as president of the BJP. Following a prolonged drama, a shoddy compromise—whereby Advani was given an honourable exit route and allowed to continue as party president till the end of the year—was effected, but by 2007 Advani was removed from his party post. Although he was rehabilitated by being named as the BJP's prime ministerial candidate for the 2009 general election, both his authority and his appeal diminished considerably. The BJP's 2009 campaign was, by its own standards, lacking in focus and enthusiasm and the results came as no great surprise.

By 2010, with Vajpayee out of action after 2007 owing to illness and Advani edged out, the BJP was confronted with a leadership vacuum. Increasingly, the party faithful began looking to the man who had successfully won two state elections, braved sustained hostility of the Congress establishment, and had made a huge mark on the quality of governance. The bid to catapult Narendra Modi into national politics was not easy. Modi had to confront the opposition of the BJP old guard led by Advani, the misgivings of an RSS leadership that perceived him as too much of an individualist, and the shrill hostility of the entire left-liberal ecosystem that painted him as a 'mass murderer' and held him responsible for the 'pogrom' in Gujarat in 2002. That Modi prevailed despite these formidable obstacles owed almost entirely to grass-roots opinion. There was just no one else that measured up even remotely to his popularity. This was finally acknowledged in September 2013 and Modi was anointed the BJP's prime ministerial candidate.

It is worth recalling that while BJP workers and sympathizers celebrated the decision, a section of the commentariat were convinced that the party had shot itself in the foot by nominating one whom they deemed unelectable. So strong was the belief that Modi was far too 'polarizing' a figure to be acceptable to the middle ground, that Bihar chief minister Nitish Kumar broke off his long-standing alliance with the BJP and made peace with his traditional adversary Lalu Prasad Yadav. Lalu was a doughty anti-BJP campaigner who had earned his 'secular' credentials by arresting Advani in 1990 during the final leg of his rath yatra from Somnath to Ayodhya. Nitish, it also seemed, was misled into believing that the BJP itself would not be united in its endorsement of Modi.

The extent to which Modi's nomination as the BJP's candidate for prime minister prompted concern has already been mentioned. In 2013, at the time of his selection by the BJP, Modi was regarded as a shade too controversial and unacceptable in global circles. His pariah-like status owed almost entirely to attempts by activists to directly implicate him in the retaliatory killing of Muslims in the aftermath of the arson attack on a railway carriage carrying Hindu activists in the Godhra railway station in Gujarat in 2002. The anger of the 'secular' activists multiplied after Modi turned the tables on his opponents and transformed the assembly election the same year into a test of Gujarati pride and identity. Needless to say, the dividing line between Gujarati pride and Hindu assertion was extremely thin. One inevitably merged into the other.

A resounding election victory did not, however, end the political persecution of Modi over his suspected role in the 2002 riots. In March 2005, Modi applied for a diplomatic visa to visit the United States (US) to address members of the Gujarati diaspora who counted among his fierce supporters. Citing a provision in its country's Immigration and Nationality Act, the US embassy turned down his application.[25] The US action was followed by many countries of the European Union (EU), including the United Kingdom (UK), ceasing all contact with the Gujarat government. Ironically, far from adding to Modi's political difficulties, the ostracism by the West added to a pre-existing feeling of Hindu victimhood, including the belief that there was a big Christian network active in undermining Hindus. Opposition parties in India often cited the denial of the US visa to argue that Modi was an international pariah and a national embarrassment. Far from lowering Modi in the eyes of Indians, the visa denial may actually have added to his appeal as a politician who was resolute in standing up for Hindu interests.

Modi, it would seem, had a twin-track strategy. On the one hand, he did absolutely nothing to counter the impression that he was being victimized by those with an anti-Hindu political agenda. On the other hand, within Gujarat, he turned his entire attention to streamlining the administration and making the state attractive to private sector investment. Modi was among the first chief ministers who took full advantage of the deregulation of the Indian economy and create a business-friendly environment in the state. He was helped immeasurably by the prevailing pro-business ethos among a large section of Gujaratis.

In the course of his thirteen years as chief minister, Modi acquired a reputation of a proactive administrator with an overriding interest in efficient governance. The Vibrant Gujarat summits aimed at securing investment for the state were a first, and they attracted huge participation from entrepreneurs. At the

2007 summit, the chairman of the Tata Group of companies, gave Modi the certificate of a lifetime by proclaiming, 'It is stupid if you are not in Gujarat.'[26] The endorsement of big industry added to the appeal of Modi and his 'Gujarat model'. The reputation of being business-friendly received an enormous boost in September 2008 when, exasperated by the problems involved in land acquisition for their proposed small car manufacturing unit in Singur, West Bengal, the Tatas abruptly decided to relocate the entire facility to Sanand in Gujarat. The speed at which Modi completed the land acquisition and other clearances for the Tatas enhanced Modi's reputation as a politician who could get things done. In an India that was then experiencing a near-dysfunctional government, Modi's single-minded determination to cut through bureaucratic hurdles and red tape became a talking point all over the country.[27]

For the BJP there was also a political shift arising from Modi's business-friendly record in Gujarat. As noted earlier, the BJP was distinctly ambivalent on issues of economic policy and was invariably guided by the interests of its support base of traders and the SMEs (small and medium enterprises). Prior to 1991, when the Congress pursued an over-regulated, public–sector-oriented, and protectionist approach, the Jana Sangh/BJP emphasized the need for lessening controls, lowering taxes, and warding off the 'inspector raj.' The liberalization of the economy initiated by Prime Minister P.V. Narasimha Rao and Finance Minister Manmohan Singh—essentially a response to a severe balance-of-payments crisis that had led to India mortgaging some of its gold reserves—threw the party into some confusion. There were aspects of the deregulation, particularly the relaxation of the licence-permit-quota raj, that found favour with the BJP. However, on the issue of globalization there were serious misgivings.

Since the 1970s, the Jana Sangh/BJP had favoured an approach that can loosely be described as national capitalism. This was personified by its adherence to swadeshi, an approach that had its origins in the freedom movement. The RSS, on its part, combined its disavowal of consumerism with a fascination for technology, welfarism, and a strong state. There was, in short, just too many contradictory strands in the thinking on economic policy in the Hindu nationalist camp.

Encouraged by a section of Indian industry that felt its pampered existence was threatened by global competition in the domestic market, the BJP became sharply critical of the globalizing facets of the liberalization programme initiated by the Congress. Murli Manohar Joshi, with his famous quip of 'computer chips, not potato chips', spelt out the need to thwart economic globalization from subverting Indian culture.[28] The BJP, egged on by the RSS, mounted an alarmist attack on India's entry into the World Trade Organization (WTO), warning that sinister multinationals would end up securing patents on neem and turmeric. At the same time, the BJP could not turn a blind eye to the fact that the urban middle classes—also among the BJP's traditional supporters—welcomed the respite from an economy built on shortages, shoddy consumer goods, and notoriously inefficient services.

These contradictions were never satisfactorily addressed at the party level. The BJP, consequently, had in its fold individuals such as Jaswant Singh whose economic orientation replicated an updated version of the old Swatantra Party approach, Murli Manohar Joshi whose disavowal of socialism was matched by his suspicion of globalization, and those who took their cue from the Integral Humanism of Deendayal Upadhyaya—a philosophy that highlights compassion, righteousness, and harmony with nature. Finally, there was the Vajpayee–Advani duo, always uncomfortable with the complexities of economics, who preferred pragmatism and common sense.

Attempting to provide coherence to the BJP's approach to economic policy was always daunting and carried the danger of exposing the fissures to public view. Consequently, it was carefully avoided. 'We will never fight an election on economic issues,' Advani once admitted to me.

The Vajpayee government attempted to tread a cautious middle path, with the upgradation of India's creaking infrastructure being its stated priority. There was no question of rolling back the tide of deregulation and technological upgradation through foreign direct investment (FDI). There was, after all, no fundamental divergence from the path taken by the Narasimha Rao government or even the two short-lived United Front governments in which P. Chidambaram was the finance minister.

The sanctions imposed by the Bill Clinton administration after the nuclear tests of May 1998 added a new dimension. As a counter-strategy to minimize any adverse effects on the Indian economy, it was decided to open the huge, and relatively untapped, domestic market to foreign capital. Combined with the announcement of 'no first use' of nuclear weapons that proclaimed India's larger non-aggressive intent, it was believed—and quite rightly as it turned out—that anxious governments would be placated by businesses eyeing the Indian market. Consequently, despite the commitment to swadeshi in the NDA's common programme, the opening up of India to global business was pursued quite actively in the Vajpayee years. But the motivation was entirely strategic—to thwart any bid to isolate India internationally and to prevent its portrayal as another rogue regime. By the time the Vajpayee government exited the stage, India and the US had kissed and made up and President Clinton even completed a highly successful visit to India.

It is sometimes tempting to attribute Modi's shift in tack from Gujarati and Hindu pride to development and governance after the victory in the 2002 assembly election to similar expediency. Certainly, there was a compelling need to lower the political temperature after the riots, and Modi was also aware of the possible long-term dividends from merging Gujarati pride with a sense of achievement at the state's progress. But more to the point, a focus on development also corresponded to Modi's own temperament and the political priorities of the BJP.

Modi was in many ways an unusual RSS swayamsevak. A compelling public speaker with a talent for organization, he was never content to be a faceless, self-effacing soldier for the organization that nurtured him. Steadfastly loyal to the RSS and its traditions, he was at the same time also a fierce individualist. In an organization where unquestioning obedience to the superior was the norm, Modi stood out for his questioning and argumentative ways.

His was also a restless mind. Whereas many RSS apparatchiks were grounded in inherited certitudes, Modi was forever pushing the frontiers of his own intellectual development. At one time he imagined a future for himself as a monk in the Ramakrishna Mission—an order established by Swami Vivekananda at the beginning of the twentieth century. When the Mission turned down his request, he resumed his life in the RSS. But what inspired him was not so much the Hindutva of the RSS stalwarts Keshavrao Baliram Hedgewar and 'Guru' Golwalkar but the message of national resurgence and activism that Swami Vivekananda blended with his spiritualism. Modi was moulded by his readings of Vivekananda and not least the Swami's sense of India's global mission.

Modi never had any formal training in economics, and nor did he have any administrative experience before he assumed charge as chief minister of Gujarat in 2001. What he did have, however, was an open mind and an appreciation of the Gujarati spirit of entrepreneurship and global orientation. Whereas Mahatma Gandhi, India's most famous Gujarati, had stressed austerity and debunked the West's idea of progress, Modi was a fanatical modernist. To him, it was a travesty that India was still riddled with poverty, backwardness and insufficient opportunities for personal growth. His exposure to the West through travel and his interaction with the successful Gujarati diaspora convinced him that India could not afford to be Third World. India too needed the best the world had to offer, both in terms of services and infrastructure. Temperamentally at least,

he was never at ease with the *chalta hai* (loosely translated as
'anything goes') attitude that often coexisted with a sense of
fatalism.

Modi was particularly attracted to technology as a means
to improve the quality of administration, enhance the average
citizen's quality of life, and connect Indians with each other. In an
earlier era, the RSS–BJP ecosystem had viewed the revolution in
technology as a Western phenomenon and linked to consumerist
lifestyles. The BJP leader from Mumbai, Pramod Mahajan, was,
for example, constantly chided for the enthusiasm with which
he used mobile phones at the time of their introduction in India
in the late 1990s. Apart from defence where technological
upgradation of the military was constantly demanded, there was
an instinctive sympathy with 'development' programmes that
stressed the overriding importance of 'appropriate technology'.

During his tenure, Prime Minister Rajiv Gandhi contributed
immeasurably in sensitizing India to the importance and the
opportunities presented by the rapid strides in information
technology (IT). Modi was certainly one of the early converts
to the idea. As chief minister, he introduced IT in different
areas of governance, particularly land registration, revenue
administration, and the regulation of transfers and postings in
the lower bureaucracy. Modi was among the first to experiment
with biometric systems to ensure attendance of teachers
and students alike in government schools. 'Perhaps no State
government,' wrote journalist Uday Mahurkar in his study of
the Modi administration in Gujarat, 'has used latest technology
to bring transparency in governance to reduce delays and red-
tape as the Modi government has.'[29]

The success of e-governance in curbing discretionary powers
of the bureaucracy—the principal source of corruption—yielded
rich political dividends for Modi in Gujarat. It also established
his reputation all over India as a politician who went beyond
ethical homilies and demonstrated that the levels of corruption
could be brought down significantly. At a time when India was

agitated by the sheer scale of the reported scams—notably the ones involving telecom licences, coal mining leases, and the organization of the Commonwealth Games—under the UPA government, Modi came through as a politician who had the courage to fight the menace head-on.

As prime minister, Modi has used the tools of e-governance in every sphere of life. From the issue of driving licences and passports to tax administration, life has become much easier for the ordinary citizen. The sheer harassment that was the hallmark of everyday existence in India has come down exponentially, and so has the incidence of petty corruption. The Aadhaar biometric system of personal identification—a scheme conceived by the Manmohan Singh government—was put into operation and has become an important instrument in ensuring tax compliance and fighting corruption.[30] Likewise, the administration of Goods and Services Tax (GST) has been marked by a parallel introduction of online systems, a move that was, however, contested by a section of traders accustomed to dodging local taxes by innovative means.

From the day he assumed charge as prime minister, toning up the administration and introducing systemic reforms have been the priorities of Modi. In his first Independence Day address from Delhi's Red Fort in 2014, he called for a moratorium on all contentious issues for ten years, a period that could be better utilized to addressing bread-and-butter issues. This prompted the charge that Modi was intent on reducing politics to a set of managerial choices. A more sinister connotation attached to his appeal was that the managerial focus would enable the BJP to rejig the fundamentals of Indian nationhood and break down the Nehruvian consensus without the glare of publicity and controversy.

The wariness and the belief that Modi was being wilfully disingenuous stemmed from the inability to grasp that the prime minister himself was not being guided by doctrinaire prescriptions. He was principally guided by considerations of feasibility, efficiency and speed.[31] Like a former president of India,

A.P.J. Abdul Kalam—a man widely respected and admired in India—Modi too believed there were aspects of nation building that were above partisan politics.

In a curious way, this approach had a lot in common with the approach of Jawaharlal Nehru, India's first prime minister who, ironically, Modi believed had exercised all the wrong choices. Nehru too felt that his grand plans of economic development through the Five-Year Plans were above politics and that the big dams, steel plants and centres of educational excellence were the new 'temples of modern India'. However, in line with the ideological predilections of the times, Nehru simultaneously believed that the state, guided by a technocratic elite, must play a pivotal role in the reconstruction of India along modern lines.

Nehru and Modi were linked by a common commitment to modernity. However, whereas Nehru emphasized the role of the state and the public sector, Modi felt that the state should merely be an efficient facilitator and focus its energies on creating a modern welfare state. The task of generating livelihood, he felt, must be left to India's entrepreneurs who had earlier been harassed and put down by an over-regulatory regime that encouraged corruption and cronyism. In the election campaign of 2014, Modi spoke about 'minimum government, maximum governance'—the first occasion any serious claimant for power had attempted to put the role of the state back in focus. To this was added civic virtues such as cleanliness, good health, adherence to laws, and respect for women. Enthused by his approach, business and industry as a whole extended substantial backing to the BJP in the 2014 election.

Modi's bid to forge a new consensus was important in another respect too. For a long time, ever since the eclipse of the Swatantra Party following its identification with privilege, the right in India had focused principally on the culture wars—issues that highlighted its cultural nationalism. Advani attempted to change this by embarking on a nationwide yatra in 1997—the fiftieth anniversary of Indian independence—to complement swaraj (self-rule) with su-raj (good governance) and the Vajpayee government emphasized 'India Shining' centred on its initiatives to upgrade infrastructure. However, it was Modi who tried to formalize the incorporation of a broad economic thinking into the party's bloodstream, something more tangible than the familiar homilies advocating development.

Unfortunately for Modi, a combination of economic circumstances and the grim realities of Indian politics intervened to slow down, if not entirely derail, the process.

Prior to the 2014 election, Modi and other senior leaders of the BJP had intensive consultations with stakeholders in business and industry. In addition, there were brainstorming sessions with economists. On the basis of the interactions, it was felt that the plummeting Gross Domestic Product (GDP) and India's overall loss of momentum owed to a dysfunctional government that was pulling in contradictory directions and rampant corruption that had undermined public confidence in the government. Consequently, it was felt that a stable government with a decisive leader at the helm who was committed to business-friendly policies would kick-start the economy and revive economic growth. The priority, it was felt, was to work overtime to improve the ease of doing business by doing away with cumbersome regulations and controls. To complement these, the government would also need to overcome its fear of taking decisions, have the political confidence of addressing complex but necessary measures such as the enactment of a GST, keep the fiscal deficit in check, and lower interest rates. Robust and visible anti-corruption measures would, in addition, bolster public confidence in the government.

In hindsight, the prescriptions overestimated the Indian corporate sector's ability to rise to the challenge. Overburdened with debt—the consequence of having rushed into expensive infrastructure projects prior to the crash of 2012—Indian businesses were not in any state of readiness to make substantial capital investments, and certainly not in the crucial infrastructure sector. A bid by the Modi government to ease land acquisition for public services and industrial parks encountered unexpected resistance from farmers and was also opposed within the BJP itself. The legislation finally had to be withdrawn altogether. By the beginning of 2015, the government came to the grudging conclusion that the costs of its ambitious infrastructure improvement plans would have to be met through public expenditure.

The implications of this shift were significant. It meant that Modi's hopes of rolling back state involvement and confining it to social welfare had to be recalibrated. It also meant that FDIs would have to play a disproportionate role in financing new capital investments. This meant readjusting the thrust of India's foreign policy to more investment-oriented objectives, particularly in East Asia and the Arab states.

Politically too the government encountered strong headwinds. The proposal to make land acquisition easier for public projects and the overall talk of improving the ease of doing business conveyed an impression that the priorities of the government were not entirely in tune with those of the hinterland. The BJP, riding the crest of the Modi wave in the general election, won state elections in Maharashtra, Jharkhand and Haryana in late 2014. However, 2015 began on a bad note for the government when, in February, the BJP was routed in the election to the Delhi Legislative Assembly. This was followed by its defeat in November 2015 in the election to the Bihar Legislative Assembly.

The lessons drawn by the BJP and the Modi government to these two unexpected, but devastating, defeats were significant. The outcome in Bihar was deemed ominous in view of the forthcoming assembly election in the neighbouring state of Uttar Pradesh fifteen months away. It was the BJP's victory in 73 of the 80 Lok Sabha seats from Uttar Pradesh in the 2014 general election that had facilitated the BJP's parliamentary majority.

The most important conclusion drawn by BJP strategists was that it would be imprudent to bank in future on securing a majority through the vagaries of the first-past-the-post system.

There was a growing likelihood that the different parties opposed to the BJP would try and set aside their differences and forge a grand anti-BJP coalition. To prevail, the BJP would have to significantly increase its share of the popular vote. Traditionally, the BJP had witnessed its strongest support from the middle classes and the upper castes. It, therefore, had to extend its reach to the sections in the lower rungs of the economic and social ladder. In other words, in social terms, the BJP's centre of gravity had to be redefined with greater support from the poorer sections of the electorate.

The approach needed deft balancing. For example, the strengthening of the legislation for the prevention of atrocities against Dalits—reversing a Supreme Court judgment that made the law less draconian—triggered an unexpected backlash among the BJP's upper-caste supporters in the assembly elections of 2018. To offset this, the Modi government was compelled to hurriedly introduce 10 per cent reservations for poorer members of castes and communities not covered by reservations.

The implications were obvious: the Modi government had to redefine its priorities. Till 2015, the government had focused its energies on improving the ease of doing business and creating employment opportunities through its 'Make in India' programme targeting foreign-owned companies. While these initiatives were neither abandoned nor diluted, the emphasis of the government's messaging changed. Addressing the concerns of rural India and designing welfare schemes for the poor became the government's paramount concerns. Additional political importance was placed on welfare schemes such as full rural electrification, subsidized cooking gas connections for underprivileged women, and a government-funded health insurance scheme for ailments for which medical treatment was relatively costly. The administration walked the extra mile to create networks of beneficiaries and the rhetoric of BJP leaders such as party president Amit Shah also acquired a definite pro-poor thrust.

The BJP's staggering victory in 325 of the 403 seats in the Uttar Pradesh Legislative Assembly election of 2017 may well be attributed to the failure of its two principal rivals to forge an alliance. However, unlike in Bihar and Delhi where the BJP's popular vote fell way below the 2014 level, the party managed to keep its level of popular support broadly intact, polling 41.3 per cent in 2017 against 43.3 per cent in 2014. According to one analysis of the election:

> [in western Uttar Pradesh] the BJP had consolidated the support of the 'leftover' castes such as the Gujjar, Tyagi, Brahmin, Saini and Kashyap who are often not counted in the typical matrix which fashioned for years on the basis of the 'dominant' groupings like the Jats, Muslims and Dalits (the Yadavs have a small presence in this region). The BJP discovered the untapped numerical potential of the unseen groupings. It not only fielded many candidates from these groups but also co-opted them in other ways.[32]

The caste dimension notwithstanding, it seems clear that the BJP's public thrust towards the welfare of the poorer sections had yielded electoral returns, but without affecting its traditional support among the upper castes and middle classes.

The Uttar Pradesh Legislative Assembly election of 2017 is revealing in another way. The election, held within a few months of the demonetization of cash holdings in November 2016, was perceived by many to be a referendum on this radical move that affected almost every Indian and caused a great deal of temporary inconvenience and hardship. In particular, demonetization hit traders in the smaller market towns traditionally accustomed to dealing in cash and largely operating outside the tax net the hardest. This section had been among the BJP's most steadfast supporters, including in the days when it was only a fringe player. Predictably, demonetization resulted in a lot of heartburn, and the media reported expressions of anger and charges of betrayal.

Yet, despite these concerns, the outcome revealed that the support for the BJP among sections most adversely affected by demonetization remained intact.

This was also the case during the Gujarat Legislative Assembly election in December 2017 when the initial unsettling effects of the newly introduced GST was most acutely felt. Like their counterparts in Uttar Pradesh, there was considerable resentment and expressions of anger. But again, the outcome clearly indicated that almost all the urban clusters had stayed loyal to the BJP.

The BJP's ability to satisfy contradictory impulses has fascinated political observers. What has also been intriguing is that despite all the talk of fighting elections on the strength of its commitment to development and economic issues, the BJP never fails to invoke emotive issues that centre on Hindu identity. The rhetoric becomes particularly strident in the final days of campaigning. In election after election, BJP campaigners have explained this sharp rise in the emotional pitch as a way of motivating the committed and invoking the latent Hindutva (Hinduness) in the community.

This approach does not work if there are other mitigating factors at work. But it is a reminder that, at the end of the day, the right in India is not driven by class and issues of economic interests alone. These play a crucial role in establishing a larger goodwill and creating overall impressions. However, what defines the Indian right, and particularly the BJP, are core beliefs that endure and often take precedence over everyday concerns. It is a dissection of these convictions and prejudices, and the different narratives governing them, that form the basis of the sections that follow.

2

Motherland, Religion and Community

There are two public faces of Narendra Modi. The first, always in evidence at official functions, is of an immaculately turned-out Modi addressing issues of governance with solemnity and with single-mindedness. With an eye for detail and always well prepared, he comes across as a politician of vision who also has a firm grip on administration. Rarely rhetorical but always passionate, his speeches invariably convey his sense of commitment to both the subject and the occasion. This is Modi in his prime ministerial avatar.

There is a very different Modi in evidence at political rallies, especially during election campaigns. Always aggressive and polemical, and with a penchant for sarcasm and mockery, this Modi is unsparing of his opponents. Cheered on by his doting fan club, forever ready to work themselves into a frenzy chanting 'Modi, Modi', he works the crowds, combining national themes with local issues. His eloquence is often mesmerizing and cuts across language barriers, especially when he invokes victimhood to full political advantage, pitting his humble origins against the arrogance of an ancien régime, bloated with its sense of entitlement. Atal Bihari Vajpayee used long pauses and wordplay to weave his oratorical magic; Modi relies on passionate eloquence.

Modi's conclusions are always characteristically robust. He leads the crowds into lusty and full-throated chants of *Vande*

Mataram, the chant that has defined Indian nationalism since the beginning of the twentieth century. When the crowds are sufficiently large and worked up, Modi does a variation: he says 'Vande' and the audience replies 'Mataram'. The effects are electrifying.

During the movement for freedom from British rule, *Vande Mataram* and the associated chant of 'Bharat Mata ki Jai' (Victory to Mother India) was associated with the Congress, although not exclusively. *Vande Mataram* was written by the Bengali writer Bankimchandra Chattopadhyay in 1875 and included in 1881 in his novel *Anandamath* as the motivational song of the sannyasi rebels taking on Muslim conquerors. It was set to music and first sung at the 1896 session of the Indian National Congress (INC) by the poet Rabindranath Tagore. The iconic cry acquired mass popularity throughout India in the wake of the swadeshi movement that accompanied the protests against Lord Curzon's Partition of Bengal in 1905. Popularized by the early nationalists, particularly Aurobindo Ghose and Bipin Chandra Pal, this ode to the motherland rapidly became India's foremost nationalist anthem. Nationalist meetings invariably began with the singing of *Vande Mataram* and protestors walked the streets and courted arrest with cries of *Vande Mataram*. Aurobindo attached great mystical significance to the discovery of *Vande Mataram* and equated it to a revelation, 'a sudden moment of awakening from long delusions'.[1]

Yet, on 24 January 1950, by a ruling of the president of the Constituent Assembly—and therefore not subject to either debate or voting—'Jana-Gana-Mana', a composition by Rabindranath Tagore was selected as independent India's national anthem. It was announced that *Vande Mataram*, 'which has played a historic part in the struggle for Indian freedom, shall be honoured equally with Jana-Gana-Mana and shall have equal status with it'.[2] Moreover, on the few official functions—such as the final day of a session of Parliament—where *Vande Mataram* is sung, it is never the full version—just the first two stanzas.

In the annals of Hindu nationalism, the story of *Vande Mataram* from being the icon of the national movement to becoming an extra—something which couldn't be repudiated but which was at the same time awkward and embarrassing—epitomized betrayal and a distortion of nationhood. For all those associated with the RSS parivar and the BJP, continuing attachment to *Vande Mataram*—without, at the same time, undermining the importance of the national anthem—has become an article of faith. It has become customary for nearly all public functions associated with the RSS to begin with the singing of *Vande Mataram*—the full song and not merely the truncated, official version. Among the more boisterous sections of the saffron fraternity, a favourite slogan is: '*Hindustan me rehena hoga, Vande Mataram kehena hoga* (If you want to live in Hindustan, saying *Vande Mataram* is obligatory).'

The combativeness over *Vande Mataram*, particularly since Independence, is inextricably linked to larger questions of nationhood. For a start, Bankimchandra envisaged India as the Mother and then proceeded to define the imagery:

> . . . O Mother, thou art love and faith,
> it is thy image we raise in every temple.
> For thou art Durga holding her ten weapons of war,
> Kamala at play in the lotuses
> and Speech, the goddess, giver of all lore,
> to thee I bow![3]

Subsequently, portraits of the Mother Goddess astride a lion with a map of India as the backdrop was popularized as the personification of Bharat Mata. This portrait of Mother India, inspired by *Vande Mataram*, soon became a central feature of nationalist iconography. There were alternative versions such as Abanindranath Tagore's 1905 painting *Bharatmata* that visualized the Mother as a saffron-robed sadhvi but serene and without weapons. Predictably, this depiction did not correspond to the mood of the times. It was also in sharp conflict with Bankimchandra's explicit invocation of power and militancy:

> Terrible with the clamorous shouts of seventy million throats,
> and the sharpness of swords raised in twice seventy million
> hands,
> who sayeth to thee, Mother, that thou art weak?
> Holder of multitudinous strength,
> I bow to her who saves,
> to her who drives from her the armies of her foemen,
> the Mother!

The imagery of Bharat Mata stemming from *Vande Mataram* was also complemented by the patriotic poetry of the times, particularly in Bengal. In later life, Tagore was to embrace universalism and shun the aggression of nationalism. However, during the swadeshi movement, he too equated the Mother Goddess with Shakti:

> From the heart of Bangladesh spontaneously
> You have emerged with such breathtaking beauty, Mother.
> In your right hand flashes the scimitar, your left hand dispels
> fear
> Your two eyes radiate a loving smile, the third eye on your
> Forehead is a fiery glow.[4]

Equally robust was the Bengali writer Dwijendralal Roy's celebration of Bharat Mata:

> The day you arose from the blue ocean, Mother Bharatavarsha,
> The world erupted in such a joyful clamour, such devotion,
> Mother, and so much laughter.[5]

On his part, Aurobindo left no scope for ambiguity. 'Nationalism is a religion,' he wrote in 1907, 'that has come from God.' He was subsequently to equate it with the Sanatan Dharma and devotion to the Goddess.[6]

The encapsulation of nationalism in Bharat Mata, the 'sacred nation', became a definitive facet of Hindu nationalist thought, and which has endured till today. The idea was not confined to Bengal. It touched the nationalist movement throughout India and became inextricably associated with the Congress. Indeed, *Vande Mataram* and the worship of Bharat Mata served to connect the earlier 'extremist' phase of the national movement with the Gandhian movements that set the tone after 1920. It also linked the critics of Mahatma Gandhi with the mainstream of nationalism. At least on this count, those committed to revolutionary violence were one with the votaries of non-violence and passive resistance.

The association of the motherland with the sacred was a central feature of the RSS, established in 1925 in Nagpur, by Dr K.B. Hedgewar. In 1940, the RSS, now undergoing a phase of steady expansion outside Maharashtra, adopted a prayer to the bhagwa dhwaj (saffron flag) that epitomized a timeless Bharat. The Sanskrit prayer was recited at the beginning of all RSS morning and evening shakhas and has continued unchanged to this day.

> Forever I bow to thee, O Loving Motherland! O Motherland of us Hindus, Thou hast brought me up in happiness. May my life, O great and blessed Holy Land, be laid down in Thy Cause. I bow to Thee again and again.
>
> We the children of the Hindu Nation bow to Thee in reverence, O Almighty God. We have girded up our loins to carry on Thy work. Give us Thy holy blessings for its fulfilment. O Lord! Grant us such might as no power on earth can ever challenge, such purity of character as would command the respect of the whole world and such knowledge as would make easy the thorny path that we have voluntarily chosen.

May we be inspired with the spirit of stern heroism, that
is the sole and ultimate means of attaining the highest spiritual
bliss with the greatest temporal prosperity. May intense and
everlasting devotion to our ideal ever enthuse our hearts. May
our victorious organised power of action, by Thy Grace, be
wholly capable of protecting our dharma and leading this
nation of ours to the highest pinnacle of glory.[7]

While the prayer introduced themes of moral resolve and
uprightness, there was a corresponding commitment to the
sacredness of Mother India, a belief that originated with *Vande
Mataram*. Even Tagore, otherwise harshly critical of the inherent
exceptionalism that nationalism promoted, was infected by it.
'Each country,' he said in a speech in Santiniketan as late as
September 1932, 'has its own inner geography where her spirit
dwells and where physical force can never conquer even an inch
of ground.' He repeated this a week later while paying birthday
tributes to Mahatma Gandhi: 'India is not merely a geographical
entity but is a living truth which they [Indians] live, move and
have their being.'[8]

The scholar Radhakumud Mookerji traced the notion of
sacred geography to the shastras. Contesting the notion that
India was a manufactured construct brought about by British
rule, he cited Vedic and subsequent texts such as *Manusmriti*,
not to mention the tradition of religious pilgrimages, to show
that 'All the conditions that make for the growth of a sense of
nationhood were fully developed and long known in ancient
India.'[9] Hindus, he wrote, 'in their heart of hearts believe that
theirs is a chosen land, where men must be worthy of final
salvation. This represents the national belief . . .'[10]

Yet, the appeal of *Vande Mataram* and the sacredness of
Bharat Mata was contested. A large section of India's Muslims
were never at ease with its explicitly Hindu symbolism and
opposed its identification with Indian nationalism. Its context
was seen as 'anti-Muslim' and its imagery 'idolatrous' and,

therefore, anathema to Islam. The Muslim League, in particular, made the repudiation of *Vande Mataram* a prestige issue and saw the Congress's attachment to it as evidence of its exclusive identification with Hindus. In the words of Muhammad Ali Jinnah, the foremost leader of the Muslim League, *Vande Mataram* 'is not only idolatrous but in its origin and substance a hymn to spread hatred for the Musalmans'.[11] He made it clear Muslims would never accept *Vande Mataram* 'or any expurgated edition of the anti-Muslim song as a binding National Anthem'.[12]

The fierce opposition of the Muslim community to *Vande Mataram* put the nationalist leadership in a quandary. Always anxious to counter the British claim that India's nationalism was essentially an exclusively Hindu phenomenon, it was hamstrung by the fact that for the foot soldiers of the nationalist cause, the idea of a free India reclaiming its destiny and *Vande Mataram* were inseparable. *Vande Mataram* was a sentiment and however much it sought to make the national movement all-inclusive, it could not really go against the popular tide. Mahatma Gandhi's anguish over a controversy that assaulted the fundamentals of everything Indian nationalism had stood for was indicative of the helplessness of the nationalist leadership:

> It never occurred to me that it [*Vande Mataram*] was a Hindu song or meant only for Hindus. Unfortunately now we have fallen on evil days. All that was pure gold has become base metal today. In such times it is wisdom not to market pure gold and let it be sold as base metal. I would not risk a single quarrel over singing *Vande Mataram* at a mixed gathering. It will never suffer from disuse. It is enthroned in the hearts of millions.[13]

Eventually, after elaborate consultations that involved the entire Congress leadership and prominent individuals such as Rabindranath Tagore, the party decided that the first two stanzas of the song were 'unobjectionable' but, in any case, singing *Vande Mataram* should involve no compulsion.[14]

The concession to Muslim misgivings to *Vande Mataram* didn't succeed in preventing the Muslim League securing a huge endorsement for Pakistan in the 1946 election. However, the controversy proved successful in preventing even a truncated version of *Vande Mataram* from becoming India's national anthem. In time, the commitment to a composite, inclusive nationalism saw even the chant being gradually substituted by Jai Hind, popularized by Subhas Chandra Bose and his Indian National Army.

The furore over *Vande Mataram* that set the political fault lines in the run-up to Independence hasn't surfaced in a significant way after 1950. Yet, the relegation of this defining symbol of the freedom struggle to history had a definite political consequence. Under the leadership of Jawaharlal Nehru, the post-Independence Congress slowly attempted to become more consciously 'secular' and shed explicit identification with Hindu imagery. In the process, it vacated a space that was gleefully appropriated by Hindu nationalism as its very own. More important, the present-day detachment of the secularists from an older tradition of nationalism, facilitated the linkage between past and contemporary Hindu nationalism. As the Congress became more and more associated with the fortunes of one family, important nationalist icons of the past such as Aurobindo, Bal Gangadhar Tilak, Bipin Chandra Pal, Sardar Vallabhbhai Patel, and Rajendra Prasad, to mention only a few, came to be incorporated in the pantheon of the Hindu right. Till the lifetime of Indira Gandhi at least, the Congress—despite many secular adjustments—broadly represented the mainstream of Indian nationalism. However, as it progressively vacated the old ground and simultaneously lost its overwhelming political dominance, traditional Indian nationalism increasingly came to be identified with forces that had hitherto been on the fringes. The slow transition of *Vande Mataram* and Bharat Mata from being a mainstay of the Congress to becoming identified with the BJP epitomized the shift.

Since Independence, but particularly after the term 'secular' was inserted into the Preamble of the Indian Constitution without any meaningful debate at the height of the Emergency in 1976, there has been a temptation to read history backwards and underplay—if not entirely gloss over—the 'Hindu' dimensions of the national movement. There is an implicit suggestion that the leadership of the Congress by Mahatma Gandhi and, subsequently, Jawaharlal Nehru ensured that the ideology which guided the struggle for freedom was accommodative and inclusive and not mired in narrow Hindu sectarianism and bigotry.

That the nationalist leadership tried to speak for the entire nation and were deeply conscious of the need to involve the religious minorities in the struggle is undeniable. Gandhi, in particular, while being devoutly religious and regarded as a saint by his followers, took exceptional care to be respectful of all faiths. On his part, Nehru believed that religious divisions could be overcome by a common economic agenda that was loosely socialist.

The grass-roots reality was, however, a little more awkward. 'In the building of a mass movement,' wrote historian William Gould in his study of Congress mobilization in Uttar Pradesh in the 1930s and 1940s, 'religion helped to provide the necessary framework, space, discipline and mobilisation, and in the process the political meaning of "Hinduism" was redefined as an idea. In the varied contexts, the Hindu people were represented as being conterminous with the Indian nation.'[15] What Partha Chatterjee concluded about the peasant disturbances in Bengal in the decade after 1926 may well be valid for the nationalist mobilization in the rest of India.

It is hardly surprising to discover that the ideology which shaped and gave meaning to the various collective acts of the peasantry was fundamentally religious. The very nature of peasant consciousness, the apparently consistent unification of an entire set of beliefs about nature and about men in the collective and active mind of a peasantry, is religious. Religion to such a community provides an ontology, an epistemology as well as a practical code of ethics, including political ethics. When this community acts politically, the symbolic meaning of particular acts . . . must be found in religious terms.[16]

From revolutionary nationalists taking the oath on the Bhagavadgita to activists twinning gau mata with Bharat Mata, upholding a way of life and the honour of the nation were inextricably connected.[17]

The protection of the cow and the abhorrence of beef eating formed an important element of modern nationalist consciousness. Throughout much of the nineteenth century, aggressive Christian missionaries had mocked the Hindu reverence for the cow and the social stigma attached to the eating of the 'forbidden' meat. This, in turn, had fostered a reaction in 'native' society against educated Indians who equated modernity with a repudiation of all Hindu norms and customs. The adherents of the Young Bengal movement who were enamoured of the idea of shocking Bengali society by flaunting their attachment to beef were treated harshly and often hounded out of society. Bankimchandra Chattopadhyay, who emerged as one of the most articulate upholders of the Hindu inheritance against attacks by Christian evangelists and others, was particularly savage in his repudiation of the British-promoted beef culture. 'And what shall I say,' he wrote in *Letters on Hinduism*, 'of that weakest of human beings, the half-educated anglicised and brutalised Bengali babu, who congratulates himself on his capacity to dine off a plate of beef as if this act of gluttony constituted in itself unimpeachable evidence of a perfectly cultivated intellect?'[18] Even the widespread respect for the literary talents of Michael Madhusudan Dutt couldn't stop the stalwarts of society decrying the poet's conversion to

Christianity. Bhudeb Mukhopadhyay, for example, could never reconcile himself to 'Madhu [sudan]'s despicable inclination to imitate'.[19] Even Ramakrishna Paramahansa who showed an inclination to familiarize himself with the fundamentals of other faiths was known to stiffen at the mention of Dutt.[20]

However, the contempt that much of bhadralok society felt at those who colluded in the undermining of Hindu society (and the food economy) did not lead to assertive opposition to cow slaughter. That was left to the Arya Samaj in Punjab and the Gau-Rakshini Sabhas that mushroomed all over Uttar Pradesh and Bihar, particularly the Bhojpuri belt, from the 1880s. These movements went beyond the landowners and rich traders that funded the gaushalas. They found a responsive audience among the intermediate castes such as Kurmis, Koeris and Ahirs, then involved in improving their ritual status—a direct consequence of the census operations that defined caste hierarchies.[21] It was the participation of these 'backward' castes in the cow protection movements that gave the early expressions of nationalism a popular and populist touch.[22] The Congress that evolved after the 1920s incorporated the traditions of the Gau-Rakshini Sabhas and cow protection became an associated feature of nationalist mobilization. 'As nationalism and communal competition stimulated the search for categories of mutual identity and for definitions of nationality, the cow took on symbolic meaning.'[23] The process, quite inevitably, led to vicious rioting as Muslims often retaliated to cow rescue operations with demonstrative slaughter.

The consequences of the cow protection movements in northern and central India were twofold. First, the defence of the cow became a key feature of the Hindu identity, overriding other social and political differences. It became, like the sacredness of the River Ganga, a facet of Hindu 'common sense'. Secondly, despite all attempts by important political leaders to gloss over its polarizing effects, cow protection was woven into the central fabric of Indian nationalism, and its fierce champions included

Mahatma Gandhi. This was to persist after Independence when, following its incorporation in the Directive Principles of the Constitution, Congress governments in many states enacted legislation to ban cow slaughter.

For at least two decades after Independence, attempts by the Hindu right—notably the Jana Sangh and the lesser-known Ram Rajya Parishad—to initiate agitations for a national ban on cow slaughter made limited headway. There were two reasons for this.

First, despite the indifference—verging on contempt—of Prime Minister Nehru to the issue, a large number of Congress leaders, particularly in the Hindi heartland, were passionately committed to cow protection, although they hesitated to impose their views on other states where eating beef by non-Hindus didn't carry a similar measure of social opprobrium. Consequently, attempts to portray the Congress as insensitive to Hindu interests didn't make too much headway. It was the police firing, leading to eight deaths, on a demonstration of sadhus before Parliament House in Delhi on 7 November 1966 that created a divide between the cow protection activists and the Congress. The prolonged fast of the Shankaracharya of Puri demanding a total ban on cow slaughter did certainly influence devout Hindus all over the country.[24] Cow protection could be said to have had some adverse impact against the Congress in the 1967 general election, though the headway made by the Jana Sangh in Uttar Pradesh and Madhya Pradesh also owed to its strident advocacy of Hindi as the sole official language.

Over the decades, the Congress's commitment to cow protection as a national issue worthy of serious political attention has waned enormously even to the point of hostility. The party's promise to establish gaushalas in Madhya Pradesh in the 2018 assembly election, for example, invited charges that it was trying to emulate the BJP. This retreat can be explained partly by the Congress's overdependence on the Muslim vote after 1989 and partly to accommodate a rising tide of Dalit assertiveness where beef eating is proudly flaunted as a badge of anti-caste politics.

Yet, regardless of the occasional rediscovery of its heritage, the Congress can be said to have vacated the cow protection space almost entirely to the BJP. As with *Vande Mataram*, a redefinition of national priorities and the attachment to 'secular' politics has seen the BJP claiming facets of the old nationalist mantle for itself.

The inheritance has not been without its share of political troubles. During its tenure, the Modi government has had to bear the political liabilities of aggressive cow vigilante squads—in most cases acting without political sanction—that have targeted beef traders. The incidents of lynching of Muslims suspected of possessing beef have provoked adverse reactions globally and made the BJP vulnerable to charges of intolerance. Given its strong identification with India's recent history of cow protection politics, the Hindu right has often found it difficult to balance the average Hindu's genuine abhorrence of cow slaughter with their distaste for the overzealousness and violent methods of self-appointed vigilantes.

One of the consequences of prolonged servitude and loss of national sovereignty is the loss of collective self-confidence of a nation. Whether India lost its powers of sovereign decision making with the Islamic conquests or British colonial rule is a subject of passionate dispute that often spills over into public life. In his legendary 'tryst with destiny' speech on the occasion of Independence at midnight on 15 August 1947, Jawaharlal Nehru referred to the 'period of ill fortune' and the lost 'soul of a nation long suppressed'.[25] However, he did not get into specifics. Narendra Modi was different. In one of his first interventions in the Lok Sabha on 11 June 2014, he left no scope for ambiguity: '*Barah sau saal ki gulami ki maansikta humein pareshan kar rahi hai. Bahut baar humse thoda ooncha vyakti mile, to sar ooncha karke baat karne ki humari taaqat nahin hoti hai* (The slave mentality of 1200 years is troubling us. Often, when we meet a person of high stature, we fail to muster the strength to speak up).'[26]

Modi was referring to the diffidence that has often been said to be characteristic of colonized peoples, especially in their dealings with the cosmopolitan world. He probably had in mind the tendency of Hindus to be embarrassed by their own traditions, their gods and goddesses, and their associated rituals that had, in the eyes of the 'enlightened' world, 'consecrated and encouraged every conceivable form of licentiousness, falsehood, injustice, cruelty, robbery, murder . . . Its sublimest spiritual states have been but the reflex of physiological conditions in disease.'[27] He may also have had in mind the tendency of India's intellectuals to mould the country's public discourse according to prevailing global fashions and to see nationhood—the so-called 'Idea of India'—in narrow juridical terms, bereft of culture and history. Modi's was an outburst against national self-flagellation.

Ever since Nehru secured total control of the Congress after the deaths of Mahatma Gandhi and Sardar Vallabhbhai Patel, India's dominant left-liberal ecosystem has regarded itself as both intellectually and aesthetically superior. Their electoral dominance was matched by their stranglehold over the centres of intellectual power, institutions where contrarian thinking and challenges to prevailing fashions were, if not regulated, actively discouraged.[28] Although the Swatantra Party managed to carve out a small niche for itself thanks to the personal reputation of its founder C. Rajagopalachari and the modest patronage of some Mumbai-based corporate houses, conventional wisdom deemed that there was no real future for right-wing politics in a country such as India.[29] The harshest treatment was reserved for the Hindu nationalists. Apart from being stigmatized for their supposed associations with the assassins of Mahatma Gandhi, they were cast as crude bigots, social reactionaries, and insular Hindi chauvinists. There was some personal regard for Atal Bihari Vajpayee's abilities as a parliamentarian but, by and large, the RSS and BJP were viewed as both lacking in intellectual depth and being anti-intellectual.[30] The perception did not change with the BJP's rising influence and its spate of election victories after 1991. The writer Aatish Taseer's snide description of the participants of a retreat hosted by a pro-BJP foundation in 2014 was representative of the dismissive scorn that was reserved for the new rulers:

> It was a ragtag coalition that collected at a sprawling resort, with a golf course and a swimming pool overlooking the Arabian Sea. In addition to the senior leaders of the B.J.P., there were right-wing Twitter personalities who had taken to social media because of what they described as the 'inherent bias' of the traditional news media; there were American Vedic experts who railed against a secular state that rejected its Hindu past; there were Muslim baiters; there were pseudo-historians who have rewritten Indian history to fit the political needs of the present.
>
> What all these people had in common was an immense sense of grievance against an establishment they had vanquished electorally, but whose ideas still defined them.[31]

In the run-up to the 2014 general election and subsequently, Modi was denounced for being an affront to the very 'Idea of India'.[32] In power, the BJP was mocked for being devoid of ideas altogether and for being a jumble of prejudices. Describing the Modi era as 'The Age of Cretinism', Pratap Bhanu Mehta wrote, 'There is no doubt that India is in a full blown reactionary moment. It is hard to grasp the nature of this reaction because it wears the garb of deep democratic legitimacy; it is an admission of despair described as the politics of hope. All the attributes of a reactionary politics are now gathered in one coherent form.'[33]

The condescension of intellectuals is not a new experience for political formations on the right. The Conservative Party in the UK has often been described as the 'stupid party' and even the 'nasty party' for its views on law and order and immigration. More than anything else, this disdain has stemmed from the general disinclination of those who consider themselves wedded to tradition to reduce their beliefs and convictions to either theoretical constructs or dogma. Indeed, the right has often been distinguished by its quasi-spiritual vagueness. In the preface to historian Arthur Bryant's tract on conservatism published in 1932, celebrated Scottish novelist Colonel John Buchan argued strongly against reducing conservatism to a dogma: 'Conservatism is above all things a spirit . . . and the fruits of that spirit are continuity and unity . . . It believes that the state is an organic not a mechanical thing, and that there should be no violent disruption in growth. It conserves what is still alive but it ruthlessly lops off the dead boughs.'[34]

On his part, the British parliamentarian Edmund Burke, often regarded as the father of modern conservatism for his opposition to the French Revolution, expressed his distaste for 'abstraction' because he was always mindful of 'human frailty and the particular circumstances of an age and nation'.[35] To philosopher Roger Scruton, the inability of conservatism to 'announce itself in maxims, formulae or aims' wasn't evidence of any intellectual shortcoming. It stemmed 'from an awareness of the complexity of human things, and from an attachment to values which cannot be understood with the abstract clarity of utopian theory'.[36] Burke was quite explicit about not rejecting 'prejudice' out of hand. 'The individual is foolish, but the species is wise; prejudices and prescriptions are the instruments which the wisdom of the species employs to safeguard man against his own passions and appetites.'[37] Consequently, apart from fascists who remain committed to radical ruptures, the traditional right has acted on the belief 'that a living society can only change healthily when it changes naturally—that is, in accordance with its acquired and inherited character, and at a given rate'.[38]

The emphasis on the context of human experiences and attitudes clearly indicates that the scope for right-wing and conservative universalism is limited. The nineteenth-century British prime minister Benjamin Disraeli's assertion that 'the Conservative Party is national or it is nothing' still holds.[39] This is despite attempts by right-wing think tanks to suggest that adherence to globalization, free trade, entrepreneurship, and fiscal prudence can be a universal bond among non-socialist formations. Within the EU, particularly in Germany and some Scandinavian countries, there is also a trend among conservative parties to discover global commonalities centred on human rights and shared sovereignty. The extent to which these post-national impulses in Europe stem from the bitter experiences of two world wars and an abhorrence of the fascist inheritance is worth considering. A study of the complex relationship between culture and politics in nineteenth-century Germany has, for example, suggested that 'cosmopolitanism quite often became a refuge for those who could not but stay aloof from national culture'.[40]

Right-wing nationalist movements are invariably rooted in specific social formations and cultures. They tend to be vastly dissimilar. Yet, there are broad common strands.

First, what distinguishes national movements with a conservative orientation against liberal tendencies is the primacy attached to community wisdom over individual choices. 'The condition of mankind,' wrote Scruton, 'requires that individuals, while they exist and act as autonomous beings, do so only because they can first identify themselves as something greater— as members of a society, group, class, state or nation, of some arrangement to which they may not attach a name but which they recognise instinctively as home.'[41] The aim of politics is to ensure that rampant individualism does not come into conflict with community interests and endanger civil order.

The community, in turn, is defined by historical memory. In explaining Burke's resolute defence of 'native' society over the depredations of the East India Company, the chronicler of conservative thought Russel Kirk argued that: 'He had defended those liberties not because they were innovations discovered in the Age of Reason, but because they were ancient prerogatives, guaranteed by immemorial usage. Burke was liberal because he was conservative.'[42] To Burke, only a small fraction of human knowledge was formally codified, with the greater part captured in instinct, common usage, customs and tradition. This may explain the recurrence in the English imagination of the idea of the 'ancient Constitution', celebrating ancestral rights that predated the Norman conquest.

Even when these myths are shown to have tenuous links to history, they serve a valuable social purpose. Political philosopher David Miller identified at least two functions: '. . .they provide reassurance that the national community of which one now forms part is solidly based in history, that it embodies a real continuity between generations; and they perform a moralising role by holding up before us the virtues of our ancestors and encouraging us to live up to them'.[43]

In practical terms, this translates into respect for what the British Conservative politician David Willets has described as the 'unreflective but deeply felt values of the normal citizen',[44] and the celebration of what Scruton described as 'ordinary prohibitions and decencies'.[45] Indeed, ordinariness has been a powerful idea when taking on an arrogant establishment committed to changing society in its own image.

Secondly, conservative nationalists, as we have seen earlier, have attached great importance to the sacred in maintaining national life. There have been attempts to rework conservatism as a secular, rational approach, but as the American conservative writer Irving Kristol quipped in 1956, 'conservative disposition is real enough but without the religious dimension, it is thin gruel'.[46] As late as 1959, in a tract for the Conservative Party for the British general election, Lord Hailsham argued that: 'There can be no genuine conservatism which is not founded upon a religious view of the basis of civil obligation, and there can be no true religion where the basis of civil obligation is treated as purely secular.'[47]

Over the years, this commitment to Christian doctrines has eroded throughout Europe—although there is a spirited fightback in countries such as Poland and Hungary. The post-Christian consensus centred on secularism, according to conservative nationalists, has undermined national unity. In the words of Cambridge historian Maurice Cowling, the 'loss of the Church's psychological reassurance' introduced 'uncertainty in the historic English personality which has made coherent feeling difficult to maintain'. Cowling attributed this transformation and collapse to liberalism which, after the late 1960s, came to be equated with 'any decent moral opinion'. In a scathing attack, he described the emergent liberalism as 'a movement for spreading what can only, with unavoidable vagueness, call "niceness". Liberals hated anything that might cause pain or stress . . . One liberalism or another operating in this idiom picked up a hostility to everything from punishment to meat, from sexual repression to academic testing.'[48]

Thirdly, while there is no uniform pattern in how nationalists view the state and its role, the tendency in conservatism is to circumscribe the authority of the state by the will of society. There is a view, at least among conservatives in the West, that the state should not impose any preconceived version of the good on a reluctant society. In the words of David Miller, conservative governments should aspire to create 'an environment in which the culture can develop spontaneously rather than being eroded by economically self-interested action on the part of particular individuals'.[49]

A more radical view suggests that the state should desist from intrusive involvement in the management of the economy. In Scruton's view, 'The state's relation to the citizen is not, and cannot be, contractual. It is therefore not the relation of employer and employee. The state has the authority, the responsibility, and the despotism of parenthood. If it loses those attributes, then it must perish, and society along with it. The state must therefore withdraw from every economic arrangement which puts it at the mercy of individual citizens.'[50] Needless to say, this purist view is not widely shared.

Finally, nationalist conservatism perceives itself as the embodiment of national identity. A conservative is much more than just a patriot; he is simultaneously a nationalist, with a primary commitment to the nation state. Although this may often imply an adherence to cultural homogeneity, the reality isn't entirely black and white. David Miller's sympathetic view of national identity in the modern context seems closer to reality: 'If we think of national cultures not as implying complete uniformity but as a set of overlapping cultural characteristics—beliefs, practices, sensibilities—which different members exhibit in different combinations and to different degrees, then . . . it is reasonably clear that distinct national cultures do exist.'[51] However, national identity naturally involves a large measure of genuflection to authority. Going by Scruton's stark formulation, the price of a national community involves 'sanctity, intolerance, exclusion and a sense that life's meaning depends upon obedience and also on vigilance against the enemy'.[52]

Such an espousal of national identity is naturally at odds with the multiculturalist view that sees the acknowledgement and even institutionalization of group differences as a compelling necessity. Apart from the old liberal desire to promote civic values to bind people, there are influential voices seeking to decouple the majority culture from the wider political culture and separate the nation from the state.[53] The tensions involving the EU and countries such as Hungary and Poland are a consequence.

In recent years, the notion of 'constitutional patriotism'—a phrase coined by the German intellectual Jürgen Habermas—has been put forward as an alternative to national identity, possibly to overcome potential internal conflicts involving nationhood. The idea originated in post-war Germany and was an attempt to create a completely new political identity that carried nothing of the troubled baggage of the past and was based entirely on rights and procedures. Since then, the idea has evolved into a prescription for post-national goals and constitutes an attempt to ensure that 'the nation-state becomes denuded of cultural content'.[54]

Adherence and commitment to a constitution is an important facet of a political democracy. It, at best, demarcates both the liberal and the conservatives from ultra-right fascists and ultra-left communists seeking the violent overthrow of the existing order. But, as David Miller has argued, 'It does not provide the kind of political identity that nationality provides. In particular, it does not explain why the boundaries of the political community should fall here rather than there; nor does it give you any sense of the historical identity of the community, the links that bind present-day politics to decisions made and actions performed in the past.'[55] Nor does it help to relegate national identity to a 'private set of cultural values'. Important as these undoubtedly are, they cannot serve as substitutes for a 'public understanding of the terms on which we are going to carry on our collective life'.[56]

This brief survey of the ideas and principles that govern nationalist conservative thought, particularly in the Anglophone democracies, may serve as pointers in locating India's nationalist conservative politics in a wider context. But two caveats are in order.

First, both English and American conservatism emerged in self-governing states with democracies that evolved and matured over centuries. India, however, had lost its sovereign status and was a subject nation until the middle of the twentieth century, this despite islands of independence and patchy bids to regain sovereignty. The manifestations of nationalist conservatism were, under the circumstances, likely to be different. In pre-Independence India there was a larger focus on custom, culture, religion and national pride than on political and state institutions.

Secondly, there is a problem posed by translation. Many of the doctrinal shorthands that emerged in Europe and America had, in many cases, no equivalents, either linguistically or conceptually, in the Indian languages. In his study of the Indian liberal tradition, Christopher Bayly referred to the unsatisfactory translation of 'liberal' as udarvadi.[57] Similar difficulties are encountered in attempting to capture the essence of 'conservatism' in Indian languages. A possible way out is to view conservatism in oppositional terms:[58]

- as the opposite of liberalism: *anudar panth*
- as that opposed to progressivism: *rudhivad*
- as anti-revolution: *kranti virodh*
- as anti-egalitarianism: *asamantavad*
- as opposed to state controls: *vaishvikta*

None of these appear entirely satisfactory, and it is a possible reason why conservatism suffers from non-usage in the Indian languages. In political discourse, it is used synonymously with *dakshin panth* (right wing) or even *pratikriyasheel* (reactionary). Even in English-language usage, the use of conservative/conservatism as implying a political orientation, rather than a set of attitudes, is rare. The expression 'Hindu right' and the deeply unsatisfactory 'Hindu fundamentalism' are the preferred choices in the media. In part this is an expression of political preference but it may also be explained by the larger unfamiliarity with the literature on the subject.

The spectacular influence of Western political thought—particularly John Stuart Mill, Jeremy Bentham, Auguste Comte, and subsequently, Karl Marx—on Indian intellectuals professing either liberalism or socialism, has been exhaustively studied and documented. By contrast, the roots of India's conservative traditions, being largely indigenous, have been less scrutinized. While some scholars have detected European influences—conscious or otherwise—on Indian political thought, the indigenous knowledge systems that shaped the minds of those stalwarts that don't fit easily into the 'progressive' mould have been relatively less explored. The study of India's conservative nationalism is still at a nascent stage.[59]

As has been noticed with the *Vande Mataram* and cow slaughter issues, there was never any clear divide between Hindu

nationalism and the Congress variants of nationalism. Both
overlapped and fed on each other. Recent misunderstandings on
the subject have entirely to do with the assumption that the rise
in nationalist consciousness from the late nineteenth century was
a direct consequence of English education and Western political
thought. Subsequent historical research has revealed that while
English-educated Indians assumed prominence and occupied
the national stage, there were other indigenous influences that
were just as important. Historian C.A. Bayly, for example, has
argued that 'the Indian national movement which emerged in the
1870s and 1880s drew upon and recast some patterns of social
relations, sentiments, doctrines and embodied memories which
had come into existence before British rule was established . . .'[60]
Ties of nationality forged by pilgrimages, notions of territoriality,
emergence of cross-caste solidarities, and even an emotional
alienation from the state after the establishment of Muslim rule
helped forge a notion of what Bayly has described as a 'sacred
landscape'. Particularly significant was the contribution of
Shivaji and his successors. 'The Marathas saw themselves, not as
usurpers of Mughal rule, but as the protectors of the boundaries
of Hindustan.'[61]

The importance that many Indians, particularly those
living outside Calcutta and Bombay, attached to indigenous
cultural forms were not eroded with the advent of colonial rule.
'Patriotism, in a distorted form, could coexist with loyalism, even
pathetic dependence on the British government. It could also
co-exist with a form of Hindu assertion.'[62] Consequently, there
was no rigid demarcation between liberalism and conservatism.'
They were, as Bayly noted, 'joined at the hip from birth'.[63]

The blurring of lines between who was 'progressive' or
traditionalist and 'reactionary' is best highlighted in the lives of
two nineteenth-century Bengal stalwarts: Pandit Ishwar Chandra
Vidyasagar (1820–91) and Raja Radhakanta Deb (1784–1867).

Vidyasagar, a distinguished principal of Sanskrit College,
Calcutta, is viewed in the popular imagination as an enlightened

social reformer who fought Hindu orthodoxy. The reputation owes significantly to the leading role he played in legitimizing Hindu widow remarriage, a measure that is seen as the next forward from the outlawing of sati during the tenure of Governor General Lord William Bentinck. While Vidyasagar's stellar role in bringing the plight of widows—especially young girls given away in marriage to much older men—was quite audacious, it is also significant that he joined hands with 'respectable' Bengali society in opposing the Age of Consent Act that raised the minimum age of marriage for girls to twelve years. Both his endorsement of widow remarriage and his resolute opposition to the colonial state tinkering with Hindu marriage customs were based on a reading of the shastras and not from secular concerns.[64]

Likewise, while seeking 'a renewal of common Hindu sensibility'[65] Vidyasagar did not disavow all existing social norms altogether, even when they were at odds with his reading of the shastras. As principal of Sanskrit College, he endorsed a scheme for the admission of Kayastha students—along with Brahmin and Baidya students who were admitted right from the inception of the College—but opposed allowing access to Sanskrit learning to Sudras, including the prosperous Subarnabanik caste. His argument was that they were 'at present lacking respectability' and their ritual status was 'very low'.[66]

Vidyasagar, it has been suggested, 'sought to influence the religious instincts of his people by explaining to them, in a new light, the scriptural texts of their own honoured and sacred authorities. It was an endeavour to initiate social reforms on the very grounds of conformity to established religion.'[67] He never sought upheaval in Hindu society.

Raja Radhakanta Deb, a contemporary of both Raja Ram Mohan Roy and Vidyasagar, has often been caricatured as the epitome of orthodoxy and bigotry for his opposition to the legislation banning sati. In hindsight, the opposition seems akin to endorsing an inhuman practice on the ground of tradition.

However, there was a specific context to his opposition. In 1829, Deb, partnered the creation of the Dharma Sabha, that sought to bring Hindus with different ritual traditions under a common umbrella, not least to be vigilant against attempts by the British government to interfere in the customs of its Hindu subjects. Interestingly, even Vidyasagar had misgivings over relying on alien rulers to usher change, but justified it on grounds of expediency and a misplaced—but not novel—belief that the 'sole object of their [British] conquest is to bring about all-round welfare of the country'.[68]

Despite his opposition to the sati legislation, there is a common thread running through the public lives of Deb and Vidyasagar. Deb, for example, served as the director of Hindu College for nearly three decades. He was also an important functionary of the Calcutta School Society and the Calcutta School Book Society. He had a special interest in women's education and co-authored a manual on women's education. According to a historical assessment, Deb 'tried to drive a wedge between English education and English ideas. The first in his view was functionally useful and the second socially unsettling.'[69] This was not very dissimilar from Vidyasagar's insistence that the teaching of Western philosophy and the Hindu shastras should be kept firmly apart.[70]

Among the reasons why the application of the modern-day liberal–conservative schism was problematic in pre-Independence India was the broadly similar concerns over colonial rule. When Clive defeated Siraj-ud-Daulah at Plassey in 1757 and acquired control over Bengal, the Indian merchants of Calcutta are said to have celebrated. Despite the severe hiccups of 'dual government' and the commercial depredations of the East India Company before the Crown stepped in, there was broad consensus in Bengali Hindu society that British rule was a marked improvement over what had prevailed earlier. Bankimchandra, in particular, believed that British rule had rescued Bengal from the disorders of Muslim rule, a theme that found reflection in *Anandamath*.[71]

In the 1890s, the writer Chandranath Basu—who coined the term 'Hindutva' for the title of his book in 1892—admonished the poet Nabinchandra Sen for upholding the glories of Siraj in Palashir yuddha: 'Why is the Hindu so remorseful if the Muslim should lose Bengal? And why may I ask, does Mohanlal lament? Is it because he is only a servant of the Muslim? And as a Hindu should you not be upset at this?'[72]

The antipathy to Muslim rule was also quite marked in the consciousness of the Maratha territories. The poet Ramdas (1608–81), the spiritual guru of Shivaji, for example, lamented: 'Many people have now become Mahomedans; some have fallen on the field of battle; many have lost touch with their native language, and have become proficient in foreign tongues. The bounds of Maharashtra have been constrained.'[73] During the riots in Benares in 1809 and 1811, involving local Hindus and Muslim weavers, the petitions to the British authorities from Hindus provided 'evidence of an articulate history of grievance and victimhood . . . (The) petitioners argued that they had suffered discrimination under the Mughal emperor Aurangzeb and his local officers, but had been too weak to act. Now, with the waning of Muslim power in India, they could reassert their ancient rights and block the pretension of the Muslim weavers on their sacred space.'[74]

The belief in British rule as deliverance waned outside the metropolitan cities of Calcutta and Bombay. It was mixed among the Brahmins that were the mainstay of Peshwa rule which, despite its many imperfections, was centred on the notions of regional pride and Hindu glory. Bayly has noted that 'the strongest resistance [to British rule] came apparently from middling or aspiring groups in society and not necessarily from the established oligarchy or upper bureaucrats, many of whom compromised with the British to retain their office and perquisites . . . Men brought up in the regional homelands and committed to their cultural and religious institutions were stubborn in their resistance than rootless aristocrats and itinerant pens men.'[75]

Yet, despite groups that rejected British rule and all forms of Western cultural influences completely, the complete political dominance of the Raj ruled out anything but qualified assertions of nationality. Consequently, loyalty to the government and fierce pride in Indianness, particularly India's heritage, existed simultaneously. The cultural self-assertion ranged from discoveries of common Aryan ancestry to believing that the core of all scientific knowledge could be discovered in ancient Sanskrit texts.[76]

There was always a realization that India had become a subject nation and lost its sovereign status. The racial discrimination and the racist slurs most Indians experienced drove home the realities of being a conquered people. The shame this generated, along with the anger over the rhetoric of Christian missionaries and suspicion of the government's cultural engineering, ensured that loyalism was never unequivocal, despite the over-abundance of flattery— some comic—for the rulers. Historian Tapan Raychaudhuri has described the convoluted and contradictory responses to British rule in nineteenth-century Bengal as 'neurotic'.[77]

'Neurotic' or not, from the 1830s, different parts of India witnessed an intellectual churning triggered by the encounter with colonial rule. In his study of Indian liberalism, Bayly has detected 'a broad and internally contested range of thought and practice directed to the pursuit of political and social liberty. Its common features were a desire to re-empower India's people with personal freedom in the face of the despotic government of the foreigners, embodied traditional authority and supposedly corrupt domestic or religious practices'.[78] At the same time, there were parallel currents that sought to preserve, strengthen, and reform indigenous institutions, blend it with the larger community reawakening processes and generate a resurgent India. Predictably, there were internal differences over how much to conserve and how much to adapt to outside influences. These differences were relatively less in evidence till Independence but formed the basis of political schisms subsequently.

In assessing why India had become a subject nation and what could be done to recover national self-esteem, there was broad agreement over the absence of national feeling—a commonality of purpose the British were seen to possess in abundance. Writing in 1901, the educationist and one-time vice chancellor of Bombay University, R.G. Bhandarkar, was explicit that: 'A regard for national interest must grow up amongst us . . . In our history as Hindus as a whole we have shown no concern for national or corporate interests, or were not actuated by the national spirit or sentiment or consequently allowed ourselves to be conquered by foreigners.'[79] Lala Lajpat Rai similarly asked in 1907: 'A question has often haunted us . . . as to why is it that notwithstanding the presence among us of great, vigorous and elevating truths, and of the very highest conception of morality, we [Hindus] have been a subject race, held down for so many centuries by sets of people who were neither physically nor spiritually nor even intellectually so superior to us . . . to demand our subjection.'[80] Like Bhandarkar, he too concluded that 'individual selfishness, greed and calculation' had prevented national unity. The political answer, he felt, was to inculcate 'a sense of social responsibility which requires each and every member of the organization to place the interests of the community or the nation above those of his own'.[81]

Bhudeb Mukhopadhyay (1827–1894), an early conservative who grappled with the issues of what to conserve and what to modify,[82] complimented the British for 'their will power, skills and mutual sympathy, the results of observing codes appropriate for their country and their faith'.[83] He felt that the British conquest of India 'was also divine dispensation: for Indians divided against themselves on the basis of race and language would now learn patriotism from the British whose love for their country transcended even their moral sense'.[84] Nor was this admiration of Britain's national character confined to the presidencies. The Hindi writer Harishchandra felt that a 'pious worldly religion and a free press working in a national language had consolidated a strong patriotism and made Britain a world power'. By contrast, India was like a train with separate first- , second- and third-class carriages but no engine to move it.[85]

Both the sneaking and explicit admiration of British character was inevitably contrasted with India's own shortcomings, particularly the distortions that had undermined Hindu traditions. Bankimchandra often contrasted British worldliness with the Hindu penchant for asceticism, abstruse philosophical speculation, and the corresponding failure to master the world of nature.

> 'Knowledge is power': that is the slogan of Western civilisation. 'Knowledge is salvation' is the slogan of Hindu civilisation . . . Europeans are devotees of power. That is the key to their advancement. We are negligent towards power: that is the key to our downfall. Europeans pursue a goal which they must reach in this world: they are victorious on earth. We pursue a goal which lies in the world beyond, which is why we have failed to win on earth. Whether we will win in the life beyond is a question on which there are differences of opinion.[86]

The absence of any worthwhile tradition of science and technical education was a perennial lament of India's nationalists, and India's failure was often contrasted with Japan's success. However, unlike the nineteenth century that had witnessed a rush to absorb every European idea and trend, the rise of political nationalism saw a demand for the Indianization of education. In 1911, Sir Rashbehari Ghosh, once the president of a Congress session, asked for 'Hindu ethics and metaphysics' to be given a 'foremost place' in the curriculum. S. Srinivasa Iyengar claimed at a conference in Madras in 1921 that the education system had 'ignored India's racial psychology, history, literature and religion, and patriotic ideals and aspiration'.[87] It was to meet some of these concerns, but without repudiating the West altogether that initiatives such as the Dayanand Anglo-Vedic colleges and the Banaras Hindu University were undertaken. Rabindranath Tagore's Viswa-Bharati in Santiniketan was altogether a very different initiative, although the cultural dimensions of nationalism were fully accommodated.

The issue of grappling with the realities of political power and evolving theories of statecraft were also issues that concerned the nationalists. Predictably, Shivaji was held up as an ideal and his ability to craft a Hindu state was widely celebrated, sometimes with a rash of European parallels. In 1934, for example, Professor S.R. Sharma, formerly of Fergusson College, Poona, published *The Founding of Maratha Freedom* where he claimed:

> Shivaji was a titanic creator in the realms of politics and nation-building. He had the vision of Mazzini, the dash of Garibaldi, the diplomacy of Cavour, and the patriotism, perseverance and intrepidity of William of Orange. He did for Maharashtra what Fredrick the Great achieved for Germany or Alexander the Great for Macedonia.

Such hyperbolic histories were denounced by Sir Jadunath Sarkar as 'pure nationalist brag and moonshine': 'We make ourselves ridiculous when we read the ideals and thoughts of the 20th century English educated nationalists into the lives of the sectarian or clannish champions of the 17th and 18th centuries.'[88]

On a more serious note, however, history was an important instrument in the hands of nationalists to highlight the importance of charitra (character) in the life of a nation. The genre of popular historical plays in Marathi contributed immeasurably to public awareness of uprightness in national life. Between 1860 and 1900 some sixty historical plays were written in Marathi; about 100 more were added by 1930, and another 170 more by 1960.[89] Many of these plays centred on the personality and deeds of Shivaji. According to a study by historian Prachi Deshpande, Shivaji was 'lionised as an important political figure and his life story was constructed as the ideal blend of tradition and modernity. In these representations, he embodied a moderate individualism that preached the necessity of individual action and enterprise but also maintained a healthy respect for religious and social tradition.' This was unlike Sambhaji who was portrayed as ill-tempered and blessed with bad habits and dodgy associates.[90]

The importance of charitra in the making of a people, or for that matter, empires, was mirrored in the writings of Sir Jadunath Sarkar, a historian of the Mughals and Marathas, whose writings exercised a tremendous influence till the 1970s. To Sarkar, 'what mediated between the "destiny" of a people and the contingency of their empirical reality was something called "character", the sheer capacity in humans for leadership, discipline, effort, mastering passions and self-cultivation. It was what separated destiny from fate and left the former open to multiple possibilities. Take away the question of character and the revealed greater purpose in human history remains unfulfilled.'[91]

Sarkar believed that British rule was a valuable, indeed, indispensable element of character building that would prepare India for self-rule. Like other admirers of British rule before him, he too believed that the way forward did not lie 'copying the externals of European civilisation' and 'plume herself in the borrowed feathers of European civilisation'. To produce a renaissance involved 'undergoing a new birth of spirit'.[92]

The idea of a cemented religion forging a resurgent Indian nationality held out a great attraction to conservative nationalists. Bal Gangadhar Tilak, in particular, attempted 'a populist reconfiguration of Hindu devotionalism and Hindu regional nationalism'.[93] Speaking at the Bharat Dharma Mahamandala in Benares on 3 January 1906, he was categorical that:

> Religion is an element in nationality . . . During Vedic times, India was a self-contained country. It was united as a great nation. That unity has disappeared bringing great degradation

and it becomes the duty of the leaders to revive that union. A Hindu of this place is as much a Hindu as one from Madras or Bombay. The study of the Gita, Ramayana and Mahabharata produce the same ideas throughout the country. Are not these—common allegiance to the Vedas, Gita and Ramayana—our common heritage? If we lay stress on it forgetting all the minor differences that exist between different sects, then by the grace of Providence we shall ere long be able to consolidate all the different sects into a mighty Hindu nation. This ought to be the ambition of every Hindu.[94]

Swami Vivekananda, who, in recent times, has often been portrayed as merely a mystic with a universal message, had earlier echoed Tilak and asserted that only religion could rescue the 'Hindu nation' that had become 'wretchedly jealous of one another' and 'gone to pieces'.

The problems in India are more complicated, more momentous, than the problems in any other country. Race, religion, language, government—all these together make a nation. The one common ground that we have is our sacred tradition, our religion. That is the only common ground, and upon that we shall have to build . . . The unity in religion, therefore, is absolutely necessary as the first condition of the future of India. There must be the recognition of one religion throughout the length and breadth of this land . . . National union in India must be a gathering up of its scattered spiritual forces. A Nation in India must be a union of those whose hearts beat to the same spiritual tune.[95]

Vivekananda was particularly concerned with asserting India's cultural sovereignty.

We Hindus . . . have been clamouring here for getting political rights and many other things . . . Rights and privileges . . . can only be expected between two equals. When one of the parties is a beggar, what friendship can there be? . . . So I must call upon you to go out to England and America, not as beggars but as teachers of religion.[96]

In asserting India's soft power in the West, Vivekananda hoped that the mental squeamishness of India's own Western-educated gentlemen over their own inheritance would give way to cultural pride. That certainly was the impact of his interventions at the World Parliament of Religions in Chicago in 1893, an event that is still commemorated in India.

While belief in the centrality of a unified Hindu identity in the framework of nationhood was a common thread running through nationalist thought till the 1920s—when alternatives such as socialism and the Constitution entered the arena—there was less agreement over how this could be brought about.

For Bhudeb Mukhopadhyay, upholding the essence of the Hindu inheritance involved adhering unflinchingly to the ritually prescribed code laid down by the shastras and upholding the family. In his view, these prescriptions, which he adhered to as a Brahmin, gave society a cohesiveness and discipline. 'In his study of Europe and contact with Europeans, he failed to discover anything which could compensate for the loss of ideals by which his forebears had lived. He saw these as still a vital, if threatened component of national life.'[97]

As opposed to Bhudeb who fell back almost entirely on inherited ritualism, Bankimchandra felt that 'the actual enemy was not some force external to oneself but one's own selfishness, sentimentalism and cowardice'.[98] He was particularly harsh on popular superstitions and the enhanced ritualism—he called it a 'monstrous fantasy'—that had come to define the Hindu faiths and felt they were the reasons for India's decline.[99] Although an upholder—for understandable reasons given his role as a high functionary of the government—of what he described as 'non-political patriotism' Bankimchandra sought to move away from the Hindu preoccupation with metaphysical abstractions and the afterlife, and link individual salvation with social cohesion—as the likes of Aurobindo and Vivekananda were to do subsequently. In a bid to construct a modern nationhood, he felt that freedom was likely to be imperfect without the people being liberated socially and intellectually. Political assertion, Bankimchandra felt, had to be preceded by the 'cultural self-discovery of a people'.[100] 'The ancients,' he wrote, 'had made a mistake by submerging patriotism into the higher love of all created things and the balance had to be redressed.'[101]

Like Bankimchandra, Vivekananda believed in the centrality of religion in reinvigorating India. However, while Bankimchandra attached greater reliance on bhakti and the Puranic traditions, Vivekananda looked to India's spiritual traditions, particularly Vedanta for guidance. He believed that a man's true potential could be unearthed by intense spiritualism. In that sense, his approach was different from his spiritual guru Ramakrishna Paramahansa's path of bhakti and personal communion with the Deity.[102] In his discourses, Ramakrishna spoke in earthy parables while Vivekananda was attached to high philosophy.

However, what distinguished Vivekananda in late-nineteenth-century India was not merely his erudition in religious matters but his ability to link his spiritual mission with a larger nation-building purpose. He was perhaps the first religious figure—one who was perceived as a monk in saffron robes—who countered the highly individualistic notion of personal salvation taking priority over a larger commitment to society.[103] He extended the notion of unity of God and man into Practical Vedanta—a commitment to daridranarayan, the belief that service to God implied service to India's poor. 'And may I be born again and again,' he wrote to an American disciple in 1897, 'and suffer thousands of miseries, so that I may worship the only God that exists, the only God I believe in, the sum total of all souls. And above all, my God the wicked, my God the miserable, my God the poor of all races, of all species, is the especial object of my

worship.'[104] He attempted to guilt-trip the educated classes into
looking beyond their immediate world and acknowledging the
pitiable state of India. But most important, he believed that
the 'common people have suffered oppression. For thousands
of years—suffered it without murmur, and as a result have got
wonderful fortitude. They have suffered eternal misery, which
has given them unflinching vitality . . .' The future of India, he
felt, belonged to them.[105]

Vivekananda created his monastic order not merely to
strengthen Hinduism but to serve the poor, the backbone
of national life. His 'schemes of social service were more
modestly conceived and also perhaps less radical in their results
when compared to Gandhian programmes but the beginning
nevertheless had been made. Vivekananda anticipated Gandhi
in probably two respects: one of which surely is the attack on
untouchability and human oppression in the name of caste; and
the other, the idea of voluntary movements and restoring the
dignity of human labour.'[106] He inspired and continues to inspire
generations of Indians who took to public life inspired by his
message.

The belief that the caste prejudice and oppression was
dragging India down was an important feature of the Hindu
nationalist movement. The role of Swami Dayanand Saraswati
and the Arya Samaj, in this context, was seminal, particularly in
northern India.

Dayanand was outright in his rejection of the entire range of
popular Hinduism which he described as 'historical degradation'.
He harked back to the authenticity of a pure Vedic religion
that was simple, pure and, above all, free from Brahmanical
distortions.[107] Lala Lajpat Rai, an Arya Samaj stalwart and a
leading nationalist figure in Punjab, traced the demise of the
Hindu nation to the period after the decline of Buddhism when 'the
genius of a jealous and perverted, sometimes corrupt and selfish
priesthood built a vast and superstructure of conventionalities
and formalities, with an almost interminable labyrinth of rituals

and ceremonies'.[108] This was echoed by another leading light of the Arya Samaj, Swami Shraddhanand in his *Hindu Sangathan*, written in 1924: 'The great Aryan nation is said, at the present moment to be a dying race not because its numbers are dwindling but because it is completely disorganised. Individually, man to man, second to none on earth in terms of intellect and physique, possessing a code of morality unapproachable by any other race of humanity, the Hindu nation is still helpless on account of its manifold divisions and selfishness.'[109]

In practical terms, the Arya Samaj undertook two programmes to restore the vitality of Hindu society. The first, in debunking the caste system, it attempted to integrate the 'untouchables' into mainstream Hindu society. Secondly, and far more controversially, it initiated a shuddhi movement to reconvert Christians and Muslims back into the Hindu fold. Many Hindu leaders in the past had flagged their concerns over conversions, particularly by Christian missionaries, but the worry had been accompanied by mere anger and helplessness. The shuddhi innovation was the response. Regardless of how many Hindu organizations were involved in reconversions, the initiative enjoyed a huge measure of passive support and has persisted in patches after Independence.

There were important differences in the approach of individuals and organizations that believed in a revitalized Hindu identity for national regeneration. However, there were important points of convergence. By far the most important of these was the disavowal of individualism in the larger project of corporate citizenship, an approach that goes against the fundamentals of liberalism.

It is this theme that has resonated strongly in the RSS. The RSS, founded by K.B. Hedgewar in Nagpur in 1925, has steered clear of choosing between Hindu belief systems and modes of worship in upholding Hindu nationhood. Instead, it has attached prime importance to moulding the character of Hindus by the implantation of worthwhile samskaras (values) in its swayamsevaks. Among the values it has consciously cherished is discipline. According to M.S. Golwalkar, the second—and by far the most influential—head of the organization, 'all our great authorities on mental discipline have ordained us not to succumb to overflow of emotions and weep in the name of God but to apply ourselves to a strict discipline of day-to-day penance. Effusion of emotions will only shatter the nerves and make the person weaker than before, leaving him a moral wreck.'[110] He was very disdainful of individualism:

> It is natural that the persons in the Sangh imbued with the correct national perspective react spontaneously to the various national problems that arise from time to time in the same manner. To mistake it for mental regimentation is to call the spirit of nationalism itself as an instrument of regimentation! It is the undigested modern ideas like 'freedom of thought', 'freedom of speech', etc, that are playing havoc in the minds of our young men who look upon freedom as licence and self-restraint as mental regimentation.[111]

Deendayal Upadhyaya, whose theory of Integral Humanism is held by the BJP to be its guiding principle, wasn't quite as brutal in his repudiation of individualism. But in his mind too, the individual was subordinated to society and dharma. While society, in his view, was a living organism with a defined *chiti* (ethos) that 'protected' the national soul, dharma was the 'innate law' that sustained individuals in a society. The power of dharma, in turn, was exemplified 'in the ideal of the family'.[112]

The Swatantra Party has often been held out as an example of a 'secular' right-wing tradition in India that was subsumed by the greater appeal of the Hindu right. While there is no doubt that the Swatantra Party showed a greater attachment to the free market, unlike the Jana Sangh and BJP that was often partial to state-sponsored redistributive programmes, the belief that it disavowed the religious underpinnings of conservatism is a myth.

The leading light of the Swatantra Party was unquestionably Chakravarti Rajagopalachari or Rajaji, as he popularly known. A veteran Congressman and close associate of Mahatma Gandhi with a reputation for intellectual sharpness and independent thinking, Rajaji fell out with Nehru on the question of excessive state involvement in the economy. However, outside the realms of day-to-day politics, Rajaji was an archetypal traditionalist in the mould of an earlier generation of conservative thinkers.

To Rajaji, the 'loosening of the religious impulse is the worst of the disservices rendered by the Congress to the nation. We must organise a new force and movement to replace the greed and the class hatred of Congress materialism with a renovated spiritual outlook emphasising the restraints of good conduct as of greater importance than the triumphs of organised covetousness.' The restraint was, to him, born of dharma that would facilitate 'an organic growth which it is our duty to respect and which we should not treat as mere Indian superstition or eccentricity'. He venerated the joint family and decried 'the cult of individuality' and 'perverted social movements'. He believed that Hindu thought was 'scientific' and based 'as a search for truth and not as a matter of dogma'. If 'our 400 million strike out religion from their lives, India will be wiped out'.[113]

Rajaji's colleague in the Swatantra Party was K.M. Munshi, another former Congressman best known for his role in facilitating the rebuilding of the Somnath Temple in Gujarat, an example that inspired those who sought the construction of a grand Ram temple on the site of the Babri Masjid in Ayodhya. Munshi's other great contribution was the establishment of the Bharatiya Vidya Bhavan that sought to give dynamic expression to the idea of Bharatiya shiksha. 'The ultimate aim of Bharatiya shiksha,' claimed the Bhavan's statement of principles, 'is to teach the younger generation to appreciate and live up to the permanent values of Bharatiya vidya which flowing from the supreme act of creative life-energy as represented by Shri Ramachandra, Shri Krishna, Vyasa, Buddha and Mahavira have expressed themselves in modern times in the life of Shri Ramakrishna Paramahansa, Swami Dayanand Saraswati and Swami Vivekananda, Shri Aurobindo and Mahatma Gandhi.'[114]

In hindsight, it can be gauged that the Indian right was characterized by a huge measure of continuity that extended from the middle of the nineteenth century. The themes that preoccupied conservative thinkers quietly resisting colonial encroachments are no doubt important as history. But many of these preoccupations did not die out with the onset of Independence and the recovery of national sovereignty. They have persisted as guiding forces in contemporary India. The idea of national resurgence is as important in a globalized twenty-first century setting as it was in the India of the mid-nineteenth century. The ideas that drove Indians of an earlier age have persisted in one form or another in shaping contemporary politics. The quest for a New India has invariably involved the rediscovery of an Old India.

3

Politics and the Hindu Narrative

On 11 January 2019, the BJP formally launched its campaign to secure re-election of the Narendra Modi government. Speaking at the National Council convention to party cadres gathered from all parts of India, BJP president Amit Shah said the election of the Modi government in 2014 was a landmark in the history of independent India and it was crucial the gains be defended. The party, he said, had won important battles but there was no room for complacency: '2019 will be a decisive contest like the third battle of Panipat. The Marathas had won over 131 battles but lost in Panipat against the forces of Ahmad Shah Abdali. The Maratha defeat led to 200 years of colonial slavery.'[1]

The historical analogy was telling. In the eyes of Hindu nationalists, the war to regain national sovereignty that had been launched with Shivaji's rebellion against Mughal rule, did not culminate in the achievement of Independence in 1947, though that was an important step. India, they believed, would reach fulfilment and realize its manifest destiny once nationhood was recrafted to reflect its larger Hindu ethos.

This belief dated back to the early nationalists groping to imagine a post-colonial vision of India. In the late nineteenth century, the Bengali writer Bhudeb Mukhopadhyay penned a novel *Swapnalabdha Bharater Itihas* (A History of India as Revealed in a Dream). He visualized a Maratha victory in the third battle of Panipat against the Afghan invaders. For him, this

victory was a decisive might-have-been moment of history and
he envisaged a prosperous, united India, ruled by a wise Hindu
monarch. The kingdom was the epitome of enlightened Hindu
virtues—the rule of dharma that incorporated Western science
and technology.[2]

The evolution of a sovereign India that blended material
progress with a strong sense of cultural rootedness was at the
heart of the conservative Hindu nationalist project from the
1930s, when the end of British rule seemed imminent. Japan,
quite predictably, was a major source of inspiration, as were
some of the princely states such as Baroda and Mysore. The
problem lay in nurturing a political vehicle that would make this
transformation possible, a vehicle that was led by enlightened
souls and relatively insulated from the distortions of mass politics.
At the first Round Table Conference in London in 1930, the
Maharaja of Rewa expressed his dismay that 'in a country whose
ways of life are so dominated by custom and tradition, there
should be no political party which calls itself Conservative.' He
expressed the hope that as British rule was eased out, 'a strong
party of experienced and responsible politicians will emerge,
which will call itself the Conservative Party'.[3]

The hope was to remain unfulfilled for another five decades.
The advent of Mahatma Gandhi as the undisputed leader of the
freedom movement after 1920 put both Hindu nationalism and
conservative politics in the shade. This is not to suggest that the
ideas that were prominent in the earlier phases of nationalism
were completely eclipsed. Far from it.

When he gave his call to achieve Swaraj in one year by
boycotting all government institutions, Gandhi seemed the
great deliverer that many Indians hoped would lift India from
bondage, humiliation and despondency. His mass appeal was
phenomenal, and he was cast in the role of a traditional guru and
a saint, attributes that appealed particularly to rural folk whose
involvement in the Congress had hitherto been nominal. Gandhi's
celebration of the Indian village and the village community,

his partiality for indigenous medicine and his message of Ram Rajya appealed to a large body of traditionalists—particularly in Middle India—who had been less touched by the prevalence of Western ideas and lifestyles in the three presidencies.

However, just as Gandhi won mass adulation, he was viewed with some suspicion by many of those who had played a role in nurturing national consciousness in the earlier part of the century. Even those who accepted his leadership on account of his connect with ordinary people, Gandhi's ideas were treated with considerable scepticism.

The doubts were broadly on account of three factors.

First, there was his steadfast refusal to accept technology—an aspect of modernity that enamoured Indians in search of national resurgence. Gandhi's rejection of modern medicine, in particular, struck even his devoted followers as eccentric. Subhas Bose, who gave up a career in the Indian Civil Service to join his political mentor Chittaranjan Das in the movement for Swaraj in a year, could, for example, never quite understand why Gandhi elevated the medieval absurdity of the charkha into a modern panacea.

Secondly, his fanatical disavowal of violence directed against the enemy seemed bizarre to those inspired by the Italian Risorgimento and the daring deeds of the Fenians in Ireland, not to mention an underlying justification of violence for a just cause, particularly the restoration of dharma, in the Bhagavadgita. Whereas Gandhi viewed non-violence as evidence of great moral strength, his political detractors saw it as cowardice. The followers of Lokmanya Tilak, in particular, pitted themselves against Gandhi and their estrangement from the Congress was to become permanent.

Finally, Gandhi's incorporation of the masses into political life—a phenomenon that contributed to rioting and peasant unrest in the Non-Cooperation movement—was viewed with profound disquiet, if not distaste. The stalwarts of the Indian National Liberal Federation who revelled in interventions on the Constitution were among those wary of the Congress's mass orientation, as was Muhammad Ali Jinnah who—in his pre-1936 avatar—was fearful that an explosive mix of religiosity and the mob would take India in dangerous directions. On his part, the poet Rabindranath Tagore expressed fears that the noble Mahatma, whom he deeply admired, had unleashed passions that would prove uncontrollable. 'An oppressive atmosphere,' he wrote at the height of the Non-Cooperation movement, 'seemed to burden the land. Some outside compulsion seemed to be urging one and all to talk in the same strain, to work at the same mill . . . Today, in the atmosphere of the country, there is a spirit of persecution, which is not that of armed force, but something still more alarming, because it is invisible'.[4]

One of Gandhi's great political experiments in 1921 was to link the Congress's movement for Swaraj with the Muslim agitation for the restoration of the Caliphate in Turkey. In tactical terms, this was a master stroke. For the first time since the uprising of 1857, British rule was confronted with significant opposition from both Hindus and Muslims. This combination made the movement particularly potent in towns and cities and neutralized to some extent Gandhi's image as a Hindu leader. With his experiences in South Africa to guide him, Gandhi probably realized that the overwhelmingly Hindu ethos of the earlier swadeshi movement had left India's largest religious minority cold. He sought to overcome this by calling for a multi-faith patriotism, which left each religious community free to do their own thing. Addressing the question of Hindu–Muslim unity in 1920, Gandhi wrote:

> I hold it to be utterly impossible for Hindus and Mahomedans to inter-marry and yet retain intact each other's religion. And the true beauty of Hindu-Mahomedan Unity lies in each remaining true to his own religion and yet being true to each other . . . What then does the Hindu-Mahomedan Unity consist in and how can it be best promoted? The answer is simple. It

consists in our having a common purpose, a common goal and common sorrows.[5]

Confronted with the question of inter-dining, Gandhi suggested that stressing its importance was 'a superstition borrowed from the West. Eating is a process just as vital as the other sanitary necessities of life. And if mankind had not, much to its harm, made of eating a fetish and indulgence we would have performed the operation of eating in private even as one performs the other necessary functions of life in private . . .'[6]

Critics of Congress's alliance with the Khilafat movement felt that Gandhi went a step too far in trying to accommodate the Muslim community. Historian R.C. Majumdar concluded that 'there seems to be no doubt whatsoever that when he launched the Non-Cooperation movement on 1 August 1920, the Khilafat wrongs were the single issue which determined his action; the Punjab atrocities and the winning of swaraj were subordinate issues which were gradually tacked on to the main issue of Khilafat, at a later date and as an after-thought'.[7]

Unfortunately for Gandhi, his gesture was never fully reciprocated by the Khilafat leadership. The Ali brothers saw the understanding with Gandhi as purely tactical—even on the question of the Mahatma's pet theme of non-violence—and they were unconcerned with the idea of a common nationalism. In a speech in Broach, Gujarat, the Khilafat leader Mohammed Ali said that while at present they would keep the sword in its sheath, 'we must reserve the right to take up arms against the enemies of Islam'. On another occasion, he made the astonishing assertion that if the Emir of Afghanistan chose to invade India, it was the duty of Indian Muslims to support him.[8] In 1925, much after the Congress–Khilafat alliance broke down and Hindu–Muslim relations nosedived, Ali couldn't conceal his distaste for Hindus. 'However pure Gandhi's character may be,' he said, 'he must appear to me from the point of view of religion inferior to any Mussalman, even though he be without character.' He repeated this assertion of Muslim superiority later by saying that 'according to my religion and creed, I hold an adulterous and a fallen Mussalman to be better than Mr Gandhi'.[9]

The Non-Cooperation–Khilafat movement was the last time that a serious attempt was made to overcome sectarian divisions and forge a common nationality on the unity-in-action principle. As communal relations between Hindus and Muslims deteriorated and rioting became a recurrent feature of public life in many parts of India, the space for Hindu nationalism reopened. But it was a space that the Congress never vacated. Gandhi may have fallen out with the Muslim leadership and community, but in the eyes of India's Hindus, his position as the supreme leader of the Congress, and by implication, the national movement was never in doubt. The Hindu Mahasabha operated on the fringes of the Congress, explicitly championing Hindu interests that the main body felt too squeamish to take up. Meanwhile, as the British government agonized over constitutional proposals that would accord a small measure of self-government to Indians without at the same time compromising imperial interests, the polarization between Hindus and Muslims deepened. Gandhi came out of his self-imposed retirement in 1929 and initiated the Civil Disobedience movement, beginning with his salt satyagraha, but the Hindu–Muslim schism did not heal.

This was the backdrop in which Hindu nationalism found its leader in Vinayak Damodar Savarkar, a former revolutionary who had been imprisoned in 1911 for a decade in the Andaman Islands. Although he was freed from prison life in 1924, Savarkar was prohibited from moving out of Ratnagiri in Maharashtra until his unconditional release in 1937. On returning to public life, he assumed charge of the then somewhat directionless Hindu Mahasabha and became its foremost leader until 1948, when he was implicated in the assassination of Gandhi but subsequently acquitted.

In many ways Savarkar was not an archetypal Hindu nationalist. A self-professed rationalist, equally at ease with both the West and the East, Savarkar almost entirely disavowed the elaborate rituals associated with the Hindu faiths. Politics was his passion and it was this passion that led him to Hindu nationalism. He was a political Hindu.

Savarkar's main contribution to Indian nationalism was to try and incorporate the different ideas of Hindu resurgence within the framework of Hindutva (Hinduness). He gave Hindu nationalism a doctrine and although this doctrine has been tempered, modified, and even sanitized over the decades, it has been the starting point of all contemporary debates on the subject.

For Savarkar, the particular beliefs and modes of worship of different Hindu denominations was not of any great consequence and had to be displaced as the foundational element of Hindu identity. He drew a sharp distinction between Hinduism and Hindutva:

> Let Hinduism concern itself with the salvation of life after death, the concept of God and the universe. Let individuals be free to form opinions about the trio. The whole universe from one end to the other is the real book of religion. But so far as the materialistic and secular aspect is concerned, the Hindus are a nation bound by a common culture, a common history, a common language, a common country and a common religion.[10]

Consequently, he was particular to debunk the notion that the Hindu Mahasabha was 'an exclusively religious organisation, something like a Christian Mission'.

> The Hindu Mahasabha is not a Hindu Mission. It leaves religious questions regarding theism, monotheism, pantheism or even atheism to be discussed and determined by different Hindu schools of religious persuasions. It is not a Hindu Dharma Mahasabha, but a Hindu National Mahasabha . . .

[The] sphere of its activity is far more comprehensive than that of an exclusively religious body. The Hindu Mahasabha identifies itself with the National life of Hindudom in all its entirety, in all its social, economic, cultural and above all political aspects and is pledged to protect and promote all that contributes to the freedom, strength and glory of the Hindu Nation . . .[11]

Savarkar drew a sharp distinction between Hinduism and Hindutva. 'Hindutva is not a word but a history. Not only the spiritual or religious history of our people, but a history in full.'[12]

An important intervention by Savarkar—and one that is at the root of many contemporary controversies—centred on the issue of who is a Hindu, a vexed question since Hindu can be defined in both religious and civilizational terms. He arrived at the conclusion that a definition of Hindu 'which is not only historically and logically as sound as is possible in the case of such comprehensive terms' was indeed possible. Explaining the idea to a political gathering in Ahmedabad in 1937, he said:

Everyone who regards and claims this Bharatbhoomi from the Indus to the Seas as his Fatherland and Holy land is a Hindu. Here I must point out that it is rather loose to say that any person professing any religion of Indian origin is a Hindu. Because that is only one aspect of Hindutva. The second and equally essential constituent of the concept of Hindutva cannot be ignored if we want to save the definition from getting overlapping and unreal. It is not enough that a person should profess any religion of Indian origin, i.e. Hindustan as his punnyabhu, his Holy Land, but he must recognise it as his pitri bhu . . . his Fatherland as well.[13]

Although sacred territoriality was a facet of his definition of Hindu nationhood, Savarkar was harsh on secular territoriality, the Congress's 'assumption that the territorial unity, a common habitat, was the only factor that constituted and ought to and must constitute a Nation'. Looking at the strains in Europe over the recrafting of national boundaries in the aftermath of the Treaty of Versailles, Savarkar came to the conclusion that 'hotchpotch Nations based only on the shifting sands of the conception of Territorial Nationality, not cemented by any cultural, racial or historical affinities and consequently having no will to incorporate themselves into a Nation' were a recipe for disaster. The Hindus, he insisted, 'are no treaty Nation but an organic National Being'.

> We Hindus, in spite of thousand and one differences within our fold or bound by such religious, cultural, historical, racial, linguistic and other affinities in common as to stand out as a definitely homogeneous people as soon as we are placed in contrast with any other non-Hindu people, say the English or Japanese or even the Indian Muslims. That is the reason why today we the Hindus from Kashmere to Madras and Sindh to Assam will to be a Nation by ourselves, while the Indian Muslims are on the whole more inclined to identify themselves and their interests with Muslims outside India than Hindus who lived next door . . .[14]

Savarkar acknowledged that the bulk of India's Muslims were converts—albeit 'forcible in millions of cases'—and 'inherit Hindu blood in their veins'. Yet, in his view, they could not be regarded as Hindus. This was not merely because they didn't regard India as their Holy Land but because they lacked commitment to a common civilization. Muslims and Christians, he claimed, '[S]ince their adoption of a new cult . . . had ceased to own Hindu civilisation (sanskriti) as a whole. They belong, or feel that they belong, to a cultural unit altogether different from the Hindu one.'[15]

This belief in the innate and unbridgeable separateness of Hindus and Muslims led Savarkar to a stark and radical conclusion. By 1937, he advised his followers to 'bravely face unpleasant facts as they are. India cannot assume today to be a unitarian and homogeneous nation, but on the contrary, there are two nations in the main: the Hindus and the Muslims, in India.'[16]

Three years later, Muhammad Ali Jinnah and the Muslim League arrived at the same conclusion; and ten years later the British departed, leaving behind India and Pakistan.

Savarkar was quite clear in his mind that: 'We are not out to fight with England only to find a change of masters but we Hindus aim to be masters in our own house.' To Muslims he threw out the challenge 'if you come, with you; if you don't, without you; and if you oppose, in spite of you'.[17] However, despite this unequivocal assertion of majoritarian nationhood, Savarkar was careful to not extend the Hindu-first principle to the Indian state.

> Let the Indian State be purely Indian. Let it not recognise any invidious distinctions whatsoever as regards the franchise, public services, offices, taxation on the grounds of religion and race. Let no cognisance be taken whatsoever of man's being Hindu or Mohammedan, Christian or Jew. Let all citizens of that Indian State be treated according to their individual worth irrespective of their religious or racial percentage in the general population . . . Let 'one man one vote' be the general rule . . . I for one and thousands of the Mahasabhaites like me have set this ideal of an Indian State as our political goal ever since the beginning of our political career and shall continue to work for its consummation to the end of our life.[18]

This assertion of the principles of a secular, non-discriminatory state assumes importance in view of the debate over the RSS advocacy of a Hindu rashtra. There is a crucial distinction here between nationhood, which is governed by Hindutva, and a modern state where the principle of equal citizenship is operational. One involves the nation—where divergent visions compete in the political space—and the other centres on the principles governing the state.

In defining the Hindu nation, the second RSS sarsanghchalak, M.S. Golwalkar, took a somewhat different tack from Savarkar. Whereas for Savarkar the Hindu nation was based on civilization and historical memory, Golwalkar injected the notion of race. 'It is superfluous,' he wrote in his controversial *We, or Our Nationhood Defined* (first published in 1939), 'to emphasise the importance of Racial Unity in the Nation state. A Race is a hereditary Society having common customs, common language, common memories of glory and disaster; in short it is a population with a common origin under one culture . . . [The] Race is the body of the Nation, and that with its fall, the Nation ceases to exist.' In India, Hindus constituted the 'National Race'.[19]

Although 'race' as defined by Golwalkar was different from the genetic orientation of the Nazi preoccupation with the Aryan race and did incorporate many of Savarkar's emphasis on civilization and history, the RSS guru went a step further by advocating an exclusionary state. The 'National Race', he maintained, 'had the indisputable right of excommunicating from its Nationality all those who, having been of the Nation for ends of their own, turned traitors and entertained aspirations contravening or differing from those of the National Race as a whole'.[20] This was accompanied by a brutal prescription to safeguard India's future:

> . . . the non-Hindu peoples of Hindustan must either adopt the Hindu culture and language, must learn to respect and hold in reverence Hindu religion, must entertain no ideas but those of the glorification of the Hindu race and culture . . . in a word they must cease to be foreigners, or may stay in the country wholly subordinated to the Hindu nation, claiming nothing,

deserving no privileges, far less any preferential treatment—not even citizen's rights.[21]

Clearly Golwalkar left no scope for ambiguity.

For decades, Hindu nationalism has had to confront charges of fascism on account of Golwalkar's iron-clad definition of nationhood that delineated the nation into two classes: Hindu citizens with rights and others who had no entitlements and lived under sufferance. The RSS ceased publication of Golwalkar's tract and, subsequently, formally disowned his views on Indian nationhood.[22] It has also been argued that Golwalkar's book didn't really carry his views but was 'an abridged version of Ganesh Damodar (Baburao) Savarkar's work, *Rashtra Mimansha*'.[23] In his three lectures to explain the philosophy and work of the RSS in September 2018, RSS sarsanghchalak Mohan Bhagwat carefully omitted any mention of Golwalkar, preferring to focus on the organization's founder K.B. Hedgewar.

The relationship between the RSS and Savarkar was always strained. The RSS focus was on the creation of model Hindu citizens, who, imbibed with the right samskaras (values) could put the Hindu rashtra on the path of renewal. Savarkar always preferred a larger canvas and was impatient, if not downright contemptuous, of the RSS preoccupation with the daily shakhas. The 'epitaph for the RSS volunteer' he is said to have once remarked, 'will be that he was born, he joined the RSS and he died without accomplishing anything'.[24]

Savarkar was passionate about politics and devoted the most productive phase of his life—between 1937 and 1948—to promoting the Hindu Mahasabha and simultaneously taking on the Congress and Muslim League. The early RSS, on the other hand, saw politics as morally degrading and Golwalkar compared it to a 'woman of the multitude' whom virtuous individuals should, ideally, stay away from.[25] When, after Gandhi's assassination and the first ban on the RSS, complete disavowal of politics was no longer a feasible option,

Golwalkar allowed members of the RSS to enter politics, but grudgingly.

The reason for this wariness of politics didn't stem from the fear of moral downfall alone. Unlike Savarkar who dwelt at length on political and state power, Golwalkar believed that the Hindu rashtra was built on the foundations of sanskriti, which incorporated religion, tradition and dharma. This, in his view, accounted for the resilience of Hindu society over centuries of hostile, alien rule. Consequently, the RSS must concentrate single-mindedly on upholding and spreading Hindu sanskriti.[26] Although the RSS subsequently shed Golwalkar's preference for political detachment and became more closely—some would say too closely—involved in the Jana Sangh and BJP, it has never wavered from the view that its main work lies in shaping Hindu society, not India's politics. However, it has never shied away from speaking out on issues affecting 'national interests' and the annual Vijayadashami speech of the RSS sarsanghchalak has always been an occasion for stocktaking.

The formation of the Bharatiya Jana Sangh in 1951 by Shyama Prasad Mookerjee, a former stalwart of the Hindu Mahasabha, was an important landmark in RSS history. The organization which had hitherto consciously kept away from involvement in India's political life, now chose to enter it, albeit hesitantly. Whatever his personal misgivings about politics, Golwalkar seconded prominent swayamsevaks to the Jana Sangh. These included Deendayal Upadhyaya, Kushabhau Thakre, Sunder Singh Bhandari and Atal Bihari Vajpayee. A large number of swayamsevaks in the states also involved themselves in the new party.

Despite his association with Savarkar and his resolute fight to uphold the interests of Hindus in Bengal—the immediate reason for his resignation from the Nehru government in 1950—Mookerjee's Hindu nationalism was a shade different from that of the RSS. Like Savarkar, his focus was exclusively political, and he saw the Jana Sangh as an important step in the creation of a right-wing alternative that would include elements of the Hindu Mahasabha, the Ganatantra Parishad in Orissa, the Tilak-ites in Bombay Presidency and the Central Provinces and even the Akali Dal in Punjab. He was at his best as a parliamentarian and constitutionalist, as was evident from his spirited opposition to the first amendment to the Constitution in 1951. The RSS had somewhat different priorities. In the words of Bruce Graham who studied the early years of the Jana Sangh: 'Mookerjee wanted to challenge Congress rule without delay, and he apparently believed that middle-class liberalism was compatible with Hindu traditionalism, if not with Hindu nationalism, but the young men of the RSS acted as though they were a brotherhood building for some future time, in which a new elite, imbued with Hindu values, would sweep aside that which had been formed under the Raj.'[27]

The different approaches were short-lived. In 1953, Mookerjee died under detention in Srinagar while leading a movement for the full integration of Jammu and Kashmir in the Indian Union. His sudden death threw the new party into crisis, and it was the discipline and cohesiveness of the RSS-linked members of the Jana Sangh that prevented it from disintegrating. In short, circumstances propelled the RSS to overcome its initial hesitation of being involved in politics. From 1954 onwards, RSS full-timers have periodically been despatched to work in the political arena. However, it is interesting to note that once assigned political work, the pracharaks are never re-accommodated as full-timers in the parent organization, but merely 'adjusted' in fraternal bodies.

The links between the RSS and the political world were further strengthened with the formation of the BJP in 1980. In 1951, the initiative to involve the RSS in politics had been taken by Mookerjee. In 1980, the formation of the BJP was directly triggered by the crisis in the Janata Party over its members' simultaneous association with the RSS. A chunk of the Janata Party—formed in 1977 with the merger of the

Congress (Organization), Bharatiya Lok Dal and the Jana Sangh—had been grudgingly forced to go their separate ways following a decision to ban 'dual membership'. Consequently, the RSS was at the very heart of the establishment of the BJP.

Critics of the Indian right are of the view that the RSS's appearance of political detachment is an eyewash. The RSS, it was held, 'wanted a kind of power which could control politics yet remain untainted by the vices of being in government or participating in politics. The strength that the Sangh envisaged would be able to leave its imprint on politics through its virtues.'[28] Even if this argument, particularly the latter assertion, is valid, it implies that the RSS had to concede a great deal of autonomy—both ideological and operational—to organizations that constituted the wider Sangh parivar. It was clear, for example, that the rigid discipline and hierarchies that distinguished the shakhas would be out of place in the rough and tumble of politics. More important, in a sphere where attracting maximum electoral support mattered most, some of the stark formulations of the RSS leadership would have to be tempered to secure larger acceptance. It is to the credit of the RSS leadership that it recognized the need for flexibility to suit specific requirements, as long as the broad commitment to nationalism was not compromised. As the present RSS chief Mohan Bhagwat put it, 'Everything can be negotiated, except the Hindu Rashtra.'[29]

To begin with, it was recognized quite early on that Golwalkar's formulations of Indian nationhood, implying the complete exclusion of Muslims and Christians from all civic life, went against the grain of nearly everything India stood for. Never mind the sections targeted, such an idea would be completely repugnant to the bulk of Hindus. The Jana Sangh/BJP, with its roots in the RSS, had to dissociate itself from such an exclusionary nationalism.

This was not a terribly daunting project. The RSS had always stressed the importance of sanskriti in holding the Indian nation together, in forging the Hindu rashtra. From this foundation, the Jana Sangh/BJP projected 'cultural nationalism' as the core attribute of Indian nationhood. The detailed elaboration of cultural nationalism in a manifesto issued by the Jana Sangh encapsulates the broad tenets of its core belief system:

> From Himalayas in the North to Kanya Kumari in the South, all Bharat has always been one and indivisible, an organic whole, geographically, historically and culturally. The living unity has manifested itself in economic, political and all other spheres. In expression of our great love and adoration for every particle of this land we have visualised and worshipped it as Bharat Mata.
>
> The vast humanity inhabiting and devoted to Bharatvarsh constitutes one people. With all its diversities, its fundamental unity has always endured unimpaired. Our diversities are no sign of disintegration or deformity; they are on the contrary an evidence of natural growth and enrichment of our cultural heritage.
>
> With this one country as its home, this one people has developed and lived a culture which is one and the same from the Himalayas to the seas. For a vast land as ours it was but natural that somewhat different patterns of life should have grown in different zones, localities and sections. But all of them stand . . . united in Bharatiya Sanskriti, which has never been tied to any particular dogma or creed. All the creeds that form the commonwealth of the Bharatiya Rashtra have their share in the stream of Bharatiya culture which has flown down from the Vedas in unbroken continuity absorbing and assimilating contributions made by different way as to make them indistinguishable part and parcel of the main current. The Bharatiya culture is thus like Bharatvarsh one and indivisible. Any talk of composite culture, therefore, is not only illogical but also dangerous for it tends to weaken national unity and encourage fissiparous tendencies.[30]

What is particularly significant about this espousal of cultural nationalism—which from the late 1980s the BJP has increasingly taken to describing as its version of Hindutva—is its sharp differences with Savarkar's Hindutva. While the notion of pitribhu and punnyabhu is subsumed in Bharat Mata, no religious connotation is attached to the veneration for the motherland. Equally, by suggesting that the people of India are one and bound by a common culture that stems from antiquity, there is a conscious attempt to suggest that Muslims and Christians are also part of the same stock and should not be viewed separately. It argues that the underpinnings of India's common sanskriti flows from the Vedas, but insists this is a common, non-denominational inheritance. The manifesto did, however, jump to the rash conclusion that the innate unity of India necessitates a unitary state, an over-reading that was corrected in subsequent years to an advocacy of cooperative federalism.

Cultural nationalism was the bedrock on which Hindu nationalism began its post-Independence journey. There was, however, a compelling need to articulate a political philosophy that would bind day-to-day policies and approaches. It was in this context that Deendayal Upadhyaya developed the philosophy of Integral Humanism that was embraced by the Jana Sangh in 1965 and reiterated by the BJP after a fleeting dalliance with Gandhian socialism.

Deendayal viewed Indian notions of nation and nationality as being a series of interconnections, a 'creative harmony' involving the individual, family, society, nation, state, and even the natural world. His ideas have been very succinctly explained by Chaturvedi Badrinath: 'The individual, having his distinct existence, his legitimate self-interest, and desires and pursuit of happiness, fulfils himself in the larger life of society: society derives the meaning of its existence from the still larger life of the nation: the nation finds its ultimate fulfilment in serving the universal interests of mankind. All these units are interconnected, not in a hierarchy, but in a natural, innate . . . reverence for life.

Here the law is not conflict and competition for the mastery of the world but harmony and co-operation, and ultimately the mastery of the self.'[31]

India's national life, Deendayal maintained, is determined by its unique national consciousness—its chiti. It is this that manifests itself in dharma—not to be confused with religion—that forms the essence of Indian civilization, sustains and upholds it, and gives it vitality. He advocated a Dharma Raj for India. He believed that only when the institutions of India were imbued by the force of dharma would it have real moral legitimacy. As Badrinath explained: 'He maintains that the State exists for the sake of the nation, and not the nation for the sake of the State. Similarly, the nation is not a means of achieving political ends; rather, policies shall have the one aim of strengthening the nation, and shall express a nation's deeper consciousness . . . The people will, rightly, decide, who is to govern; but neither those who are thus elected . . . nor the people, can determine what principles will govern such governance; that can be determined by dharma alone.' To Deendayal, 'neither the State, nor the majority of the people, nor the government, is sovereign. The force that is sovereign above them all is dharma.'[32]

Integral Humanism has been deified by the BJP and countless welfare schemes and public institutions have been named after Deendayal, but the extent to which his vision actually shapes the political direction of Hindu nationalism is debatable. In many ways, Integral Humanism has become what Gandhism became for the Congress—some writers have detected similarities in the organic-utopian facets of both ideas: ideas that can be selectively drawn on when expedient.[33] Certainly, at a time when the public debate has come to centre on the Constitution, constitutional patriotism and constitutional morality, the notion of dharma has few takers in the entire political space. The BJP has often rued the increasing tendency of political discourse to be influenced by Western concerns masquerading as universal principles—also one of Deendayal's recurring complaints. Unfortunately for it,

Integral Humanism hasn't quite become a weapon of alternative discourse.

However, there is one facet of Deendayal's political philosophy that has made a dent in the dominant right: the innate suspicion of both unbridled market economics and socialism.

Traditionally, the right has often been equated in many countries with privilege, and increasingly, with market capitalism. Deendayal, in line with others in Nehru's India, had an innate suspicion of big business, and by implication, global corporations. According to him, 'Concentration of power is repugnant to democracy and human freedom. Subject to considerations [of] national unity, economic power should be decentralised both horizontally and vertically . . . Small-scale mechanised industries, small traders and farms that can be run and managed under individual, family or cooperative ownership should be the basis of our economy.'[34] In subsequent years, this partiality for medium and small enterprise was extended by the BJP to freedom from excessive state regulations—the inspector raj—and demands for low taxation. Traders and small businesses, in fact, became reliable support centres of Hindu nationalism precisely because their economic interests and their conservative social orientation coincided with that of the BJP.

Narendra Modi's focus on creating a welfare architecture surprised many of his supporters who interpreted his commitment to 'minimum government, maximum governance' to mean the rolling back of the frontiers of the state. But again, like in its disavowal of big business, the BJP's advocacy of unhindered individual initiative is qualified by its sense of social obligations. The ideas can be traced back to Deendayal, who felt dharma would suffer for the want of artha. Equally it would also suffer from excessive affluence. He believed that it was 'the responsibility of society to arrange for the upkeep of every child . . . and to provide him with education which would enable him to develop his individuality' that would enhance the quality of society and, in turn, the nation. He argued that 'right to a minimum living standard, education, employment and social security and welfare will have to be accepted as fundamental rights'.[35] Deendayal felt that: 'Society has the authority, and often it becomes its duty, to alter property rights. There is no such thing as an absolute and immutable right of property.'[36] In short, the interventionist state—albeit guided by the right motives—has, therefore, always been a part of the BJP's political personality. It is the belief that decision making must not be doctrinaire and should be guided entirely by practical and nation-building considerations that sets the BJP apart from both the Congress and the left.

The Swatantra Party was more conventionally right-wing in its economic orientation. It enjoyed the support of big business and also had articulate spokesmen in India's two last Parsi politicians, M.R. Masani and Piloo Mody. But its parallel alliance with India's erstwhile princes, while important in states such as Rajasthan, Gujarat and Orissa, proved an image liability in other parts of India, and not least in urban India. After an encouraging performance in the 1967 general election, the Swatantra Party faded out completely, taking with it the political articulation of market economics.

For the Indian right, economics has always been an incidental extra, although it was a crucial incremental extra that propelled Modi's clear victory in the 2014 general election. What preoccupied it, helped it gain mass traction and even set the political agenda, was the debate over secularism that has waged since Independence. India's political fault lines have been delineated by the battle over the distinctions between competing versions of secularism.

India's first prime minister Jawaharlal Nehru set the terms of the debate. In 1958, the French intellectual André Malraux, then a minister in the De Gaulle government, visited him in Delhi. Over an exchange of ideas, Malraux asked Nehru to identify his greatest challenges in his eleven years as prime minister. 'Creating a just state by just means,' Nehru replied unhesitatingly. Then, after a slight pause, he added: 'Perhaps, too, creating a secular state in a religious country.'[37]

That Nehru considered institutionalizing secularism in a 'religious country' as one of his foremost challenges may seem surprising. In 1958, both he and the Congress party were at the height of their political power. Nehru had overcome all internal challenges within the Congress, seen off the challenges of Hindu traditionalists to the reforms in Hindu personal laws, and the general election of 1957 had given his programme of state-sponsored modernization a resounding mandate. The Indian Constitution, though not mentioning 'secularism' explicitly (that improvisation took place in 1976, in controversial circumstances during the Emergency imposed by Indira Gandhi) had guaranteed freedom of religious worship, codified minority rights and outlawed faith-based discrimination.

In 1958, Nehru faced no real political challenge to the idea of a secular state. Hindu nationalism hadn't quite recovered from the ignominy of being seen to be associated with the killers of Gandhi and Muslim separatism had been orphaned after the creation of Pakistan, its earlier supporters having moved en masse from the Muslim League to the Congress. Identity politics hadn't evaporated completely but the focus had shifted from religious to linguistic and regional identities. Apart from the challenges of institution building, the issues that Nehru faced were primarily economic and linked to India's poverty, low productivity, crippling shortages, and technological deficiencies. Twelve years after the country witnessed the most devastating religious conflict that led to Partition and the uprooting of millions of people from their ancestral homes, sectarian conflict didn't count as one of the intractable problems of independent India—at least not in 1958.

Was Nehru's remark to Malraux, therefore, a clever exaggeration aimed at showcasing his own commitment to modernity under difficult circumstances? Was he cynically pandering to 'Orientalist' stereotypes of an India bogged down by tradition, superstition and prejudice—a portrayal that only served to juxtapose his own enlightenment? Alternatively, was Nehru gripped by a sense of foreboding? Was he deeply conscious that underneath the surface there were forces readying for a counter-revolution? Did Nehru anticipate India's 'agony over religion' that was to define Indian politics from the 1980s?

The 'progressive', democratic socialist that appealed instinctively to Nehru envisaged no place for religion in either political mobilization or public life. India's bitter experience with sectarian politics during the final phase of the freedom struggle had served to reinforce the belief, among modernists at least, that the 'false consciousness' of religion had to be uprooted and replaced by 'real' nationalism based on economic interests and even class consciousness. Nehru had lived in constant denial of the rising tide of communal feelings and sectarian conflict from the mid-1920s. He believed that the demand for Pakistan which captured the Muslim imagination all over India—and particularly in the Muslim-minority provinces—was a passing fad that would disappear once Muslims recognized their 'real' economic interests. 'The day of national cultures is rapidly passing,' he wrote with astonishing confidence in his *Autobiography* (published in 1936), 'and the world is becoming one cultural unit . . . The real struggle today is not between Hindu culture and Muslim culture, but between these two and the conquering scientific culture of modern civilisation.'[38]

At the same time, Nehru, in one of his more candid moments, did admit to being quite puzzled by the hold of religion among the masses. After campaigning during the 1946 election, he confessed that: 'An unknown factor . . . creeps in when God and the Koran are used for election purposes.'[39] He could hardly have thought otherwise since in that election the Hindu–Muslim polarization was total.

The Nehruvian penchant for what is sometimes called 'secular fundamentalism' was, however, not universally shared within either the Congress or the wider nationalist fraternity.

Gandhi, for example, was deeply suspicious of Nehru's attempt to disentangle religion from politics altogether. 'I cannot conceive politics,' he wrote in 1940, 'as divorced from religion. Indeed, religion should pervade every one of our actions. Here, religion does not mean sectarianism. It means a belief in ordered moral government of the universe.' In Gandhi's eyes, as historian Judith Brown observed, 'men and women were human in virtue of their capacity for religious vision . . . [If] this was stifled by the individual or by political and economic structures then people were degraded and dehumanised.'[40]

This celebration of religious values didn't imply that Gandhi was against a secular state. 'I swear by my religion,' he told a Christian missionary in 1946, 'I will die for it. But it is my personal affair. The state has nothing to do with it. The state would look after your secular welfare, health, communications, foreign relations, currency and so on, but not your or my religion. That is everybody's personal concern.'[41] His vision of a moral order envisaged an India where people remained attached to their religion and explored the ethical underpinnings of faiths. Gandhi, suggests Bhikhu Parekh, 'de-theologised Hinduism' and 'reduced it to a set of such basic principles as truth, love and ahimsa (non-violence) . . . To belong to a religious tradition was to share allegiance to its central principle, not to be committed to upholding its historically contingent practices and beliefs.'[42]

Gandhi's concerns over the moral and ethical dimensions of public life meant that the Indian state was never indifferent to religion. Mirroring Gandhi, it aspired to be an association of believers, a sort of defender of faiths. Its secularism lay in the fact that it was not explicitly partial to any religion—the Hindi term for secularism in the Constitution is 'panth nirapekshata'—and strove to establish a respectful balance between all organized expressions of faith; the clearest expression of which was the even-handed distribution of public holidays for religious occasions. Religion, therefore, wasn't banished from the public sphere—as Nehru, perhaps, may have wished. It was repackaged as a celebration of religious diversity and multiculturalism.

The incorporation of religion led to secularism acquiring distinctive and uniquely Indian meanings. In Indian popular usage, the antithesis of secularism isn't religion but intolerance or communalism or xenophobia. Mother Teresa, a devout Roman Catholic whose international reputation stemmed from her work among Kolkata's dying and destitute, was routinely portrayed as a symbol of secularism and even accorded a state funeral, complete with a military guard of honour. In her case, secularism was made synonymous with the state's respect for religious pluralism and even multiculturalism. The Aligarh Muslim University, an institution that has sought to promote modern education while preserving its denominational character, is also painted as a 'secular' institution. Here, the term was blended with the special guarantees for minority faiths in the Constitution. Likewise, the opulent iftar parties hosted by politicians—at least during Congress rule—were flaunted as celebrations of secularism. It is therefore curious that similar 'secular' certification for Hindu religious occasions, or even the innocuous Holi milans hosted by Hindu-minded politicians, has been invariably absent. In West Bengal, during the prolonged rule of the communist-dominated Left Front, the popular Durga Puja celebrations were gradually repackaged as a Saradotsav (autumn festival) from Durgotsav (festival of Durga) to airbrush the religious dimension. In India, the usage of secularism has been whimsically context-specific.

With characteristic irreverence, historian Mukul Kesavan has taken this argument a step further. To India's metropolitan elite, anxious to not be regarded as provincial in cosmopolitan surroundings, secularism was very much a 'style choice' and a 'marker of modernity and good taste': 'Because Partition and the Nehruvian Congress had shown that communalism was a bad thing, the metropolitan elite decided by a kind of default that secularism was a good thing . . . More often than we like to imagine, people were secular because their neighbours were secular; put another way, secularism was a hegemonic style—it was fashionable . . . (S)ecularism-as-ambiance encouraged many people to pay lip service to an idea they had learnt by rote.'[43]

The argument that Indian secularism was an alien, Nehruvian imposition on a deeply sceptical society wasn't a view from the fringes of the political spectrum. The sociologist T.N. Madan has argued that the major religious traditions in India do not have a history of 'privatising' religion and detaching it from secular life. Secularism, he wrote, 'is the dream of a minority which wants to shape the majority in its own image, which wants to impose its will upon history but lacks the power to do so under a democratically organised polity. In an open society the state will reflect the character of the society.'[44]

Madan's searing attack on the 'moral arrogance' of secularists who 'stigmatise the majority as primordially oriented' has also been echoed by Ashis Nandy, arguably India's best-known 'anti-secularist', no friend of the BJP. To Nandy, the idea of secularism in India 'is borrowed from Western history and has been during the last hundred years or so, a symbol of the efforts to internalise that history and redesign contemporary Indian history according to the demands of that history'.[45]

Secularism, it would seem, was an important facet of the Nehruvian quest for modernity. However, its status as a holy mantra wasn't matched by a corresponding measure of clarity over what it represented.

Perhaps this was understood by the makers of the Constitution, and maybe even by Nehru. For the first twenty-six years of the Republic, the implicit secularism of the Constitution was not accompanied by a formal declaration of the secular nature of the state. In 1976, however, at the height of the Emergency, Prime Minister Indira Gandhi rushed through a Constitution amendment that injected secularism—and, for that matter, socialism—into the Preamble. By subsequent Supreme Court judgments, the Preamble constituted an important facet of the 'basic structure' of the Constitution and deemed to be inviolable.

The rationale behind the move was 'progressive' grandstanding, in keeping with the mood of the times. Unfortunately, its long-term impact was not as inconsequential. It may not be entirely coincidental that most of the vicious political battles over secularism began after the champions of modernity deemed it necessary to codify a hitherto nebulous set of values. By exposing it to sustained scrutiny and trying to evolve a common understanding, Nehru's daughter unwittingly nurtured a conflict over India's secular future. She gave the Indian right, particularly the BJP, a booster dose of oxygen.

Apart from Jammu and Kashmir, which became a battleground between India and Pakistan, the seventeen years of Nehru's premiership witnessed an astonishing respite from sectarian tensions. The early years saw political tensions over the fate of the Hindu minority in East Pakistan and led to the resignation of Shyama Prasad Mookerjee from the Cabinet. Mookerjee who went on to establish the Bharatiya Jana Sangh with the cooperation of the RSS, also opposed Nehru on the issue of a 'special status' for Jammu and Kashmir. The abrogation of Article 370 of the Constitution giving 'special status' to that state has since become one of the BJP's key political demands.

However, neither the presence of large numbers of dispossessed Hindu and Sikh refugees from Pakistan nor the communal riots that broke out periodically in northern and eastern India affected the Congress' complete political dominance throughout the country. Nehru often denounced the 'RSS mindset' of Congress leaders in the Hindi heartland, but more than posing a real political challenge to the secular edifice, Hindu nationalists often played the role of juju men: the more the prime minister attacked them, the more the Congress was seen as the saviour and protector of India's large Muslim minority. Indeed, it took nearly two decades (and after Nehru's death in 1964) for the Hindu nationalists to mount their first mass movements of consequence—the Hindi-language movement of 1965–66 and the anti-cow slaughter agitation of 1966–67.

In hindsight, Nehru's prime ministership was the age of secular triumphalism. In a perceptive account of the mood of the early 1960s, Nirad C. Chaudhuri proffered an account of the likely response of a 'person belonging to the present ruling class' to suggestions that traditional 'Hindu India was alive and kicking: Hinduism is dying, if it is not already dead. Our industrial revolution will kill it, and that would be right. We have proclaimed a secular state, and to try to bring into it an out-of-date religious notion is rank obscurantism. That might do for Pakistan, a backward, theocratic country, but India is progressive, and is admired by the whole world for her progressive outlook and activities.'[46] It was this smugness, verging on arrogance, of the Nehruvian elite that prompted him to despair of 'a social class whose outlooks, ideas, behaviour, and social role are utterly different from those of the traditional and numerically stronger part of the middle class'. The latter, he noted, 'can only regard the Westernised type of Indian only as a renegade or usurper'.[47]

In his lifetime, the future of the secularism that Nehru sought to promote seemed assured. At the same time, there were issues that were left unresolved and awaiting their moment of political expression. This happened once the Congress's position as the unchallenged dominant party started eroding after the general election of 1967.

The first of these unresolved issues was the contentious relationship between secularism and culture—the entire issue of cultural nationalism.

Among the notable facets of the freedom movement was—despite Savarkar—the conscious disentanglement of religion from nationality. Whereas the Pakistan movement was built on the assumption that the Muslims of India, by virtue of Islam's separateness from Indic religions, constituted a separate nation, the Congress sought to build an Indian nationality on the strength of geography and rights of citizenship. Speaking in the Constituent Assembly on 11 December 1946, philosopher

S. Radhakrishnan decried the mindset that had fuelled Muslim separatism: 'the people—whether they are Hindus or Muslims, princes or peasants—belong to this country . . . If they try to disown it, their gait, their cast of countenance, their modes of thought, their ways of behaviour, they will all betray them. It is not possible to think that we belong to separate identities.'

On his part, Nehru, speaking at the convocation of the Aligarh Muslim University, the intellectual nerve centre of the Pakistan movement, in January 1948—a mere five months after Partition—posed a series of awkward questions to the Muslim community:

> I have said that I am proud of our inheritance and our ancestors who gave an intellectual and cultural pre-eminence to India. How do you feel about this past? Do you feel that you are also sharers in it and inheritors of it and, therefore, proud of something that belongs to you as much as to me? Or do you feel alien to it and pass it by without understanding it or feeling that strange thrill which comes from the realisation that we are the trustees and inheritors of this vast treasure . . . You are Muslims and I am a Hindu. We may adhere to different religious faiths or even to none; but that does not take away from that cultural inheritance that is yours as well as mine.

Nehru, in fact, echoed the champions of Hindu nationalism by suggesting that 'political changes have had little effect on the growth of this variegated and yet essentially unified culture'.[48]

Nehru's Aligarh speech has been frequently invoked by those uneasy with what they perceive is a warped and contrived secular consensus. If 'cultural inheritance' was indeed going to be a hallmark of nationhood, could Hindu inheritance that linked an overwhelming majority of Indians be put in cold storage in the guise of anti-majoritarianism? The controversy over the Somnath temple highlighted the divergent perceptions.

In 1951, the rebuilding and restoration of the Somnath temple, located in the erstwhile princely state of Junagadh, was completed. The temple which had been a special target of Mahmud of Ghazni's raids and repeatedly vandalized and desecrated had become an important symbol of Hindu pain over the widespread destruction of temples by Muslim rulers over the centuries. The restoration was undertaken by a trust with some state assistance. Two ministers in Nehru's government—Food and Agriculture Minister K.M. Munshi and Home Minister Sardar Vallabhbhai Patel—took a special interest in the matter. However, rather than leave the temple as a monument under the Archaeological Survey of India as some desired, Patel argued that 'Hindu sentiment' wouldn't 'be satisfied by mere restoration of the temple . . . The restoration of the idol would be a point of honour and sentiment with the Hindu public.'[49]

It was Sardar Patel's insistence that was crucial in overcoming Nehru's misgivings over the government's involvement in the project that was religious in nature. After Patel's death in 1950, the prime minister became more insistent in his objections and berated Munshi at a Cabinet meeting: 'I do not like your trying to restore Somnath. It is Hindu revivalism.' In a letter to Nehru on 24 April 1951, Munshi retorted very sharply: 'I can assure you that the "Collective Subconscious" of India today is happier with the scheme of reconstruction of Somnath sponsored by the Government of India than with many other things that we have done and are doing.' Replying to Nehru's invocation of secularism, Munshi wrote: 'I cannot value India's freedom if it deprives us of the Bhagavad Gita or uproots our millions from the faith with which they look upon our temples and thereby destroy the texture of our lives.' He wrote that 'this shrine once restored to a place of importance in our life will give to our people a purer conception of religion and a more vivid consciousness of our strength, so vital in these days of freedom and its trials'.[50]

The controversy resurfaced after it was proposed that President Rajendra Prasad would inaugurate the restored temple and participate in the consecration of the Jyotirlinga. Nehru objected strongly to the presence of the head of state on such an occasion. Prasad disagreed and went ahead. At the inauguration, his speech articulated a vision that seemed very normal in those times but would probably trigger a culture war today.

> By rising from its ashes again, this temple of Somnath is proclaiming to the world that no man and no power in the world can destroy that for which people have boundless faith and love in their hearts . . . Today, our attempt is not to rectify history. Our only aim is to proclaim anew our attachment to the faith, convictions and to the values on which our religion has rested since immemorial ages.[51]

Nehruvians, if not Nehru himself, considered the president 'of inferior intellectual quality and with a social outlook which belonged to the eighteenth century'.[52] In his fortnightly letters to the chief minister, Nehru gave vent to his profound disappointment with the president's action over Somnath: 'Our frequent declarations that we are a secular state are appreciated abroad and raise our credit. But they are not wholly believed in . . . The recent inauguration of the Somnath Temple, with pomp and ceremony, has created a very bad impression abroad about India and her professions.'[53]

Nehru's fears of negative impressions of India were largely in his own mind—and probably limited to his social circle of 'progressives': the 'pomp and ceremony' in a remote part of Gujarat attracted little attention in the pre-television age. Nor did his firm warning against any state identification with religious ceremonies become the norm. It has become routine for state and political functionaries to attend religious and quasi-religious functions, including those hosted by god-men, as a show of respect for religious India. Indira Gandhi was a fierce opponent of Hindu nationalism and professed her father's secularism, but she was a passionate temple-goer and patron of religious gurus. Her successors have kept up the tradition but more as necessary political gestures, particularly during elections.

The bone of contention between Nehru and his colleagues on Somnath was not the involvement of the state per se in religious activity but the quantum of association with Hindu culture. Nehru's anxieties stemmed from the need to maintain distinction between an appearance of even-handedness and majoritarianism. According to the assessment of Nehru's 'official' biographer, S. Gopal, the likes of Sardar Patel, Rajendra Prasad, and even the Jana Sangh founder Shyama Prasad Mookerjee 'believed not so much in a theocratic state as in a state which symbolised the interests of the Hindu majority'.[54] It was this failure to maintain the pro-Hindu tilt by the relatively inexperienced Rajiv Gandhi that fuelled Hindu resentment and shifted the social consensus in favour of explicit majoritarianism. The restoration of the Somnath temple in 1951 led to a sense of quiet satisfaction among Hindus but it was not accompanied by boisterous muscle-flexing. However, by the time BJP leader L.K. Advani chose the Somnath temple as the start of his rath yatra to Ayodhya to press for the building of a Ram temple on the site of a sixteenth-century mosque, 'soft Hindutva' was rapidly becoming a diminishing option. To Advani, the restored Somnath temple served as 'a sobering reminder that a weak nation that cannot defend itself against external attacks stands to lose more than its political freedom; it risks losing its cultural heritage'.[55]

Much of the sparring over secularism in the past three decades has centred on perceptions of 'cultural heritage'. In 2001, a political storm erupted after the education ministers of Congress and left-ruled states boycotted a conference convened by the Union minister for HRD Murli Manohar Joshi in the Atal Bihari Vajpayee's BJP-led government. Their objection was to the fact that the ceremonial inauguration included the invocation to Saraswati, worshipped by Hindus as the goddess of learning. The Congress-left protests were perhaps calculated to focus attention on Joshi's larger 'saffron' agenda that included the rewriting of history textbooks to rid them of their supposed 'anti-Hindu' bias. But by directing their ire on the singing of the Saraswati Vandana, an incantation that is broadly comparable to the genuflection to Nataraj that precedes a Bharatanatyam dance performance, the secularists reinforced a stereotype of themselves as being unmindful of the Hindu underpinnings of India's cultural heritage.

To the cultural nationalists such as Advani and Joshi, Indian secularism had become distorted over time and had steadily acquired an anti-Hindu bias. In Nehru's value system, 'the problem of minorities was basically one for the majority community to handle. The test of success was not what Hindus thought but how Muslims and other communities felt . . .'[56] Now this asymmetry was sought to be turned on its head, not by discarding secularism altogether, but in repudiating what Advani famously dubbed pseudo-secularism. What has propelled contemporary Hindu nationalism was a simmering anger that the Hindus were being taken for granted because they were not either religiously or politically organized as Hindus. In an article on the need to support the Vishwa Hindu Parishad (VHP), the head of the Chinmaya Mission, Swami Chinmayananda, stressed the need for Hindus to acquire a corporate identity.

> I know that religious organisation is against the very principle of Hinduism, but we have to move with the times. We seem to have entered today all over the world . . . into an age of organisation . . . If disorganised, there is no strength, no vitality. Therefore, in the spiritual field, even though the individuals proceed forward and develop, if religion wants to serve the society, it also has to get organised.[57]

The VHP sought to provide coherence to the fragmented world of Hinduism.

Since Independence, the population of Hindus in the Indian Union has not fallen below 80 per cent, although there have been significant regional shifts, particularly in eastern India. In view of the overwhelming preponderance of what may be loosely called the 'majority' community, it may seem surprising that Indian politics from the mid-1980s was marked by a rising tide of Hindu assertion. More surprising, perhaps, was that this assertiveness arose from a profound sense of grievance. The target of Hindu ire was the sustained policy of what is dubbed 'minorityism'.

The genesis of the phenomenon may well be located in another of the loose ends of Indian secularism: the special privileges granted to religious minorities. In particular, minorities (and minorities alone) were given the right to manage their own religious, cultural and educational institutions without state interference. That India's secular Constitution felt obliged to create a differentiated citizenship was itself a departure from the idealized, Western versions of secularism based on state indifference to religion. But the recognition of group rights (along with a charter of uniform rights) was dictated by the legacy of the freedom struggle.

First, there was Gandhi's sustained campaign against an iniquitous caste system that condemned a significant section of the people to pariah status. For Gandhi, the abolition of untouchability and the right of all self-professed Hindus to enter temples were integral features of the national resurgence that had to accompany political independence. Since Hindus were made up of diverse communities and lacked any ecclesiastical command structure, the project of social reform had to have a large measure of state involvement—as it indeed did under imperial rule.

Secondly, in the wake of the creation of Pakistan and the exodus of large numbers of Muslims from independent India, the leaders of the Congress, and Nehru in particular, felt a compelling need to assure the large Muslim minority which remained in India that their faith and identity would be statutorily protected.

It was made sufficiently clear that common citizenship and integration did not automatically imply assimilation. Muslims, it was decreed, could retain their distinctive Muslim-ness and still be good Indians.

Finally, as political philosopher Rajeev Bhargava argued, 'India needed a coherent set of intellectual resources to tackle inter-religious conflict, and to struggle against oppressive communities not by disaggregating them into a collection of individuals or by derecognising them but by somehow making them more liberal and egalitarian.' The state was conferred the right to balance aloofness from religious affairs with the 'demand for equality and justice which necessitates intervention in religiously sanctioned social customs'. In recent times, it has been the courts rather than the legislature that has been at the forefront of reformist interventions. The Supreme Court has declared the iniquitous triple talaq divorce among Muslims to be illegal and permitted the entry of women into the Ayyappa temple in Sabarimala, much to the distress of the local community. Indian secularism, Bhargava had argued, was based on keeping a 'principled distance' from matters of faith and custom.[58]

The problem lay in defining the red lines. On 9 December 2006, for example, Prime Minister Manmohan Singh, told a meeting of the National Development Council, 'We will have to devise innovative plans to ensure that minorities, particularly the Muslim minority, are empowered to share equitably the fruits of development. These must have the first claim on resources.'[59] Did he cross those lines then? Was the National Advisory Council led by Sonia Gandhi being even-handed when it, in a draft Communal Violence Bill in 2011, defined victims of communal violence as 'a religious or linguistic minority, in any state . . . or Scheduled Castes and Tribes', thereby ruling out the possibility of any member of the 'majority' community being victims?[60]

One of the first important legislation undertaken by the Nehru government after the Constitution came into force was a series of changes in the personal laws of Hindus. Among other things, the modified personal laws outlawed polygamy and gave women equal inheritance rights. There was resistance from Hindu conservatives who argued against tampering with traditional laws and customs, but the resounding victory of the Congress in the 1952 general election—where the reforms were a talking point—settled matters conclusively. Unfortunately, the reforms governing Hindus were not accompanied by initiatives to modify the personal laws of the Muslim community, which continued to be governed by the regressive provisions of the Muslim Personal Law (Shariat) Application Act, 1937.

The Constituent Assembly had recognized that all Indians should be governed by common laws relating to marriage and inheritance. However, at the urging of the leadership, which felt that the time was not yet ripe to expose a Muslim community still suffering the trauma of Partition, to such radical change, the issue—along with the Gandhian pipedream of prohibition and Nehru's quest for a 'scientific temper'—was listed as one of the Directive Principles of state policy. It was further felt that the demand for a uniform civil code had to come from within the Muslim community rather than be thrust on it by well-meaning modernizers.

For nearly four decades, the uniform civil code issue lay in cold storage. It was occasionally raised by Hindu nationalist parties not so much as a part of a modernizing agenda but as an instrument to combat the 'emotional separatism' of Muslims. From within the Muslim community, no meaningful reform movement arose. The community itself remained preoccupied with issues such as representation in legislatures, the status of Urdu, the character of Aligarh Muslim University, and ever-recurring communal riots.

All that changed in 1986 following a Supreme Court judgment directing nominal alimony payment to one Shah Bano. In his judgment, Justice Chandrachud also referred in passing to the forgotten promise of a uniform civil code for India.

The instinctive response of the Rajiv Gandhi government, still enjoying a political honeymoon after its staggering electoral win in 1984, was to welcome the judgment. One of its Muslim ministers, Arif Mohammed Khan, took up cudgels for gender rights. Unfortunately for the government, the Muslim community reacted viscerally to the judgment. There were large protests throughout the country, and it was made clear that the Congress would have to confront organized Muslim opposition in future elections unless it remedied the situation. It was suggested that the Supreme Court judgment was the thin end of the wedge and that there was a threat to Sharia law from a uniform civil code.

The turmoil in the Muslim community had an instant political fallout. A nervous Rajiv signalled a U-turn. Khan resigned from the government and a Muslim Women's Bill overturning the divorced Muslim woman's right to alimony was rushed through Parliament. The only spirited opposition came, predictably, from the BJP and, to a lesser extent, the Communist Party of India (Marxist).

For the religious and political leadership of the Muslims, overturning a Supreme Court verdict was a famous victory. For the first time since Independence, the Muslim community demonstrated its political clout and asserted the right to insulate its own personal laws from outside interference. The agitation against the Shah Bano judgment also highlighted the pivotal role of bodies such as the Deoband seminary and the Muslim Personal Law Board as the custodians of Muslim social and religious interests.

It is significant that shortly after the excitement over the Shah Bano case subsided, the Rajiv government reacted with indecent haste to Syed Shahabuddin's denunciation of Salman Rushdie's *Satanic Verses*. India became the first country to ban the book.

If the Muslim reaction to the Supreme Court judgment in the Shah Bano case was fierce, it generated a countervailing Hindu reaction. The groundwork of a Hindu political consolidation of sorts had actually been laid during the 1984 election, which took place just three months after Indira Gandhi's assassination and the vicious anti-Sikh riots in Delhi. In the face of widespread concern over a possible break-up of India, a fear the Congress exploited in a shrill campaign, large numbers of Hindus departed from traditional political allegiances and voted for Congress as an affirmation of faith in Indian nationalism. One of the biggest casualties was the BJP, which was reduced to just two seats in the Lok Sabha. Although it is over-simplistic to describe the 1984 verdict as a 'Hindu vote' for the Congress, it is undeniable that Rajiv's resounding victory had a subliminal Hindu dimension to it. In its editorial comment after the election, *Organiser*, the RSS weekly wrote that the verdict 'was a conscious Hindu vote, consciously and deliberately solicited by the Congress party as a Hindu party'.[61] In the exhaustive, but private, deliberations that followed the electoral decimation it was decided that the party needed to assert its credentials as a Hindu party and never again be upstaged on that count.

It is also facile to speak of any composite Hindu reaction to the Shah Bano controversy, an issue that affected only the Muslim community and, perhaps, the courts. However, it wouldn't be inaccurate to suggest that the government's feeble capitulation raised concerns over the might of an organized Muslim vote bank, a fear the BJP was quick to exploit. Its claims of the political 'double standards' nurtured by 'minorityism' struck a responsive chord. At the ground level, crude suggestions of 'five wives and twenty-five children' found appreciative audiences.

The Shah Bano affair didn't by itself trigger a communal polarization. However, it created an environment for a larger Hindu questioning of differentiated citizenship.

To complicate matters, the passage of the Muslim Women's Bill, overturning the Shah Bano judgment, coincided with a district court in Faizabad, Uttar Pradesh, opening the doors of the Babri Masjid, which had been turned into a Ramjanmabhoomi shrine in 1948, for public worship. Although it would take Hindu nationalists another three years to transform this localized dispute into an overriding national issue, the Shah Bano case became a reference point for the brewing disquiet over the lack of even-handedness in Indian secularism.

The emotive controversy over the site that local tradition in Ayodhya suggested was the birthplace of the epic hero of the Ramayana dominated Indian politics for at least fifteen years. The Ayodhya years witnessed widespread and vicious Hindu–Muslim clashes, led to the decimation of the Congress in the largest Indian state of Uttar Pradesh, and contributed substantially to the BJP's emergence as the largest party in Parliament in the general elections of 1996, 1998 and 1999. Till the mid-1980s, the communist left, kisan populists and Hindu nationalists had occupied the non-Congress space in equal measure. Following the Ram shila pujas of 1988–89 that led to nearly 167, 000 consecrated bricks, mainly from individual villages; L.K. Advani's highly symbolic rath yatra from the rebuilt Somnath temple in Gujarat; and, finally, the kar seva that led to the demolition of the Mughal shrine on 6 December 1992, the BJP emerged as the alternative pole of national politics and the principal opponent of the Congress. By 2014, the political world had been divided into BJP and anti-BJP.

In its bid to emerge as the alternative pole of Indian politics, the BJP initially banked on both religiosity and a critique of 'pseudo-secularism'. In rural India, and particularly among women, the appeal of a Ram temple in his birthplace at Ayodhya had a deep emotional appeal grounded in uncluttered religiosity. With the BJP complemented by Hindu religious figures who toured the country delivering impassioned speeches on Ram the maryada purshottam (the ideal man), the Ayodhya campaign simultaneously evolved into an assertion of Hindu pride—'*Garv se kaho hum Hindu hain* (Say with pride I am a Hindu)'—that in turn was twinned to national pride. 'Reverence for Ram,' Advani proclaimed, 'is a unifying factor; not only for Hindu society, but for the whole nation.'[62]

However, the BJP was simultaneously mindful that it was a political party and not, as Vajpayee told the party's National Council in 1991, a dharma sabha (religious gathering). The theme of pseudo-secularism was repeated endlessly to emphasize the political establishment's double standards: one set for the Muslim personal laws, another for the Ram temple. Advani—who became the political face of the Ayodhya movement—also contrasted the 'real' secularism of Sardar Patel and Rajendra Prasad with the pseudo-secularism of Nehru on the Somnath temple issue. He contrasted the nationalism of the early Congress leaders with the 'minorityism' and 'vote bank politics' of the present-day Congress. Gandhi's celebration of 'Ram rajya' was also invoked. The implication was that the BJP was the rightful inheritor of the nationalist mantle.

In time, this ideological battle was extended to the Nehruvian consensus with the implied promise that the BJP was aiming not merely for a change of government but a more fundamental transformation—what Modi, subsequently, was to call his battle against the Lutyens Delhi elite. To Girilal Jain, a former editor of *The Times of India*, who emerged as one the intellectual advocates of the new Hindutva resurgence, the demolition of the Babri shrine was a portent of bigger changes in India:

> The structure as it stood, represented an impasse between what Babur represented and what Ram represents. This ambiguity has been characteristic of the Indian state since Independence . . . [In] my opinion, no structure symbolised the Indian political order in its ambivalence, indecisiveness and lack of purpose, as this structure. The removal of the structure has ended the impasse and marks a new beginning.[63]

To Jain, the time had come to address the civilizational–cultural issues that Nehru and the entire tradition of secular nationalism had so far wilfully skirted. Yet, the new political project, could not be based on the aggressive affirmation of Hindu civilization alone:

The Nehru order . . . did not rest on the secular pillar alone. It would have collapsed long ago if it had. The Nehru structure has stood mainly on three pillars in conceptual terms—socialism, secularism and non-alignment—and these concepts have been interlinked. Nehru's was an integrated world view. As such, it is only logical that if one of them becomes dysfunctional, the others must get into trouble. In my opinion, they have.[64]

In effect, Jain was calling for a regime change that would overturn the warped and 'un-Hindu disregard for power, economic and military, and the illusory belief that social equity is possible in conditions of economic weakness'.[65] Two decades later, these precise themes resonated in Prime Minister Modi's New India project.

The Ayodhya movement was mercilessly flayed by the dominant sections of the Indian intelligentsia. 'Never before,' wrote a left academic in visible anger, 'has there been such a comprehensive and single-minded assault on the founding principles of the Indian Constitution and state.'[66] Hindu nationalism was equated with fascism in Europe in the 1930s and a distinguished American professor of law, in an unexpected foray into Indian politics, described the BJP-led coalition government of Vajpayee as 'increasingly controlled by right-wing Hindu extremists'. Developments in India, she wrote ominously, pose 'a serious threat to the future of democracy in the world'.[67] In 2014, an article in *The New York Times* argued that 'retrograde 1920s-style nationalist dogma . . . is making a big comeback in India, especially since last year, when Mr Modi . . . overcame the taint of various suspected crimes to launch his bid for supreme power'.[68]

In hindsight, the prognosis of radical change heralding India's descent into darkness after the Ayodhya demolition seems wildly, if not wilfully, overstated. In the past three decades, there have been no amendments to the Constitution that have either compromised or diluted the protection to minorities. If anything, the Places of Worship Act of 1991 decreed that no religious shrine could undergo a denominational change—Ayodhya was left out of its purview because it was sub judice—and ruled out possible attempts by Hindu nationalists to reclaim the sites of demolished temples in Mathura and Varanasi. Under Modi, the BJP negotiated an unlikely power-sharing arrangement in March 2015 with the pro-autonomy People's Democratic Party (PDP) in Jammu and Kashmir. One of the conditions set by the PDP was a commitment from the BJP that the status quo on Article 370—giving Jammu and Kashmir a special status—would be maintained. This inevitably triggered charges that the BJP was compromising on one of its foundational principles for which its icon Shyama Prasad Mookerjee had died under detention in Srinagar in 1953.

Yet, despite the appearance of relative stillness, India has witnessed one profound change in the past three decades: it has witnessed the emergence of a significant, self-conscious Hindu bloc—both electoral and otherwise—that is unwilling to countenance any real or perceived assaults on 'Hindu' interests. This phenomenon has stretched far beyond any nominal support to the BJP during elections. Yet, what are the implications of this phenomenon for India's Hindu nationalism?

It is apparent that the loyal core of the BJP, and indeed the wider Sangh Parivar, has a distinctive understanding of India's history and civilization, and the post-Independence experience. Nehru too grappled with these issues unendingly, even agonized over them and some of his tentative conclusions formed the basis of the secular consensus as it has prevailed. The BJP leaders, whose perceptions of India's civilizational ethos flowed from an understanding of Aurobindo, Vivekananda, Savarkar, Golwalkar and Upadhyaya, often as imparted through the boudhik sessions of the RSS, had divergent perceptions.

The departures centred on the centrality of Hinduism—both as belief systems incorporating the Sanatan Dharma and as a way of life—in the 'idea of India'. According to his biographer's description, Nehru felt that India's heritage transcended faith: 'If all Indians had been converted to Islam or to Christianity, their culture would still have remained the same.'[69] This assessment was sharply different from Savarkar's who believed that a departure from the Hindu fold was also accompanied by a change of nationality. To those who grew up offering a prayer to the bhagwa dhwaj at RSS shakhas each day, Hindutva or Hindu-ness was at the core of India's nationhood, not necessarily as a religion but as a culture. The BJP sees itself as a Hindu party, but this rarely meant a commitment to religious practices, only to a larger cultural ethos. Its disagreement with the 'secular fundamentalism' of the Nehruvians was not over the freedom of faith and the non-discriminatory features of the Constitution, but on the centrality of Hindu cultural forms in the symbolism associated with the state. This was coupled with unrelenting hostility to any special treatment or affirmative action for religious minorities. The mantra of 'justice for all, appeasement of none' has guided the movement since 1947. The tirade against 'biryani for terrorists and bullets for kar sevaks' that the BJP used quite effectively in the 1990s was a crude but telling articulation of how it perceived the double standards of the secularist Congress. The BJP was perhaps the only sustained voice against the secular squeamishness over the ethnic cleansing of Hindu Pandits from the Kashmir Valley in 1990. Its stated hostility to 'vote bank politics' practised by the 'secular' parties was a coded invitation to Hindus to assert their numerical clout and vote as Hindus.

To this divergence on the features of nationhood was a belief that India had been in a state of servitude since the establishment of the Delhi Sultanate in the eleventh century. Like the early nationalists, the BJP's pantheon of national heroes included Maharana Pratap, Shivaji, and Guru Govind Singh who had waged war against Mughal rule. Whereas the Nehruvians were inclined to view the Mughal experience as high point of a syncretic and composite culture—what is often called the Ganga-Jamuni tehzeeb—Hindu nationalists yearned for a recovery of Hindu honour and self-esteem that never quite happened after Independence. The Muslim that Hindu nationalists have profoundly admired has been the former president of India A.P.J. Abdul Kalam who combined his contribution to India's missile programme with deep reverence for Hindu cultural forms.

In 1993, Advani stated quite tellingly that Hindutva was the BJP's 'permanent ideological mascot'. However, the extent to which the mascot was brought to the fore has always depended on political compulsions. When the Jana Sangh merged itself into the Janata Party in 1977, the Hindu nationalists were careful to underplay their political ancestry. 'We have left the politics of Jana Sangh far behind,' said Vajpayee in 1979. 'We should forget these things now and . . . participate . . . in the only nationalist stream of the Janata Party . . .'[70] In an interview to the RSS Hindi weekly *Panchjanya* in 1980, Advani was categorical that in India 'a party based on ideology can at the most come to power in a small area. It cannot win the confidence of the entire country—neither the Communist Party nor the Jana Sangh in its original form.'[71] In 1996, shortly before the general election, Advani—without any consultations—announced that Vajpayee would be the BJP's prime ministerial candidate. His logic was based on the realization that the BJP was likely to get the 'Hindu vote' in any case, but to win it needed an incremental vote that only Vajpayee, with his benign liberal image, could secure.[72] His assumption proved correct. While the BJP couldn't quite secure the numbers in 1996, Vajpayee's appeal proved a magnet for regional parties to ally with the BJP in the elections of 1998 and 1999.

As a general rule, the BJP has stressed its anti-Congress credentials while in coalition with regional parties that have a following among Muslims and Christians. It has been less inhibited when it fights in what Advani once called 'majestic isolation' or is in a commanding position. In 2014, the BJP defied all expectations and won a majority on its own in the Lok Sabha but remained in a coalition with smaller parties. At the same time, not having a majority in the Rajya Sabha, it was dependent on other parties to push through legislation.

It was an awkward imbalance, made more so by the awareness that Hindutva was only a part of the broader social coalition that won the 2014 general election for the BJP. This was driven home by the outcome of the Bihar Legislative Assembly election of 2015 when a grand alliance of secular parties easily defeated the BJP. The BJP drew two important conclusions from this defeat. First, it realized that overemphasizing Hindu nationalism would lead to a secular consolidation that would be electorally damaging. Secondly, it concluded that the only way to retain electoral dominance—apart from exploiting the quirks of the first-past-the-post rule—was to enlarge the social base of the party. A conscious effort was therefore made to shift the BJP's social centre of gravity lower down the class and caste scale by also appealing to poorer voters on the strength of governance.

Effective governance was always Modi's priority as chief minister of Gujarat for thirteen years. It was his ability to blend Hindutva and Gujarati pride with efficient administration that saw him win three consecutive assembly elections. Indeed, good governance became a BJP mantra ever since it secured control over three state governments in 1989. As prime minister, Modi has single-mindedly tried to make economic modernization and efficient delivery of state-run programmes the hallmark of his tenure. It is not that the fight against 'distorted' secularism has been put in cold storage. In power, the BJP has made interventions in the cultural sphere that were calculated to raise the hackles of a hostile intelligentsia and upholders of the Nehruvian legacy. After an event in Kerala in 2015, an angry editorial in the left-wing *Economic and Political Weekly* observed:

Excerpts from Modi's speech at a 'national celebration' of the elevation to sainthood of a priest and a nun from Kerala on 17 February at which he proclaimed his government's commitment to Indian secularism, namely 'equal respect and treatment for all faiths', are intriguing. The Constitution's principles of secularism, Modi states, has its 'roots in the ancient cultural traditions in India' and now, if the Prime Minister is to be believed, following what is 'in the DNA of every Indian', 'the rest of the world too is evolving along the lines of ancient India.' The problem with all of this is that the kind of secularism deriving from Vedic times and 'values' has no resemblance to what is understood as secularism in the post-Enlightenment world. The former, a revivalist secularism, is oozing with religiosity, even as the 'secular' Indian state sets itself up as the underwriter of all faiths with its chief executive affirming the glory of Hinduism. In this sense, as India becomes more secular, it becomes more Hindu, with neo-Vedantic Hinduism being claimed not merely as a religion but a way of life for all Indians . . .[73]

The indignation, although polemically overstated, wasn't, however, entirely misplaced. Just as Nehru shifted the terms of the culturalist discourse after 1947, Modi has acquainted Indians with another approach—a cocktail of pre-Nehruvian nationalism and the BJP's cultural nationalism. Throughout his five years in office, Modi has chipped away at the Nehruvian legacy—sometimes quite explicitly—through symbolism. Whether it the installation of Sardar Patel's gigantic statue on the banks of the Narmada, the importance attached to the memory of Netaji Subhas Chandra Bose, and the renaming of Delhi's Aurangzeb Road to A.P.J. Abdul Kalam Marg, Modi has subtly tried to recast the old consensus.

There has, of course, been a larger questioning of Nehruvian principles in the directions set for the economy and foreign policy. At his first Independence Day speech in August 2015, Modi abolished the Planning Commission, a Nehruvian institution to foster state control and supervision. Other legacies of the old consensus had already been whittled down by others, notably Prime Minister P.V. Narasimha Rao, but Modi took things further. Brushing aside the old concerns over Muslim sentiment, Modi became the first Indian prime minister to visit Israel and, in a symbolic gesture, ensuring his hotel stay in Jerusalem. Despite encountering huge opposition in Assam and the north-eastern states, the Modi government has also tried to ensure a 'right of return' for all Hindus, Sikhs and other non-Muslims from Pakistan, Bangladesh, and Afghanistan—those unfortunate to be stranded on the 'wrong' side after Partition.

Of the three pillars on which the Congress sought to build its India, the secular consensus was the only one that had remained somewhat intact. That is because it was crafted in the realm of ideas and approaches. For pragmatic and strategic reasons, neither Modi nor the BJP would wish to do away with it altogether. But the motifs on the pillar may well have features that reflect India's cultural inheritance.

Change in India has always proceeded at an unhurried pace. Nehru was able to nudge India away from its Hinduized nationalist legacy because he ruled without any opposition for fourteen years and was succeeded (after a very brief interval) by his daughter, grandson, and others in the family who ruled directly or indirectly until very recently. And even now the Congress continues to be led by Indira Gandhi's grandson and swears by the family's inheritance. The forces of Hindu nationalism will need much more time, elbow room and even a greater show of political imagination before India can acquire an alternative common sense. Additionally, they will need to create a counter-establishment, not least to extend a political battle into the realm of ideas. The outcome of the 2019 general election will indicate whether the process will be halting or uninterrupted.

Readings

Introduction to the Readings

Politically speaking, the right is an omnibus term. It is not doctrinal, although certain doctrines exercise disproportionate influence, and may best be characterized as a set of approaches and attitudes towards public life. In India, for reasons that have much to do with the intellectual dominance of the left, the right has been loath to describe itself as such, preferring, in most cases, the relatively unexceptionable term 'nationalist'. More significant, whereas the right has of late begun to define itself in terms of its approach to economic policy, the Indian right—with the possible exception of the Swatantra Party that proffered a sharp critique of state-led development—has focused principally on issues of nationhood. This was true of the movement for Independence and has persisted after Independence.

The inspiration for the Indian right is rich but varied. Beginning from the late nineteenth century, nationalist thinkers such as Bankimchandra Chattopadhyay, Swami Vivekananda and Bal Gangadhar Tilak attempted to connect the recovery of national honour and sovereignty with the evolution of a modern corporate identity. However, even within this framework there were important differences. The importance of Hindu social reform was, for example, stressed by the likes of Swami Vivekananda, M.G. Ranade and R.G. Bhandarkar. However, there was an equally important strand of opinion that opposed state interference in the social life of Hindus.

The set of readings that follow does not aim to provide a comprehensive documentation of the influences on the Indian right.* They aim instead to give readers a flavour of the different attitudes that have characterized interventions of the right in public life. Most of the readings originated in the English language and, predictably, suffer from a metropolitan bias. A more comprehensive documentation of the Indian right's pedigree must await translations from the Indian languages.

Nevertheless, some of these interventions have exercised influence and some of the texts have been chosen because they mirror attitudes. Sita Ram Goel, for example, was a lone warrior and crossed swords with the BJP–RSS establishment on a regular basis. His views were regarded as too extreme and politically imprudent. However, his influence in shaping a strand of contemporary Hindu nationalism shouldn't be underestimated. Likewise, Girilal Jain—once a pillar of the old Congress establishment—was a significant voice of the relatively undocumented intellectual ferment that accompanied the Ayodhya movement.

History was a particularly important concern of nearly all strands of the right. In viewing the past, the search was not merely for inspiration but for the missteps that led to India's loss of its sovereignty. A dissection of the past also played a pivotal role in shaping contemporary attitudes towards the 'Muslim question', a theme that has preoccupied the right for the past 100 years and more. The readings also indicate that what is decried today as revisionism or simply distortion, was conventional wisdom yesterday. The interpretations of Swami Vivekananda by his disciple Sister Nivedita and historian R.C. Majumdar are a case in point.

India's right too had its share of intellectuals. Many of them have subsequently been airbrushed from the intellectual imagination. The

---

* For a more exhaustive account see Christophe Jaffrelot (ed.), *Hindu Nationalism: A Reader*, Permanent Black, Ranikhet, 2007.

involvement of Ramananda Chatterjee, a stalwart of the Brahmo Samaj and editor of the influential *Modern Review*, in the Hindu Mahasabha has, for instance, been largely forgotten.

The accompanying extracts are a small attempt to narrow the apparent mismatch between the Indian right's political clout and the disdain with which it is viewed in the citadels of intellectual power.

Part I
The Motherland and Nation Building

4

Is Nationalism a Good Thing?[*]

Bankimchandra Chattopadhyay

For many years now India has been in bondage. Why? The common people's answer to this question generally is because Indians are weak. 'Effeminate Hindoos' is a pet phrase of the Europeans. And yet, the same Europeans often praise the Indian soldiers for their bravery. Our British masters have conquered Kabul on the strength of these weak Indian fighters and have put them to use in winning over India itself. Even though the British hesitate to admit it, they have themselves lost many battles against these 'weak' Hindus of Maharashtra and equally 'weak' Sikhs of the Punjab. Whatever toughness and bravery the Indians may have today, no doubt, is less than what they had in the past. Many years of subjugation have blunted their power. My conviction is that in the past Indians had excelled in their capacity to strike back.

I know how difficult it is to prove my point in this matter as Indians have not chronicled their past battles. Indians have never written the accounts of their bygone days. The books known as

[*] 'Bharat Kalanka', *Bankim Rachanabali*, Dwitiya Khanda, edited by Subodh Chakravarty and published by Kamini Prakashan in 1991, pp. 234–41. Extracted from *Many Threads of Hinduism* by Bankimchandra Chattopadhyay, translated by Alo Shome (Harper Element, NOIDA, 2015, pp. 143–49).

Puranas in this country are not really history even though the word 'purana' means an account of olden days. Whatever facts the Puranas carry are overshadowed by imagined, unnatural stories and exaggerations. So we have to depend upon accounts by others to discover our own history. This, unfortunately, comes with the risk of the reports being biased in others' favour. We find glorious pictures of men killing lions and not lions killing men simply because men are the painters of these pictures. As we can expect, there are very few historians who praise their rivals honestly for the sake of truth.

In any case, we must consider ourselves lucky to have two instances in the documents of foreigners where India's military prowess has been mentioned.

Firstly, there are the accounts of the Arabs. The Arab at one time were world-beaters. Soon after their conversion to Islam they captured whichever country they invaded—except France in the West and India in the East. The Arabs had subdued Egypt and Syria within five to six years, Turkey within eight years, Persia within ten years and Kabul within eighteen years of Muhammad's death (632 CE). They had taken only one year to conquer Africa and another year to conquer Spain. However, they had not succeeded in defeating India even after three hundred years of endeavour. Muhammad bin Qasim had occupied Sindh. But he was defeated in his confrontation with Rajputana. And Sindh was brought back under Rajput control soon after bin Qasim's death.

India was invaded and subdued by the Pathans more than five hundred years after its first encounter with the Arabs. In between, the Turks also attacked India but failed to conquer it. The Pathans, in capturing India, only completed the mission left unfinished by the Arabs and the Turks. Thus it follows that around five hundred and fifty years were needed for three groups of invaders—the Arabs, the Turks and the Afghans—to end India's free status.

The above account is recorded by Muslim witnesses. And this instance of India's bravery transpired, we must remember, in spite of the decay that had occurred in Hindu society by that time. The Indians of the pre-Christian era were, no doubt, a more courageous lot.

The Greeks confronted the Indians in 327 BCE and found them proud and brave. Themselves great warriors, they have praised the Indians highly for their courage and fighting skills. They admitted they had not found such worthy combatants in any other province in Asia during their conquests. In their march to subdue countries across several continents they had suffered the largest loss of lives in their encounter with India. Yet, in spite of these facts, the current impression in the modern world is that Hindus are cowardly. Three reasons are offered for this:

1. The Hindus have not written their own account of bravery.
2. They have fought only for their defence and not to attack any other country. Generally only attacking forces win fame for their 'glory'.
3. Hindus have lived in subordination for many years now.

Who would want to believe that they actually are brave? I do not agree with the proposition that even though the Hindus could have been brave once, they are subordinate now because of their current state of cowardice. I argue that there are other reasons for them to have lost their independence. Two of these reasons are elaborated in this essay.

The First Reason

Indian (that is Hindus, Buddhists, Jains and people of many other religious sects of India) do not have a passion for independence.

The common belief is that a kingdom is a king's property. It does not matter from which country the king is, provided there is good governance. Maybe Indians have a vague feeling that it is better to have someone from their own country ruling them. But for most of the citizens that vague feeling does not translate into desire. For many centuries now, Indians have not been passionate enough to lay down their lives for their country's freedom. In contrast, many European countries, even in the past, had highly developed loyalty for their individual nations.

The reason for the Indians' habitual disinterest in passionately protecting their country is also not far to seek.

The early Aryans coming to India had found the land fertile and the climate pleasant. Survival, here, was easy for the elite of the community. This gave them enough leisure to reflect and wonder. So their minds turned to poetry and metaphysics. Their intellectual engagement was with the limitlessness of the universe and the timelessness of creation. They found peace and joy in these abstract ideas. Material possessions seemed insignificant compared to that inner delight. They, therefore, advised others to treat worldly wealth lightly. Indeed, India's disinterest for political independence is only a form of their general low regard for any kind of worldly possessions.

Somebody who gives little credit to his belongings would hardly endeavour to preserve them. In the Vedas, in Buddhism (and Jainism) and in the Puranas, detachment for worldly property is glorified. Mukti, moksha or nirvana, each of which means an ultimate disconnect with the material world, is considered the supreme goal of life.

How come, then, if Indians do not love independence, have they resisted multiple foreign invasions for one thousand and five hundred years before being subdued by the Afghans?

The answer is, the Hindus and other communities of India never made special efforts to defend their country; the kingdoms at the borders of India did. Individual monarchs attempted to dissuade the invaders to protect their property, for a monarch's duty is to defend his land and its people. Individual soldiers fought well because a soldier's job is to fight. When victory came, it had to come out of these simple arrangements.

The Second Reason

The second reason for India losing its independence is related to the first. It is India's lack of national unity. However, before coming to India's attitude to unity, let me tell you that, frankly speaking, nationalism—an intense loyalty for one's country/community/race—may not be a purely virtuous or faultless proposition. Let me explain. Suppose the Hindus wanted something of advantage to them. Suppose that advantage was likely to cause suffering for non-Hindus. If the Hindus were fiercely loyal to their own cause, they would not care even if the non-Hindus suffered. Conversely, if some disadvantage to the others promised some advantage to the Hindus, the Hindus would not hold back from hurting others.*

On the whole, then, group loyalty is not an entirely healthy attitude. This ill practice has caused much damage in Europe. Many fiery wars have been fought in that continent due to this flawed sentiment. Currently, this passion of dominant nationalism is a leading trend there. Italy has strongly united itself. The German authority is determined to build a huge empire by force. Who knows what else will happen in Europe under the influence of racial or nationalistic sentiments?†

We notice, however, that, virtuous or not, nationalism or unity among a clan of people and their racial pride give a people

---

* Bankimchandra clearly finds nationalistic feeling a defective emotion. Yet, in his book *Dharmatattwa* there is a chapter called 'Swadeshpriti' which means love for one's own country. There he describes this category of love as a highly desirable attitude. Is Bankim contradicting himself? The answer is: no. He dislikes the European pattern of nationalism and patriotism, including sanctioning encroachment of others' property and freedom. By swadeshpriti, Bankim means a dedication to improving the conditions of one's habitat and upholding the rights of its people. This, Bankim holds, conforms to the universal Dharma of preserving life on earth.

† Bankim prophetically anticipates the two World Wars of 1914–18 and 1939–45.

immense strength to assert themselves over others. I do not claim that ancient Bharatvarsha never had a united, dominant race that tried to establish itself as a superior force over others.

The Vedas were written during the first Aryan invasion of India. In the verses of the Vedas and in books composed soon after them, we find several examples of the dominance of a united power. The way the seniors of the Aryan society of India at that time organized their community highlights their power over others. The sharp divisions between high-caste Aryans and the Shudras are merely an outcome of the social codes laid down by the inconsiderate Brahmins to rule over the non-Aryans.

By and by, the population of the Aryan community grew. The race had to regroup themselves into many smaller communities to settle in far-flung territories of India. This gradually weakened the former unity of the Aryans. Interactions with diverse local traditions began to distinguish one group of Aryans from the others in minute details. The country as a whole became a land of diversity. Soon, Buddhism rose to become a prominent religion with many followers. Now, people differed from one another in their languages, religion, local customs. Later, Muslims overpowered the land. Many of my countrymen embraced Islam either to win favours with the victors or out of fear of them. Now there was more diversity in India. So much variety brought intense disunity to the country.

At present the English people are doing us a great favour. They are teaching us new lessons—lessons that we have not learnt for centuries. They are teaching us that being patriotic and united will give us strength.

5

On Caste[*]

(22 September 1907)

Sri Aurobindo

Caste was originally an arrangement for the distribution of functions in society, just as much as class in Europe, but the principle on which the distribution was based in India was peculiar to this country. . . . A Brahmin was a Brahmin not by mere birth, but because he discharged the duty of preserving the spiritual and intellectual elevation of the race. And he had to cultivate the spiritual temperament and acquire the spiritual training which could alone qualify him for the task. The Kshatriya was a Kshatriya not merely because he was the son of warriors and princes, but because he discharged the duty of protecting the country and preserving the high courage and manhood of the nation, and he had to cultivate the princely temperament and acquire the string and lofty Samurai training which alone fitted him for his duties. So it was with the Vaishya whose function was to amass wealth for the race and the Sudra who discharged the humbler duties of service without which the other castes could not perform their share of labour for the common good. Essentially

[*] Extracted from *Sri Aurobindo and India's Rebirth: Revolutionary Writings 1893–1910*, edited by Michel Danino, Rupa Books, Delhi, 2018.

there was, between the devout Brahmin and the devout Sudra, no inequality in the single *virat purusha* (Cosmic Spirit) of which each was a necessary part. Chokha Mela, the Maratha Pariah, became the Guru of Brahmins proud of their caste purity; the Chandala taught Shankaracharya: for the Brahman was revealed in the body of the Pariah and in the Chandala there was the utter presence of Shiva the Almighty . . ..

Caste therefore was not only an institution which ought to be immune from the cheap second-hand denunciations so long in fashion, but a supreme necessity without which Hindu civilization could not have developed its distinctive character or worked out its unique mission.

But to recognise this is not to debar ourselves from pointing out its later perversions and desiring its transformation. It is the nature of human institutions to degenerate, to lose their vitality, and decay, and the first sign of decay is the loss of flexibility and oblivion of the essential spirit in which they were conceived. The spirit is permanent, the body changes; and a body which refuses to change must die. The spirit expresses itself in many ways while itself remaining essentially the same but the body must change to suit its changing environments if it wishes to live. There is no doubt that the institution of caste degenerated. It ceased to be determined by spiritual qualifications which, once essential, have now come to be subordinate and even immaterial and is determined by the purely material tests of occupation and birth. By this change it has set itself against the fundamental tendency of Hinduism which is to insist on the spiritual and subordinate the material and thus lost most of its meaning. The spirit of caste arrogance, exclusiveness and superiority came to dominate it instead of the spirit of duty, and the change weakened the nation and helped to reduce us to our present conditions.

6

Revival or Reform?[*]

Sister Nivedita

'How did the Pope go to Avignon?' says a European proverb. 'En protestant—as a protestant.'

Even the Pope, then, in face of a usurper, may, till he is reinstated, act the part of a protestant. Even a Hindu, in a similar place, may call himself a reformer. It would be sad, however, if the Pope, in love with the attitude of a protestor, were permanently tinged with the originality and discontent of that character. The great church of which he is the head, divided thus against herself, could no longer stand intact under the blows that would then be dealt her by her chief pastor. And similarly of the reformer. The work of reform is always limited in any given direction, and nothing can be more mischievous than the temper of the professional reformer. One reform there indeed is, which may be pursued day and night, in season and out of season, but this is the reform effected by pure ideas. The same universality does not belong to reform proper, that is to say, to the displacement of one institution by another. Never, for instance, can we sufficiently realise, never can any sufficiently

---

[*] First appeared in the *Indian World*, January–July 1907, in *Sister Nivedita's Lectures and Writings*, Vol. V, Ramakrishna Sarada Mission, Calcutta, October 1955, pp. 82–88. Emphasis as in the original.

aid us to realise, the highest ideal of faithfulness in woman. But who could presume to dictate to another the form in which this should be pursued? . . .

Only the pure idea, the concept of faith and purity itself can be universal. The form must always be of localised application. Only the crusader of the ideal, then, can claim passports without limitation. The rights of the reformer of institutions are definite, and have a beginning and an end. . . .

All the world must prostrate itself before women who were capable of performing Sati. But Ram Mohun Roy was indubitably right to forbid women in future that liberty. The patriot admires the heroic wifehood and admired even the lion-hearted reformer. Hinduism has appropriated, in this matter, the labours of the agitator. Hindus know well that his stern prohibition must be eternally enforced. They hold only that in his person—original as was his impulse, national as was his whole upbringing—it should be recognised that a Hindu and not foreigners, put an end to the custom. Ram Mohun Roy's was the apostolate. The response of his own people was the sanction. All that foreigners contributed was the assistance of the Police, on definite occasions.

This is indeed the mode of all social progression. Custom grows rigid or becomes exaggerated. Protest arises in the person of seer or saint or teacher, and society opens her arms, embraces her rebel son, and takes her or becomes exaggerated. Protest arises in the person of seer or stand henceforth on that wider basis which his work has built for her.

Or to put it otherwise, a healthy reform group represents an experiment in the laboratory of social growth. The Brahmo Samaj in Bengal may be looked upon as a community segregating itself from Orthodox society for the purposes of working out certain results that were quite requisite to that society itself. It was desirable to show that Hinduism was capable of offering all that Christianity could offer in the religious life and organisation, without de-nationalism.

The tragedy of Christianity in India is its imperialistic character. It may be quite true that the under-dog is not always in the right, still, no self-respecting under-dog will wag its tail over the upper-dog's statement of his own ideals! But congregational worship, the weekly sermon, the Sunday school and the mutual aid of sectarian organisation were undoubtedly valuable contributions to the social site of religious activity.

On the purely human side again, by opening up society to women, Brahmoism silently made the important assertion that men stand or fall by their obedience to as high a moral standard as is required of their wives and sisters. . . . The beautiful old reverence of the orthodox for womanhood was not lost; the exquisite reserve of the Indian householder, guarding the privacy of his home, remained. Only for those who were proved worthy of the honour, there was now opened a social sanctum where fine men might meet good women and make an exchange of courtesy and thought.

Freedom as to food and marriage did not mean the transcending of social limitations. The Brahmo appears to the outsider to be as much a man of his own class as any other. But wherever he may have come from, he belongs to a caste now that is determined by its education and any newcomer may join it, by reaching the required development. . . .

The Pope went to Avignon as a protestant, true. But he came back. But when he did return, it was as a good Catholic, glad to be at home, in familiar places, glad to be freed from the necessity of protesting against everything. So of reforms in general. A good deal of dust is stirred up by their inception. A good deal of antagonism and mutual conflict is required at first, partly to weed the ranks of recruits who might not be helpful. But in the end there assuredly comes a time when the pioneer-stage of the labour is incumbent to appropriate consciously all that the social experiment has achieved or evolved. On the reformers it is desirable to draw closer the bonds that unite them to the old fold and sentiments from which, for a while, they were necessarily isolated.

Then arise fresh and still more living ideals. The divided consciousness of conservatism on one side and new moulding on the other gives place to the sense of a great task of up-building to be performed in common. Men realise that they are after all but the children of their own fathers; that if they could reach the fullest significance of their own institutions, the achievements would be tantamount to the most perfect reform. The radical sees that his own moral fervour and love of integrity were handed down to him from his orthodox forbears, who must have been to the full as good men as himself. The orthodox man, on his side, realises that a mere religion of the kitchen would never represent Dharma. Instead of casting stones at others for their errors of sympathy, it is his duty to widen his own activity. The Brahmo is no longer to be blamed for abandoning the ancient forms of caste, and neither is the orthodox to rest content with his own petrifaction of custom. For nationality has arisen, as the goal of all sections of society, alike, and side by side must work brothers of all shades of opinion, of all forms of energy, for the recreating of the Dharma, for the building anew, in the world, the Maha-Bharata, Heroic India.

Our watchword, then, is no longer Reform. In its place, we have taken the word 'Construct'. We have to re-create the Dharma. We have to build again the Maha-Bharata. It was said that the church und its protestants society and the reformer are now to exchange achievements and become fused once more. For, after all, humanity is greater than any church. Society was made for Man, not Man for society.

It is essential then, that a rich efflorescence of such opportunities be produced. It is essential then that the brain of the race be set out to the task. Every industry created, every factory established, however insignificant it may appear in itself, is a school of a manhood, an academy where shrewdness and responsibility and integrity are to be studied in the lesson book of experience, an Ashrama where young souls may ascend the first steps of the ladder to Rishihood. The task is creating of a nation to take possession of its country. The men are to be produced by hard experience. The method is to be unity. But where is this unity to be learnt? The reformers have taught us the value of fixed congregation, a pride in the achievements of its own members. But it could not be expected, it could not even be desired, that the body of the orthodox should drift into the camp of the heretics. How, then, can they appropriate the results of their experiments? It could not be asked that the reformers should return to the city from which for conscientious reasons they set out, and abandon in the eyes of the world all for which, in the past, they have fought. Where, then, are the two parties to meet and confer together? Where are they to attack the common problems? Where and round what standard are they to assert in their unity?

The answer is simple. They are to meet on the common ground of place. For rebuilding the Maha-Bharata, the village is to be the work-room. The city is the factory. The whole country is the site of the new building. In all that concerns the interests of India the neighbours are Indians, willing to avail themselves of all that can be learnt, from far and near, ready to obey anyone, whatever his personal convictions on other subjects, who has the strength and wisdom necessary to lead . . .

The power of steam is not a whit greater today, though it drives the railway engine and the ship, than it was of old, when it merely made the cover rattle over the pot where the rice was cooking. Steam is not more powerful than it was. But man has recognised his power. Similarly, one may stand paralysed in all our strength for ages, all for want of knowing that we had that strength. After we faced the fact, there still remains the problem of how to control and use it. And long vision is not given in this kind to any of us. Only now and then, for hard prayer and struggle, do mists flow to one side a little, letting us for a moment catch the glimpse of the mountain path. Yet, without recognition of our strength, there can be no possible question of using it. Without right thought, there cannot possibly be right action. To us, then, the recognition; to us, the thought. India is not divided and subdivided in any effective sense of those words. She is not divided in any way that could possibly hinder the working out of a great nationality. We are working comrades, not because we speak the same language or believe the same creeds. Should I cease to be the brother of my own mother's son because he went abroad and learnt a foreign tongue, or took up the worship of Mahadeva instead of that of Vishnu or Parthasarathi? We are working comrades on no basis so limited as that of creed or language, which, after all, would limit us geographically to a province and spiritually to a single line of development. We are working comrades because we are Indians, children of a single-roof tree, dwellers around one bamboo clump. Our task is one, the rebuilding of Heroic India. To this, every nerve and muscle of us tingle with response. Who is foolish as to imagine that a little political letting and pampering can make half a nation forget its kinship with the other half? Nonsense! We are one! We have not become one. We are one. Our sole need is to learn to demonstrate our unity.

7

Hinduism and Organisation[*]

Sister Nivedita

Hinduism is one of the finest and most coherent growths in the world. Its disadvantages arise out of the fact that it is a growth, not an organisation; a tree, not a machine. In an age in which the whole world worships the machine, for its exactness, its calculableness, and its dirigibility, this fact, while it makes for a greater permanence, also involves a certain number of desiderata. The fruits of the tree of Hinduism are of an excellence unparalleled; but it is not easy to reach by its means those benefits that do not occur spontaneously, ends that have to be foreseen and deliberately planned and arranged for. For instance, alone amongst the world's faiths perhaps, ours has no quarrel of any sort with truth. Under its sway, the scientific mind is absolutely free to pursue to the uttermost its researches into the Infinite Nescience of things, the philosopher is encouraged to elucidate his conclusions, and simple piety does not dream of passing judgment on things admittedly too high for it. All this is true of Hinduism. At the same time, what has it done to grasp the highest scientific education for its children, or to impel its people forward upon the pursuit of mastery in learning or in ministering to social service? There is nothing in Hinduism

---

[*] Extracted from *The Complete Works of Sister Nivedita*, Volume III, Ramakrishna Sarada Mission, Calcutta, 1955, pp. 400–40.

to forbid an attempt on our part to compass these things, and the only thing that could drive us to make the effort—namely, a vigilant and energetic sense of affairs, a public spirit that took account of things as a whole—was undoubtedly indicated by Swami Vivekananda, as part of what he meant by Aggressive Hinduism. We ought to make our faith aggressive, not only internationally, by sending out missionaries, but also socially, by self-improvement; not only doctrinally, by accepting converts, but also spiritually, by intensifying its activity. What we need is to supplement religion by public spirit—an enlightened self-sense in which every member of the community has a part. Class preference is obsolete in matters of education. The career of the intellect is now for him who has the talent. By us, this principle has to be boldly and enthusiastically accepted. Even as the school is open to all, so must every form of social ministration be made. The college, the orphanage, the hospital, the women's refuge, these must be opened by such as have the devotion and energy for the task, and nothing must be said of the birth of the servant of humanity. By virtue of his consecration, he becomes a saint, even as, by his Jnanam, the philosopher makes himself a Rishi. Activity is eased and heightened if it is socialised: that is to say, if it is the work of a body, espousing a common conviction, and not of a solitary individual, wandering the world, and divided between his idea itself and the question of its support. This common conviction, driving into work, is the reason why small religious sects are so often the source of vast movements of human amelioration. Many of these outstanding problems of Hinduism have been attacked, for instance, by the Brahmo Samaj, with considerable success. The little church forms a background and home for the worker. It sends him out to his task, rejoices over his success, and welcomes him back with laurels, or with ministration, when he turns home to die. Without some such city of the heart, it is difficult to see how the worker is to keep up his energy and courage. The praise and pleasure of our own little group of beloved ones is very sweet to all of us, and quite properly spurs us on to surmount many an obstacle that we should not otherwise attempt. Let the soul grow, by saying 'not this!' 'not this!' to what height it will; but let it have the occasion for practising this discrimination. We must take up our problems, then, as social groups. Let no man enter on the apostolate that is to shake the world, alone. Everything done, every discovery made, even every poem written, and every dream dreamed, is a social achievement. Society has contributed to it, and will receive its benefits. Let the missionary, then, on whom the effort seems to rest, not reckon himself to be the chief actor. There must be some two or three, knit together by some well-wrought bond, in every undertaking that is to benefit humanity. Perhaps they were comrades at school and college. Perhaps they are disciples of a single master. Possibly they belong to the same village. Maybe they are fellow-workmen in some common employment. Whatever be the shaping force, there must be association of aim and co-operation of effort, if there is to be success, and there must be a strong bond of love amongst those few ardent souls who form the central core. Voluntary association, the desire of a body to take on corporate individuality, is thus the point of departure within Hinduism for civic activity. But we must not forget how much every activity owes to the general movement of society around it. Work must be done by the few as the servants, not as the enemies, of the many. Every single movement needs other counter-movements to supplement it, if it is to maintain itself in vigour. Thus, the difficulty about technical education in India is not want of funds, which have been poured in in abundance; but want of general industrial development, in the society around. There is a fixed ratio between education and development which cannot be passed, hence only by definite and alternating increments to the one and to the other can progress take place. Again, there is a fixed proportion between the total of these and the community's need of the highest scientific research, which cannot be contravened. And all these alike must find themselves inhering in an inclusive social energy, which takes account of its own needs, its own problems and its own organs. The vivifying of this general social sense is the first of all our problems. We have to awaken it, to refresh it, and to keep it constantly informed. What this social sense has now first and foremost to realise, is our want of education, the need of a real ploughing of the mind.

Aggressive Hinduism

I. *The Basis*

'*The True* Hinduism, that made men work, not dream.'
—Dr J.C. Bose

One of the most valuable generalisations of the modern era is that which was first arrived at, just about the time of the French Revolution, that the *individual, in his development, follows the race.* Each man and woman, that is to say, when perfectly educated, becomes an epitome of the history either of his or her own race, or of Humanity as a whole. This great perception made itself felt as a definite element in a new scheme of education, through Pestalozzi—the saint and Guru of teachers in the twentieth century West. Pestalozzi saw that, if there were ever to be hope for the people, it must be through an education at once modern, that is liberal, psychological, that is founded on a knowledge of mental laws, and in accordance with the historic development of man. The problem which the young student Pestalozzi, son and lover of the people, had to face at the end of the French Revolution, in Switzerland, was of trifling magnitude compared with that which confronts the son and lover of India today. And yet, in their innermost nature, the two are identical. For this, like that, consists in the difficulty of opening up the human field to a new thought-harvest, while at the same time avoiding the evils of mere surface-culture. The soil that has brought forth the mango and the palm ought not to be degraded to producing only gourds and vetches. And similarly, the land of the Vedas and of Jnana-Yoga has no right to sink into the role of mere critic or imitator of European Letters.

Yet this is the present condition of Indian culture, and it appears likely to remain so, unless the Indian mind can deliberately discipline itself to the historic point of view. To do this is like adjusting oneself to a new dimension. Things which were hitherto merged in each other all at once become distinct. That which till now was instinctive is suddenly seen to have a goal—which is capable, in its turn, of clear definition. The social and the religious idea, under Hinduism as under Islam, were in the past indistinguishable. Philosophically, of course, every tyro could detach one from the other; in practice, however, they were one, and could not be separated. For religious reasons, as was supposed, we must eat in a certain way, wear specified clothing, and fulfil a definite scheme of purification. Suddenly, through the modern catastrophe, the sunlight of comparison, contrast, and relativity is poured over the whole area, and we discover that by living up to custom, we have been not accumulating pious merit, but merely approximating to that ideal of absolute refinement, cleanliness, and purity, which is the dream of all fine human life, and which may as well, or better, be achieved by some other canon as by our own. Seeing the goal thus clearly, we become able to analyse and compare various methods; to add to our own conduct the virtues of others, and to eliminate from it the defects of all. Above all, we find out how to distinguish effectively between the social idea and religion. It is thus that it becomes possible to talk of 'aggressive Hinduism'.

Aggression is to be the dominant characteristic of the India that is today in school and class-room—aggression, and the thought and ideals of aggression. Instead of passivity, activity; for the standard of weakness, the standard of strength; in place of a steadily yielding defence, the ringing cheer of the invading host. Merely to change the attitude of the mind in this way is already to accomplish a revolution. And the inception of some such change will have become evident to us all within a dozen years.

But before the first step can be taken, there must be clear thought about essentials. The object of all religious systems is the formation of character. Theocratic systems aim at the construction of character through the discipline of personal habit. But at bottom it is character and not habit that they desire to create. No one will dispute that her ideals are a still prouder fruit of Hinduism than her widespread refinement. It is true that India is the only country in the world where a penniless wanderer may surpass a king in social prestige. But still grander is the fact that the king may be a Janaka, and the beggar a Shuka Deva.

Let us, then, touch on the comparative study of the value of habit as a factor in the evolution of character. We find in India that society watches a man all the years of his life, ready to criticise him for the hour at which he bathes and eats and prays, the mode of his travel, the fashion in which, perhaps, he wears his hair. To attempt a serious innovation on social custom in such directions as marriage or education seems to horrified public opinion not merely selfish, but also sacrilegious. And this kind of criticism becomes more and more powerful over the individual as the villages empty themselves into the cities. For the man who might have had the courage to make his mark in the smaller community would think it presumptuous to go his own way in the larger. Hence the aggregation of men tends to become the multiplication of their weaknesses and defects. It is the mean and warped judgment that gains fastest in weight.

But let us look at a community in which active ends and ideals are energetically pursued. Here a certain standard of personal refinement is exacted of the individual, as rigidly as in India itself. But public opinion, being strong enough to kill, does not stoop to discuss such points. The learning of the method is relegated to the nursery, where it is imparted by women. Having passed through this stage of his education, it is not expected that the hero will fall short in future of its standards;

but if he did so, society would know how to punish him, by ignoring his existence. Both he and society, meanwhile, are too busy with other efforts to be able to waste force on what is better, left to his own pride. For a whole new range of ideals has now come in sight. From the time that a Western child steps out of the nursery, it is not quietness, docility, resignation, and obedience, that his teachers and guardians strive to foster in him, so much as strength, initiative, sense of responsibility, and power of rebellion. Temper and self-will are regarded by Western educators as a very precious power, which must by no means be crushed or destroyed, though they must undoubtedly be disciplined and subordinated to impersonal ends. It is for this reason that fighting is encouraged in our playgrounds, the only stipulation being for fair play. To forbid a boy to undergo the physical ordeal, means, as we think, undermining his sincerity, as well as his courage. But for him to strike one who is weaker than himself is to stand disgraced amongst his equals.

That is to say, a social evolution which in Asia has occupied many centuries is in the West relegated to, at most, the first ten years of a child's upbringing, and he then passes into the period of chivalry. Indeed if, as some suppose, the ten Avatars of Vishnu are but the symbol of a single-perfect life, India herself has not failed to point this lesson. For after the stages of fish, tortoise, boar, and man-lion are all safely and happily passed, and the child has become 'a little man', it still remains for him to be twice a Kshatriya before he is able to become a Buddha. What is this but the modern generalisation that the individual in his development follows the race? And in the last sublime myth of Kalki, may it not be that we have the prophecy of a great further evolution, in which Buddhahood itself shall plunge once more into a sovereign act of redeeming love and pity, and initiate, for every individual of us, the triumph of active and aggressive ideals?

Let us suppose, then, that we see Hinduism no longer as the preserver of Hindu custom, but as the *creator* of *Hindu character*.

It is surprising to think, how radical a change is entailed in many directions by this conception. We are no longer oppressed with jealousy or fear, when we contemplate encroachments on our social and religious consciousness. Indeed, the idea of encroachment has ceased, because our work is not now to protect ourselves but to convert others. Point by point, we are determined, not merely to keep what we had, but to win what we never had before. The question is no longer of other people's attitude to us, but, rather, of what we think of them. It is not, how much have we kept, but, how much have we annexed? We cannot afford, now, to lose, because we are sworn to carry the battle far beyond our remotest frontiers. We no longer dream of submission, because struggle itself has become only the first step towards a distant victory to be won.

No other religion in the world is so capable of this dynamic transformation as Hinduism. To Nagarjuna and Buddhaghosha, the Many was real and the Ego unreal. To Shankaracharya, the One was real and the Many unreal. To Ramakrishna and Vivekananda, the Many and the One were the same Reality, perceived differently and at different times by the human consciousness. Do we realize what this means? It means that CHARACTER IS SPIRITUALITY. It means that laziness and defeat are not renunciation. It means that to protect another is infinitely greater than to attain salvation. It means that Mukti lies in overcoming the thirst for Mukti. It means that conquest may be the highest form of Sannyasa. It means, in short, that Hinduism has become aggressive, that the trumpet of Kalki is sounded already in our midst, and that it calls all that is noble, all that is lovely, all that is strenuous and heroic amongst us, to a battlefield on which the bugles of retreat shall never more be heard.

8

The National Significance of Swami Vivekananda's Life and Work[*]

Sister Nivedita

Of the bodily presence of him who was known to the world as Vivekananda, all that remains today is a bowl of ashes. The light that has burned in seclusion during the last five years by our riverside, has gone out now. The great voice that rang out across the nations is hushed in death.

Life had come often to this mighty soul as storm and pain. But the end was peace. Silently, at the close of even song, on a dark night of Kali, came the benediction of death. The weary and tortured body was laid down gently and the triumphant spirit was restored to the eternal Samadhi.

He passed, when the laurels of his first achievements were yet green. He passed, when new and greater calls were ringing in his ears. Quietly, in the beautiful home of his illness, the intervening years with some few breaks, went by amongst plants and animals, unostentatiously training the disciples who gathered round him, silently ignoring the great fame that had shone upon his name. Man-making was his own stern brief summary of the work that was worth doing. And laboriously, unflaggingly, day after

[*] Extracted from *The Complete Works of Sister Nivedita*, Volume I, Ramakrishna Sarada Mission, Calcutta, 1967, pp. 373–82.

day, he set himself to man-making, playing the part of Guru, of father, even of schoolmaster, by turns. The very afternoon of the day he left us, had he not spent three hours in giving a Sanskrit lesson on the Vedas?

External success and leadership were nothing to such a man. During his years in the West, he made rich and powerful friends, who would gladly have retained him in their midst. But for him, the Occident, with all its luxuries had no charms. To him, the garb of a beggar, the lanes of Calcutta, and the disabilities of his own people, were more dear than all the glory of the foreigner, and detaining hands had to loose their hold of one who passed ever onward toward the East. What was it that the West heard in him, leading so many to hail and cherish his name as that of one of the great religious teachers of the world? He made no personal claim. He told no personal story. One whom he knew and trusted long had never heard that he held any position of distinction amongst his Gurubhais. He made no attempt to popularise with strangers any single form or creed, whether of God or Guru. Rather, through him the mighty torrent of Hinduism poured forth its cooling waters upon the intellectual and spiritual worlds, fresh from its secret sources in Himalayan snows. A witness to the vast religious culture of Indian homes and holy men he could never cease to be. Yet he quoted nothing but the Upanishads. He taught nothing but the Vedanta. And men trembled, for they heard the voice for the first time of the religious teacher who feared not Truth.

Do we not all know the song that tells of Shiva as he passes along the roadside, 'Some say He is mad. Some say He is the Devil. Some say—don't you know?—He is the Lord Himself!' Even so India is familiar with the thought that every great personality is the meeting-place and reconciliation of opposing ideals. To his disciples, Vivekananda will ever remain the archetype of the Sannyasin. Burning renunciation was chief of all the inspirations that spoke to us through him. 'Let me die a true Sannyasin as my Master did,' he exclaimed once, passionately, 'heedless of money, of women, and of fame! And of these the most insidious is the love of fame!' Yet the self-same destiny that filled him with this burning thirst of intense Vairagyam embodied in him also the ideal householder—full of the yearning to protect and save, eager to learn and teach the use of materials, reaching out towards the reorganisation and re-ordering of life. In this respect, indeed, he belonged to the race of Benedict and Bernard, of Robert de Citcaux and Loyola. It may be said that just as in Francis of Assisi, the yellow robe of the Indian Sannyasin gleams for a moment in the history of the Catholic Church, so in Vivekananda, the great saint, abbots of Western monasticism are born anew in the East.

Similarly, he was at once a sublime expression of superconscious religion and one of the greatest patriots ever born. He lived at a moment of national disintegration, and he was fearless of the new. He lived when men were abandoning their inheritance, and he was an ardent worshipper of the old. In him the national destiny fulfilled itself, that a new wave of consciousness should be inaugurated always in the leaders of the Faith. In such a man it may be that we possess the whole Veda of the future. We must remember, however, that the moment has not come for gauging the religious significance of Vivekananda. Religion is living seed, and his sowing is but over. The time of his harvest is not yet.

But death actually gives the Patriot to his country. When the master has passed away from the midst of his disciples, when the murmurs of his critics are all hushed at the burning-ghat, then the great voice that spoke of Freedom rings out unchallenged and whole nations answer as one man. Here was a mind that had had unique opportunities of observing the people of many countries intimately. East and West he had seen and been received by the high and low alike. His brilliant intellect had never failed to gauge what it saw. 'America will solve the problems of the Shudra, but through what awful turmoil!' he said many times. On a second visit, however, he felt tempted to change his mind, seeing the greed of wealth and the lust of oppression in the West, and comparing these with the calm dignity and ethical stability of the old Asiatic solutions formulated by China many centuries ago. His great acumen was yoked to a marvellous humanity.

Never had we dreamt of such a gospel of hope for the Negro as that with which he rounded on an American gentleman who spoke of the African races with contempt. And when, in the Southern States he was occasionally taken for 'a coloured man', and turned away from some door as such (a mistake that was always atoned for as soon as discovered by the lavish hospitality of the most responsible families of the place), he was never known to deny the imputation. 'Would it not have been refusing my brother?' he said simply when he was asked the reason of this silence.

To him each race had its own greatness, and shone in the light of that central quality. There was no Europe without the Turk, no Egypt without the development of the people of the soil. England had grasped the secret of obedience with self-respect. To speak of any patriotism in the same breath with Japan's was sacrilege.

What then was the prophecy that Vivekananda left to his own people? With what national significance has he filled that Gerrua mantle that he dropped behind him in his passing? Is it for us perhaps to lift the yellow rags upon our flagpole, and carry them forward as our banner? Assuredly. For here was a man who never dreamt of failure. Here was a man who spoke of naught but strength. Supremely free from sentimentality, supremely defiant of all authority (are not missionary slanders still ringing in our ears? Are not some of them to be accepted with fresh accessions of pride?), he refused to meet any foreigner save as the master. 'The Swami's great genius lies in his dignity,' said an Englishman who knew him well. 'It is nothing short of royal!' He had grasped the great fact that the East must come to the West, not as a sycophant, not as a servant, but as Guru and teacher, and never did he lower the flag of his personal ascendancy. 'Let

Europeans lead us in Religion!' he would say, with a scorn too deep to be anything but merry. 'I have never spoken of revenge,' he said once. 'I have always spoken of strength. Do we dream of revenging ourselves on this drop of sea-spray? But it is a great thing to a mosquito!'

To him, nothing Indian required apology. Did anything seem, to the pseudo-refinement of the alien, barbarous or crude? Without denying, without minimising anything his colossal energy was immediately concentrated on the vindication of that particular point, and the unfortunate critic was tossed backwards and forwards on the horns of his own argument. One such instance occurred when an Englishman on board the ship asked him some sneering question about the Puranas, and never can any who were present forget how he was pulverised, by a reply that made the Hindu Puranas, compare favourably with the Christian Gospels, but planted the Vedas and Upanishads high up beyond the reach of any rival. There was no friend that he would not sacrifice without mercy at such a moment in the name of national defence. Such an attitude was not, perhaps, always reasonable. It was often indeed frankly unpleasant. But it was superb in the manliness that even enemies must admire. To Vivekananda, again, everything Indian was absolutely and equally sacred—'This land to which must come all souls wending their way Godward!' his religious consciousness tenderly phrased it. At Chicago, any Indian man attending the Great World Bazaar, rich or poor, high or low, Hindu, Mohammedan, Parsi, what not, might at any moment be brought by him to his hosts for hospitality and entertainment, and they well knew that any failure of kindness on their part to the least of these would immediately have cost them his presence.

He was himself the exponent of Hinduism, but finding another Indian religionist struggling with the difficulty of presenting his case, he sat down and wrote his speech for him, making a better story for his friend's faith than its own adherent could have done!

He took infinite pains to teach European disciples to eat with their fingers, and perform the ordinary simple acts of Hindu life. 'Remember, if you love India at all, you must love her as she is, not as you might wish her to become,' he used to say. And it was this great firmness of his, standing like a rock for what actually was, that did more than any other single fact, perhaps, to open the eyes of those aliens who loved him to the beauty and strength of that ancient poem—the common life of the common Indian people. For his own part, he was too free from the desire for approbation to make a single concession to newfangled ways. The best of every land had been offered him, but it left him still the simple Hindu of the old style, too proud of his simplicity to find any need of change. 'After Ramakrishna, I follow Vidyasagar!' he exclaimed, only two days before his death, and out came the oft-repeated story of the wooden sandals coming pitter patter with the Chudder and Dhoti, into the Viceregal Council Chamber, and the surprised 'But if you didn't want me, why did you ask me to come?' of the old Pundit, when they remonstrated.

Such points, however, are only interesting as personal characteristics. Of a deeper importance is the question as to the conviction that spoke through them. What was this? Whither did it tend? His whole life was a search for the common basis of Hinduism. To his sound judgment the idea that two pice postage, cheap travel, and a common language of affairs could create a national unity, was obviously childish and superficial. These things could only be made to serve old India's turn if she already possessed a deep organic unity of which they might conveniently become an expression. Was such a unity existent or not? For something like eight years he wandered about the land changing his name at every village, learning of every one he met, gaining a vision as accurate and minute as it was profound and general. It was this great quest that overshadowed him with its certainty when, at the Parliament of Religions, he stood before the West and proved that Hinduism converged upon a single imperative of perfect freedom so completely as to be fully capable of intellectual aggression as any other faith.

It never occurred to him that his own people were in any respect less than the equals of any other nation whatsoever. Being well aware that religion was their national expression, he was also aware that the strength which they might display in that sphere, would be followed before long, by every other conceivable form of strength.

As a profound student of caste—his conversation teemed with its unexpected particulars and paradoxes!—he found the key to Indian unity in its exclusiveness. Mohammedans were but a single caste of the nation. Christians another, Parsis another, and so on! It was true that of all these (with the partial exception of the last), non-belief in caste was a caste distinction. But then, the same was true of the Brahmo Samaj, and other modern sects of Hinduism. Behind all alike stood the great common facts of one soil; one beautiful old routine of ancestral civilisation; and the overwhelming necessities that must inevitably lead at last to common loves and common hates.

But he had learnt, not only the hopes and ideals of every sect and group of the Indian people, but their memories also. A child of the Hindu quarter of Calcutta returned to live by the Ganges-side, one would have supposed from his enthusiasm that he had been born, now in the Punjab, again in the Himalayas, at a third moment in Rajputana, or elsewhere. The songs of Guru Nanak alternated with those of Mira Bai and Tanasena on his lips. Stories of Prithvi Raj and Delhi jostled against those of Chitore and Pratap Singh, Shiva and Uma, Radha and Krishna, Sita-Ram and Buddha. Each mighty drama lived in a marvellous actuality, when he was the player. His whole heart and soul was a burning epic of the country, touched to an overflow of mystic passion by her very name. Seated in his retreat at Belur, Vivekananda received visits and communications from all quarters. The vast surface might be silent, but deep in the heart of India, the Swami was never forgotten. None could afford, still fewer wished, to ignore him. No hope but was spoken into his ear—no woe but he knew it, and strove to comfort or to rouse. Thus, as always in the case of a religious leader, the India that he saw presented a spectacle strangely unlike that visible to any other eye. For he held in his hands the thread of all that was fundamental, organic, vital; he knew the secret springs of life; he understood with what word to touch the heart of millions. And he had gathered from all this knowledge a clear and certain hope.

Let others blunder as they might. To him, the country was young, the Indian vernaculars still unformed, flexible, the national energy unexploited. The India of his dreams was in the future. The new phase of consciousness initiated today through pain and suffering was to be but the first step in a long evolution. To him his country's hope was in herself. Never in the alien. True, his great heart embraced the alien's need, sounding a universal promise to the world. But he never sought for help, or begged for assistance. He never leaned on any. What might be done, it was the doer's privilege to do, not the recipient's to accept. He had neither fears nor hopes from without. To reassert that which was India's essential self, and leave the great stream of the national life, strong in a fresh self-confidence and vigour, to find its own way to the ocean, this was the meaning of his Sannyasa. For his was pre-eminently the Sannyasa of the greater service. To him, India was Hinduistic, Aryan, Asiatic. Her youth might make their own experiments in modern luxury. Had they not the right? Would they not return? But the great deeps of her being were moral, austere, and spiritual. A people who could embrace death by the Ganges-side were not long to be distracted by the glamour of mere mechanical power.

Buddha had preached renunciation, and in two centuries India had become an Empire. Let her but once more feel the great pulse through all her veins, and no power on earth would stand before her newly awakened energy. Only, it would be in her own life that she would find life, not in imitation; from her own proper past and environment that she would draw inspiration, not from the foreigner. For he who thinks himself weak is weak: he who believes that he is strong is already invincible. And so for his nation, as for every individual, Vivekananda had but one word, one constantly reiterated message:

Awake! Arise! Struggle on,
And stop not till the
Goal is reached!

Perhaps the distinguishing feature of the Swami's patriotism was the fact that it was centred in the country itself. Like all religious teachers in India he had a more complex and comprehensive view of what constituted the nation than could be open to any lay mind. And he hoped for nothing from the personality or the methods of the foreigners. He occasionally accepted Europeans as his disciples, but he always disciplined them to the emphatic conviction that they 'must work under black men'.

Before meeting his own guru, Ramakrishna Paramahamsa, he may be said to have imbibed completely all that the Europeanising movement among his own people had to give. His whole life from this point becomes a progressive recapture of national ideals. He was no student of economic sociality, but his Asiatic common sense and brilliant power of insight were of themselves enough to teach him that the labour-saving mechanism of the far West—where vast agricultural areas have to be worked single-handed—could only be introduced to the remote East—where a tiny plot of land maintains each its man or men—at the cost of overwhelming economic disaster. He was eager indeed to see the practicability of modern science developed among his own people, but this was rather with the object of giving a new and more direct habit of thought than with any outlook on the readjustment of conditions. He probably understood as well as any university student of the West (for scholars are the only people who understand the actual bearing of national and economic questions! statesmen certainly do not!) that the problem of Asia today is entirely a question of the preservation of her old institutions at any cost, and not at all of the rapidity of innovation. He was no politician: he was the greatest of nationalists.

9

Swami Vivekananda: A Historical Review[*]

R.C. Majumdar

Practical Vedanta

But the most distinctive feature of Swami Vivekananda's teaching is that he applied his philosophic principles to the affairs of everyday life. He laid emphasis on the fact that we shall seek salvation, not so much in the traditional way, by renouncing the world and taking to the life of a recluse, as by serving the God in man. We have seen above how this practical Vedanta was the foundation on which the whole structure of his monastic organization was built. Reference has also been made above to the opposition of his own brother-disciples to this new mode of salvation propounded by Swamiji. He, however, not only stuck to his gun, but even went to the other extreme of denouncing every other form of salvation. His retort to his critics, that he would follow this path even if it go against the teachings of Ramakrishna, indicates the depth of his feeling in the matter. The same spirit appears in a more pronounced form when he pours out his heart in a letter to Mary Hale on 9 July 1897:

[*] Extracted from *Swami Vivekananda: A Historical Review* by R.C. Majumdar, Advaita Ashram, Kolkata, 2013, pp. 97–109.

Only one idea was burning in my brain—to start the machine for elevating the Indian masses, and that I have succeeded in doing to a certain extent.

It would have made your heart glad to see how my boys are working in the midst of famine and disease and misery-nursing by the mat-bed of the cholera-stricken pariah and feeding the starving chandala, and the Lord sends help to me to them, to all . . . I feel my task is done—at most three or four years more of life are left. I have lost all wish for my salvation. I never wanted earthly enjoyments. I must see my machine in strong working order, and then, knowing for sure that I have put in a lever for the good of humanity, in India at least, which no power can drive back, I will sleep without caring what will be next.

And may I be born again and again, and suffer thousands of miseries, so that I may worship the only God that exists, the only God I believe in, the sum total of all souls. And above all, my God the wicked, my God the miserable, my God the poor of all races, of all species, is the especial object of my worship.

Swamiji's Vision of India's Future

The words 'in India at least' in the above passage seem to be significant. Indications are not wanting that Swamiji's insistence on the service of God in man (*daridra-Narayana*) was largely the result of his view about the future regeneration of India. He denounced the upper classes in the severest language. 'You, the upper classes of India, do you think you are alive? You are but mummies ten thousand years old: It is among those whom your ancestors despised as "walking carrions" that the little of vitality there is still in India is to be found; and it is you who are the real "walking corpses".' He emphasized again and again that the masses were the real foundations of National life. 'It is through their physical labour only are possible, the influence of the Brahmans, the progress of the Kshatriyas, and the fortune of the Vaishyas.'

He holds out the following vision of India's future greatness. 'Let her arise—out of the peasants' cottage, grasping the plough, out of the huts of the fisherman, the grocer's shop, from beside the oven of the fritter-seller. Let her emanate from the factory, from marts and from markets. Let her emerge from the groves and forests, from hills and mountains. These common people have suffered oppression for thousands of years—suffered it without murmur, and as a result have got wonderful fortitude. They have suffered eternal misery, which has given them unflinching vitality . . . Such peacefulness, such contentment, such love, such power of silent and incessant work, and such manifestation of lion's strength in times of action—where else will you find these! Skeletons of the past, there, before you, are your successors, the India that is to be. Throw those treasure-chests of yore and those jewelled rings among them—as soon as you can; and you—vanish into air, and be seen no more.'

Swamiji's National Ideal: Influence on Arabinda, Rabindra and Gandhi

It is not difficult to understand why Swamiji, who always dreamt of the rise of a puissant Indian nation and looked upon the uplift of the masses as sine qua non for the purpose, should have put the whole emphasis of his position and personality on the solution of the problem of Indian masses. Indeed, the development of religion and spirituality and the regeneration of the downtrodden Indian masses formed the two chief planks in his programme for the future of India. It is interesting to note that the two greatest Indians of the twentieth century, Arabinda Ghosh and Mahatma Gandhi, took up these two aspects of Swamiji's programme as the chief aims of their activities. Some of the poems of Rabindranath indicate that he was also influenced by Swamiji's ideas of living; and working among men, and serving the God in man. In one of his poems, the great poet denounces the attitude of the Hindus towards the low castes almost in the same vigorous language as Swamiji used, and he actually uses the word manusher narayana, corresponding to daridra narayana of Swamiji. Thus the three greatest Indians of the twentieth century were all inspired by him. And this has been openly admitted by Arabinda and Gandhi.

Swamiji always stressed the fact that the best approach to Hindu mind and one sure to move it was through religion. So he put the organized and devoted service to the masses for their all-round regeneration in intellectual, religious, moral, and material conditions, not as a political programme, but on a religious basis as a means of salvation to every individual in accordance with the neo-Vedanta or practical Vedanta preached by him.

Similarly he put the other important factor of national regeneration—growth of self-confidence and self-reliance and development of physical and moral strength—also on a religious basis.

'First of all, our young men must be strong. Religion will come afterwards. Be strong, my young friends; that is my advice to you. You will be nearer to heaven through football than through the study of the Gita. These are bold words; but I have to say them, for I love you . . . You will understand the Gita better with your biceps, your muscles, a little stronger.'

'What I want is muscles of iron and nerves of steel, inside which dwells a mind of the same material as that of which the thunderbolt is made. Strength, manhood, Kshatra-Virya, Brahma-Teja.'

'Strength, strength is what the Upanishads speak to me from every page. This is the one great thing to remember, it has been the one great lesson I have been taught in my life; strength, it says, strength, O man, be not weak.'

'In spite of the greatness of the Upanishads, in spite of our boasted ancestry of sages, compared to many other races, I must tell you that we are weak, very weak. First of all is our physical weakness. That physical weakness is the cause of at least one-third of our miseries. We are lazy, we cannot work . . . What we want is vigour in the blood, strength in the nerves, iron muscles and nerves of steel, not softening Indians again an namby-pamby ideas.'

He reminded the Indian of the Vedantic doctrine that we are all parts of God and therefore divine, and we must therefore shed all fears. The ignorance of this truth through maya or illusion makes us feel that we are weak and powerless. He cited the story of a lion, brought up from its birth in the company of a flock of sheep, which regarded itself as one of them and behaved as such. One day a lion from the forest fell upon the sheep and saw the baby lion running in fear along with them. The older lion tried in vain to convince the baby that it was a lion and not a sheep, but as soon as they came to the edge of a tank and the baby saw its own image in water, it at once recognized the truth and joined the other. So, said Swamiji, as soon as we realize that we are really the divine children of immortal bliss, we shall be able to cast our fear and gather strength of mind and body. The following passage may be quoted as a specimen.

> Let us proclaim to every soul: 'Arise, awake, and stop not till the goal is reached.' Arise, awake! Awake from this hypnotism of weakness. None is really weak; the soul is infinite, omnipotent, and omniscient. Stand up, assert yourself, proclaim the God within you, do not deny Him! Too much of inactivity, too much of weakness, too much of hypnotism, has been and is upon our race.
>
> O ye modern Hindus, de-hypnotize yourselves. The way to do that is found in your own sacred books. Teach your selves, teach everyone his real nature, call upon the sleeping soul and see how it awakes. Power will come, glory will come, goodness will come, purity will come, and everything that is excellent will come, when this sleeping soul is roused to self-conscious activity.

Swamiji also stressed the fact that this body is merely the garb of the soul which is our real self. The body perishes, but the soul is immortal, nothing can kill it. As a man casts off old tattered garment and puts on a new one, so a man who dies merely changes one body for another, but his soul remains unchanged. There is thus no cause of real fear on earth. It is significant to note how many a revolutionary hero in India fearlessly faced bullet or gallows, not to speak of lesser pain, with these words of Vivekananda on their lips and engraved on their hearts.

Swamiji's Contribution to the Growth of Indian Nationalism

This brings us to the question of Swamiji's contribution to the growth and development of Indian nationalism. In order to understand this we must lay stress upon certain distinctive features in Swamiji's conception of nationalism. First of all is his patriotism or love for India. This is so much evident throughout his writings and speeches that it will suffice to quote only one or two passages.

> India! Wouldst thou attain, by means of thy disgraceful cowardice, that freedom deserved only by the brave and the heroic? Oh India! forget not that the ideal of thy womanhood is Sita, Savitri, Damayanti; forget not that the God thou worshippest is the great Ascetic of ascetics, the all renouncing Shankara, the Lord of Uma; forget not that thy marriage, thy wealth, thy life are not for sense-pleasure, are not for thy individual personal happiness; forget not that thou art born as a sacrifice to the Mother's altar; forget not that thy social order is but the reflex of the Infinite Universal Motherhood, forget not that the lower classes, the ignorant, the poor, the illiterate, the cobbler, the sweeper are thy flesh and blood, thy brothers. Thou brave one, be bold, take courage, be proud that thou art an Indian, and proudly proclaim: 'I am an

Indian, every Indian is my brother.' Say: 'The ignorant Indian, the poor and destitute Indian, the Brahman Indian, the Pariah Indian is my brother.' Thou, too, clad with but a rag round thy loins proudly proclaim at the top of thy voice: 'The Indian is my brother, the Indian is my life, India's gods and goddesses are my God, India's society is the cradle of my infancy, the pleasure-garden of my youth, the sacred heaven, the Varanasi of my old age.' Say brother, 'The soil of India is my highest heaven, the good of India is my good,' and repeat and pray day and night: 'O Thou Lord of Gauri, O Thou Mother of the Universe, vouchsafe manliness unto me! Thou Mother of Strength, take away my weakness, take away my unmanliness, and Make me a Man.'

On the eve of his departure from London, an English friend had asked him, 'Swami, how will you like your motherland after three years' experience in the luxurious and powerful West?' His significant reply was: 'India I loved before I came away. Now the very dust of India has become holy to me, the very air is now holy to me, it is the holy land, the place of pilgrimage.'

Though an ascetic, Vivekananda was a patriot of patriots. The thought of restoring the pristine glory of India by resuscitating among her people the spiritual vitality which was dormant, but not dead, was always the uppermost thought in his mind. His great disciple, Sister Nivedita, who was his constant companion, has remarked: 'Throughout those years, in which I saw him almost daily, the thought of India was to him like the air he breathed.'

Urged by such an intense feeling of patriotism, Swamiji, though he kept himself aloof from politics, held the ideal of political freedom before his countrymen, specially the young men, as their immediate goal. To a group of young men who met him at Dacca during his tour in 1901, and asked for his advice, he said: 'Read Bankim Chandra and emulate his deshabhakti (patriotism) and Sanatana Dharma (principles of the heroic band of Sannyasins as depicted in the *Ananda-Math*). Your duty should be service to motherland. India should be freed politically first.'

Referring to the policy followed by the Indian National Congress, he told them: 'That is not the way to build up Patriotism anywhere. Beggar's bowl has no place in a Banik's (merchant's) world of machine, mammon and merchandise. Everything has got to be controlled and directed by the invocation of human conscience, that is Mahamaya's voice—the latent energy in man . . . First thing first, and body-building and dare-devilry are the primary concerns before the buoyant young Bengal.'

Then Swamiji observed: 'India had a glorious past, India will have a future certainly more majestic. . . . The soul-stirring death-defying Mantram, Abhaya—fearlessness—will shake off age-long vestiges of slave-mentality, superstition and inferiority complex. In order to march boldly in equal pace side by side with other materially advanced nations of the world—ye, young Bengal, emulate the manly ways of Lakshmi Bai, the Rani of Jhansi, whose gallantry the English Commander has recognized. . . . Imitate the virtues of other nations, cultivate their technical skill and qualities of life. . . . And then, with a modern standard of morale and efficiency attained, pay them, the foreign usurpers, in their own coins in your own country to unfasten the alien octopus-hold on the citadel of Oriental Culture. But know it for certain, mere imitation will lead you nowhere.'

In his lecture on the 'Future of India' he said that we lack unity and fellow-feeling which are the secrets of national greatness. He cited the example of Japan and showed how those two factors enabled compact little nations to rule huge unwieldy nations. Then he continued: 'And the bigger the nation, the more unwieldy it is. Born, as it were, a disorganized mob, they cannot combine. All these dissensions must stop . . . If one of our countrymen stands up and tries to become great we all try to hold him down, but if a foreigner comes and tries to kick us, it is all right. We have been used to it, have we not? And slaves must become great Masters! So give up being a slave. For the next fifty years this alone shall be our keynote—this, our great Mother India. Let all other vain gods disappear for the time from our minds. This is the only god that is awake, our own race.'

Swamiji pointed out that disunion and jealousy of each other have been the greatest defects in our national life. Here are his denunciations.

'We cannot combine, we do not love each other; we are intensely selfish, not three of us can come together without hating each other, without being jealous of each other.'

'Why should the Hindu nation with all its wonderful intelligence and other things have gone to pieces? I would answer you, Jealousy. Never were there people more wretchedly jealous of one another, more envious of one another's fame and name than this wretched Hindu race. And if you ever come out in the West, the absence of this is the first feeling which you will see in the Western nations.'

'Why is it, to take a case in point, that forty million of Englishmen rule three hundred million of people here? What is the psychological explanation? These forty million put their wills together and that means infinite power, and you three hundred million have a will each separate from the other. Therefore to make a great future India, the whole secret lies in organization, accumulation of power, co-ordination of wills.'

According to Swamiji, true nationalism in India can only be based on unity of religion. 'The problems in India are more complicated, more momentous, than the problems in any other country. Race, religion, language, government—all these together make a nation. The one common ground that we have is our sacred tradition, our religion. That is the only common ground, and upon that we shall have to build. In Europe, political ideas form the national unity. The unity in religion, therefore, is absolutely necessary as the first condition of the future of India. There must be the recognition of one religion throughout the length and breadth of this land. What do I mean by one religion?

Not in the sense of one religion as held among the Christians, or the Mohammedans, or the Buddhists. We know that our religion has certain common grounds, common to all our sects, however varying their conclusions may be, however different their claims may be. So there are certain common grounds; and within their limitations this religion of ours admits of a marvellous variation, an infinite amount of liberty to think and live our own lives. . . .It is not only true that the ideal of religion is the highest ideal in the case of India, it is the only possible means of work; work in any other line, without first strengthening this, would be disastrous. Therefore, the first plank in the making of a future India, the first step that is to be hewn out of that rock of ages, is the unification of religion. . . . National union in India must be a gathering up of its scattered spiritual forces. A Nation in India must be a union of those whose hearts beat to the same spiritual tune.'

Thus the ideal of nationalism preached by Swamiji was based on the four solid rocks of:

1. The awakening of the masses who form the basis of the nation.
2. Development of physical and moral strength.
3. Unity based on common spiritual ideas.
4. Consciousness of, and pride in, the ancient glory and greatness of India.

These were the four pillars on which, according to Swamiji, Indian nationality must rest, and it can be hardly denied that he was the first who clearly emphasized these ideas and directly contributed, perhaps more than anybody else, to sow the seeds of national development on this line.

10

Revival and Reform: The Eleventh Social Conference—Amraoti, 1897[*]

M.G. Ranade

The Hon'ble Mr. Justice Ranade said:—Mr. President and gentlemen,—This time last year, when we met in the metropolis of India, I ventured to say that the gathering of the Conference was held under the shadow of a great calamity. Few of us then fully realised the accumulation of miseries and sorrows which this unhappy year now about to close had in store for us. The shadows darkened and deepened in their horrors as the year advanced, and it almost seemed as if the seven plagues which afflicted the land of the Pharaohs in old time were let loose upon us, for there is not a single province which had not its ghastly record of death and ruin to mark this period as the most calamitous year of the century within the memory of many generations past. No province has suffered more from these dire visitations than the Presidency of Bombay, and we are still carrying the yoke of this hard discipline of sorrows with a patience, and, I might add, courage, which baffle all description. The fight has been very unequal, and we have been worsted at every point, our activities have been paralysed, and

---

[*] Extracted from *The Miscellaneous Writings of The Late Hon'ble Mr Justice M.G. Ranade*, Sahitya Akademi, Delhi, 1992, pp. 179–97.

our losses great beyond all previous anticipations. Speaking on an occasion like this, I cannot but give expression to the grief which presses heavy on our hearts, as we remember the faces, once so familiar in these Conference gatherings, conspicuous by their absence here to-day—soldiers of God in the great fight with evil, who have been taken away from us in the full bloom of their manhood, and whose places we can never hope adequately to fill up. One such earnest soul, the late Rao Bahadur Chintaman Narayen Bhat, was the life and light of this movement. I had fondly hoped that it would be my privilege to hand over to him the charge of this great service, for which the many great and good qualities of his head and heart fitted him so well. But this was not to be, and we have now to console ourselves with the mournful satisfaction that he died a martyr to his self-imposed labour of love and charity. In another place I have described our sense of the loss suffered by us by the death of another veteran in the fight—the universally lamented Mr. Waman Abaji Modak. Though disabled for a time for active work, his soul was ever alive to the call of duty for which he lived and died. Friends who knew Mr. Gokuldas Leula of Sind have paid a similar tribute of their sorrow to the memory of this sincere worker, who died a victim to the plague, while administering relief to those who suffered from its ravages. A tribute of respect is also due to the memory of Mr. Kasinath Punt Natu of Poona, and Mr. Vaman Daji Oka, well-known in these parts. I might recall to your mind the names of many more whom it has pleased Providence to take away from us, but this is hardly necessary to convince you that the year's casualties in our ranks have been very heavy. When people in their impatience complain that our friends here and elsewhere are only glib talkers, and fail badly when they are called on to act, they seem to forget the most prominent feature of our experience of these great visitations— namely, that in every town and city, where distress in any form prevailed, whether it was due to famine, or plague, or earthquake, or floods, or hurricane, the members of the various

Reform Associations and their sympathisers have always been the first to volunteer their help, and if they have lost heavily, this loss is due to the perseverance with which they maintain the fight. We, who have been spared till now, may pay this tribute of respect to their memories on an occasion like this, when we meet together to reckon our gains and losses for the year.

As might be expected, the reports of this year's work which have been received from nearly sixty Associations, large and small, and which have been summarised up to date, complain that their work for the year has not been as successful as in the previous two years. And yet to those who can read between the lines, there are manifest signs which show that the work has been as earnestly pursued as ever. To instance a few cases:—Under the head of female education, the Bethune College of Calcutta, the Girls' High Schools at Poona and Ahmedabad, the Kanya Maha Vidyalaya at Jullundar, the Singh Sabha's Girls' School at Lahore, the Maharani's Girls' School at Mysore, the Mahakali Pathshala organised by Mataji Tapaswini Bai, a Maratha lady in Calcutta, and the Sylhet and Mymensingh Unions, all show a record of progress each in its own line of development. There is not a single Reform Association of any position in the country which has not lent its best efforts to raise the standard and popularise the system of female education. Many Associations, Sabhas and Samajas maintain independent girls' schools of their own, and others have their home classes more or less actively employed in carrying on the work of the schools to educate the more advanced students. Others again have their lectures for ladies, and Ladies' Associations, such as at Ahmedabad, Bombay, and Madras, started and maintained by the ladies themselves. Though the condition of female education is still very backward, and though the experiments that are now carried on are on different lines, the signs are clearly visible that throughout India, the national awakening to the necessity of developing the moral and intellectual capacities and aptitudes of our sisters has found universal recognition. As regards another sign of this liberal movement which seeks to do equal justice to the rights of the female as of the male sex, it is satisfactory to note that though the number of widow marriages this year has been smaller than that of the previous years, still all the provinces have taken part in the movement. The reports show that in all 25 widow marriages were celebrated throughout India during the past year:—Punjab 10, Bombay 6, Central Provinces 4, Madras 3, North-West Provinces and Bengal 1 each. The widow marriages in the Central Provinces have been all brought about directly or indirectly by the persistent efforts of Rao Bahadur Kolhatkar, the President of this gathering. For the re-marriages in Punjab the credit is due to Dewan Santaram and his friends of the Widow Marriage Association there, and in regard to Bombay the same honour is due to Mr. Bhagawandas, the son of the late Madhavdas Raghunathdas in whose house two re-marriages were celebrated. The credit of the widow-marriages celebrated in Madras is due to Rao Bahadur Viresalingam Pantulu. There was thus not a single province in which friends of the cause did not manifest their active interest in it, which remark does not equally hold good for the previous years. The paucity in the total number was partly due to the calamities of the year, and partly to the prohibition of all marriages due to the year being a Sinhast year.

Another good sign of the times which may be noted is the fact that some of the castes, in which no re-marriages had been celebrated before, joined in the movement for the first time this year. It was also reported in the papers that the Maharajah of Nabha, in the Punjab, had exercised his influence in favour of bettering the condition of Hindu widows, and inducing influential Hindu gentlemen to support the widow-marriage movement. In the Chandraseniya Kayasth Prabhu caste of Bombay, a similar pronouncement was made by the leaders of the community in favour of re-marriage, and it was resolved to bring up the subject before the next Kayasth Prabhu Conference to be held at Baroda. Another satisfactory indication of the times is furnished by the fact reported from Guzerat, that the Audich Brahmin community at Damun made a similar pronouncement in favour of widow marriage in their caste. The Widows' Homes at Baranagar and Poona have also been successfully maintained notwithstanding pecuniary difficulties, and the number of widows attending the homes has slightly increased, thanks to the efforts of Mr. Sasipada Banerjee of Baranagar and Professor Karve of Poona.

As regards foreign travel, the year has had a good record to show. Several Saraswata gentlemen have returned from England, and though the *Guru* of the caste has refused admission to them, the reform party at Mangalore and in North Canara have succeeded in openly showing their sympathy with these men. Raja Nowlojee Rao Gujar, a scion of the princely house of Nagpur, returned from England, and was well received, and Messrs. Booti and Alonikar of Nagpur, Mr. Krishna Rao Bholanath of Ahmedabad, Professor Gokhale of Poona, and Mr. Ketkar of Gwalior, have similarly, though not formally, been admitted by some of their caste people, and the opposition has not ventured to place any difficulties in their way. Two Bhatia gentlemen, for the first time in that community, left for England with the full support of their caste. In the Punjab, several young men in the Biradari castes, who had been to England, were admitted back without any opposition. Two young men from the Aurorbans caste went to England last year. The liberal section of the Cashmere Pundits' Sabha is strongly in favour of foreign travel. These instances show that slowly but surely in all parts of the country, the prejudice against foreign travel is on the wane, and that before long the orthodox community or the communities will learn to tolerate these departures from custom as an inevitable change.

In regard to the question of inter-marriage, the Bengal papers announced an inter-marriage in high life between two sub-divisions of the Kayastha community which hitherto kept aloof. In the Punjab, there was a betrothal between two sub-castes of the Serin community. This was the first instance of an inter-marriage between these two sub-divisions. Many of the widow-marriages have also been instances of inter-marriages, and for the first time last year two instances of inter-marriage between Madrasee and Bengalee gentlemen and ladies occurred. The North-West Provinces reports show instances of similar fusion between sub-divisions of the Kayastha caste there, and in Guzerat there is a similar tendency manifest in some of the castes to amalgamate together.

As regards the postponement of infant marriages, the reports from all provinces show a decided tendency to increase the limits of marriageable ages of girls and boys. In the Punjab, the Aurorbans Sabha has passed a resolution that no girl belonging to the caste should be given in marriage unless she has completed her twelfth year. In the Madras Presidency, the opinion is gaining ground that the time has now come for applying to Government for legislation on the subject to fix at least the marriageable age for boys, if not for girls and to lay down a maximum limit of age for old persons who marry young girls, on the plan adopted by the Mysore Government. The Madras Provincial Social Conference and the Godavari District Conference expressly passed resolutions on this subject. The Hindu Social Reform Association at Madras has also appointed a committee to draw up a memorial with the same object. The Hon'ble Mr. Jambulingam Mudaliar is reported to be contemplating the introduction of a Bill into the local Council there on this subject. There have also been individual instances in some parts of the country where grown-up girls have been married without experiencing any very bitter opposition from the caste.

Nearly all the Associations have been pledged to support the Purity movement, including the anti-*nautch* and temperance agitation and the work done during the year shows considerable progress under both these heads.

To turn next to another question in which the Conference has been interesting itself for the past few years,—the admission of converts from other faiths—some progress has been made during the year. The Shuddhi Sabha admitted nearly 200 Mahomedan converts this year. Hitherto the movement for the re-admission of converts to other faiths back into the Hindu society was chiefly confined to the Punjab. This year, however, there have been also instances of such conversions in Bengal, the North-West Provinces, and far away in Burmah, one of them being a convert Christian and the others Mahomedans. The Shuddhi Sabha of Lahore and the Arya Samaj there have deservedly taken the lead in this movement, and it will be a source of great strength to them that the movement has been taken up in the other Provinces also. The Central Provinces Reports for the year show that Mr. Shanker Shastri of Jubbulpore has published a pamphlet on the subject, and it is a strange coincidence that Professor Rajaram Shastri Bhagwat of Bombay read this year a paper before the branch of the Asiatic Society there, showing how in old times the non-Aryan races were brought within the fold of the Aryan system.

As regards the reduction of extravagant expenses in marriage, a very important movement was started in Calcutta under the auspices of leading Kayastha gentlemen, including such men as Sir Romesh Chandra Mittra and the Hon'ble Mr. Chunder Madhub Ghose, who met at Babu Ramanath Ghose's house, and passed several resolutions which are likely to be attended with good results. Nearly every one of the reports of the North-West Provinces contain details of the manner in which the Kayasthas, the Bhargavas, the Chaturvedis, the Vaishyas, the Jains and other castes have tried to lay down sliding scales of marriage expenditure, curtailing extravagance under many heads, abolishing *nautch* parties, fireworks, and other useless items. In the Punjab, the Aurorbans have very considerably reduced the extravagance in marriage expenses. On the Bombay side, the Bhatia *mandal* and the Dasa Oswal Jains have successfully worked in the same direction. Even in far off Baroda, the Dasa Porwad Bania caste people have been moving in the matter. Following the example of the Rajputra Hitkarni Sabha, many non-Rajpoot castes in Rajputana and Malwa have laid down rules which are enforced by the same sanctions as those of the principal Sabha.

As regards Conference work generally, it may be noted that caste Conferences are the order of the day in all parts of India. I have, on previous occasions, mentioned the gatherings annually held this week in several large towns in the North-Western Provinces of the Kayastha and the Vaishya community. This year was distinguished by the holding of the first Provincial Social Conference in Madras, in which Presidency also we have had two district Conferences, one on the East Coast in the Godavari District, and the other on the West Coast at Mangalore. New associations are being formed under very favourable auspices in many parts of the country, notably in the Bombay and Madras Districts, to support the work of the Conference, and to give effect to its resolutions.

Encouraged by the success which has attended the efforts of the Mysore Government, and the Malabar Marriage Law passed in the Madras Council, two Bills of great social importance have been introduced, one in the Imperial Council, to bring under better control religious charities and endowments, and another has been introduced in the Madras Council to remove all doubts in and codify the law in regard to what constitutes self-acquired property under the Hindoo joint family system. Both these Bills have suggested subjects for discussion at the ensuing Conference this year, and it is not therefore necessary for me to enlarge upon their importance.

There is a third measure before the Viceroy's Council which though it relates to a particular section of the Mahomedan community, has a wider bearing which interests us all. The Memon section of this community in Bombay were originally Hindoo converts, and though they embraced Mahomedanism, they retained their old Hindoo customs in regard to inheritance and succession, and these customs were recognised by our Law Courts. A majority of that community, however, now desire that in place of the Hindoo customs, the Mahomedan Law should govern their succession to the property of deceased persons. The Government of India accordingly intend to pass a sort of a permissive measure, by which a member of this community may retain or abandon the old rules by a formal declaration of his choice, which choice, once made, will be final. The subject bristles with difficulties, but the permissive legislation, if it proves a success in actual operation, will furnish a precedent which may prove of considerable help to those who wish to have more liberal laws of inheritance and succession without change of religion.

Such, gentlemen, is the brief record of the principal social events of the year. Many ardent spirits amongst us will no doubt be very much dissatisfied with the poverty of this record. At the same time, we must bear in mind that hundreds and thousands—nay millions of our countrymen will regard this poor record as very revolutionary, and condemn this as one of the unseen causes which has brought about physical and moral catastrophie upon the land by way of punishment for the sins of the reformers. These are two extreme sides of the question, and it is not for me to say to an audience like this on which side the balance of truth may be found. The *Arya Patrika* of the Punjab, which is a recognised organ of the Arya Samaj there, has in its words of advice to the Conference expressed its view that we are radically in the wrong in seeking to reform the usages of our society without a change of religion, and it seriously suggests that we should, in the first instance, become members of their Samaj and this conversion will bring with it all desired reforms. Many enthusiastic friends of the Brahmo Samaj entertain similar views and give us similar advice. All I can say to these welcome advisers is that they do not fully realise the situation and its difficulties. People have changed their religion, and yet retain their social usages unchanged. The Native Christians for instance, especially the Roman Catholic section among them, and many sections of Mahomedans are instances in point. Besides, it has been well observed that even for a change of religion, it is too often necessary that the social surroundings must be liberalised in a way to help people to realise their own responsibilities and to strengthen them in their efforts. Lastly, these well-meaning advisers seem to forget that the work of reform cannot be put off indefinitely till the far more arduous and difficult work of religious conversion is accomplished. It may take centuries before the Arya or Brahmo Samaj establish their claims for general recognition. In the meanwhile what is to become of the social organisation? Slowly but surely, the progress of liberal ideas must be allowed to work its way in reforming our social customs, and the process cannot be stopped even though we may wish it. In the case of our society especially, the usages which at present prevail amongst us are admittedly not those which obtained in the most glorious periods of our history. On most of the points which are included in our programme, our own record of the past shows that there has been a decided change for the worse, and it is surely within the range of practical possibilities for us to hope that we may work up our way back to a better state of things without stirring up the rancorous hostilities which religious differences have a tendency to create and foster. There is no earthly reason whatsoever why we should not co-operate with these religious organisations, or why they should not rather co-operate with us in this work in which our interests are common, because the majority of our countrymen hold different views about religion from those which commend themselves to these Samajas. I am speaking these words with a full sense of my responsibility, for I am in my humble way a member of one, if not of both the Samajas, and I am a sincere searcher after religious truth in full sympathy with the Arya and Brahmo Samaj movements, and I hope therefore that these advisers of ours will take my reply in the same spirit, and will not misunderstand me. Schismatic methods of propagation cannot be applied with effect to vast communities which are not within their narrow pale.

On the other side, some of our orthodox friends find fault with us, not because of the particular reforms we have in view, but on account of the methods we follow. While the new religious sects condemn us for being too orthodox, the extreme orthodox section denounce us for being too revolutionary in our methods. According to these last, our efforts should be directed to revive, and not to reform. I have many friends in this camp of extreme orthodoxy, and their watch-word is that revival, and not reform, should be our motto. They advocate a return to the old ways, and appeal to the old authorities and the old sanction. Here also, as in the instance quoted above, people speak without realising the full significance of their own words. When we are asked to revive our institutions and customs, people seem to be very much at sea as to what it is they seem to revive. What particular period of our history is to be taken as the old? Whether the period of the Vedas, of the Smritis, of the Puranas or of the Mahomedan or modern Hindu times? Our usages have been changed from time to time by a slow process of growth, and in some cases of decay and corruption, and we cannot stop at a particular period without breaking the continuity of the whole. When my revivalist friend presses his argument upon me, he has to seek recourse in some subterfuge which really furnishes no reply to the question—what shall we revive? Shall we revive the old habits of our people when the most sacred of our caste indulged in all the abominations as we now understand them of animal food and drink which exhausted every section of our country's Zoology and Botany? The men and the Gods of those old days ate and drank forbidden things to excess in a way no revivalist will now venture to recommend. Shall we revive the twelve forms of sons, or eight forms of marriage, which included capture, and recognised mixed and illegitimate intercourse? Shall we revive the Niyoga system of procreating sons on our brother's wives when widowed? Shall we revive the old liberties taken by the Rishis and by the wives of the Rishis with the marital tie? Shall we revive the hecatombs of animals sacrificed from year's end to year's end, and in which human beings were not spared as propitiatory offerings? Shall we revive the Shakti worship of the left hand with its indecencies and practical debaucheries? Shall we revive the *Sati* and infanticide customs, or the flinging of living men into the rivers, or over rocks, or hook swinging, or the crushing beneath Jagannath car? Shall we revive the internecine wars of the Brahmins and Kshatriyas, or the cruel persecution and degradation of the aboriginal population? Shall we revive the custom of many husbands to one wife or of many wives to one husband? Shall we require our Brahmins to cease to be landlords and gentlemen, and turn into beggars and dependents upon the king as in olden times ? These instances will suffice to show that the plan of reviving the ancient usages and customs will not work out salvation, and is not practicable. If these usages were good and beneficial, why were they altered by our wise ancestors? If they were bad and injurious, how can any claim be put forward for their restoration after so many ages? Besides, it seems to be forgotten that in a living organism as society is, no revival is possible. The dead and the buried or burnt are dead, buried, and burnt once for all, and the dead past cannot therefore be revived except by a reformation of the old materials into new organised beings. If revival is impossible, reformation is the only alternative open to sensible people, and now it may be asked what is the principle on which this reformation must be based? People have very hazy ideas on this subject. It seems to many that it is the outward form which has to be changed, and if this change can be made, they think that all the difficulties in our way will vanish. If we change our outward manners and customs, sit in a particular way or walk in a particular fashion, our work according to them is accomplished. I cannot but think that much of the prejudice against the reformers is due to this misunderstanding. It is not the outward form, but the inward form, the thought and the idea which determines the outward form, that has to be changed if real reformation is desired.

Now what have been the inward forms or ideas which have been hastening our decline during the past three thousand years? These ideas may be briefly set forth as isolation, submission to outward force or power more than to the voice of the inward conscience, perception of fictitious differences between men and men due to heredity and birth, passive acquiescence in evil or wrong doing, and a general indifference to secular well-being, almost bordering upon fatalism. These have been the root ideas of our ancient social system. They have as their natural result led to the existing family arrangements where the woman is entirely subordinated to the man and the lower castes to the higher castes, to the length of depriving men of their natural respect for humanity. All the evils we seek to combat result from the prevalence of these ideas. They are mere corollaries to these axiomatic assumptions. They prevent some of our people from realising what they really are in all conscience, neither better nor worse than their fellows, and that whatever garb men may put on, they are the worse for assuming dignities and powers which do not in fact belong to them. As long as these ideas remain operative on our minds, we may change our outward forms and institutions, and be none the better for the change. These ideas have produced in the long course of ages their results on our character, and we must judge their good or bad quality, as St. Paul says, by the fruits they have borne. Now that these results have been disastrous, nobody disputes or doubts, and the lesson to be drawn for our guidance in the future from this fact is that the current of these ideas must be changed, and in the place of the old worship we paid to them, we must accustom ourselves and others to worship and revere new ideals. In place of isolation, we must cultivate the spirit of fraternity or elastic expansiveness. At present it is everybody's ambition to pride himself upon being a member of the smallest community that can be conceived, and the smaller the number of those with whom you can dine or marry, or associate, the higher is your perfection and purity, the purest person is he who cooks his own food, and does not allow the shadow of even his nearest friend to fall upon his cooked food. Every caste and every sect has thus a tendency to split itself into smaller castes and smaller sects in practical life. Even in philosophy and religion, it is a received maxim that knowledge is for the few, and that salvation is only possible for the esoteric elect with whom only are the virtues of sanctity and wisdom, and that for the rest of mankind, they must be left to wander in the wilderness, and grovel in superstition, and even vice, with only a colouring of so-called religion to make them respectable. Now all this must be changed. The new mould of thought on this head must be, as stated above, cast on the lines of fraternity, a capacity to expand outwards, and to make more cohesive inwards the bonds of fellowship. Increase the circle of your friends and associates, slowly and cautiously if you will, but the tendency must be towards a general recognition of the essential equality between man and man. It will beget sympathy and power. It will strengthen your own hands, by the sense that you have numbers with you, and not against you, or as you foolishly imagine, below you.

The next idea which lies at the root of our helplessness is the sense that we are always intended to remain children, to be subject to outside control, and never to rise to the dignity of self-control by making our conscience and our reason the supreme, if not the sole, guide to our conduct. All past history has been a terrible witness to the havoc committed by this misconception. We are children, no doubt, but the children of God, and not of man, and the voice of God is the only voice which we are bound to listen. Of course, all of us cannot listen to this voice when we desire it, because from long neglect and dependence upon outside help, we have benumbed this faculty of conscience in us. With too many of us, a thing is true or false, righteous or sinful, simply because somebody in the past has said that it is so. Duties and obligations are duties and obligations, not because we feel them to be so, but because somebody reputed to be wise has laid it down that they are so. In small matters of manners and courtesies, this outside dictation is not without its use. But when we abandon ourselves entirely to this helpless dependence on other wills, it is no wonder that we become helpless as children in all departments of life. Now the new idea which should take up the place of this helplessness and dependence is not the idea of a rebellious overthrow of all authority, but that of freedom responsible to the voice of God in us. Great and wise men in the past, as in the present, have a claim upon our regards, but they must not come between us and our God—the Divine principle enthroned in the heart of every one of us high or low. It is this sense of self-respect, or rather respect for the God in us, which has to be cultivated. It is a very tender plant which takes years and years to make it grow. But there is the capacity and the power, and we owe it as a duty to ourselves to undertake the task. Revere all human authority, pay your respects to all prophets and all revelations, but never let this reverence and respect come in the way of the dictates of conscience, the Divine command in us.

Similarly there is no doubt that men differ from men in natural capacities, and aptitudes, and that heredity and birth are factors of considerable importance in our development. But it is at the same time true that they are not the only factors that determine the whole course of our life for good or for evil, under a law of necessity. Heredity and birth explain many things, but this law of *Karma* does not explain all things. What is worse, it does not explain the mystery that makes man and woman what they really are, the reflection and the image of God. Our passions and our feelings, our pride and our ambition, lend strength to these agencies, and with their help the Law of Karma completes our conquest, and in too many cases enforces our surrender. The new idea that should come in here is that this Law of Karma can be controlled and set back by a properly trained will, when it is made subservient to a higher will than ours. This we see in our everyday life, and Necessity, or the Fates are, as our own texts tell us, faint obstacles in the way of our advancement if we devote ourselves to the law of Duty. I admit that this misconception is very hard to remove, perhaps the hardest of the old ideas. But removed it must be, if not in this life or generation, in many lives and generations, if we are ever to rise to our full stature.

The fourth old form or idea to which I will allude here is our acquiescence in wrong or evil doing as an inevitable condition of human life, about which we need not be very particular. All human life is a vanity and a dream, and we are not much concerned with it. This view of life is in fact atheism in its worst form. No man or woman really ceases to be animal who does not perceive or realise that wrong or evil doing, impurity and vice, crime and misery, and sin of all kinds, is really our animal existence prolonged. It is the beast in us which blinds us to impurity and vice, and makes them even attractive. There must be nautches in our temples, say our priests, because even the Gods cannot do without these impure fairies. This is only a typical instance of our acquiescence in impurity. There must be drunkenness in the world, there must be poverty and wretchedness and tyranny, there must be fraud and force, there must be thieves and the law to punish them. No doubt these are facts, and there is no use denying their existence, but in the name of all that is sacred and true, do not acquiesce in them, do not hug these evils to your bosom, and cherish them. Their contact is poisonous, not the less deadly because it does not kill, but it corrupts men. A healthy sense of the true dignity of our nature, and of man's high destiny, is the best corrective and antidote to this poison.

I think I have said more than enough to suggest to your reflecting minds what it is that we have to reform. All admit that we have been deformed. We have lost our stature, we are bent in a hundred places, our eyes lust after forbidden things, our ears desire to hear scandals about our neighbours, our tongues lust to taste forbidden fruit, our hands itch for another man's property, our bowels are deranged with indigestible food. We cannot walk on our feet, but require stilts or crutches. This is our present social polity, and now we want this deformity to be removed; and the only way to remove it is to place ourselves under the discipline of better ideas and forms such as those I have briefly touched above. Now this is the work of the Reformer. Reforms in the matter of infant marriage and enforced widowhood, in the matter of temperance and purity, inter-marriage between castes, the elevation of the low castes, and the re-admission of converts, and the regulation of our endowments and charities, are reforms only so far and no further, as they check the influence of the old ideas, and promote the growth of the new tendencies. The Reformer has to infuse in himself the light and warmth of nature, and he can only do it by purifying and improving himself and his surroundings. He must have his family, village, tribe, and nation recast in other and new moulds, and that is the reason why Social Reform becomes our obligatory duty, and not a mere pastime which might be given up at pleasure. Revival is, as I have said, impossible; as impossible as mass-conversion into other faiths. But even if it were possible, its only use to us would be if the reforms elevated us and our surroundings, if they made us stronger, braver, truer men with all our faculties of endurance and work developed, with all our sympathies fully awakened and refined, and if with our heads and hearts acting in union with a purified and holy will, they made us feel the dignity of our being and the high destiny of our existence, taught us to love all, work with all, and feel for all. This is the Reformer's true work, and this in my opinion is the reason why the Conference meets from year to year, and sounds the harmonies in every ear which can listen to them with advantage.

11

Presidential Address at the Ninth Indian Social Conference Held in 1895[*]

R.G. Bhandarkar

Ladies and Gentlemen—I must in accordance with the usual practice begin by thanking you for having elected me your Chairman. On the present occasion, however, this is not a mere matter of routine and formality. Certain circumstances have this year very widely evoked enthusiasm for the cause of Social Reform, and have led to a sort of constitution being given to this conference similar to that which the Political Congress possesses. I have before me to-day a large number of my countrymen, who, I believe, are sincere advocates of social reform, as calculated to improve the fortunes of our country, and to place her in a condition to enable her to maintain her position in the keen competition and rivalry that is now going on between the different countries and races of the world. To be the Chairman

---

[*] Extracted from *Collected Works of Sir R.G. Bhandarkar*, Volume II, edited by Narayan Bapuji Utgikar, Bhandarkar Oriental Research Institute, Poona, 1928, pp. 487–526.

of a body of such true lovers of their country is an honour that cannot but be highly appreciated. . . .

And first, a good many of the proposals have reference to the condition of the female portion of our society. Gentlemen, one half of the intellectual, moral and spiritual resources of our country is being wasted. If our women were educated as they ought to be, they would be a powerful instrument for advancing the general condition of our country. They will bring up every new generation in a manner to perform its duty, efficiently, and will shed the influence of the benign virtues peculiar to them on men and, so to say, humanise them. All the means of educating women, therefore, that have been indicated in the propositions, you will, I feel sure, approve of. You will see that the opening of High Schools is one of them. That necessarily implies that the study of English language and literature is considered to be beneficial for our women. Though there has been some difference of opinion as regards this point, still I believe the necessity of such education has been recognized by the majority. But I think it still remains an open question whether our ideal for the education of women ought to be the same as that for the education of men, whether after they finish their High School education, they ought to be made to go through the whole University Course up to the M.A. Degree. . . .

The misery of our widows has been the subject of frequent remarks; I will therefore not detain you long by a full exposition of it. I will only make a general observation that that society which allows men to marry any number of times even up to the age of sixty, while it strongly forbids even girls of seven or eight to have another husband after one is dead, which gives liberty to a man of 50 or 60 to marry a girl of eleven or twelve, which has no word of condemnation for the man who marries another wife within fifteen days after the death of the first, is a society which sets very little value upon the life of a female human being, and places women on the same level with cattle and is thus in an unsound condition, disqualifying it for a successful competition with societies with a more healthy constitution.

Oftentimes the marriage of a girl under certain circumstances proves her death warrant. This matter has within the last few years forced itself powerfully upon my observation. A young man of thirty or thirty-five loses his first wife; straightway he proceeds to marry another, who is a girl of ten or twelve. That girl dies by the time she reaches the age of twenty; another takes her place; immediately after, she too dies similarly; then comes a third who meets with the same fate; and a fourth is married by the persevering man and is eventually left a widow before she is out of her teens. A great many such cases have occurred within the last few years and amongst our educated men. The medical men, whom I have consulted, say that the results are due to the marriages being ill-assorted, i.e., to the great inequality between the age of the girl and of the strong and vigorous man. I do not know how else to characterize these cases except as cases of human sacrifice. Surely, if the men who have married girls successively in this manner are educated men, their refined sentiments and feelings ought to make them spare poor innocent girls and marry grown up women, widows, if unmarried ones are not to be had. Gentlemen, this case of ill-assorted marriages deserves greater condemnation at our hands than the other, which is the only one that seems to be contemplated in one of the resolutions to be brought forward and in which an old man of even fifty or sixty marries a girl of ten or twelve.

I will next call your attention to those points in the resolutions which concern the institution of castes. And first of all, allow me to observe that a very great revolution has been effected in this matter by the mere fact that we are governed by a people, amongst whom the sense of equal justice for all classes of people, has received a high development. A Sudra at the present day is not more heavily punished than a Brahmana for the same crimes. Manu, Yajnavalka and others have been set aside in this respect, and the privileges which in the eye of the criminal law, men of the highest caste enjoyed, have been taken away from them. I remember about 45 years ago when a Brahman was hanged for committing a murder at Ratnagiri, it created a stir among the people, since such a punishment for a Brahman was opposed to all past traditions of the country. But of course the change did not provoke active hostility and has been acquiesced in on all sides. Similarly a Sudra's tongue is not now cut off for repeating the letters of the Vedas. On the contrary if a teacher in a Government school refuses to teach the sacred Mantras to a Sudra, he is apt to be dismissed from service. In our schools and colleges we have to teach Sanskrit literature including the Vedas to all castes and classes. But it is very much to be regretted that the treasures of knowledge which has thus been thrown open to all, is not availed of by the lower castes to the extent to which they should. This is to be accounted for in a great measure by the fact of the old traditional feeling not having gone out—education is not what the Sudras think of first, nor are endeavours made by others to induce him to educate himself and smoothen his path, to a University Degree. Similarly the railways have been effecting a silent revolution. A holy Brahman does not scruple to sit in a third class carriage by the side of a Mahar, whose very shadow is an abomination on ordinary occasions.

The Mahars and Mangs on this side of the country and the Pariahs on the other, who form the lowest classes, have been entirely neglected. They are the outcasts of Hindu Society, and have been from the remotest times in a very degraded condition. The reference made to this fact by a Mahar Haridasa in his prefatory remarks, while performing a Kirtana at my house a few years ago, was very touching. He said, 'The Vedas and Sastras have cast us aside, but the Santas or saints of the middle ages have had compassion on us.' And be it said to the credit of the Santas of Maharashtra headed by the Brahman Ekanatha, and to the Santas of other provinces, that they had compassion for the outcasts of Hindu Society, and admitted their claims to religious instruction and a better treatment. If then in those olden days, these pious men, with their hearts elevated by faith and devotion, admitted the lowest Sudra to religious communion and instruction, shall we, upon whom a greater variety of influences have been operating, refuse to exert ourselves for bringing enlightenment in the dense darkness in which his mind is shrouded? And I believe from the opportunities I have had of observation, that the despised Mahar possesses a good deal of natural intelligence and is capable of being highly educated. So that to continue to keep him in ignorance, is to deprive the country of an appreciable amount of intellectual resources.

And generally allow me to observe that the rigid system of castes, which prevails among us, will ever act as a heavy drag on our race towards a brighter future. To tie men down to certain occupations, even when they have no aptitude for them, renders those men less useful to the country. When all men belonging to a certain caste must follow a certain occupation only, the field is overstocked and poverty is the result. You can get a Brahman school master for five or six rupees a month, but a good carpenter or stone-mason cannot be had unless you pay from twenty to twenty-five rupees per mensem. And unless perfect freedom is allowed to men in this respect, and each allowed to make the best possible use of his own powers, the country cannot economically advance. Special privileges enjoyed by certain castes must keep the members of others in a disadvantageous position in the rivalry and competition of life. In order that a nation as a whole must put forth all its power, it is necessary that there should be no special privileges and special restrictions.

Again the principle of caste has throughout our history operated in such a way that each caste has now come to form a separate community with distinct usages, even as to the kind of food that is eaten and the manner in which it is cooked. And there is no social inter-communication between them of a nature to bind them together into one whole. Hence, instead of there being a feeling of sympathy between different castes, there is often a feeling of antipathy. As long as this state of things lasts, I shall feel greatly obliged to anyone who will explain to me how it is possible to form a united Hindu nation. If therefore we feel at all concerned as regards the future of our country in the great struggle that is going on in the world, something must be immediately done to induce a feeling of unity among these distinct communities, and to convert active antipathy into active sympathy.

And I will here make bold to assert that the chronic poverty of the agricultural classes and the depredation of the proverbial Savakar or money-lender constitute a great social evil. The Government has been endeavouring to do a good deal by means of mere special legislation; but that does not seem to have remedied the evil, and the money-lender continues to charge interest from 18 to 25 per cent on loans raised on the security of lands, and two or four pice per rupee per month, i.e., 37½ or 75 per cent on smaller sums lent for shorter periods; and there are also enhancements of interest when the money is not paid at the stipulated time. In this manner, the poor peasant is everywhere a prey to the rapacity of the money-lender and is never allowed to raise his head. This is a political as well as a social question. The Government has been on several occasions urged to establish Agricultural Banks, but it has not yet seen the wisdom of doing so, and we too, whose countrymen the agriculturists are, have not shown particular solicitude to remedy the evil by establishing banks of our own. I do not think any special banking institution with elaborate machinery, such as has been recently proposed, is wanted. An ordinary bank with agencies at the District towns, and sub-agencies for circles with a radius of about 10 miles, will, I think, fully answer the purpose. Money should be lent on the security of land at an interest from 9 to 12 per cent, payable about the same time as the land revenue. Sympathetic, though firm, treatment should be accorded to the peasants, and the agents employed should not be unscrupulous men exacting perquisites for themselves. But I will not trespass on the province of the man of business, and whatever be the scheme that may be considered suitable and whatever its details, this I feel certain about—that shrewd men ought not to be allowed to prey upon the ignorance and entire helplessness of the agricultural classes, and perpetuate their wretched condition.

Then there are other points in the resolutions, the aim of which is to remove positive obstacles of our healthy development. The early marriage of boys and girls is of this nature, since its effect is to undermine the strength of both, and bring forth a progeny of weak children. The growth of the parents themselves, intellectual as well as physical, is stunted; and in the course of evolution our race must become incapable of that energy and stillness of application, which are so necessary, under the conditions brought into existence by the rivalry and competition of races. The prohibition of travel in foreign countries I would put under the same head, since the game acts as an obstacle to the free expansion of our energies and capacities.

These are the principal points aimed at by the Social Reformer. You will see that what is necessary in order that these reforms may come into practice, is that there should spring up in our hearts a sense of justice, a keen sympathy for the sufferings of others, and a love for one's own country and race, and an anxiety for their future well-being. If the feelings have been awakened in us with any degree of intensity, they cannot fail to realise themselves in some sort of action, and I believe that the contrary holds true that when no action follows, the feelings are either not awakened at all, or if really awakened, are very weak. It is this fact and also the general conservatism of our nature as well as the fear of excommunication, that hold us back, and we devise a number of excuses for our inaction.

Sometimes we are disposed to leave the whole matter to the action of time, thinking that all that we desire will come into practice just as the rigidity of caste rules is being gradually lessened by railway travelling and such other circumstances. But time is not a force—it is simply a conception of the mind to connect events together—and cannot work any changes. If therefore any changes have come on in the course of time, they must be brought about by the force in the human heart that leads to action. As a matter of fact, such changes are often very extensive and important. For instance, the practice of early marriage of girls, and of female infanticide and Kulinism have come into existence in comparatively recent times. But if you examine their origin, you will find that the first owes its introduction probably to the circumstance that when the girls grew up, they went wrong in some cases. In order to prevent such a result, they were tied down to a husband before they were of an age to go wrong. To avoid sin was of course a laudable object, but the desire was not under the guidance of reason. Consequently the many evil effects of early marriages were overlooked, and the attainment of that one object was exclusively attended to. If, however, the desire to prevent the evil had been under the guidance of reason, other modes would have been devised for avoiding it than the one actually chosen.

Similarly the practice of female infanticide and of Kulinism must in the beginning have arisen from family pride. One's daughter should not be married into a family possessing no importance or distinction. To marry her into a high family requires a heavy expenditure of money, which the father cannot afford, and in the case of Kulinism, such a family is not available. Hence rather than suffer the disgrace of allying himself with a low family, he allowed his daughter to be destroyed, and in the other case to be married to one who had innumerable wives already. Here again you will see that the motive of action was not under the guidance of the higher feelings of love and tenderness for a human being, and especially for one's own child.

Thus then what time brings about is very often not under the guidance of reason or the higher feelings of our nature, and consequently, very often, degradation is the result and not elevation. It will, therefore, not do to leave reform to time or the slow or unconscious operation of causes. It must be effected from a conscious intention, and the motive force should be, as above remarked, a sense of justice, a keen sympathy and an anxiety for the future of one's own country. Unable to appreciate the

feelings of the true reformer, we often accuse him of being hasty
in desiring to do everything at once, we sometimes say that if he
had adopted a particular way, the reform he desires would have
long come into practice. Comments such as these I always suspect,
especially when they come from a man who has done little or
nothing practical. I am, however, not an advocate of headlong
action. The motive forces of reform should be powerful in our
hearts, but they must be tempered in a manner not to lead us to
cut ourselves from a vital connection with the past. We should
not adopt the procedure of the French Revolution, but imitate
the mode of action of the English people, whose pupils we are.
They have realised as great changes as the French Revolution
sought to effect, but in a manner which connects them with the
past history of the country. It will not be impossible to devise
such a mode of action. One who has returned from foreign
travels should live like an ordinary Hindu. A remarried widow
should conduct herself just like an ordinary Hindu lady. And
even as regards caste, we should behave towards each other
in ordinary matters as if no such distinction existed between
us; while as to eating together and inter-marriage, they must
come in by and by, especially when the sharp distinctions as to
usages and customs between the several castes are obliterated
by a closer intercommunication than that which exists at the
present day.

But the great danger of delayed reform is that in a short
time the feeling which dictated it becomes cool, and the necessity
for it is entirely forgotten. To prevent this result it is essential
that the motive springs of reform should always be kept alive
in our hearts. We should make an earnest effort never to lose
sight of the goal we have to reach. But the modest proposal that
will be laid before you as regards these two matters, viz., inter-
communication as regards eating, and marriage-alliance between
members of the sub-divisions of the same castes, involves no
violent change whatever; consequently, there is, I believe, no
excuse for delaying its realization.

Generally it may be observed that what we have to avoid is the formation of a separate caste cut off from all social intercourse with any of the existing Hindu caste, that is to say, we should avoid such complete isolation, as for instance, conversion to Christianity leads to. And most of the reforms we advocate involve no break of continuity. Some of them will be welcomed by the orthodox people themselves, and as regards a great many others, what we propose is merely to go back to the more healthy condition in which our society once existed. In ancient times girls were married after they had attained maturity, now they must be married before; widow marriage was in practice, now it has entirely gone out, women were often highly educated and taught even music and dancing, now they are condemned to ignorance and denied any accomplishments. The castes were only four in number, now they are innumerable. Inter-dining among those castes was not prohibited, now the numberless castes that prevail cannot have inter-communication of that nature. Consistently with the maintenance of continuity in this manner, there ought to be, I think, as much action as possible. A strong public opinion must be created among the whole body of educated natives condemning any departure from the programme of reform, while no mercy should be shown to one who does what even the orthodox disapprove, and at sixty, marries a girl of ten or twelve, or another wife immediately after the death of the first. The exhibition of any caste partiality must also be severely condemned, as no religious rules require it. Unless we act in this manner, all our advocacy of reform will sink into the merest sentimentality more demoralising in its effects than sturdy orthodoxy.

But even sentimental advocacy is an homage done to a right cause, and consequently is better than stolid indifference or active hostility. This, however, is unfortunately the mental attitude of a great many educated natives in all parts of the country. In Bengal, as was pointed out by our friend the Honourable Mr. Justice Ranade the other day, social reform is now confined to

Brahmos. The great body of educated Bengalees, who are not Brahmos, are indifferent or hostile. The late Ishvara Chandra Vidyasagara, who inaugurated the reform about widow-marriage, and first ransacked our Smriti literature to be able to make out that it was sanctioned by the Sastras, and worked for a lifetime to make it popular, was in his later days filled with despondency, and expressed his conviction to visitors from this side of the country that Hindus as Hindus would never accept Social Reform. It is certainly a matter of the deepest regret that it should be confined to a religions body. We on this side have not come to this pass yet, though we have our full share of indifference and hostility. The aim of the reformers here has always been to reform our society—our nation. I am happy to find that our Madras friends agree with us in this respect. Reform through the agency of caste, which is attempted in some parts of the country, is very unsatisfactory. Very little can be effected in this way. The reduction of marriage expenses and measures of this nature only can be carried out by its means, and the great danger of this method is that caste which has corroded the vitals of this country, will be strengthened by it.

Thus then we should nurture in our hearts the great forces which bring about the reform of society, viz., truth, justice and sympathy. Two of the greatest historians of England have told us that the Moral Law governs the affairs of the world; its observance alone ensures national prosperity. One of these I have quoted elsewhere, and will now ask your attention to the observations of the other. The strongest of the forces, which are steadily bearing nations onward to improvement or decay are, according to Lecky, the moral ones. 'Their permanent political well-being,' he says, 'is essentially the outcome of their moral state.' The Moral Law seeks to purify private life and to effect social justice, and through these alone is the political well-being of a nation possible.

And Evolutionary Science is beginning to teach us the same lesson. Competition and rivalry are the necessary conditions of progress towards a higher condition among men as well as among the lower creatures. This competition and this rivalry tend to establish the supremacy of the stronger individual over the weaker; his race propagates itself and that of the other disappears. It is this law that is leading or has led to the extinction of the aboriginal races in the presence of the stronger European races in America, Australia, New Zealand and other islands. This competition and rivalry need not assume the form of an actual war of extermination. It has been clearly ascertained that even in the midst of profound peace, the primitive races show a tendency to disappear. If this law was in operation in our country, our future must be very gloomy. But our climate will, I think, come to our rescue, as it has been ascertained that the stronger races of Western Europe cannot, if settled here, exhibit the same energy and perseverance that they do in temperate regions. Colonization of India by the European races is, therefore, an impracticability; but does not deliver us from the dangers of competition and rivalry with them. And again that law must be in operation among us to ensure our own progress. But to estimate its full effects we must understand the conditions under which it acts in the case of man.

Man is a social animal, and the competition that comes into operation in his case is a competition between societies. The ancient history of the human race consists of wars between such societies and the triumph of one and subjugation of another. This competition and rivalry between different societies is going on still, and in order that a society may carry on the contest to a successful issue, it is necessary that it should be so organized, that the individuals composing it, should not be borne down by artificial restrictions, but be able to put forth their best powers and capacities.

The history of England, for example, shows a gradual emancipation of the classes that were once in a condition of little better than slavery, and a renunciation of their privileges by the dominant classes. The effect of this has been to place the

individual in a more advantageous position to conduct the battle
of life, and thus to render the society, of which he is a member,
fitter for competition and rivalry with other societies. But it
is the development of sympathetic or altruistic feelings only
amongst the privileged classes and the society generally, that can
lead to the removal of the disabilities of others and the redress
of their grievances. Without such feelings, internal dissensions
and eventual degradation must be the rules. And these feelings
are now leading the English people to devise means for relieving
the chronic poverty of the lower classes, to readjust the relations
between labour and capital, and undertake a variety of schemes
to relieve distress and misery. It is a patent fact acknowledged by
all disinterested persons that the English people have developed
the altruistic feelings in a higher degree than any other European
nation, and by the way, this constitutes the basis of our hopes in a
future for our country. Just as England has been endeavouring to
remove the disabilities and sufferings of the lower classes of her
population, so shall efforts not be wanting on her part to remove
our disabilities and sufferings, but the law of social evolution
cannot cease to operate, and in order that our society may be
able to hold its own in the competition and rivalry with other
societies, which is inevitable, we must abide by the conditions
of that law. That law is thus stated by the latest writer on the
subject, whose book has created a great stir: 'That the moral
law is the unchanging law of progress in human society is the
lesson which appears to be written over all things. No school
of Theology has ever sought to enforce this teaching with the
directness and emphasis, with which it appears that evolutionary
science will in the future be justified in doing. In the silent and
strenuous rivalry, in which every section of the race is of necessity
continually engaged, permanent success appears to be invariably
associated with certain ethical and moral conditions favourable
to the maintenance of a high standard of social efficiency, and
with those conditions only.'

If then social efficiency and consequent success are what we desire in our contest with other races, we must, because the law is immutable, endeavour to realise those ethical and moral conditions. We must cultivate a sense of justice and a love and sympathy for others, relieve the poor widow of her sufferings, remove the disabilities of woman-kind and of the lower classes, and allow free play to the energies and capacities of all.

Part II
History

12

Shivaji's Genius Analysed[*]

Jadunath Sarkar

The greatest of Shivaji's genius can be fully realised not from the extent of the kingdom he won for himself, nor from the value of the hoarded treasure he left behind him, but from a survey of the conditions amidst which he rose to sovereignty.

He was truly an original explorer, the maker of a new road in mediaeval Indian history, with no example or guide before him. When he chose to declare his independence, the Mughal Empire seemed to be at the height of its glory. Every local chief who had, anywhere in India, revolted against it had been crushed. For a small jagirdar's son to defy its power, appeared as an act of madness, a courting of sure ruin. Shivaji, however, chose this path, and he succeeded.

His success can be explained only by an analysis of his political genius. First and foremost he possessed that unfailing sense of reality in politics, that recognition of the exact possibilities of his time (*tact des choses possibles*) which Cavour defined as the essence of statesmanship. His daring was tempered and guided by an instinctive perception of how far his actual resources could carry him, how long a certain line of action or policy was to be followed, and where he must stop. For the lack of this political

---

[*] Extracted from *Shivaji and His Times* by Jadunath Sarkar, Orient Blackswan, Delhi, 2017, pp. 301–05.

insight his rash son Shambhuji came to a miserable end and undid the work of Shivaji's life.

Shivaji possessed the true master's gift of judging character at sight and choosing the fittest instruments for his work. This is proved by the successful execution of his agents in his absence. Many of the distant expeditions of his reign were conducted not by himself but by his generals, who almost always carried out his orders according to plan. This is a novel feat in an Asiatic monarchy, where everything depends on the master's presence. It was the training gained in Shivaji's service, aided by the Maratha national character for personal independence and initiative, that enabled the disorganized Maratha people to stand up against the resources of the mighty Aurangzeb for eighteen years after the murder of Shambhuji and ultimately to defeat him, even though they had no king or capital.

His reign brought peace and order to his country, assured the protection of women's honour and the religion of all sects without distinction, extended the royal patronage to the truly pious men of all creeds (Muslims no less than Hindus), and presented equal opportunities to all his subjects by opening the public service to talent irrespective of caste or creed. This was the ideal policy for a State with a composite population like India.

His gifts were peace and a wise internal administration. The stability of these good conditions was the only thing necessary for giving permanence to Shivaji's work and ensuring national consolidation and growth. But that stability was denied to his political creation. Only his example and name remained to inspire the best minds of succeeding generations with ideals of life and government, not unmixed with vain regrets.

Did Shivaji merely found a Krieg-staat? Was he merely an entrepreneur of rapine, a Hindu edition of Alauddin Khilji or Timur? I think it would not be fair to take this view. For one thing, he never had peace to work out his political ideas. The whole of his short life was one struggle with enemies, a period of preparation and not of fruition. All his attention was necessarily devoted to meeting daily dangers with daily expedients and he had not the chance of peacefully building up a well-planned political edifice.

In the vast Gangetic valley and the wide Desh country rolling eastwards through the Deccan, Nature has fixed no boundary to States. Here a kingdom's size changes with daily changes in its strength compared with its neighbours'. There can be no stable equilibrium among them for more than a generation. Each has to push the others as much for self-defence as for aggression. Each must be armed ready to invade the others, if it does not wish to be invaded and absorbed by them. Where friction with neighbours is the normal state of things, a huge armed force, sleepless vigilance, and readiness to strike the first blow are the necessary conditions of the very existence.

He was himself a Hindu, sincere in belief and orthodox in practice, and yet he had a number of Muhammadan officers in the highest positions, such as Munshi Haide (Chief Justice of the Mughal empire on entering Aurangzeb's service), Sidilik and Daulat Khan (admirals), besides commanders like Siddi Halal and Nufli. He gave legal recognition to the Muslim qazis in his dominions.

The evil could be remedied only by the establishment of a universal empire throughout the country from sea to sea. Shivaji could not for a moment be sure of the Delhi Government's pacific disposition or fidelity to treaty. The past history of the Mughal expansion into the Deccan since the days of Akbar, was a warning to him. The imperial policy of annexing the whole of South India was as unmistakable to Shivaji as to Adil Shah or Qutb Shah. Its completion was only a question of time, and every Deccani Power was bound to wage eternal warfare with the Mughals if it wished to survive. Hence Shivaji lost no chance of robbing Mughal territory in the Deccan.

With Bijapur his relations were somewhat different. He could raise his head or extend his dominion only at the expense of Bijapur. Rebellion against his liege lord was the necessary condition of his being. But when, about 1662, an understanding was effected between him and the Adil-Shahi ministers, he gave up molesting the heart of the Bijapur kingdom. With the Bijapuri barons whose fiefs lay close to his dominions, he had, however, to wage war till he had wrested Kolhapur, North Kanara and South Konkan from their hands. In the Karnatak division, viz., the Dharwar and Belgaum districts, this contest was still undecided when he died. With the provinces that lay across the path of his natural expansion he could not be at peace, though he did not wish to challenge the central Government of Bijapur. This attitude was changed by the death of Ali II in 1672, the accession of the boy Sikandar Adil Shah, the faction-fights between rival nobles at the capital, and the visible dissolution of that Government. But Shivaji helped Bijapur greatly during the Mughal invasion of 1679.

Shivaji's real greatness lay in his character and practical ability, rather than originality of conception or length of political vision. Unfailing insight into the character of others, efficiency of arrangements, and instinctive perception of what was practicable and most profitable under the circumstances, these were the causes of his success in life.

To these must be added his personal morality and loftiness of aim, which drew to his side the best minds of his community, while his universal toleration and insistence on equal justice for all gave contentment to all classes subject to his rule. He strenuously maintained order, and enforced moral laws throughout his own dominions, and people were happier under his sway than anywhere else.

His splendid success fired the imagination of his contemporaries, and his name became a spell calling the Maratha race to a new life. His kingdom was lost within nine years of his death. But the imperishable achievement of his life was the raising of the Marathas into an independent self-reliant people, conscious of their oneness and high destiny, and his most precious legacy was the spirit that he breathed into his race.

The mutual conflict and internal weakness of the three Muslim Powers of the Deccan were, no doubt, contributory causes of the rise of Shivaji. But his success sprang from a higher source than the incompetence of his enemies. I regard him as the last great constructive genius and nation-builder that the Hindu race has produced. His system was his own creation and, unlike Ranjit Singh, he took no foreign aid in his administration. His army was drilled and commanded by his own people and not by Frenchmen. What he built lasted long: his institutions were looked up to with admiration and emulation even a century later in the palmy days of the Peshwas' rule.

Shivaji was illiterate; he learnt nothing by reading. He built up his kingdom and Government before visiting any royal Court, civilized city, or organized camp. He received no help or counsel from any experienced minister or general. But his native genius, alone and unaided, enabled him to found a compact kingdom, an invincible army and a practical and beneficent system of administration.

Before his rise, the Maratha race was scattered like atoms through many Deccani kingdoms. He welded them into a mighty nation. And he achieved this in the teeth of the opposition of four great powers like the Mughal Empire, Bijapur, Portuguese India, and the Abyssinians of Janjira. No other mediaeval Hindu has shown such capacity.

Before he came, the Marathas were mere hirelings, mere servants of aliens. They served the State, but had no lot or part in its management. They shed their life-blood in the army, but were denied a part in the conduct of war or peace. They were always subordinate never leaders.

Shivaji was the first to challenge Bijapur and Delhi and thus teach his countrymen that it was possible for them to be independent leaders. Then, he founded a State and taught his people that they were capable of administering a kingdom in all its departments. He has proved by his example that the Hindu race can build a nation, found a State, defeat enemies; they can conduct their own defences; they can protect and promote literature and art, commerce and industry; they can maintain navies and ocean-trading fleets of their own, and conduct naval battles on equal terms with foreigners. He taught the modern Hindus to rise to the full stature of their growth.

He has proved that the Hindu race can still produce not only jamadars (non-commissioned officers) and chitnises (clerks), but also rulers of men, and even a king of kings (Chhatrapati.) Emperor Jahangir cut the Akshay Bat tree of Allahabad down to its roots and hammered a red-hot iron cauldron on to its stump. He flattered himself that he had killed it. But lo! within a year the tree began to grow again and pushed the heavy obstruction to its growth aside!

Shivaji has shown that the tree of Hinduism is not really dead, that it can rise from beneath the seemingly crushing load of centuries of political bondage, exclusion from the administration, and legal repression; it can put forth new leaves and branches; it can again lift its head up to the skies.

13

The Guiding Principle of the New Maratha Strategy, Aggression— Not Merely Defence[*]

V.D. Savarkar

The most important reason why since the time the Marathas assumed the military leadership of the Hindu nation, the Hindus alone went on winning victories, all over the vast subcontinent of India whenever they joined battle with the Muslims, was that these Marathas with their daring valour, had at once purged the Hindu mind of that pernicious epidemic of the perverted sense of virtues, which had afflicted and paralysed most of the Hindu society all over India and which had given birth to the false notion of chivalry, deeming it highly despicable from the ethical point of view, a veritable sin, as it were to lead a military attack—even against the direst enemy.

In fact the creed of every national army is to march upon the enemy even before the latter attacks—to lead a blatant aggression not merely to stage defensive formations! The first successful attempt to inspire this aggressive mentality amongst the Hindus was made at the time of the establishment of the Vijaynagar

---

[*] Extracted from *Six Glorious Epochs of Indian History* by Veer Savarkar, Abhishek Publications, Chandigarh, pp. 368–70.

empire against the Muslims, even before the Marathas took the lead. But it was restricted to the south alone and the terrible defeat at Talikota deterred the Hindu mind from invading the Muslims. It was then that the Marathas inspired the Hindus with a new war-like spirit by successful inroads upon the Muslims.

To invade the enemy territory is the chief aim or the chief duty of a national military strength. The nation which maintains armed forces just strong enough for the purpose of defence—and does not build it up so as to be capable to undertake an invasion and considers it improper to do so—is either basically coward at heart or is labouring under a delusion. Perhaps it is to camouflage that inward cowardice that such high sounding declarations are made. A nation whose armed might is evidently built up on the basis of its aggressive capacity is certainly capable of self-defence.

Again, the Hindu aggression against the violent and unjust political domination of the Muslim rulers was basically not an aggression at all. The really unjust aggression was that of the Muslims who had invaded the territories of the Hindus. The aggressive risings of the Hindus against the outrageous Muslim rule can never be called revolts or rebellious. For, the aggression of the Muslim rulers against the independent and rightfully established Hindu states was itself mutinous and revolting. The rising of a robber against the rightful owner to chastise the rebellious freebooters! It is, therefore, to inspire with indomitable courage the majority of the Hindu society all over India, which had taken fright of these Muslim freebooters, that Shree Ramadas raised his war-cry from every peak of the Sahyadri: 'It is the Muslim-insurrection! The insurgents are the Muslims and not the Hindus! In order to punish them severely invade them from all sides all at once!'

(One should court death for the sake of religion [But] while dying one should kill [the enemies] and by thus killing them, one should win back one's kingdom.)

14

Hinduism: A Religion to Live By[*]

Nirad C. Chaudhuri

This can be most conclusively demonstrated by taking the very thing which creates the impression that the south is different from that the north. Those who see the two regions exclaim: 'Oh, the south is a land of great temples!' But the simple historical explanation of this fact is that in the south the temples have survived, and in the north they have not. Over seven centuries from the eleventh to the end of the seventeenth all the great cities of northern India dating from Hindu times were sacked by the Muslim invaders and conquerors of India. All the temples there and in all other centres of Hinduism were systematically destroyed. None were left standing at Ujjain, Ajmere, Delhi, Mathura, Brindaban, Kanauj, Prayag, or Benares—which were the centres of the political, cultural, and religious life of the Hindus. In most of these places mosques were built on the sites of the temples, and in some with pillars taken from them. This religious vandalism also worked its fury on the Buddhist centres. Moreover, it was not simply that the great temples in the cities were destroyed; so were the village temples. For most of the period of Muslim rule, there was a ban on building new temple and rebuilding the old in the regions the Muslims controlled.

[*] Extracted from *Hinduism* by Nirad C. Chaudhuri, Oxford India Paperback, 1996, pp. 125–29.

The ban was lifted by Akbar, but this was a short respite. It was then that one of the most original and beautiful temples of northern India was built. It was that of Govindaji at Brindaban. It could not be finished, but like the *Unfinished Symphony* of Schubert remains a great work of art. The ban on temples was re-imposed, and a period of iconoclastic fury was witnessed under Shah Jahan (himself the son of a Hindu princess) and Aurangzeb, when even the rebuilt temples were again razed. It was only with the rise of Maratha power in the latter half of the eighteenth century that the destruction ceased and rebuilding began. The Marathas rebuilt Benares. The new temple of Visvanath—the old having been converted into a mosque by Aurangzeb—was built by the Maratha princess Ahilya Bai of the Holkar family, and the then famous waterfront of Benares was the creation of other Maratha princes and one Rajput prince.

So it is impossible to judge what Hindu temple architecture was like in its homeland in the greatest age of Hindu civilization. We can only guess from scattered references in secular Sanskrit literature. One Sanskrit epic, written at the end of the twelfth century, laments the destruction of the temples at Ajmere. It was meant to celebrate the victory of Prithviraj, the Chauhan king, over Muhammad of Ghur in the first battle of Tarain, but the next year this king was defeated and killed, and so the poem was not finished. But it was given a prologue in which the burning of the temples and crashing of their steeples are described.

During all those centuries, all over northern India only ruins of the temples were to be seen. But the Hindus did not forget the houses of their gods. When at the beginning of the eighteenth century the Jesuit priest and mathematician Tiffenthaler travelled from the west coast of India to Malwa he saw in the evenings the flickering lights of the earthen lamps placed in these ruins by the villagers at some risk to themselves. It was only in the regions where Muslim power could not penetrate on account of their inaccessibility that the temples escaped destruction, and two of the most notable groups which have survived are those at

Khajuraho and Mahoba in Bundelkhand and at Bhuvaneswar, Puri, and Konarak in Orissa. Both the regions were protected by hills and jungles. Even so Orissa suffered a short spell of vandalism in the sixteenth century. Thus temple architecture in northern India is represented by examples which are provincial and for the most part late. Yet even these examples are so impressive that they are included among the greatest temples to be found in India. The temples at the centres of Hindu political power in the Gangetic plain and in Malwa must have been more numerous and splendid. But they have disappeared, and those which are now seen in these areas are not only smaller but also in a style considerably influenced by Islamic architecture. All this has induced modern observers to give pre-eminence to the south as the land of temples at the expense of the Aryavarta—the home of Hindu culture.

What happened to the temples in northern India happened also to the Hindu princely order and the aristocracy. A majority of them were just exterminated, and the rest fled to the Himalayan foothills. The social and cultural vacuum thus created was filled up by Turkish, Persian, and Afghan colonists and a Muslim aristocracy, and in northern India that substitution was a disaster for every expression of Hindu culture, including religion. The dominant culture in the Gangetic plain became Islamic, and the Hindus became a cultural proletariat. They never recovered their old cultural status during the whole of British rule, and have not done so even today.

Nothing illustrates the transformation of Hindu life in the northern plain better than the change in the economic status and manner of living of the two upper castes, the Brahmins and the Kshatriyas, i.e., the priestly and the fighting castes. They were born necessarily dependent on the Hindu kings for providing them with livelihood as priests and soldiers, their caste vocations. Deprived of the patronage, both the castes largely adopted agriculture as their main source of living and became peasants. The establishment of British power in India

gave both of them a military function, and a majority of the
sepoys of the Bengal army, i.e., the north Indian army of the
East India Company, came from these two castes. It was they
who rose in rebellion against the British at an imagined threat
to their religion, and the ruthless suppression of that rising
gave a further blow to the higher expression of Hinduism in
Hindustan.

This new name of Hindustan for the Gangetic plain is
significant in itself. In Sanskrit this plain, the homeland of
Brahmanism, was called the Aryavarta, i.e., the land of the
Aryas or Aryans. The new name was Persian. Thus the course
of political history in northern India reduced Hindu culture and
religion to the level of a folk culture and folk religion by depriving
it of its élite. Both lost their sophistication and pride. Sanskrit
learning virtually disappeared from the region, and orthodoxy in
the mores became less rigorous. The festivals became more and
more democratic, although patronized by the wealthy. Under
Muslim rule there remained in northern India only one social
order which still carried on the tradition of a high social and
religious culture, and that was the wealthy Bania or commercial
class. The Muslims could not do without this class, and by means
of its wealth it continued a kind of Hinduism which though not
at the old level, was higher than the Hinduism of the common
people of the region.

Nevertheless, an overall denudation could not be avoided.
This is comparable to the geographical change that has come
over the Gangetic basin through deforestation and denudation
of the soil. The forests of that region have become scrub; so have
culture and religion in a figurative sense. Thus Hindu culture
here wears an appearance of poverty which was not its old
condition. It is the religious expression of this culture, which is
the 'popular Hinduism' of English writers. In reality it was only
the remnant, the detritus of the old Hinduism. Comparison of
this kind of survival with a higher kind in the south created an
impression of the superiority of the latter.

The contrast was noticed even by the earliest writers on India. They were led to think that in northern India Hinduism hardly existed, because they had made their first acquaintance with it in the more elaborate form it had in the south. Robert Orme, the first historian of British India, noted in the first volume of his history published in 1763 that the northern nations of India, although idolaters, having scarce a religion, when compared with the multitudes of superstitions and ceremonies which characterize the inhabitants of southern countries, were easily induced to embrace Mahomedanism. In saying this Orme was really mistaking the effect for the cause. The Hindus of northern India did not embrace Islam because they had no religion; their religion was reduced to its lowest denominator owing to the Muslim Conquest. It should, however, be kept in mind that within these two very blocs of Hinduism created in north and south India by history, there were differences which created smaller blocs.

In the south the Tamil-speaking Hindus constituted the most important and typical group, while those who spoke Telugu, Canarese and Malayalam were associated groups, not minor in themselves, but less assertive and with less prestige derived from the places of pilgrimage and temples than the Tamil area. In the north, on the other hand, the Hindus of the Punjab had a form of religion which was simpler even than that of the Gangetic plain. In their manners and external ways they were very largely Islamized, and most of them till recently read even their own religious books in Urdu translations, because they could not read the Devanagari script. But so far as writing was concerned, it must be remembered that the north-west of India had the right-to-left style of writing from very ancient times.

Under Muslim and also with competition facing them from both Islam and Sikhism, the Hindu content of their faith became very elementary. To sum up the matter, the Muslim conquest pulverized Hinduism in the northern plain, but left it as an old and yet inhabited building in the south. There is no reason to assume that before the Muslim conquest Hindu culture and religion were in any significant way different in the two regions. It must not be forgotten the most famous commentator of the Vedas, Sayana, and the greatest exponent of philosophic Brahmanism, Samkara, came from the south.

15

Critics of Hinduism[*]

Bankimchandra Chattopadhyay

I suggested to Mr. Hastie that before putting himself forward as the assailant of the Hindu religion, he should study the Hindu scriptures in the original, and under the guidance of native scholars who believe in them. That Mr. Hastie does not choose to accept my advice does no harm either to me or to my cause. It is no loss to the Hindu religion that assailants do not choose to be better armed than they are. But beneath Mr. Hastie's scornful rejection of my advice, there lurk errors which are not confined to him, but are shared by a large class of Europeans, whose numbers, position and influence and sincere good feeling for Indian populations give them an importance far superior to what can arise out of this shallow and somewhat worn-out controversy.

The first of these errors consists in the assumption that, because European Sanskritists are competent scholars, the translations from Sanskrit which they produce must necessarily teach all that the Originals have to teach. A brief consideration will convince Mr. Hastie, and others who think with him, that no translation from the Sanskrit into a European language can truly or even approximately represent the original.

---

[*] Extracted from *Essays and Letters* by Bankimchandra Chattopadhyay, Rupa & Co, Delhi, 2010, pp. 114–18.

Let the translator be the profoundest Sanskrit scholar in the world—let the translation be the most accurate that language can make it, still the disparity between the original and the translation will be, for practical purposes, very wide. The reason is obvious. You can translate a word by a word, but behind the word there is an idea, the thing which the word denotes, and this idea you cannot translate, if it does not exist among the people in whose language you are translating. The English or the German language can possess no words or expressions to denote ideas or conceptions which have never entered into a Teutonic brain. Now, a people so thoroughly unconnected with England or Germany as the old Sanskrit-speaking people of India, and developing a civilisation and a literature peculiarly their own, had necessarily a vast store of ideas and conceptions utterly foreign to the Hindu. These, which form the spirit and the matter of religious and philosophical treatises, are entirely distorted and, as a matter of necessity, misrepresented in every translation—even in the best. And the best translations—not translations merely, but all comments and expositions in any language so widely differing as the European languages differ from Sanskrit—must, thus, to a great extent be misleading.

And who is best qualified to expound the ideas and conceptions which cannot be translated—the foreigner who has nothing corresponding to them in the whole range of his thoughts and experiences, or the native who was nurtured in them from his infancy? If obviously the latter, what is the meaning of this towering indignation at my suggestion that Mr. Hastie should resort to the latter for instruction? I added that he should take his lesson not merely from a Brahmin, but from a Brahmin who believed in them. Was it so very unreasonable as to call down a protest from Mr. Hastie on behalf of the helpless, ill-treated scholars of Europe? Does Mr. Hastie believe that any department of human thought which has had its influence on a large portion of the human race, will yield any valuable results without a loving and reverential study? If Mr. Hastie thinks that he can comprehend the vast complicated labyrinth of Hindu religious belief without studying it in the original sources of knowledge, and in a spirit of patient, earnest, and reverential search after truth, he will meet with bitter disappointment. He will fail in arriving at a correct comprehension of Hinduism, as—I say it most emphatically—as every other European who has made the attempt has failed. And if he thinks that this eloquence alone will enable him to demolish the oldest and the most enduring of all religious systems without a correct knowledge of its doctrines— why, I can only wish for an Indian Cervantes to record his achievements.

Mr. Hastie has unnecessarily complicated the question by his protest on behalf of European Sanskritists. No one questions their scholarship. I can assure him that men like Max Mueller and Golstucker, Colebrook and Muir, Weber and Roth[*] do not stand in need of a champion like Mr. Hastie. I yield to none in my profound respect for their learning, their ability, and the large-hearted philanthropy which leads them to devote themselves to pursuits from which my countrymen often recoil in fear and despair. And I, as a native of India, would be certainly shamefully wanting in gratitude, if I did not acknowledge their great services in the dissemination of the Sanskrit language and Sanskrit literature—but that they are much better understood in Europe and America than they are in India, I decline to follow. It is, I believe, one of the most monstrous assertions ever made; but what gives it importance is that not a few Europeans, and possible some anglicized natives—Hindus I cannot call them— who do not mix with their own race, believe it to be true. The principal ground for this belief is, I think, to be found in the circumstance that these Europeans and natives are more familiar with what European scholars have written on Indian languages

---

[*] Rudolph Roth (1821–93): German Indologist; founder of Vedic philology and author of *On the Literature and History of the Vedas* (1846); honorary member of the Asiatic Society of Bengal.

and Indian literature than with the writings of native scholars. A few natives like Dr. Rajendralal Mitra and Dr. K.M. Banerjee write in English. Those not less estimable men, who are more anxious to address the vast mass of their own countrymen than a few European scholars, prefer writing in their own vernacular. The existence and the scholarship of those who choose to write in their own vernacular, in preference to Mr. Hastie's, remain to him and to those who think with him as things unknown. I am also willing to confess that as the native scholars have written much less than European writers address, the scientific value of their writings is necessarily proportionately inferior. But the inference does not follow that native scholars are less at home in the language and literature of their own country than European Sanskritists.

The question is, however, hardly relevant. European scholars may be all that Mr. Hastie says that they are; no one seeks to depreciate their merits. What I said of them was—'They cannot teach what they do not understand; the blind cannot lead the blind.' This of course is a mere truism on the surface, but it is not the mere truism which has induced Mr. Hastie to explode. I did mean to say that the fundamental doctrines of the Hindu religion and its vast details are what no European scholar understands, what no European scholar is competent to teach. This I did mean to say, and this I again positively assert. I will add that there are many other things in Indian literature and Indian philosophy— other things than the religious doctrines which European scholar understands, and no European scholar is competent to teach. I will also assert with equal emphasis that in these cases, the native scholar is decidedly a better teacher than the European.

16

Education in India[*]

Ananda K. Coomaraswamy

What are the essentials in the Indian point of view, which for their intrinsic value, and in the interests of the manysidedness of human development, it is so important to preserve? Space will not admit of their illustration at any length, but these appear to the writer to be some of the ideals that must be preserved in any true education system for India:-

Firstly, the almost universal philosophical attitude, contrasting strongly with that of the ordinary Englishman, who hates philosophy. For every science school in India to-day, let us see to it that there are ten to-morrow.[†] But there are wrong as well as right ways to teaching science. A 'superstition of facts' taught in the name of science were a poor exchange for a metaphysic, for a conviction of the subjectivity of all phenomena. In India, even the peasant will grant you that 'All this is *maya*',

---

[*] Extracted from *Essays in National Idealism* by Ananda K. Coomaraswamy, Munshiram Manoharlal, Delhi, 2013, pp. 104–08.

[†] There is of course a danger of a new kind threatening Indian education at present—the desire to restrict free development, and confine instruction to such subjects and books as are not likely to awaken the spirit of progress or revolt. This conspiracy—it is no less—can only be properly checked if the entire control of Indian education is assumed by Indians themselves. My suggestions are based entirely on this assumption.

he may not understand the full significance of what he says; but consider the deepening of European culture needed before the peasant there could say, however blindly, that ' The world is but appearance, and by no means Thing-in-itself'.

Secondly, the sacredness of all things—the antithesis of the European division of life into sacred and profane. The tendency in European religious development has been to exclude from the domain of religion every aspect of 'worldly' activity. Science, art, sex, agriculture, commerce are regarded in the West as secular aspects of life, quite apart from religion. It is not surprising that under such conditions, those concerned with life in its reality have come to feel the so-called religion that ignores the activities of life, as a thing apart, and of little interest or worth. In India, this was never so; religion idealises and spiritualizes life itself, rather than excludes it. This intimate entwining of the transcendental and material, this annihilation of the possibility of profanity or vulgarity of thought, explains the strength and permanence of Indian faith, and demonstrates not merely the stupidity, but the wrongness of attempting to replace a religious culture by one entirely material.

Thirdly, the true spirit of religious toleration, illustrated continually in Indian history, and based upon a consciousness of the fact that all religious dogmas are formulas imposed upon the infinite, by the limitations of the finite human intellect.

Fourthly, etiquette—civilisation conceived of as the production of civil men. There is a Sinhalese proverb that runs, 'Take a ploughman from the plough, and wash off his dirt, and he is fit to rule a kingdom.' 'This was spoken,' says Knox, 'of the people of Cande Uda (the highlands of Ceylon) because of the civility, understanding, and gravity of the poorest men among them. Their ordinary Plowmen and Husbandmen do speak elegantly, and are full of compliment. And there is no difference between the ability of speech of a Country-man and the Courtier.' There could be said of few people any greater things than these; they belong to a society where life itself brought culture, not books alone.

Fifthly, special ideas in relation to education, such as the relation between teacher and pupil implied in the words of *guru* and *chela* (master and disciple); memorizing great literature, the epics as embodying ideals of character; learning a privilege demanding qualifications, not to be forced on the unwilling, or used as a mere road to material prosperity; extreme importance of the teacher's personality.

'As the man who digs with a spade obtains water, even so an obedient (pupil) obtains the knowledge which lies in his teacher' (Manu II. 218). The view is antithetic to the modern practice of making everything easy for the pupil.

Sixthly, the basics of ethics are not any commandments, but the principle of altruism, founded on the philosophical truth: 'Thy neighbour is thyself.' Recognition of the unity of all life.

Seventhly, control, not merely of action, but of thought; concentration, one-pointedness, capacity for stillness.

These are some of the points of view which are intrinsic in Indian culture, and must be recognized in any sound educational ideal for India; but are in the present system ignored or opposed. The aim should be to develop the people's intelligence through the medium of their own national culture. For the national culture is the only *Aussichtspunkt* from which, in relation to a wider landscape, a man can rightly *sich am Denken orientiren*. To this culture has to be added, for those brought into contact with the modern idea, some part of that wider synthesis that should enable such an one to understand what may be the nature of the prospect seen from some other of the great headlands, the other national cultures, wherefrom humanity has gazed into the dim sea of the Infinite Unknown. To effect this wider synthesis, are needed signals and interpretations, rather than that laborious backward march through the emptiness of a spiritual desert where one may perish by the way, or if not so, then weary and footsore arrive at last upon one of those other headlands, only to learn, it may be, that there is to be found a less extensive prospect and a more barren soil.

17

Shortcomings in Indian Historiography[*]

R.C. Majumdar

So far about the British historians. As regards the Indian historians the chief defect arose from national sentiments and patriotic fervour which magnified the virtues and minimized the defects of their own people. It was partly a reaction against the undue depreciation of the Indians in the pages of British histories like those of Mill, and partly an effect of the growth of national consciousness and a desire for improvement in their political status. It is a noticeable fact that these defects gained momentum with the movement for political reforms, and later, in the course of the struggle for freedom.

An extreme example is furnished by K.P. Jayaswal. The repeated declarations of British historians that absolute despotism was the only form of Government in Ancient India provoked Indian historians, who, following the footsteps of Rhys Davids, emphasized the existence of republican and oligarchical forms of Government. This reaction was, generally speaking, kept within reasonable limits of historical truth; but Jayaswal carried the whole thing to ludicrous excess in his Hindu Polity, by his

---

[*] Extracted from *Historiography of Modern India* by R.C. Majumdar, Asia Publishing House, London, 1970, pp. 47–57.

theory of a Parliamentary form of Government in Ancient India, which is a replica of the British Parliament including the formal Address from the Throne, etc.; and many other statements of the kind. Similarly, historical discussions on social and religious matters are not unoften coloured by the orthodox views on the subject. The recent acrimonious discussion on the killing of cows shows how even clearly established facts of history are twisted to suit present views. A truly scientific spirit of history is often sacrificed in discussions of such subjects as, 'Did the Aryans come to India from outside?', 'Was there a caste system in the Ṛgveda?', and conscious attempts are often made to explain away, ignore, or minimize, the harsh treatment accorded by the high caste Hindus to the lower castes, particularly Sūdras and Caṇḍālas.

So far as Medieval India is concerned, there is a distinct and conscious attempt to rewrite the whole chapter of the bigotry and intolerance of the Muslim rulers towards Hindu religion. This was prompted by the political motive of bringing together the Hindus and Musalmans in a common fight against the British. A history written under the auspices of the Indian National Congress sought to repudiate the charge that the Muslim rulers ever broke any Hindu temple, and asserted that they were the most tolerant in matters of religion. Following in its footsteps a noted historian has sought to exonerate Mahmūd of Ghaznī's bigotry and fanaticism, and several writers in India have come forward to defend Aurangzīb against Jadunath's charge of religious intolerance. It is interesting to note that in the revised edition of the *Encyclopaedia of Islam*, one of them, while rewriting the article on Aurangzīb originally written by Sir William Irvine, has expressed the view that the charge of breaking Hindu temples brought against Aurangzīb is a disputed point. Alas for poor Jadunath Sarkar, who must have turned in his grave if he were buried. For after reading his *History of Aurangze*b, one would be tempted to ask, if the temple-breaking policy of Aurangzīb is a disputed point, is there a single fact in the whole recorded history of mankind which may be taken as undisputed? A noted historian has sought to prove that 'the Hindu population was better off under the Muslims than under the Hindu tributaries or independent rulers'. While some historians have sought to show that the Hindu and Muslim cultures were fundamentally different and formed two distinct and separate units flourishing side by side, the late K.M. Ashraf sought to prove that the Hindus and Muslims had no cultural conflict. But the climax was reached by the politician-*cum*-historian Lala Lajpat Rai when he asserted 'that the Hindus and Muslims have coalesced into an Indian people very much in the same way as the Angles, Saxons, Jutes, Danes and Normans formed the English people of today'. His further assertion 'that the Muslim rule in India was not a foreign rule' has now become the oft-repeated slogan of a certain political party. The pity of the whole thing is that history books which do not incorporate these views are not likely to be prescribed as textbooks, and anyone who challenges these statements would be included in the black list of the Government of India.

Coming to the British period, national sentiments prejudiced a calm consideration of several episodes. Two of these are, (1) the Black Hole Tragedy and character of Sirāju'd-daulah; and (2) the nature of the outbreak of 1857. Having myself written on both these topics I would not like to dwell on the merits of the different points of view. Reference has already been made above to other episodes where historians have been influenced by racial or national sentiments. To these may be added many questions concerning economic and administrative systems; in almost all of which the British and Indian views have been influenced more or less by national or patriotic feelings.

To this long array of defects of modern historiography in India, may be added another charge mostly levelled by Indians in recent times. It is said that the historians merely collect facts but do not make any generalizations or frame laws on their basis, while the real task of history is to reveal the spirit of humanity and trace the course of progress towards liberty. I do not think the charge is a legitimate one and would try to rebut it by the observations of some eminent scholars. The views of Fisher already quoted by me have been rebutted by other eminent historians like Acton who looks upon history as 'the unfolding story of human freedom'. A.L. Rowse also refutes Fisher's view and says: 'No; there is no one rhythm or plot in history, but there are rhythms, plots, patterns, even repetitions. So that it is possible to make generalizations and to draw lessons.' On the other hand, Sir Charles Oman in a way supports Fisher.

'History', says he, 'is a series of interesting happenings, often illogical and cataclysmic, not a logical and orderly development from causes to inevitable results. In short, history is full of "might have beens", and these sometimes deserve as much attention as the actual, but by no means necessary, course of events.' But whatever view we may adopt in this matter so far as the history of Europe is concerned, our very inadequate knowledge of data in Indian history renders such generalizations a difficult and risky process. I fully share the views expressed by Sir Jadunath Sarkar in the course of his estimate of Sir William Irvine as a historian. He observes: 'Some are inclined to deny Mr. Irvine the title of the Gibbon of India, on the ground that he wrote a mere narrative of events, without giving those reflections and generalizations that raise the *Decline and Fall* to the rank of a philosophical treatise and a classic in literature. But they forget that Indian historical studies are at present at a much more primitive stage than Roman history was when Gibbon began to write. We have yet to collect and edit our materials, and to construct the necessary foundation—the bed-rock of ascertained and unassailable *facts*—on which alone the superstructure of a philosophy of history can be raised by our happier successors. Premature philosophizing, based on unsifted facts and untrustworthy chronicles, will only yield a crop of wild theories and fanciful reconstructions of the past like those which

J.T. Wheeler garnered in his now forgotten *History of India*, as the futile result of years of toil.'

During the post-Independence period, certain new trends are noticeable among the Indian historians in addition to those noted above. Strangely enough, these were foreseen by the great Arab historian Ibn Khaldun. He includes, in a long list of defects of historians, 'a very common desire to gain the favour of those of high rank, by praising them, by spreading their fame, by flattering them, by embellishing their doings and by interpreting in the most favourable way all their actions'. He then justly observes that all this gives a distorted version of historical events. This characteristic is a growing menace to historiography in Modern India. The evil is enhanced by the fact that the Government, directly or indirectly, seeks to utilize history to buttress some definite ideas, such as the Gandhian philosophy of non-violence, the artificial conception of fraternal relation between the two great communities of India sedulously propagated by him, and several popular slogans evoked by the exigencies of the struggle for freedom. These have been accepted as a rich legacy by the Government, even though it practically means in many cases the sacrifice of truth, the greatest legacy which Gandhi meant to bequeath to mankind.

Thus the cult of non-violence is an ideal devoutly to be wished for, but when historians of India seriously maintain that this ideal has been followed throughout the course of Indian history, one rubs his eyes with wonder, for not only are all the known facts of Indian rulers against the assumption that they were averse to war, but war has been recommended by political texts as a normal practice and sanctioned by religion through the aśvamedha sacrifice and eulogy of digvijaya. The Court-poets flattered the patron king by giving him the proud epithet of 'hero of hundred fights'.

Such distortion of history can never be excused even in the name of Mahatma Gandhi. Similar distortions have been made on other topics mentioned above. The net result has been that the oft-quoted phrase, 'History is past politics', is likely to be substituted soon by a new phrase, 'History is present politics'. The attitude of the British Government towards Cunningham who dared include unpalatable truths in history, has not quitted India along with the British, and an Indian historian today is not always really free to write even true history if it is likely to offend the ruling party. I know from personal experience that any expression of views, not in consonance with the officially accepted view, is dubbed as anti-national, and is likely to provoke the wrath of the Government.

No wonder that even eminent historians feel shy of, even if not prevented from, telling the whole truth. An apt illustration is furnished by the official history of the 'Freedom Movement in Bihar' (1957). Much has been said in it of Kunwar Singh as the local organizer and a hero of the great 'War of Independence' in 1857. But no mention has been made of a document which shows that the local sepoys, *who had already mutinied*, threatened to plunder his house and property if he did not join them. It can hardly be excused on the ground of ignorance, for it was the author of this history who first brought this document to light and published it in a local magazine. Some other documents of similar nature have also been withheld.

When I was writing out the first draft of this lecture, the Proceedings of the Indian History Congress in 1964 and 1965 reached my hands. The Address of the General President in the 1964 session contains an elaborate presentation of the trends and concepts of history which appear to me to be a great departure from the ideals and concepts of history which I have outlined above. It may be reasonably assumed that these trends and concepts dominate at least a section of Indian historians today, and as such deserve careful scrutiny. 'History,' we are told, 'has a mission and obligation to lead humanity to a higher ideal and nobler future. The historian cannot shirk this responsibility by hiding his head into the false dogma of objectivity, that his job is merely to chronicle the past. His task is to reveal the spirit of

humanity and guide it towards self-expression.' Some concrete
steps are suggested for achieving this noble end. History must
not call to memory 'ghastly aberrations of human nature, of
dastardly crimes, of divisions and conflicts, of degeneration and
decay, but of the higher values of life, of traditions of culture
and of the nobler deeds of sacrifice and devotion to the service
of humanity'. In other words, history should record the spread
of Buddhism by Aśoka, but not the horrors of the Kaliṅga war,
carefully avoid all references to the devastation and massacre of
Mahmūd of Ghaznī, destruction of temples by Aurangzīb, the
Jallianwala Bagh massacre by General Dyer, the holocaust during
communal riots, and so on. The reason for these omissions is that
such things bring some 'unhealthy trends which militate against
the concept of national solidarity or international peace'. We are
further told that 'the purpose of history was to trace the course
of progress towards liberty'. To crown all, it is declared that
even '*facts* of Indian history and the Process of its march have to
be judged by the criterion of progress towards liberty, morality
and opportunities for self-expression'. So far as I understand, all
these mark a definite departure from the accepted principles of
historiography. As a concrete instance of the radical difference
in the ideals of historiography which animates the post-
Independence era in India, I may quote another passage from
the Presidential Address: 'The most important subject awaiting
the critical touch of the historian, however, is the national
movement, particularly the age dominated by Mahatma
Gandhi, which restored the independence of the country. The
historian has to get behind the external of the events and detect
the spirit which animated them, and thereby reveal the soul of
India. That approach alone will help to surmount the danger
of provoking communal, regional, linguistic and class hatreds
which unfortunately beset history writing.'

I must confess that in writing the 'History of Freedom
Movement' I have not kept all this high ideal before me. I have
preferred to follow the footsteps of Ranke, and may say in his

words: 'My book does not aspire to such lofty functions as are laid down in the Presidential address. Its aim is merely to show what actually occurred, with such comments as are obviously suggested by it.'

For a similar reason I demur to the principle that the purpose of history is to trace the course of progress towards liberty, and that even *facts* have to be arranged and judged by that criterion. The real purpose of history is to report correctly the progress of events, which did not in all cases mark the progress towards liberty. When all this is coupled with a definite instruction for avoiding mention of violent deeds, or even such *facts* as militate against the concept of national solidarity or international peace, we cannot but feel that Gandhian philosophy, which sought in vain to regenerate politics by infusing morality into it, has succeeded in inoculating history with his moral ideas. It may be a laudable project, but then, I would humbly suggest that history as a subject of study be omitted from our curriculum and replaced by books containing Gandhi's philosophy and morality. The lack of knowledge of history may perhaps be made good by development of moral character.

I would cite only one more example which gives a forecast of the shape that Indian history would take in the future. The President of Section II (Medieval India) of the Indian History Congress held at Allahabad in 1965 begins his address by pointing out the chief errors of Sir Henry Elliot and other Anglo-Indian writers of Medieval India. One of these is, to quote his own words, 'the wholly impossible and erroneous conclusion that the Musalmans, as such, were a governing class, while the Hindus, as such, were the governed'. Another error is that 'while pointing out the crimes of the medieval kings and their governing classes they quite overlooked what was happening at the same time in contemporary Europe'.

The President then refers to 'India's contact with Islam which had a deep impact on social, cultural, political and economic life of the country'. The net result of this is reflected in the following successive stages in the evolution of Medieval India. First, the *Turkish State* of the Ilbarites; second, the *Indo-Muslim State* of the Khaljī and the Tughlaqs, and third, the emergence of the *Indian State* of the Mughals. We are told that 'Akbar's political outlook was an outcome of the accumulated political wisdom of the generations that had gone by and was a logical development inherent in the very nature of the situation'. Unfortunately, nothing is said about his successors, particularly Aurangzīb, though it is claimed that on account of the continuity in this cultural evolution, the Mughal empire lasted longer than the whole of the Sultanate period.

There is hardly any doubt that the modern trends of Indian historiography noted above are inspired, or at least influenced to a large extent, by the attitude of the Government in deliberately seeking to utilize history for the spread of ideas which they have elevated to the rank of national policy to their own satisfaction. They are not willing to tolerate any history which mentions facts incompatible with their ideas of national integration and solidarity. They do not inquire whether the facts stated are true or the views expressed are reasonable deductions from facts, but condemn outright any historical writings which in their opinion are likely to go against their views about such things as Hindu-Muslim fraternity, the non-existence of separate Hindu and Muslim cultures on account of their fusion into one Indian culture, etc. I mention these particular instances, as I am in a position to substantiate them by documentary evidence, but reference may be made to many other illustrations, less susceptible to positive evidence. All these things are done in the name of national policy, which is at best the policy of a political party. But it violates the only national policy, which cannot be challenged by any party, namely 'Truth shall prevail', the motto engraved on our national emblem. This policy also underlies the most advanced ideal of historiography, as I have discussed above, and was expressed more than fifty years ago by the greatest historian of India, Sir Jadunath Sarkar, as chairman of a historical conference in Bengal. The following is a literal English translation of the original Bengali passage: 'I would not care whether truth is pleasant or unpleasant, and in consonance with or opposed to current views. I would not mind in the least whether truth is or is not a blow to the glory of my country. If necessary, I shall bear in patience the ridicule and slander of friends and society for the sake of preaching truth. But still I shall seek truth, understand truth, and accept truth. This should be the firm resolve of a historian.'

Later, when Dr. Rajendra Prasad launched a scheme to write a comprehensive national history of India on a cooperative basis and requested Jadunath to become its chief editor, Jadunath wrote to him on 19 November 1937: 'National history, like every other history worthy of the name and deserving to endure, must be true as regards the facts and reasonable in the interpretation of them. It will be national not in the sense that it will try to suppress or whitewash everything in our country's past that is disgraceful, but because it will admit them and at the same time point out that there were other and nobler aspects in the stages of our nation's evolution which offset the former. . . . In this task the historian must be a judge. He will not suppress any defect of the national character, but add to his portraiture those higher qualities which, taken together with the former, help to constitute the entire individual.'

In his reply to the above, dated 22 November 1937, Dr. Rajendra Prasad wrote: 'I entirely agree with you that no history is worth the name which suppresses or distorts facts. A historian who purposely does so under the impression that he thereby does good to his native country really harms it in the end. Much more so in the case of a country like ours which has suffered much on account of its national defects, and which must know and understand them to be able to remedy them.'

I solemnly hope and pray that these words would be remembered by the present and future generations of Indian historians, for I see great dangers lurking ahead. I was reading recently a book entitled *Contemporary History in the Soviet Mirror* published in 1964. I was struck by many passages, a few of which I quote at random.

'The present official line in historiography is, if anything, even more militantly partisan than it was in Stalin's day.'

'The Soviet politicians have a narrow and utilitarian view of the functions of scholarship.'

'Nothing could be more destructive of historical scholarship than the claim that the party is the repository of supreme wisdom. . . . In the Soviet Union today historians, like everyone else, are required to believe that, by some mysterious process unfathomable to an ordinary mortal, the party has been infallible.'

'The partisan approach to history prevents the observer from recognizing the sanctity of objective facts and requires him, where necessary, to deny the evidence of his senses; for there are occasions when he must subordinate his own personal concept of truth to that held by an individual or group of individuals, namely the party.'

I hope it would be obvious to most people that these symptoms constitute dangerous impediments to the growth of true historiography. What is less obvious is that our country, dominated by party system, is rapidly moving towards the same tragic end.

18

India's Secularism: The Emerging National Vision[*]

Sita Ram Goel

I feel that it is presumptuous on my part to speak about the national vision before an audience from Bengal, particularly before an audience from this city of Calcutta. It was in this land of Bengal, it was in this city of Calcutta, in the opening decades of this century that we obtained a clear picture of the national vision. You have only to read the works of Bankimchandra, Vivekananda and Sri Aurobindo and listen to the songs of Rabindranath in order to know what that national vision was, as also to understand what that vision is likely to be when it revives and is reaffirmed. I have nothing to add to what these great men have written and expounded and what they have shown in their own lives. I am only a poor interpreter of their vision as it should unfold, as it should emerge in the present situation.

The national vision which was expounded by these great men rose to its heights, reached a high watermark, attained its acme in the Swadeshi Movement. The same imperialist forces, that is, Islamic imperialism (or the residues of Islamic

---

[*] Speech delivered on Sunday, 4 December 1983, at the Yogakshema monthly meeting at Calcutta; extracted from *India's Secularism* by Sita Ram Goel, Voice of India, Delhi, 2016, pp. 53–72.

imperialism) and British imperialism, had combined to partition
Bengal, to partition a land which God had made one. But at
that time, the conspiracy was frustrated. The game was defeated
because the national vision was very clear, very firm. In fact, the
Swadeshi Movement was the beginning in real earnest of the
national struggle for freedom which was earlier confined to some
distinguished people meeting together and passing a number of
resolutions. It was for the first time that India witnessed in the
history of the freedom movement a mass mobilization of her
people. The echoes of the Swadeshi Movement were heard far
and wide, all over India, particularly in Maharashtra and the
Punjab, as also the mantras that were given during the Swadeshi
Movement—the mantra of Swadeshi, the mantra of Swarajya,
the mantra of 'Vande Mataram' which pulsated with all the
aspirations of an awakened nation. That was a complete picture
of the national vision as it had to be.

But, unfortunately, in the hands of the latter-day leadership
in the later phases of the freedom struggle, that vision got diluted.
It was obscured by certain other visions. It lost its clarity and the
result was the tragedy of partition. We know what happened
and how the events unfolded. Bengal has suffered the most due
to that tragedy. The wounds which Bengal has suffered and
which have now become running sores—well, I do not have to
dwell on the subject. You know it all. I have only to point out,
it is my painful duty to point out, that this land of Bengal which
has suffered so much due to the loss of the national vision, has
neglected that vision to a greater extent than the rest of this
country. It is, therefore, the duty of Bengal to resurrect that
vision, to recover that vision, to reaffirm that vision, and thus
reclaim its lost leadership of India.

Bengal today feels neglected. But the fault is not of the rest
of India. The fault lies with Bengal itself. Bengal has neglected
its own heritage. Bengal has ignored its own vision which it had
once given to the whole of India and which, in turn, had given
to Bengal the leadership of India. I need not go into details.

You know what is happening in Bengal today. It is not only the perspective but also the personal character of its great men which is being questioned. As I read the various debates going on in the Bengali press, in Bengali novels and other writings, I am really pained. How can things go down to such a low level in a land which had once raised India to such great heights?

What was that national vision which these great men gave us and which inspired India to launch such a great struggle for freedom? Remember the revolutionaries which India produced at that time. They were great men and women, those revolutionaries who mounted the gallows with the Gita in hand and with 'Vande Mataram' on their lips. They were not like the latter-day revolutionaries. I can say with a full sense of responsibility that quite a few of the latter-day revolutionaries sound like ordinary criminals. The earlier revolutionaries were of a different character because their vision was of a different character.

What was that vision? In a way, it was nothing new. It was only a restatement in modern language, in a modern setting, of the ancient Vedic vision as unfolded in the Vedas, in the Upanishads, in the Jainagama, in the Tripitaka, in the Ramayana and the Mahabharata, in the Puranas, in the Dharmashastras, and in the latter-day poetry of saints and siddhas. We have had countless spokesmen of that vision throughout our history.

The first dimension of that vision was that India was the land of Sanatana Dharma. That was the first and foremost point of that vision. In fact, Sri Aurobindo had said in his Uttarpara Speech that India would rise with the rise of Sanatana Dharma, that India would sink if Sanatana Dharma sank, and that India would die if it were at all possible for Sanatana Dharma to die. This is not the occasion for me to talk about Sanatana Dharma. All I want to say is that Sanatana Dharma is a natural religion that is in harmony with the development of human nature, with the growth of human aspirations. . . . It is not a set of mechanical beliefs constructed by the outer mind of man and imposed upon its followers.

The second dimension of that vision was that of a vast and variegated culture. According to ädhära and adhikära, the various sections of our population, various segments of our society, various regions of our country, developed their own culture, developed their own art, developed their own literature. We have a vast literature—sacred, secular and scientific—which grew in different regions of this country, in different social and cultural surroundings. We have a lot of art and literature. But its spirit is the spirit of Sanatana Dharma. It is informed by Sanatana Dharma in all its details. That was the second dimension of that national vision.

The third dimension of that vision was that this great society, the society which we describe as Hindu society today, was reared on the basis of spirituality, on the basis of Sanatana Dharma, on the basis of a great culture created by Sanatana Dharma. The Varnashrama Dharma which has shaped this great society has been corrupted today into a single English phrase—the caste system, which everybody is busy accusing of all sorts of crime. But it was Varnashrama Dharma that created a complex social system that has survived till today with vitality and vigour. In spite of all vicissitudes of fortune, in spite of so many foreign invasions, throughout these countless ages, Varnashrama Dharma has been defended by all our great men in recent times. It was defended by Swami Dayananda, it was defended by Bankimchandra. It was defended by Vivekananda. It was defended by Mahatma Gandhi, by Madan Mohan Malaviya, by Lokamanya Tilak. All these great men have been unanimous that Varnashrama Dharma has saved Hindu society from destruction—the destruction which overtook so many societies outside India at the hands of Christianity, Islam and communism. That was the third dimension of that national vision.

The fourth dimension of that national vision was that this great society, this Hindu society, had a history of its own—a history of how this society arose, how it developed, how it created a spirituality which was akin to the spirituality of many ancient nations like Greece, Rome, China, Egypt, Persia. We were told that the history of India was the history of Hindu society, of Hindu culture, of Hindu spirituality, that it was the history of the Hindu nation and not the history of foreign invaders as we are being taught today.

And the last dimension which these great men stressed, which they affirmed again and again, was that this land of Bharatavarsha was one indivisible whole; that it was the cradle of Hindu society, of Hindu culture, of Hindu spirituality, that it was the homeland of the Hindu nation; and that other communities were welcome to live in this land provided they came to terms with Hindu society and Hindu culture. They did not think in terms of Afghanistan, Pakistan, Hindustan and Bangladesh. Today Bharatavarsha stands divided into several units which are not only politically but also culturally hostile to each other and we seem to have become reconciled to that division. But the vision that was given to us by our great men was that of Bharatavarsha as an indivisible whole, not only geographically but also culturally. That vision rose before us during the Swadeshi Movement, in the first decade of this century.

There were some other visions also, struggling for supremacy at the same time. Those other visions had an advantage on their side because of the educational system provided by the British, imposed on us by the British. This was the same educational system which we have in this country today. This educational system has been sponsoring and spreading those other visions of India.

There was the vision of Islamic imperialism. It said that India like pre-Islamic Arabia and pre-Islamic Persia and like so many other ancient lands conquered by Islam, was a land of darkness. It said that India had to be brought to the 'light' of Islam, converted into a dar al-Islam.

Later on, another vision was provided by Christian imperialism. It also said that India was a land of darkness, of heathenism, of paganism, of unbelievers. It said that the 'light' of Christianity had to be brought to India, that India had to be converted into a land of Christ.

A third vision came to us in the shape of the White man's burden. This vision shared somethings of the crusading zeal of Islamic and Christian imperialism. But it spoke in the language of rationalism and humanism. It spoke in an enlightened language. It said that India was a land of poor, illiterate, downtrodden, exploited and emasculated human beings who had to be given bread, who had to be educated, who had to be given health, who had to be given some sort of self-confidence by the British mentors or by Western culture imported from this foreign country or that.

Later still, another imperialist vision came from the West in the shape of communism. This vision said that India was a colonial and semi-colonial society, divided into exploiting and exploited classes, into the oppressors and the oppressed, and that it was the duty of the Communist Party to liberate India from all this sloth and exploitation, this deadening of the forces of production. This was the fourth imperialist vision of India.

The cumulative effect of all these imperialist visions combining together has been rather serious, rather disastrous for us. Today the vision that prevails, particularly amongst our ruling classes, amongst the Hindu intellectuals, amongst the Hindu elite, is quite the opposite of the national vision provided by the Swadeshi Movement, provided by our own great men.

Today we are told that Bharatavarsha is not one indivisible whole, that it is not one country. We are told that India is a subcontinent and that its division that has taken place into Afghanistan, Pakistan, Hindustan and Bangladesh is the natural outcome of various nationalities struggling for their own pieces of homeland. As a result, India can no more be claimed as its own homeland by any particular society, least of all by the Hindu society.

Then we are told that the history of this subcontinent is not the history of Hindu society, of the Hindu nation. This country is now regarded as some sort of a dharmashālā into which all sorts of invaders have poured in from the West and the East and other directions. The history of India has become the history of foreign invaders. So when you look at the teaching of history in our universities, colleges and schools, you find that there is an ancient Hindu period, you find that there is a medieval Muslim period, and you find that there is a modern British period. Now we are also informed of a contemporary period, the post-Independence period, with its own architect and father.

Next we are told that Indian society is not a homogeneous society. India, we are told, is multi-racial, multinational, multi-linguistic and multi many other things. We are also told that Indian culture is not Hindu culture, that it is a composite culture made out of many cultures, indigenous and imported. It makes me laugh sometimes. When we talk of Indian music, we find that it is Hindu music. When we talk of Indian sculpture, we find that it is Hindu sculpture. When we talk of Indian architecture, we find that it is Hindu architecture except for a few minor details added by foreign invaders. Indian literature, almost ninety-nine per cent of it, is Hindu literature. All this is Hindu heritage. It was the Hindus who created it, it is the Hindus who have sustained it. It is the Hindus who are still adding to it, elaborating it and expanding it. Yet, when it is pointed out that the culture of this country is Hindu culture and that the history of this culture is Hindu history, everyone seems to get annoyed. People who talk of Hindu culture are accused of being communalists.

But the strangest thing that has happened is that the religion of this country is no more Sanatana Dharma. Sanatana Dharma is now supposed to be some sort of a primitive superstition. Some people take up Vedanta and talk a lot about it. Some others take up the Gita and talk about the Gita. Some others take up and talk about other aspects of Sanatana Dharma, Yoga and so on. They acquire name and fame, write books and give lectures. But when it is pointed out that it was Sanatana Dharma which created all this spirituality, all this philosophy, all these laws, all this culture, not many people are prepared to accept it. A new religion has taken the place of Sanatana Dharma. This new religion is secularism.

We are now told that it will be through secularism that India will become a united nation, that there will be national integration on the basis of secularism. So we have a National Integration Council. . . . We are now required to accept Islam as an Indian religion, as a religion which must have as much pride of place in India as her own Sanatana Dharma. The logic has not yet been extended to the so-called British period of our history. But tomorrow there may be voices which demand that the British should not be regarded as invaders and injurers because, after all, they gave us English education, English literature, hospitals, schools, colleges, roads and all sorts of modern paraphernalia.

This is the state of things that is now prevailing in this country. The national vision which had arisen during the Swadeshi Movement, which had mobilized the masses in India and which had taken her ahead in the fight for freedom, is now more or less completely eclipsed. It is not so much eclipsed elsewhere in India as in Bengal or in Kerala or in certain other parts where English education has spread faster than in other places. This is the situation that obtains today.

Let us take secularism. It is a concept which we have imported from modern Europe. The Christian Church had created a lot of bloodshed in Europe, 100 years' wars and 200 years' wars. A dark night had descended over Europe with the coming of Christianity. Humanism, rationalism, universalism and all other values which are known as human values had been buried under the dead weight of Christianity. Some people in Europe started questioning the character of Christianity, particularly the stranglehold of the Church over the state. There was a revival of humanism, rationalism and universalism due to Europe's contact with India, China and some other great ancient civilizations.

There was a struggle against the Christian church and over a period of time the state was freed from its stranglehold. It was this struggle which gave birth to the concept of secularism in Europe. . . . This is still a very healthy concept for countries suffering under the yoke of Islam.

But in India today people prescribe secularism to Hindu society which has never known any religious conflicts, which has never known any religious strife. Recently I was travelling in the Far East and met some Buddhist monks from China. I said to them, 'Buddhism came to China from outside. But you had ancient religions of your own. You had Confucianism. You had Taoism. Did Buddhism come in conflict with Confucianism, or Taoism?' They said: 'No, never.' There was not a single instance of conflict because Confucianism also came from the same deepest source of the Spirit, because Taoism also came from the same source from which Sanatana Dharma springs, from which Jainism springs, from which Vaishnavism springs. All these are different names of the same spiritual message for mankind. I also talked to some people in Japan in order to find out if Buddhism came in conflict with Shintoism which is their ancient religion. They also said, no, the two religions never came into conflict. The two religions are coexisting in mutual harmony till today. I met a taxi driver who was quite an intelligent man. He said: 'I am both a Shintoist and a Buddhist.' So also in ancient Greece, in ancient Rome, in the whole ancient world, all over Asia and Europe. The world had never known any religious wars before the rise of Christianity.

Religious wars started with the coming of Christianity. They became very, very bloody with the rise of Islam. But Europe had a wave of humanism, rationalism and universalism which broke the stranglehold of Christianity over the state. That is how the concept of secularism arose. As I have said, it was a very healthy concept in the context of Europe. As a result of it, European society has travelled so far, European science has developed, European technology has developed and the social welfare system for the people of Europe has improved. All these things have come out of the concept of secularism.

Hindu society, however, has always been a naturally secular society. Hindu society has never known any theocratic state. You take for instance any Hindu king. You will find a bigot who favoured this or that sect. Personally he may have belonged to Buddhism or Jainism or Vaishnavism or any other sect. But in his court, in his kingdom, all religions were equally welcome, all religions were equally patronized. In fact it was the religious people who patronized the king rather being patronized by him. It was not like the Archbishop of Canterbury who has to wait on the king of England, the king being Defender of the Faith. The Hindu king had to go to rishis, munis and sadhus in order to seek their advice.

It is in such a land, in such a society that the concept of secularism has been imported from Europe. Not only that. The concept of secularism has also been turned against Hindu society. Today you know what secularism means. Whenever the word 'secularism' is uttered, you can sense an anti-Hindu animus. Secularism in India today means denunciation of Hindu society, denunciation of Hindu culture, denunciation of Hindu history. It means denunciation of everything which is Hindu. The word 'Hindu' itself has become a dirty word. In the language of India's secularism, Muslims are a minority, Christians are a minority. But the Hindus are a 'brute' majority. This is the religion of secularism which is replacing Sanatana Dharma. This is the new vision which has replaced the vision of Sanatana Dharma, the vision of a society and a culture and a history and other things based on Sanatana Dharma.

The excesses of this secularism, its anti-Hindu animus, have gradually led to a widespread feeling among the Hindus that there is something seriously wrong somewhere. The so-called minorities have become more and more aggressive under the protection of this secularism. . . . It is due to all these circumstances, due to this seeing through secularism, due to a renewed aggression from the old imperialist forces which were lying dormant for some time, that Hindu society has experienced some sort of reawakening, some sort of resurgence. We find that Vishwa Hindu Parishad is playing a leading role in consolidating this resurgence, in giving leadership to this resurgence. But I feel that this effort will not get completed, will not acquire a strong core unless the national vision of the Swadeshi Movement days is recovered, resurrected, reaffirmed and reinterpreted in the new situation. This is what I am trying to do today in my own small measure.

The first thing we have to do to reassert the national vision, is to proclaim to the whole world, without any fear or hesitation, that this ancient land, this Bharatavarsha is one indivisible whole and that we do not recognize its partition into Afghanistan, Pakistan, Hindustan and Bangladesh. It has often happened in the history of many countries that certain imperialist forces have encroached upon them and have run away with some parts of their lands. We must be very clear in our minds that what are known as Afghanistan, Pakistan and Bangladesh today are parts of the Hindu homeland and that we are going to reclaim them. We should say it fearlessly that the consolidation of Islamic imperialism, a thousand years of Islamic aggression against India, in the shape of Afghanistan, Pakistan and Bangladesh is not going to be tolerated, that sooner or later we shall undo this division of the motherland, and that we shall reclaim our brethren who have been alienated from us by Islamic imperialism.

Some of our people are now known as Muslims, some are known as Christians. All these are our own people. We have nothing against them. But we shall not tolerate imperialism surviving in this country in the form of Islam or in the form of Christianity. . . .

The second thing which we should say very clearly and fearlessly, is that the history of India is the history of Hindu society, of the Hindu nation, and that we do not recognize any Muslim or British of this history. We do not recognize any age of

Mamluks or Khiljis or Tughlaqs or Lodis or Mughals. We shall instead read our history in terms of our own heroes, in terms of an age of Prithviraj Chauhan, an age of Rana Sanga, an age of Krishnadevaraya, an age of Rana Pratap, an age of Shivaji, and so on. We shall not concede that there ever was a Muslim Empire in India. We shall instead interpret that period as a long-drawn-out war of national resistance, of national liberation, in which Islamic imperialism was worsted. Similarly, we shall not recognize any British viceroys or governors-general except as imperialist intruders. The imperialist versions of Indian history which are being taught at present in our schools and colleges have to go.

Take the case of the so-called Muslim empire in India. Within a few years of its prophet's death, Islam had conquered large chunks of Asia and Africa. But it took it seventy long years to put its first step in India, another 500 years to reach Delhi, and a few hundred years more to reach south India. Soon after, Islamic imperialism started retreating before a national struggle for liberation. It started folding up with the rise of Shivaji. So what we had was a long-drawn-out war, a prolonged national struggle against Islamic imperialism. This war, this national struggle should not be described as the Muslim conquest of India or as the Muslim period of Indian history.

The third thing which we have to proclaim in order to reaffirm the national vision, is that the national culture of India is Hindu culture, the culture of Sanatana Dharma. It is a vast and variegated culture. But at the same time, it is a culture which is natural to mankind. There is nothing artificial about this culture, nothing which has been constructed by the outer mind of man, nothing which has been imposed by force as is the case with the cultures of Christianity and Islam and communism. Any culture which is not prepared to come to terms with Hindu culture, the culture of Sanatana Dharma, has to go. There is no place for any alien culture to flourish on the soil of India in the name of 'minority rights'.

The fourth thing which we have to proclaim, is that Hindu society is the national society in India. This is a vast society which has permitted endless expressions of human nature, which has sanctioned all types of social traditions. Today we are accused of neglecting our so-called tribals. This is an accusation which is made against us very often. But when you read Hindu history, you find that we never interfered with the lifestyle of any segment of our society. We wrote forty Dharmashastras in order to accommodate the customs and traditions and institutions of various regions and communities. Then we wrote 4000 commentaries on the Dharmashastras adapting them to different jātis, to different varnas, to different regions. So Hindu society is a vast and complex society. Any community which is not prepared to come to terms with Hindu society has no place in India any more. We shall not permit such alien communities to call themselves minorities and claim special rights and privileges.

Finally, we have to proclaim that the only religion which Hindu society recognizes, which has a place in Bharatavarsha, is the natural spirituality of Sanatana Dharma. It is a religion which accommodates all types of human aspirations including atheism, agnosticism, materialism. What it cannot accommodate is force and fraud practised in the name of religion. Any religion which wants to flourish in India has to come to terms with the spirituality of Sanatana Dharma. . . .

This, then, is the emerging national vision. The whole of Bharatavarsha is the Hindu homeland. The history of Bharatavarsha is the history of Hindu society. The national culture of Bharatavarsha is Hindu culture. And the national religion of India is Sanatana Dharma. This is the national vision which we have to reaffirm.

Part III
Fault Lines

19

Presidential Address[*]

Ramananda Chatterjee

The twelfth session of the All-India Hindu Mahasabha commenced at Surat on the 30th March at 5 in the afternoon amidst scenes of great enthusiasm in the big pandal on the Surat-Aswanikumar Road near the railway station. The pandal was decorated with photos of Shivaji, Pratap Singh, Lala Lajpat Rai, Dr. Rabindranath Tagore, Swami Shradhananda and Lokamanya Balgangadhar Tilak.

Prominent among those present were Dr. Moonji, Dr. Choitram, Swami Chiddananda, Pandit Radhakunt Malaviya. Bhai Paramanand, Dr. Suniti Chaterji, Mr. Padmaraj Jain and Dr. Sawarkar. Among the Gujrat leaders present were Dr. M.K. Dixit, Rao Bahadur Bhimbhai Naik, Rao Saheb Dadubhai and Mr. Waman Mukadam, members of the Bombay Council.

After the singing of the national song, Dr N.M. Raeji read his welcome address. Bhai Paramanand then formerly proposed Mr. Ramananda Chatterjee to the chair, describing him as a man of international fame. He also observed that Mr. Chatterjee was one of the three luminaries of Bengal, the other two being Dr. Rabindranath Tagore and Sir J.C. Bose. The proposal, after

---

[*] Extracted from *The Indian Annual Register 1929*, Volume 1, edited by N.N. Mitra, Gyan Publishing House, New Delhi, n.d., pp. 353–58.

being seconded by leading men from different provinces, was adopted, and Mr. Chatterjee took the chair.

Amidst deafening cheers, the President unfurled the Hindu flag all standing. The flag was of triangular shape in saffron colour, bearing the design of a sword and sun. The flag was then fixed in the centre of the rostrum.

The President then ascended the rostrum to deliver his address which he read for a short time, and then requested Dr. Moonji to read. The following is a detailed summary of his address:

Just as internationalists of an extreme type forget in their condemnation of nationalism that nationalism may be of two kinds, so nationalists forget that devotion to the welfare of the religious community to which one belongs may not necessarily deserve the name of communalism in an opprobrious sense. Nationalism is bad when it means 'My country, right or wrong', when it seeks to aggrandise one's own country at the expense of other countries. Nationalism has come to have a sinister significance because in Europe it has been generally of the predatory sort. But Indian nationalism is not of that character. It only wants the restoration of the birth right of Indians in India; it does not seek to deprive any foreign people of their rights in their countries. Similarly, the Hindu Mahasabha does not seek to have for Hindus any political, economic or civic rights or privileges to which they are not entitled by their numbers, educational and other qualifications, character, ability, public spirit and tax-paying capacity. And, in particular, the Hindu Mahasabha does not want for Hindus any fixed share of which it may indirectly leave an inequitable portion for others. It stands for open and fair competition, for an open door for talent irrespective of considerations of race, creed or complexion. It is one of its objects 'to promote good feelings between the Hindus and other communities in India and to act in a friendly way with them with a view to evolve a united and self-governing Indian nation'. Its other objects are concerned mainly with the internal affairs of the Hindu community. The promotion of the political interests and rights of the entire Hindu community is mentioned last. And it is added in a note that 'the Mahasabha shall not side or identify itself or interfere with or oppose any political party'. This leaves the members of the Mahasabha free in their individual capacity to join or not to join any political party.

'Political Activities—Surely Defensive.'

The history of the Mahasabha shows that its political activities have been purely of a defensive character. It has put in an appearance in the political arena only when in its opinion the political interests of the Hindus have been jeopardized. And, so far as my knowledge goes, it has not been as active in certain political matters as it could justifiably have been. Whether this has been due to forbearance or some other causes, I do not know.

Perhaps what has more than anything else made the Hindu Mahasabha unpopular with the bulk of Indian Mussalmans is its effort 'to preserve and increase the numerical strength of the Hindus' which is one of its declared objects. Non-Hindu communities in India, like the Mahomedan and the Christian, particularly the former, have increased vastly at the expense of the Hindus and the aborigines of India. Therefore, anything done to arrest this process cannot be looked upon with favour by the followers of those non-Indian faiths. Still more unpleasant must the reversal of the process be to them. But I do not see how one can logically and justly object to the Hindus doing what the others have been doing for centuries—particularly as the Hindus have not gone in for the accession to their ranks of non-Hindu woman abducted or confiscated and obliged to be converted, of men tempted to come over by the prospect of marriage, of persons induced to be converted by the prospect of economic advantage and of person forced to be converted by terrorism of any kind. The Hindu Mahasabha and Hindu missions connected with it, formally or informally, want reconversion and conversion only by fair, open and legitimate means.

Question of Conversion to Hinduism

Non-Hindus allege that Hinduism has never been a proselytizing faith, and that, therefore, conversion to Hinduism is a new departure and hence an aggressive move. Assuming that Hinduism has never been a proselytizing religion I do not see what spiritual, moral, rational or legal object there can be to Hindus adopting a new method to meet a new situation. Every individual and every group has an inherent right to take all legitimate steps for self-preservation and maximum usefulness. 'New occasions teach new duties' and 'new times demand new measures'. That a new situation has arisen is quite plain. In most provinces of India the Hindus form a smaller percentage or the population than they did fifty years ago, the percentage showing a decline of each successive census. This is true also of India as a whole. The main cause of these decreases is not conversion to non-Hindu faiths. But whatever the causes and the extent of their responsibility for these decreases, the Hindus must try to combat all of them by all fair and scientific means. It is to be noted that in some other areas conversion is a cause of considerable decrease.

I have hitherto taken it for granted that Hindus had not until recently admitted non-Hindus into their ranks. This, however, is not a historical fact. The Hindu methods of proselytism may have been different from the methods of non-Hindu religions. But from time immemorial, Hinduisation has gone on continually. According to the definition of the Hindu Mahasabha, Buddhists are also Hindus. Vincent A. Smith says that both Buddhism and Jainism may be regarded as offshoots of Hinduism. In the opinion of Prof. Rays Davids, the Buddha was the greatest and wisest and best of Hindus. Weber holds that Buddhism may be regarded as a reformed phase of Hindu religious and ethical activity. Now, it is well-known that Buddhism was the earliest and foremost of proselytizing religion both in and outside India. The Hindu Mahasabha considers Sikhism also to be a form of Hinduism, which originated some centuries ago. It also has initiated both Hindus and non-Hindus into its faith. I need not refer to the activities of the modern Brahmo and Arya Samaj movements.

Indianisation succeeded to such a great extent in many an Asiatic land, because India's spiritual and cultural ambassadors and workers there were not the sappers and miners, the scouts, the spies, or the agents, abettors and camp follower of imperialists and exploiters. Love of humanity and of the truth impelled them to cross snow-capped mountains, the parched and burning sands of deserts and the storm-swept waves of the ocean. Many lost their lives in the pursuit of humane enterprise. Unlike many European Christian nations, the ancient Hindus neither enslaved nor exterminated any races in foreign lands less civilized than themselves. Unlike the Muslim Arabs and the Christian Spaniards, English, Americans and others, the ancient Hindus were never slave-catchers and slave-traders. And here I must beg leave to remind our very orthodox touch-me-notists, that whatever the origin of the wicked and accursed custom of untouchability may be in India itself, in the India-civilized Indian Archipelago and further India, our modern Indian travellers have not found any trace of the natives there having been assigned the inferior social position of the Negroes in America and South Africa or of the untouchables in some parts of India. Let us all learn from our ancient colonizing ancestors the lesson that we became strong, immortal and manlike not by despising and depressing the lowly but by loving and respecting them and uplifting them to our own level—nay, by helping them to rise higher even than ourselves. The true Brahman is he who is the selfless helper and servant of all, not the self-righteous conceited person who places his feet on the heads of others.

Elevation of Depressed Classes

Like the work of conversion and reconversion there are some other items in the programme of Hindu Sabhas and Missions which have brought upon them the charge of communalism and made them unpopular with Christian and Muslim propagandists. One such item is the amelioration and improvement of the condition of the so-called low castes of the Hindu community and of the aborigines of India. It is from these classes that the Christians and Muslims have got the largest number of their converts. So if the 'lower' classes of the Hindus are raised in the social scale and their economic condition is improved, and if the aborigines are similarly uplifted by the Hindus, there would not be as much scope for their conversion to Christianity and Islam as hitherto. But Hindus cannot leave the field entirely to non-Hindus. Let me say here once for all that, as Hindus are responsible and thinking beings who always can and ought to judge and act for themselves as circumstances demand, they are entitled for their own preservation and welfare to take whatever legitimate steps they think fit, even if in the scriptures, tradition or history of themselves or others there be no precedents for such steps. But this uplift work is not new to Hindus. It is, no doubt, our shame that there are still so may Hindus and so many indigenes suffering from dire poverty, ignorance, superstition and social indignity. Without vain regret for the past, let us gird up our loins and do our utmost for these sisters and brethren of ours, not in the spirit of condescending patrons and benefactors, but in that of devoted and selfless fraternal service and in that of repayment of the debt we owe them. For it is they who feed us, house us, clothe us, help us in locomotion, and, as sweepers and scavengers, keep our houses, villages and towns clean and sweet and healthy.

Our sisters and brethren, the so-called low-caste Hindus are human beings just like ourselves. It would be wicked and shameful to treat them as if they were not. It is suicidal to give them better social recognition when they are converted to some non-Hindu faith than when they remain Hindus.

Permanent and hereditary untouchability is not only wicked and shameful, but it is also an absurdity. Those who believe in untouchability not only sort of tacitly and indirectly give greater rights to various lower animals, including plague-carrying rats, than to human beings. Those who are holy and pure ought to be able to raise and purify those who are not, by their company and contact. The sun purifies every impure thing it shines upon, its rays and itself are not made impure thereby. Can noisome fogs and mists obliterate the sun? God is the purifier of all. Nobody can make Him or any symbol of His impure by his approach or touch.

In order to improve the condition of the depressed classes educational facilities, both general and vocational, should be provided for them to an adequate extent. The Hindu Mahasabha itself ought to take action in this direction, as well as get pressure to be brought to bear on the Government and local bodies for them to take such action. Social status cannot be improved without economic improvement. The provision of land and the supply of raw materials for home industries are suggested as some of the means to be adopted in addition to vocational education.

I have been obliged to refer to some of my fellow countrymen as the depressed classes. But the sooner the use of this expression is given up in the Census and other Government reports, and by us and these classes themselves, the better. When under the necessity doing so, we occasionally refer to the example of Japan as an oriental country which is politically free, independent and progressive. But we should at the same time always bear in mind that the Japanese have abolished untouchability, and their untouchables the *henin* or eta, are no longer outcasts but have in actual practice the same social and political rights as others. The higher and privileged classes of Samurai and others have of their own accord given up their special privileges; so that there is at present no caste feeling in Japan, and no Japanese need suffer from the inferiority complex. Everyone there can walk erect and hold his head high.

I have said that the sooner the expression 'depressed classes' falls into disuse the better. Another thing to be guarded against is the exaggeration of their number. It is generally thought and said by our critics that these people number six or more than six crores. But it has been recently admitted officially that the number is somewhere near three crores; possibly it is still less. I long for the day when we shall all be known only as Hindus, all in the enjoyment of equal social dignity.

The Hindu Mahasabha should give hope to the lowest of the low in the Hindu community, taking off the incubus of social indignities and disabilities from their backs. Hope deferred maketh the heart sick. It will not, therefore, do to tell them that their lot may improve at their next birth. Just as we, politically-minded Indians, want full political freedom during our own lifetime, so do they want social freedom and respectability during theirs. If they lose hope as Hindus, they will either go over to Islam or Christianity or die out.

In Hinduising the Aborigines regard should be had to the conservation of their play-instinct and their joy and zest in life, while reforming degrading customs and amusements, if any.

Our Marriage Customs

The evil custom of 'bride-price' prevents many persons in parts of the country from marrying at all and others from marrying while they are young. This leads to decline in the population of some castes and to other evils. Similarly, the custom of 'bridegroom price' is a great evil. When our young men realize how mean, ungentlemanly and dishonourable it is to demand money for marrying a girl and when they want to be true lovers and real gentlemen then this disgraceful system will disappear.

The introduction of inter-subcaste and inter-caste marriages will widen the field of choice or brides and bridegrooms. This will be one remedy for 'enforced' celibacy, late marriages and marriages of elderly bridegrooms with brides very much younger than themselves all of which go against due continuance and propagation of species.

The amelioration of the condition of Hindu women is another object of the Hindu Mahasabha. Hindu idealism relating to woman is unsurpassed in the world. But many of our customs fall so short of this idealism as to make us ashamed. In order that our women may be what according to our ideal they ought to be, there should be physical culture (including the arts of self-defence) moral training and heart culture and intellectual culture and training in domestic science for all our girls and young women. In order that there may be ample time for the education of girls, child marriage and premature motherhood should be put a stop to. I am glad that the 7th session of the Hindu Mahasabha under the presidentship of Pandit Madan Mohan Malaviya 'enjoined upon all Hindus not to marry their girls, before the age of sixteen' which leaves it optional to keep unmarried a few years longer if necessary. Child marriage and premature motherhood is injurious not only to the girls but also to their progeny and decreases the fecundity of the mothers.

Need for Military Training

The encroachments on Hindu rights are many. I will not dwell on them in detail. But as the Hindus along with some others have been deprived of the right and duty of defending the country, I will refer to it in particular. With the expansion of the British Empire and the gradual evolution of British imperialistic policy in India, recruitment for the sepoy army has gradually receded from province after province in British India with the growth of political self-consciousness there and, sepoys are now for the most part recruited from some Indian States, from trans-frontier Muslim territory and from Nepal. The result is that the descendants of those who at one time fought valiantly against or for the British are practically declared unfit for self-defence. British India is thoroughly emasculated, and as Hindus outnumber other communities, they are the greatest sufferers. Proportionately there are more Muslims than Hindus in the Army. The division of the people into martial and unwarlike is unscientific, unhistorical and based on falsehood. No such classification exists in any other civilised country. There should be recruitment from all provinces and religious communities, as far as practicable. As an aid to the realization of this ideal, there should be gymnasia and sporting clubs all over the country. Both our girls and boys should be taught the arts of armed and unarmed, individual and collective self-defence. They should be placed above the fear of getting wounded and of bleeding. The Hindu Mahasabha should give the greatest possible attention to this matter. I lay stress on this subject not for any aggressive purpose, but in order that we may get rid of softness caused by over-civilization and may be able to acquire the strength, courage and secure position which alone entitle and enable men to preach and practise ahimsa and maitri which constitute India's message to the world.

With regard to our political interests and rights I shall say only this in brief that as in the past, so at present and in the future, the Hindus will not shrink from facing all dangers and making all the sacrifices necessary for winning freedom *for all communities*. In order to obtain the co-operation of the other communities, the Hindu community will honourably stand by as it has hitherto stood by the Hindu-Muslim agreements arrived at as recorded in the Nehru Committee's reports, provided there is no going back from those agreements on the part of others. But if there be such going back, and if the Mussalmans persist in opposing the Nehru Report as passed by the All Parties Convention at Calcutta, the Hindus on their part will be fully justified in going back to their original national, logical and just position that there is to be no reservation of seats for any community anywhere and that the electorates for all legislatures are to be everywhere joint and mixed.

There can be no greater confession of want of confidence in the capacity of the Muslim community than for any of them to demand any reservation of a proportionate number of seats even where they are in a majority. Such a demand practically means that in their opinion there must be perpetual Moslem Raj in the Moslem-majority provinces. On the other hand, our great departed leader Lala Lajpat Rai who was also a great national leader has declared it 'as a fact that the bulk of the Hindus do not want a Hindu Raj. What the latter are striving after is a National Government founded on justice to all communities, all classes and all interests.' 'In my judgment,' he said, 'the cry of a Hindu Raj or a Muslim Raj is purely mischievous and ought to be discouraged.'

I respectfully request all to always bear in mind some facts relating to the origin and continuance of political power. The British people, nay the entire White people inhabiting the British Empire, are a minority; whereas the Indian people even the Hindu community by itself, form the majority. Yet the British people are masters of the situation. They did not become masters by virtue of any pact or compromise. When the Moslems became master of India, that was not by the force of any agreement. Power is gained or lost, whether there be or be not any verbal or written guarantees, pacts and things of that description, though they have their value.

People's fates are determined by their possession or lack of character, strength, ability, intellectual calibre, efficiency, firm resolve and sacrifice for the cause of the whole people. Let not Hindus, therefore, be under any delusion that their mere numerical strength will be a safeguard against loss of rights and power in the future, any more than it has been in the past. Let not Moslems, too, be under any delusion that reservation of seats for them, both where they are in minority and in the majority, will secure for them a perpetual lease of powers and rights any more than the possession of supreme political power in the past in India and elsewhere has prevented their downfall. The present generation of neither Hindus nor Moslems have the right or the power to make any artificial, unjust and illogical agreements binding on their descendants. Still less can the present or any other generation make such agreement binding on the Power that rules the destinies of nations.

In addition to communal strife, conflicts between labour and capital and between cultivators and landholders have begun to loom large on the horizon. It is necessary in highest interests of the Hindu community and of all other communities that the points at issue between the parties should be settled by mutual consultation and agreement. Nay, these points should not arise at all. There are Hindus among labourers and peasants and their leaders and among capitalists and landholders. I appeal to them all not to take to the war-path in Occidental fashion, not at least till the fullest trial has been given to methods of arbitration and conciliation.

In all climes and ages givers have been richer than receivers. The teacher, the man who has to impart spiritual, moral or intellectual truth, must be superior in his possessions to the man who acquires knowledge for himself alone. Hence for India to be rich in the possession of inward treasure, her sons and daughters must be in a position to give. They must not be mere learners and borrowers. Let them again prepare themselves to take up their ancient roles. A few have already in modern times become world teachers. This is the way to promote our religious, moral and intellectual interests.

But in order to give, one must also receive. He alone can give who has life. Life connotes adaptation to environment, assimilation of that which is good and elimination of that which is injurious.

Second Day—31st March 1929

To-day's sitting of the Mahasabha commenced at 9 in the morning. Mr. W.S. Mukadam, Secretary of the Mahasabha, read messages received from various parts of India, including those from Mr. N.C. Kelkar and Mr. M.S. Aney. Non-controversial resolutions passed last night in the subjects committee were taken up. The following are the text or the resolutions:

1. Tribute to Lalaji

The Mahasabha expressed profound sorrow at the death of Lala Lajpat Rai, ex-President of the Hindu Mahasabha, a patriot and statesman, and condemned the assault of the police on Lalaji and other Punjab leaders, as also the action of the Punjab Government and the Government of India in not accepting the popular demand for an open and independent inquiry. The resolution stated that the elected Indian members of the Punjab Council had forfeited the confidence of the people by turning down that resolution. The resolution further approved wholeheartedly the proposal for raising an All-India Hindu Mahasabha Memorial to Lalaji in the shape of a society of life workers called the Servants of Hindu Society.

2. Godhra Riots

The second resolution expressed abhorrence at the murder of Mr. Purshottam by Moslem ruffians at Godhra and condemned the atrocious act and offered sympathy to the bereaved family and called upon the Hindus, particularly of Gujarat, to perpetuate his memory.

3. Hindu Sangathan

The Hindu Mahasabha calls upon every Hindu to devote himself heart and soul to the sacred work of Hindu Sangathan and to organise Hindu Sabhas in every village and town with a view to carry out the objects and resolutions of the Hindu Mahasabha. The Mahasabha expects every Provincial Hindu Sabha and all Hindu leaders to establish Hindu Sabhas during this year in places where they do not exist at present.

4. Shuddhi
The Hindu Mahasabha calls upon Hindus, irrespective of whatever sects of Hinduism they may belong to, to give their wholehearted support to the movement of Shuddhi and to offer every facilities to those willing to be converted or reconverted to enter the Hindu fold or for the enjoyment of the rights and privileges of the caste, they may have previously belonged to.

5. Removal of Untouchability
This Hindu Mahasabha declares that the so-called untouchables have equal rights with other Hindus to study in public schools, to take water from public wells and other sources of drinking water, to sit with others in public meetings and to walk on public roads. The Mahasabha calls upon all Hindus to remove such restraints as may be existing anywhere at present in the way of the so-called untouchable Hindus exercising these rights.

This Mahasabha declares that the so-called untouchables are fully entitled to have Dev Darshan and this Hindu Mahasabha calls upon all Hindus in general and all Hindu Sabhas in particular to arrange for the provision of the same facilities for Dev Darshan to them as are enjoyed at present by other Hindus.

This Mahasabha calls upon Purohits (Priests), barbers and washermen to offer their services to the so-called untouchables also as they do to other Hindus.

This Mahasabha is of opinion that every Hindu, to whatever caste he may belong, has equal social and political rights.

This Mahasabha looks upon the practice of appointing the representatives of the depressed classes by nomination by the Government to the local bodies, provincial Councils and the Assembly as most harmful and injurious to the true interests of the country and the self-respect of those classes and considers that this practice will become a source of creating a great gulf in the near future between other Hindus and the so-called untouchable. In the opinion of the Mahasabha, the right course to compel the Government to put a stop to this practice is to set up and back proper candidates belonging to the so-called untouchable classes to the elected bodies named above for election.

6. Physical training for Hindus

(a) The Hindu Mahasabha calls upon the Hindus to establish Akharas and Gymnasiums for imparting physical training, military drill and rifle practice to Hindu youths and for popularising and organising indigenous games with the object of arresting the progressive decay of the Hindu youths, and

(b) In the opinion of the Hindu Mahasabha the time has arrived for the organisation of the Hindu youth movement carrying on the work of Hindu Sangathan in an organised manner so as to prepare the Hindus to take their full share in the struggle for Swaraj.

The Mahasabha at this stage adjourned till the evening. When the Sabha re-assembled at six in the evening, Dr. B.S. Moonji moved the following resolution regarding the Nehru Report:

7. Future Constitution of the Government of India

That the Hindu Mahasabha has consistently and all along been of the opinion that communalism, in no shape or form, should be introduced in the political administration of the country, either in the matter of representation in the Legislatures or in any of the other elective bodies or in the services. Notwithstanding this, however, in order to bring about an agreement between Hindus and Moslems, the Hindu Mahasabha might have favourably considered the recommendation in respect of the Moslem demands of the Report of the Nehru Committee as amended and adopted by the All-Parties Convention: but as Moslem opinion, as represented in All-India Moslem Conference held at Delhi during the Christmas week, has rejected that Report, the Hindu Mahasabha, reiterating its original essentially nationalistic position, calls upon all Hindus to work for and support the

Constitution based on principles which were propounded by the last Jubbulpore Session of the Hindu Mahasabha, and are restated as below in a slightly amended form to suit the present circumstances:

1. (a) That there shall be uniformity of franchise for all communities in each province; (b) that elections to all elective bodies shall be by mixed electorate; (c) that there shall be no reservation of seats on communal considerations in any of the elective bodies and educational institutions; (d) the basis of representation of different communities such as, voting strength or taxation, shall be uniform. There shall be no communal representation in the public services, which must be open to all communities on the basis of merit and competency ascertained through open competitive tests. Redistribution of provinces in India if and when necessary, shall be made on their merits in the light of principles capable of general application with due regard to administrative, financial, strategic and similar other considerations; but no new province shall be created with the object of giving a majority therein to any particular community.

2. That in the case of provinces like the N.W.F. Province, Baluchistan and the scheduled districts, steps should at once be taken to secure, with as little delay as possible, the benefits of a regular system of administration, financial, judicial and executive.

3. That with regard to Moslem demands for separation of Sind from the Bombay Presidency and for the reservation of one-third of the elected seats in the Central Legislatures for Moslems, the Hindu Mahasabha resolves that in view of the fact that (a) the creation of new provinces primarily or solely with a view to increase the number of provinces in which a particular community shall be in a majority, is fraught with danger to the growth of sound nationalism in the country and will divide India into Hindu-India and

Moslem-India, (b) the redistribution of any province without the consent and agreement of the two major communities residing in that province is likely to increase the area of communal conflict and endanger the relations between the two major communities, not only in that province but throughout India and (c) the separation of Sind will not only be a costly financial proposition, but would also arrest its economic development and its educational advancement and deprive the people of Sind of many undeniable benefits of their association with the advanced people of other parts of Bombay Presidency in their economic as well as political developments, Sind should not be separated from the Bombay Presidency.

In view of the fact that the prime object of the Mahasabha is to exorcise communalism as rapidly as possible from the public administration of the country, the Hindu Mahasabha is unable to agree to the reservation of one-third of the elected seats in the Central Legislatures for Moslems.

Dr. Moonji, commending the resolution for the acceptance of the House explained the political situation existing at present and stated that it was considered till now that Mr. Jinnah had declared in favour of separate representation for Moslems and rejected the Nehru Report, the Hindu Mahasabha had to adopt this resolution. Bhai Paramanand seconded the resolution.

An Amendment Carried

Mr. Das Ram Bagai of Dera Ismail Khan moved an amendment to Clause 2 of the resolution relating to the N.W.F. Province which ran: 'The Reforms scheme in its entirety or otherwise will neither be workable nor beneficial in the N.W.F. Province owing to the peculiar conditions, geographical, financial and political, obtaining in this Province, and it is sure to be detrimental to good government, and highly prejudicial to all interests.'

Dr. Moonji, while admitting the difficulties experienced by the N.W.F. Province as mentioned by the mover of the amendment, expressed inability to accept the amendment.

When discussion was resumed on the amended resolution, Dr. Choitram (Sind), speaking on it, strongly opposed it. He contended that since the Nehru Report was accepted in December by the All-Parties Convention at Calcutta, representing not less than 56 organizations including the Hindu Mahasabha, they should not go back upon their previous decision.

Pandit Harischandra Bajpai also opposed the resolution, saying that it was impossible, at the present juncture, for the Hindu Mahasabha to withdraw the support, which it had, after full consideration, accorded to the Nehru Report. Further, the Congress had declared that if a constitution on the lines of the Nehru Report was not accepted by the bureaucracy by the end of the year, it would have to declare complete independence. It was on the strength of Hindu support that the attitude was taken up by the Congress, because most of the Mahomedans were opposed to it then. He considered it stultifying to the nation and their great leader Gandhiji, who had moved the resolution in the Calcutta Congress, to pass the present resolution.

Dr. Moonji replying declared that if Mr. Jinnah, at any moment, consented to accept the Nehru Constitution, he would also immediately be prepared to do so.

Pandit Devaratna Sharma, on behalf of the President, put the resolution to the vote of the House. Almost an equal number of hands were raised for and against. Disorderly scenes were witnessed for a few minutes, when the President had come to the rostrum and again took votes by a show of hands. The President declared the resolution carried by a majority. The declaration was followed by loud uproar and disorder which subsided after a few minutes.

8. The Music Question
The last resolution passed on this day related to the music question:

In view of the fact that participation in the conducting of musical procession along the King's highways and public thoroughfares is the inherent right of every citizen generally, and oftentimes the religious right of the Hindus particularly, and in view of the fact that this right has been recognized by the Privy Council, the highest Court of Justice in the British Empire and is the logical corollary of the principle of religious neutrality to which the government is pledged, this Mahasabha is pained at and emphatically condemns all attempts that are often made by the Executive authorities in several places for curtailing and circumscribing this right of the Hindus by the improper use of the powers given under the Criminal Procedure Code and the Police Act for meeting temporary exigencies of the situation. Under these circumstances, the Hindu Mahasabha considers it justifiable on the part of the Hindus to stand up boldly for their rights by all legitimate measures and calls upon the Hindus to insist upon their free and unmolested enjoyment of this right.

Third Day: 1st April 1929

Resolutions passed on this day included those expressing feelings of brotherly love and sympathy to all Hindu Brahmins or Buddhists residing outside India and to all others who in common with Indians derive their spiritual culture from the great mother culture of ancient India, and emphasising the necessity for reviving the ancient connections between India and Siam, Cambodia, Java, the Hindu island of Bali and China and Japan with a view to brotherly cooperation, for the benefit of the whole of humanity.

The Mahasabha authorized the Working Committee to do everything needful which it might think best in respect of the forthcoming elections to the legislatures.

The Mahasabha expressed wholehearted sympathy with the Hindus in Afghanistan in their sufferings and requested the Government to provide facilities for their removal to India.

Another resolution referred to the decisions of the Delhi and Patna sessions regarding protection of cows, Hindu orphans and widows. The Mahasabha enjoined on the Working Committee to give them full publicity.

The Mahasabha urged the Hindus to boycott foreign cloth and adopt the use of Khaddar.

The following resolution was moved from the chair and unanimously adopted:

In view of the fact that Moslems have been persistently agitating for larger and larger employment of Moslems in the public services of the country, the Hindu Mahasabha draws the attention of the Government to the fact that in the police service, particularly in many provinces even where they are in a minority and also in the military forces, Moslems have been recruited in large numbers quite out of proportion to their numerical strength or educational efficiency, and therefore requests the Government to take immediate steps to increase the recruitment of Hindus to such service.

The Mahasabha also resolved to make changes in the present constitution of the Working Committee, which is to consist of a President, a Working President, 2 Vice-Presidents, 2 Secretaries and 1 Treasurer and 11 members.

The President, Mr. Ramananda Chatterjee, in bringing the session to a close thanked the Reception Committee, the delegates and others, and expressed great satisfaction at the presence of a number of Gujarati ladies. He said: 'We must give not only passive assent, but active co-operation to make the resolutions passed during the session matters of actual history. It will not do for us to leave them printed on paper.' The singing of 'Vande Mataram' song by Surat ladies brought the proceedings to a close.

20

On Minority Rights[*]

Sardar Vallabhbhai Patel

Sir, I am sorry to see that so much time has been taken on this amendment which I thought was going to be withdrawn and on which there would not be much debate. So far as the Scheduled Castes are concerned, I do not think very much has to be said on this amendment, because I got a representation from a large majority of the Scheduled Castes representatives in this House, except one or two or three, that they were all against this amendment (*Hear, Hear*), and Mr. Nagappa knew about it. But Mr. Nagappa wanted to move his amendment to fulfil a promise or undertaking or at least to show his community that he was not purchased by the majority community! Well, he has done his job, but other people took him seriously and took a lot of time.

So far as the amendment moved by the representative of the Muslim League is concerned, I find that I was mistaken in my impression and if I had believed this, I would certainly not have agreed to any reservation at all. (*Hear, Hear.*) When I agreed to the reservation on the population basis, I thought that our friends of the Muslim League will see the reasonableness of our attitude and allow themselves to accommodate themselves to the changed conditions after the separation of the country.

---

[*] Extracted from *Constituent Assembly Debates: Official Report*, Volume V, Lok Sabha Secretariat, 2014, pp. 270–72.

But I now find them adopting the same methods which were adopted when the separate electorates were first introduced in this country, and in spite of ample sweetness in the language used there is a full dose of poison in the method adopted. (*Hear, Hear.*) Therefore, I regret to say that if I lose the affection of the younger brother, I am prepared to lose it because the method he wants to adopt would bring about his death. I would rather lose his affection and keep him alive. If this amendment is lost, we will lose the affection of the younger brother, but I prefer the younger brother to live so that he may see the wisdom of the attitude of the elder brother and he may still learn to have affection for the elder brother.

Now, this formula has a history behind it and those who are in the Congress will be able to remember that history. In Congress history this is known as the Mohammad Ali Formula. Since the introduction of separate electorates in this land there were two parties amongst the Muslims. One was the Nationalist Muslims or the Congress Muslims and the other the Muslim League members, or the representatives of the Muslim League. There was considerable tension on this question and at one time there was a practical majority against this joint electorate. But a stage was reached when, as was pointed out by the Mover of this amendment in Allahabad, a settlement was reached. Did we stand by that settlement? No. We now have got the division of the country. In order to prevent the separation of the country this formula was evolved by the nationalist Muslims, as a sort of half-way house, until the nation becomes one; we wished to drop it afterwards. But now the separation of the country is complete and you say, let us introduce, it again and have another separation. I do not understand this method of affection. Therefore, although I would not have liked to say anything on this motion, I think it is better that we know our minds perfectly each other, so that we can understand where we stand. If the process that was adopted, which resulted in the separation of the country, is to be repeated, then I say: Those who want that kind of thing have a place in Pakistan, not here. (*Applause.*) Here, we are building a nation and we are laying the foundations of One Nation, and those who choose to divide again and sow the seeds of disruption will have no place, no quarter, here, and I must say that plainly enough. (*Hear, Hear.*) Now, if you think that reservation necessarily means this clause as you have suggested, I am prepared to withdraw the reservation for your own benefit. If you agree to that, I am prepared, and I am sure no one in this House will be against the withdrawal of the reservation if that is a satisfaction to you. (*Cheers.*) You cannot have it both ways. Therefore, my friends, you must change your attitude, adapt yourself to the changed conditions. And don't pretend to say, 'Oh, our affection is very great for you.' We have seen your affection. Why talk of it? Let us forget the affection. Let us face the realities. Ask yourself whether you really want to stand here and cooperate with us or you want again to play disruptive tactics. Therefore when I appeal to you, I appeal to you to have a change in your heart, not a change in the tongue, because that won't pay here. Therefore, I still appeal to you: 'Friends, reconsider your attitude and withdraw your amendment.' Why go on saying, 'Oh, Muslims were not heard; Muslim amendment was not carried.' If that is going to pay you, you are much mistaken, and I know how it cost me to protect the Muslim minorities here under the present condition and in the present atmosphere. Therefore, I suggest that you don't forget that the days in which the agitation of the type you carried on are closed and we begin a new chapter. Therefore, I once more appeal to you to forget the past. Forget what has happened. You have got what you wanted. You have got a separate State and remember, you are the people who were responsible for it, and not those who remain in Pakistan. You led the agitation. You got it. What is it that you want now? I don't understand. In the majority Hindu provinces you, the minorities, you led the agitation. You got the partition and now again you tell me and ask me to say for the purpose of securing the affection of the younger brother that I must agree to the same thing again, to divide the country again in the divided part. For God's sake, understand that we have also got some sense. Let us understand the thing clearly. Therefore when I say we must forget the past, I say it sincerely. There will be no injustice done to you. There will be generosity towards you, but there must be reciprocity. If it is absent, then you take it from me that no soft words can conceal what is behind your words. Therefore, I plainly once more appeal to you strongly that let us forget and let us be one nation.

To the Scheduled Caste friends, I also appeal: 'Let us forget what Dr. Ambedkar or his group have done. Let us forget what you did. You have very nearly escaped partition of the country again on your lines. You have seen the result of separate electorates in Bombay, that when the greatest benefactor of your community came to Bombay to stay in bhangi quarters it was your people who tried to stone his quarters. What was it? It was again the result of this poison, and therefore I resist this only because I feel that the vast majority of the Hindu population wish you well. Without them where will you be? Therefore, secure their confidence and forget that you are a Scheduled Caste. I do not understand how Mr. Khandekar is a Scheduled Caste man. If he and I were to go outside India, nobody will find out whether he is a Scheduled Caste man or I am a Scheduled Caste man. There is no Scheduled Caste between us. So those representatives of the Scheduled Caste must know that the Scheduled Caste has to be effaced altogether from our society, and if it is to be effaced, those who have ceased to be untouchables and sit amongst us have to forget that they are untouchables or else if they carry this inferiority complex, they will not be able to serve their community. They will only be able to serve their community by feeling now that they are with us. They are no more Scheduled Castes and therefore they must change their manners and I appeal to them also to have no breach between them and the other group of Scheduled Castes. There are groups amongst themselves, but everyone tries according to his own light. We are now to begin again. So let us forget these sections and cross-sections and let us stand as one, and together.

21

On the Hindu Marriage Bill*

N.C. Chatterjee

Shri N. C. Chatterjee: The other day when we met to discuss the matter, I was making my submission to the hon. Minister of Parliament that in a social legislation of this revolutionary character, if we are to be consistent with the tenets of democracy, we should have a definite mandate from the people before we enact such a legislation of far-reaching consequences, making very radical alterations in the Hindu social organisation. I maintain that the way that you are proceeding is not in conformity with the principles of democratic Government. Such a radical legislation should easily wait for a year or so, because the elections are again coming, and it is quite clear that never did the Party in power or in office have the mandate of the nation on this subject. I would therefore ask them seriously to consider that these votaries of democracy should act according to genuine principles of democracy, and they should make this an issue in the next elections. If the Party in power gets the mandate, then it will be justified in proceeding with a measure of this character.

An Hon. Member: It has been a part of the election manifesto.

---

* Extracted from *Lok Sabha Debates 1955*, Volume IV, Part II, pp. 6835–56.

Shri N. C. Chatterjee: You, Sir, and all sections of the House, know that there is considerable feeling over this measure. A considerable section of our people is opposed to this measure, especially because its provisions are repugnant to the fundamental principles of the Hindu social system. Before you introduce this kind of a thing simply because you have a big majority or a sledgehammer majority, it is only fair and right to place this measure before the nation, educate our real masters, that is, the electors, get their definite verdict, and then proceed with the measure.

I am making four points today for the considerations of my hon. colleagues in this House. My first point is this. Is this kind of a communal legislation not repugnant to the spirit of our Constitution? Is it consistent with the Directive Principles which we have definitely and consciously embodied in our organic law, i.e., the Constitution of the Indian Republic? Article 44 in Part IV of the Constitution clearly says: 'The State shall endeavour to secure for the citizens a uniform civil code throughout the territory of India.'

My first question is: Are you not defying this mandate of the Constitution-makers? Are you securing a uniform civil code throughout the territory of India?

The cardinal principle on which our Constitution-makers worked was that there should be not diverse civil codes, not one law or one communal legislation for Hindus, another piece of communal legislation for Muslims, another piece of communal legislation for Christians and so on, but the Constitution-makers enjoined, and it is an injunction binding on Parliament, that this Parliament should secure for the citizens of India a uniform civil code throughout the territory of India. May I know why you are not acting according to the principles solemnly embodied in Article 44?

The Prime Minister has been good enough to remind us from time to time that the Directive Principles are of very great importance; they are not mere maxims to be kept in this Part IV without any meaning. He drew our attention to the opening Article 37 in Part IV when we were discussing the Constitution (Fourth Amendment) Bill the other day. He was emphasising the supreme importance of the Directive Principles. He said that the Fundamental Rights are there, but if the working of the Fundamental Rights comes into conflict with the clear Directive Principles then the Constitution should be amended and the Directive Principles must be given due recognition.

Now, are you giving due recognition to the clear Directive Principle in Article 44? What was the point in enacting Article 44? The point was that you shall not have diverse communities in this country. You do declare, you proclaim, and you take some pride in proclaiming that this is a secular State, and that you have got a secular Constitution. If you think that you are really a secular State, and that you believe in a secular Constitution, that you believe in the solemn injunctions definitely and consciously embodied herein, then why do you go counter to that Directive Principle? Why do you have a Hindu marriage law or a Hindu Divorce Bill? This is not in accordance with the spirit of it.

I know it may be pointed out that this is not a justiciable matter. I do not maintain that when by Article 37 you have said that the Directive Principles embodied in this Part are fundamental in the governance of the country and it shall be the duty of the State to apply those principles in making its laws, then that means that whenever Parliament will make any law, Parliament must remember that in framing laws it must give effect to those fundamental principles. And these fundamental principles are fundamental in the governance of the country. Why are you departing from those principles? Why do you not have one common law for all citizens, if you think that is the proper thing to do?

I point out that there is considerable force in this argument, and it is not right, unless very cogent arguments are brought forward, to make a departure from, or to run counter to the clear directive in our Constitution.

The second point I am making is that this is not consistent with the Fundamental Rights which you have given in the Constitution. Are you not really defying the guaranteed freedom of equality? Are you not going against it? I find that Shri Indra Vidyavachaspati—we know he is the son of the late Swami Shraddhanandaji—has pointed out in his Minute of Dissent that this Bill is contrary to the Fundamental Rights laid down in the Constitution of India, because it discriminates by law against a community or a particular religion. What right you have to enact such a law? What right have you to say that monogamy must be made compulsory for all Hindus, for all Hindu men and for all Hindu women? If you honestly feel that this is a blessing and polygamy is a curse, then why not rescue our Muslim sisters from that curse and from that plight? What right have you to enact that this shall be made compulsory only for one community and not for others? That is what Shri Indra Vidyavachaspati has pointed out. If you believe that this monogamy is a benefit and polygamy is a curse, then not only the Hindu women but the Muslim women also should be saved from it.

You have not got the courage to be logical and to be consistent. You pay lip homage to the Constitution. When it comes to actual practice, you fall short of your declared standards, and you are going against the Constitution. I do maintain that this is not right. This is certainly something by which you are enforcing inequality by your sledgehammer majority. You are defying your Fundamental Rights. You are going contrary to your fundamental declaration of equality, equality not for one community or for the members of one community, but equality for all the citizens of the Indian Republic, for all those who swear allegiance to it. What business have you to defy that doctrine of equality? You say that everyone in this Republic of India, every citizen in this country, shall be guaranteed equality before the law. Are you guaranteeing equal treatment and equal protection? Are ages different, standards different, yardsticks different, divorce laws different, norms different, and so on? Is that fair? It is no good looking at it from a purely legalistic point of view. You have got to appreciate the spirit of our Constitution. You have got to pay real homage to the spirit of the Constitution. That spirit you are not observing. That spirit you are defying and I do agree with Shri Indra Vidyavachaspati that it is not right.

Thirdly, Sir, I am maintaining that the *raison d'être* of this Bill has to a large extent disappeared and there is absolutely no necessity unless you want to satisfy some emotional people who indulge in language of denunciation and take particular pleasure in condemning the Hindu marriage system or in deriding it in language which degrades this Parliament and degrades also our nation. I think you should drive them out. Now, you have— rightly or wrongly, that is the decision of the Parliament—on the statute book an Act you have passed, a piece of legislation known as the Special Marriage Act. There you have put it down that it shall be operative not only on the people who had registered their marriages under the Special Marriage Act of 1872, but you have deliberately extended the provision of that Act of Hindus who married according to the strict orthodox Hindu rites some 20, 25 or 30 years back who have got children and whose children have also married under the sacramental form of marriage according to strict Hindu notions. They can also avail of the Special Marriage Act and get divorce under suitable circumstances under prescribed conditions. Then, Sir, may I ask of the Prime Minister and the hon. Minister to tell this Parliament and tell the country, what is the necessity of having the provision of divorce here? I pleaded that that should not be done in the Special Marriage Bill. But anyhow that has been done. I am now pointing out that when you have done it; when you have made retrospective the applicability of the provisions of the Special Marriage Act and thereby under certain conditions you have made provisions for treating sacramental marriage as civil contracts, dissoluble, violable and terminable under certain circumstances by the will of parties and added to that the *imprimatur* of the court, then why for heaven's sake have again the provision of divorce and tamper with sacramental marriages and wound the feelings, sentiments and religious susceptibilities of millions and millions of people in this country. What is the point in doing it? I will not use the language which was used on the floor of the House which I deeply deplore, making all allowances for hysteria and neurosis and that kind of thing coming from ladies. I do maintain that if any man or woman, or any gentleman or lady who wants to have divorce because of certain cogent grounds they can easily do so under the Special Marriage Act, then why for heaven's sake are you again introducing this kind of thing? Why duplicate? What is the point of duplication? Even I am prepared to go further. I am going to make a suggestion that has been made by a gentleman of great position, of great erudition, who is not a partisan and who is not a member of any political party—Shri Pataskar knows him—Professor Deshpande. He is a professor of Hindu jurisprudence in the University of Benares, a man whose contributions on this subject are appreciated by every thoughtful person. He has made a suggestion that if any lady or any gentleman points out any lacuna in the Special Marriage Act and if any lady thinks that having regard to the circumstances of our country, having regard to the economic backwardness of our country, having regard to the poverty or having regard to the disability of our women under present conditions, she should have recourse to the Special Marriage Act by unilateral declaration, then we are prepared to consider the conditions under which that can be done. Therefore, all restrictions can be removed and all the reasonable safeguards can be imposed. You know, Sir, under the Special Marriage Act, for both the Hindu wife and the Hindu husband if they find that they cannot live together, there are certain conditions which justify termination or divorce or dissolution of the marriage. They can approach the court and do that. But, if you feel that in some cases, extreme cases, difficult cases or some marginal cases a Hindu wife should be given unilateral right without any bilateral agreement, to have the marriage registered and to get the benefit of the Special Marriage Act, then that matter can be discussed and Prof. Deshpande, the Professor of Jurisprudence, has prepared a note on it and has circulated it. Some Members of this Parliament must also have read it. He is a great writer. I am sorry the other day Shri Pataskar was ridiculing some of his contributions on the subject. This is not a matter of ridicule. I have great respect for Shri Pataskar. I am sorry that he is taking a partisan view and ridiculing a person of unimpeachable character, great erudition and the highest integrity. He should not have used the language. He was alleging that this Prof. Deshpande had been acting as Miss Mayo, trying to find out filth and publish a drain inspector's report.

The Minister in the Ministry of Law (Shri Pataskar): I did not refer to his books. The book I referred to was *Memorandum on Sexual Life*. I do not think he wrote it.

Shri N.C. Chatterjee: *Memorandum on Sexual Life* is written by Prof. Deshpande. He should have known the author before he started ridiculing him. Anyhow it is the ministerial prerogative to ridicule people. I do not blame him for that.

What I am saying is this. He is pointing out that in Western countries, they are themselves tired of the disruption of society because of the rise in tempo of divorces in those countries. They are trying to tighten it up and we are now going to put the hand of the clock back by simply trying to imitate those countries. In England, you know, 30 out of every hundred go to divorce courts and in America which is more progressive, there it has gone up to 50 per cent. Now, they are finding that this is a thing which should be stopped and it is no glory for any civilization, country or society. The author has quoted Judge Lindsay. Now, do not ridicule Judge Lindsay. He was not a pettifogging lawyer of ordinary standing. But, he was a great thinker and a social worker. He had to administer matrimonial law in one of the biggest States and his contribution on this subject has been appreciated deeply by all sensible people and by men interested in the development of marital relations on true lines. He has not quoted only Judge Lindsay. He has quoted different authors from different countries and pointed out the steady degradation of the so-called progressing civilization due to rising tempo of divorce and easy dissolution of the marital tie.

Fourthly, I want to make one point and that point is this. It is, I am sorry to say, completely misleading the country when a responsible Minister says that Hindu marriage has never been considered sacramental according to Hindu *Dharma Shashtra*.

Shri Raghunath Singh (Benares Distt.-Central): Who says?

Shri N.C. Chatterjee: Then, I am sorry you have not done the courtesy of reading Shri Pataskar's speech. Shri Pataskar, standing on the floor of this House of Parliament of the Republic of India declared: 'It is not true that our ancient law-givers ever regarded marriage as indissoluble or marriage as sacramental.' I am shocked.

Shri Pataskar: Yes.

Shri N.C. Chatterjee: If Shri Pataskar had sat for a Hindu Law examination in any University he would have been ploughed and he would have got zero. I do not know what basis there is for that statement.

Shri Pataskar: You can refute it by references.

Shri N.C. Chatterjee: I am shocked to know that a Minister of Law in the Republic of India is saying this that it was not sacramental and the Hindu law-givers never thought it was sacramental.

Sir, the greatest authority in this country—I am reading Mayne's *Hindu Law and Usage*—has said this. His first sentence on this important subject is: 'Marriage is one of the necessary *sanskaras* or religious rites for all Hindus whatever be the caste, who do not desire to adopt the life of perpetual Brahmachari or of a *Sanyasi*.'

Shri Pataskar: *Sanskara* is not the same thing as sacramental form of marriage.

Shri N.C. Chatterjee: This is a thing which he ought not have said, I am not saying this because Mayne has said it. You know Mayne's book is treated as authority on the subject. But, this book was edited by one of the greatest Hindu jurists of modern India, Mr. Srinivasa Iyengar, who was President of the Indian National Congress, also Advocate-General of Madras and who was one of the recognised leading lawyers in the country. This edition which I am reading—11th Edition—was edited by Mr. Justice Chandrasekhara Iyer who was Judge of the Supreme Court of India and who is recognised as one the leading jurists in this branch of the law.

You know, Sir, and every lawyer who has anything to do with Hindu Law knows the greatest authority on this branch of law is Sir Gooroodas Banerjee, who was a Judge of the Calcutta High Court. But Mr. Pataskar says that the *sanskara* theory of marriage has been manufactured by European lawyers and by European Judges. Nothing of the kind. I am reading to you from the Tagore Law Lectures of Justice Gooroodas Banerjee on *The Hindu Law of Marriage and Stridhana*, page 31. The heading of the paragraph is 'Marriage in Hindu law a sacrament'. When he is saying that he is not thinking of any obsession derived from European Judges or jurists. He is one of the greatest Sanskritists in this country in modern times. This is what he says: 'Marriage in Hindu law a sacrament. The importance of the institution of marriage is too well recognized to require any comment. It is the source of every domestic comfort from infancy to old age; it is necessary for the preservation and the well-being of our species; it awakens and develops the best feelings of our nature; it is the source of important legal rights and obligations; and in its higher forms, it has tended to raise the weaker half of the human race from a state of humiliating servitude. To the Hindu, the importance of marriage is heightened by the sanctions of religion. In Hindu law it is regarded as one of the ten *sanskars*, or sacraments . . .'

If Mr. Pataskar has ever read or would care to read Sir Gooroodas Banerjee he would give up his opinion. Dr. Banerjee says, 'It is regarded as one of the ten *sanskars*, or sacraments, necessary for regeneration of men of the twice-born classes, and the only sacrament for women and *Sudras*.'

Mr. Pataskar has gone further and said: 'I do not know what basis there is for that view. At the most, it can be said *Manu Smriti* does not lay down any procedure for divorce. To that extent I am prepared to go.' Fortunately Manu and Yajnavalkya were not buried; otherwise they would have turned in their graves at this utterance of the modern Yajnavalkya. Dr. Ambedkar was the modern Manu and Mr. Pataskar is the modern Yajnavalkya. And he has declared that sacrament is of recent origin. I am sorry, I have respect for him, I do not know whether he married according to sacramental rites but if he did and his memory serves him right . . .

Shri Pataskar: May I appeal to the hon. Member with all his passions that what I have been saying was, there are *sanskaras*—my knowledge may not be so vast as his—but *sanskaras* and sacrament do not, according to me, mean the same thing.

Pandit K.C. Sharma (Meerut Distt.-South): They do not mean the same thing.

Shri N. C. Chatterjee: The Vedic *slokas* have to be uttered by every Hindu at the time of *panigrahan*: (*Hindi 4 Lines*) Rg. X, 85, 36. I will give the translation. The translation of the *sloka* given by Mahamahopadhyay Kane who is the greatest authority on this branch of the law, is in that remarkable book *History of Dharmasastra*, Vol. II, page 526: 'I take thy hand for prosperity (or love) so that you may grow to old age with me, thy husband; the gods, Bhaga, Aryaman, Savita, the wise Pusan, have given thee to me for performing the duties of a householder.

There is one book written fortunately not by a lawyer but by a sociologist of great eminence, by Dr. Pandhari Nath Prabhu, Fellow of the Society for Psychology in the United States of America and Professor in the Tata Institute of Social Sciences, Bombay. He is also saying it is a *sanskara* and it has been in vogue from the Rig Veda, not of recent vogue according to the recent theory of Mr. Pataskar. And what is the translation he gives? That you must recite the Vedic *mantra* when you perform *panigrahan*.

'I take thy hand in mine.
Yearning for happiness;
I ask thee,
To live with me
As thy husband,
Till both of us,
With age, grow old,
Know this,
As I declare,
That the Gods
Bhaga, Aryama,
Savita and Purandhi
Have bestowed thy person
Upon me,
That I may fulfil
My Dharmas of the householder
With thee.'

I shall read only one sentence from Mahamahopadhyay Kane's book. I do not know if anybody has stolen it—thank God, I have got it. The first sentence in Mahamahopadhyay Kane's celebrated book on Dharmasastra is this. You know, Sir, he has received a very big distinction, one of the awards from the President. And his first sentence in that book is this, that this is a sanskara. And this is recognised as a sanskara by all the dharmasastras, by all the shrutikaras, and by all the sages Gautam, Baudhayana, Apastamba, Vashishtha, Manu and Yajnavalkya. Each one has said it is not of recent origin—unless my friend Mr. Pataskar was a class-fellow of Yajnavalkya or Manu. In the Dasama Mandala of the Rig Veda, in the Tenth Mandala you will find it. From that day it has been there. I do not know what made my friend say that.

You know even in the latest edition of Mulla's Hindu Law which has been edited by the present Chief Justice of India who is one of the greatest jurists in this branch of law, that is Hindu Law, the first thing he has said is this. The latest edition is by Mr. Justice Bijan Kumar Mukherjee who is now the Chief Justice of India, and the first thing he has said is that this is a sacrament. I am reading the first sentence: 'Marriage, according to Hindu law, is a holy union for the performance of religious duties. It is not a contract.' And he emphasises it by certain citations. I am pointing out that give up this notion that it was not a sacrament. If there was any sacrament it was this Hindu marriage, and for women this was the only sacrament. And it was the sacrament which was meant for upliftment of human personality. Hindu marriage is not a contract. There is nothing to be ashamed of it, everything to be proud of it. You ought to be bold and declare that for thousands and thousands of years we have kept alive one virtue, one ideal, one standard.

Dr. Radhakrishnan has praised this concept in his Kamala Lectures in the Calcutta University. He has said that whatever you may say, compared to any other country he knows—England and America and other countries much better than many of us here—he has said that this doctrine of eternal fellowship is the cardinal principle of the Hindu sacramental marriage. This is perpetual fellowship not for material gains, not for secular gains, not for cardinal pleasure, not for lust, not for selfish things but for faithful fellowship, for integration of the family, for the development of society and for the development of the State. This is what Dr. Radhakrishnan has said. He has said that it is the greatest thing which you ought to remember. I do not for one moment claim to be so egotistical as to declare that my system is perfect or that in my social organisation there is absolutely no flaw. But, I do maintain, Sir, with all the emphasis I can command, that, compared to other systems of law and other personal laws, this Hindu system of marriage gives a higher family life, a nobler ideal of womanhood than any other country in the world has been able to achieve and has been able to sustain.

[MR. BARMAN in the Chair]

I want to read with your permission, Sir, only one portion of Dr. Radhakrishnan's book. He is saying that marriage is not a mere contract. I am reading from his Kamala Lectures delivered at the Calcutta University. 'Marriage is not a mere contract; it is a part of the life of the soul. Risk and hardship are part of human life, and we must be prepared to face both. We must meet as human beings and companions full of faults, weaknesses and desires common to both; and adjustment is a long process. In the Catholic Church, the parties contracting marriage receive the Cross and Sword on their heads bent towards each other, the one as the symbol of their tragic, courageous trust in a higher order than the human, the other as the symbol of the unfailing wrath for every infraction of the law of the Cross. In the faith that love is the sign and pledge of the loveableness of the ultimate ground from which all things arise, the sacramental view requires us to face risks, and not to admit defeat in the great enterprise.'

Dr. Radhakrishnan was the Professor of the Calcutta University and also Spalding Professor at Oxford.

I am asking Mr. Pataskar and all those who think with him to take this particular view of life and not to admit defeat in the great enterprise. We enter into marriage relationship for the development of the individual and for the enrichment of our lives. Without it there is no happiness for the individual or society. Dr. Radhakrishnan is pointing out that: 'This traditional view has still a strong hold on Indians, among whom stable marriages are more numerous, and family affections much stronger, than perhaps in any other country.'

Sir, I think that is the honest verdict of a great thinker and philosopher. He is not the man to applaud his own nation or his own country just for the sake of applauding. Although it is now the fashion of the day to decry our marriage system and indulge in language of unfortunate denunciation and declamation unworthy of this great country and her culture and civilisation, still it will be saying nothing improper or unhistorical if we say that whatever you may say, among our nation stable marriages are more numerous than in any other country and family affections much stronger than in any other country.

Sister Nivedita, you know, Sir, was a disciple of the great Vivekananda. She was an Irish lady but she came out to India and lived in Calcutta and Bengal and other parts of India and spent and consecrated all her life to India for the sake of our people and the women folk. She said that we should be careful not to disrupt our Institutions and not to disrupt our ways of life. Sister Nivedita said, when all is said and done, from the standpoint of purity the Indian woman, the Hindu woman—I am quoting Sister Nivedita—'The so-called tyrannised and tortured Hindu woman is a near perfection as any human being can be.'

That is the verdict of a European woman. She says 'the so-called tyrannised and tortured Hindu woman'.

We come to Parliament, we fight here with the Speaker, I go to the Supreme Court; I fight even with the Judges of the Supreme Court; but when we go home, we know where we are. This is what Sister Nivedita says: 'The so-called tyrannised and tortured Hindu woman is a near perfection as any human being can be. Once a wife, always a wife, even though the bond be shared with or remain always only a name. That other men should be only as shadows to her, that her feet should be ready at all times to go forth on any path, even that of death, as the companion of her husband, those things constitute the purity of the wife in India. Purity in every one of its forms is the central pursuit of Indian life.'

The central purity of Hindu life, this great standard of purity. I do maintain, has been, to a large extent made possible by our sacramental system of marriage. It is that marriage which has given that unique fellowship; do not try to disrupt it.

I am very sorry that my friend Shri Pataskar has used language of derision against one of our greatest countrymen and has cast aspersions unworthy of him against one of our greatest jurists in India today. He has castigated Dr. Radha Binod Pal.

After all, who is Dr. Radha Binod Pal? Dr. Radha Binod Pal has placed India on the map of the world. Our Prime Minister is placing India on the international map due to his great efforts in the international sphere. But, there is one man who has put India on the juridical map of the world and given her a place of great distinction and honour as a Judge of the International Tribunal which tried Marshal Tojo at Tokyo. The Minister of State for law forgot the decencies of life when he actually stood up and said that the conveners of the Convention which met here on the Hindu Code Bill compelled him to utter certain things. His language is this. I marked that language. There is neither wit nor humour in it but it is very crude, and this is what he said: 'In a democratic age, because a few members in the minority do not find things that are being done by the majority agreeable to them, they should make a very eminent jurist to come and sit down and make him say such a thing is not proper.'

This is an insinuation which is thoroughly unfair and thoroughly unworthy of him and it is not true. I know it is not true. I was one of the conveners of the Convention. I can assure

Mr. Pataskar and men of his thinking that Dr. Radha Binod Pal is not the man to be dictated to by any minority, however vocal it may be. He is not the man to be dictated. I honestly say that I never saw that speech until it was printed and he never consulted any one of the conveners of the Convention. He is not the man to be dictated to by anyone. He was not only one of the greatest lawyers and advocates of the Calcutta High Court but he was also a very eminent Judge. Mr. C.C. Biswas, the Law Minister, if he were here, would have paid his tribute to his character, to his integrity and to his complete independence. He is not the man to be cowed down. What has he said? What improper things has he said? He has pointed out that you should be particularly careful, before you, in a precipitate manner, try to violate the old traditions and traditional systems. He has said nothing improper. He is right. Shri Pataskar reads it as a language of threat. It is not a language of threat. It is a warning; it is an appeal; it is an admonition; it is an appeal, admonition, caution all combined. That is the fact. Why do you take it as a language of threat? I am bold to declare that we are unfit to unlace the shoes of that great jurist. If he had been on the International Court at the Hague, he would have again placed India on the map of the world. I know, you know, everybody knows, everybody who has anything to do with law knows, everybody who is votary of Themis knows that Dr. Radha Binod Pal's services have been requisitioned by the League of Nations, and international organisations. He is going to Geneva as a representative of this country, I take it, to draft the International Law Code for the whole world. That is a great honour. To say that a man of that character, a man of that experience, a man of that standing, a man of that eminence would be dictated to by a few people who are in the minority in a Parliament, is a preposterous suggestion unworthy of Shri Pataskar. I am sorry to say this, he should not have said so.

What has Dr. Pal said? He has simply pointed out: 'Our legislators would do well to remember that the instruments they are now trying to use may be the creature of their desires.' Then he says: 'I am warning you that the instruments they are now trying to use may be the creature of their desires, but they will evoke, modify and deflect people's desires in turn and in course of time will take complete revenge upon us all.'

I may tell you that a very thoughtful writer has made a patient study and research into the working of the monogamy laws in the States of Madras and Bombay. Do you know what the experience has been? The experience has been . . .

An Hon. Member: Monogamy laws?

Shri N.C. Chatterjee: Yes; Prevention of Bigamy Acts. The experience has been that it has not been really beneficial for women. It has been beneficial for men. It has been in the sense that they have a handy charter for discarding their wives, for getting newer, fresher, lovable, agreeable companions at an advanced stage of life. That has been unfortunate. I can give Shri Pataskar or any Member of this House data, facts, statistics collected as a result of great research and industry and study of the working of these particular measures in the different States. Don't think that they have been very beneficial. Women have been really placed at a greater disadvantage. They have proved to be convenient handles for men to get rid of their old wives. I am therefore saying that these points may be carefully considered.

Why go against the Directive Principles; why trespass upon those doctrines of equality and go against Fundamental Rights? Why not frame, if you have got the courage and wisdom to do it, one uniform civil Code? You proclaim from the house tops that there shall be no communal legislation. Why are you then proceeding with communal legislation? There are secular countries which have divorced personal law from religion. That is the ideal which we have also embodied. Why not act up to that ideal? You know that the Muslim community does not like interference with its personal laws. That is why you are really violating the clear directives of our Constitution.

That is what you should not do. If you are logical, if you have courage, if you have wisdom, you must implement that Directive Principle. I am pointing out that your so-called monogamy may be a legislation of polygamy in other shapes and other forms. It really comes to one husband at one time or one husband and wife at a time. By this kind of periodical marriages and changes, you can have plurality. That is not the way of real monogamy.

I am sorry to say that Shri Pataskar quoted one verse from Manu's Manava Dharma Sastra in some part of his wonderful thesis. I think he read out from Chapter 9 (verse No. 46) (Hindi 2 lines). This does not support Shri Pataskar's great thesis; this goes against his thesis. It says that there shall be no dissolution of the marital tie. If you try to desert your wife, if you sell your wife, even then, the marital bond can never be disrupted. Shri Pataskar does not need any commentator. He is the 20th Century commentator of Manu. He says that this verse shows that you could desert your wife and there was no necessity for a formal divorce. On the other hand, the verse says that under no circumstances is the marital bond broken. Manu was thinking of the great example of Shri Ramchandra. Manu was not thinking of fashionable people walking along the boulevards, going to Connaught Circus in the evening. He was thinking of the noble type of people, Shri Ramchandra deserting Sita or Shri Harischandra being compelled to sell himself and his family including his wife. Even in these cases, Manu says that the marital tie was never to be disintegrated. Under any conditions it was inviolable.

This is the law which I know, which Manu knows, but, Shri Pataskar does not know, created by the maker of the universe from ancient times. May I make a present of this to Shri Pataskar? He has not read it.

Shri Pataskar: I have read and re-read it carefully. It need not be presented to me.

Shri N.C. Chatterjee: May I point out one more *sloka*, a last gift in all humility to Shri Pataskar? (Hindi 3 lines.) Manu himself says that Vedic marriage is *sanskara*. That is a solemn injunction. It is an inviolable union, an indissoluble union; it is an interminable union; it is an external fellowship; it is a perpetual union. It is said that once you marry, it is a *sanskara* and it is a sacrament. In all humility I say, whatever you think of monogamy, I appeal to all sections of the House, don't tamper with the Hindu sacramental marriage and introduce divorce into it. I am pointing out in all humility, but with all earnestness that having regard to the law which we have already passed, there is absolutely no necessity for this. If anybody wants divorce, he or she can have it. While you are keeping the sacramental form, for heaven's sake, do not introduce this divorce here. There is absolutely no necessity for this. I am therefore submitting that this will be undemocratic, this will be unconstitutional, this will be repugnant . . .

Some Hon. Members: Why undemocratic?

Shri N.C. Chatterjee: You provoke me to start once again. I am prepared. It is undemocratic because such a radical legislation disrupting the basic factors of Hindu social organisation which is cherished by millions and millions of people under which we have lived not for ages and centuries but for thousands of years should not be passed except by a clear and definite mandate from the people.

Mr. Chairman: May I put in a word? In view of the limitation of our time, there should be no interruption because in that case the speeches will be longer and other Members who might otherwise have a chance may not have a chance to speak. Let the speaker speak out his own mind.

Shri N.C. Chatterjee: I may conclude by saying that this has been the only Vedic sacrament for our ladies; this sacramental system of marriage has given us a standard of life, a way of civilisation, a very pure, much purer and nobler and higher life than has been the fortune of other countries to enjoy. And that is the keynote of our culture and our civilisation. That is why Hindu civilisation has lived, and is still living, and nothing should be done so as to disrupt the basic factors which have kept up our civilisation and our heritage in such a glorious manner.

22

Bhiwandi Riots: Now Hindus Will Not Take a Beating[*]

Atal Bihari Vajpayee

Sir, with your permission I stand to initiate a discussion on the situation created in various parts of the country by communal disturbances. Today I would like to do some plain speaking. This is not the time for goody goody things. The situation is serious. The nation's unity is at stake. The nation's boat is heaving on the high seas of communalism. The waters are rising up to our heads. The need of the hour is some serious thinking and plain speaking.

Sir, it is a matter of coincidence that Bhiwandi is in Maharashtra. It is also a matter of coincidence that there is an 'Indicate' Government in office in Maharashtra. But these coincidences have no direct relationship with the disturbances there. There can be a Bhiwandi in any State of India and a communal conflagration can spread under any Government. In Bihar there was a communal disturbance in Chaibasa, but there is an Indicate Government there. There were nearly 25 communal disturbances when a joint front was in power. Sparks of

---

[*] Speech delivered on 14 May 1970 while initiating discussion on the situation created by communal tension in the country. Extracted from *Four Decades in Parliament*, Volume 1, by Atal Bihari Vajpayee, edited by N.M. Ghatate, Shipra, pp. 256–75.

communalism were lighted in Calcutta, Howrah, Telanipara, Jagatdal, and there was loss of life and property. The other day in April, a procession of small children in Chamrajnagar in Mysore was attacked by 300 goondas in an organised manner. Before this, riots have occurred in Chikmagalur, Ramnagar, Chennapathan. Currently there is a Syndicate Government in Mysore. I repeat that communal riots can take place anywhere, any time and under any government. So sacrificing the Gujarat government if there is a riot in Ahmedabad, taking the Indicate Government of Maharashtra to task if there is a riot there may be necessary to some extent, but it does not solve the problem.

The Government of Gujarat made mistakes and we pointed our fingers at it. We shall also refer in the House to the mistakes of the Government of Maharashtra. But all I want to say is that communal riots are not a party matter. In conditions prevailing in the country today a disturbance may occur at any place. The people are in such a state of mind that anywhere they may resort to violence and arson and break the law and order. We will have to take down partisan blinkers to look at these riots. I wish Comrade Dange does so, and I am happy he has done it. We have to rise above party interests. We have to forget votes and care for the nation.

The Question of Communalism

After the riots in Ahmedabad it was demanded that the Gujarat government must resign. I do not include my united socialist friends among those who made the demand. Whom I mean should be clear. They are not demanding the Maharashtra Government's resignation. Was what flowed in Ahmedabad was blood and what flowed in Bhiwandi water? Will there be different standards for measuring communalism? Were they not Indians who died in Ahmedabad, Bhiwandi and Jalgaon ? Can we not rise above partisan interests even on this question on national importance? Can we not act with the nation's unity in view? This discussion will decide what attitude this House, the parties represented in it, and their spokesmen adopt towards this important problem. We must face the truth. However harsh and terrible it may be, we will have to reveal it. No whitewash will do. Nobody's sin may be covered up.

The first question is, who starts these riots . . . (*Interruption*) . . . The second question is, why are they started? The third is, why do they spread? And the fourth question is, what short-term and long-term steps need to be taken to prevent them? About who starts them I do not want to say anything, but I have the report prepared by the Home Ministry. With your permission I could place it on the floor of the House. The National Integration Council has set up a subcommittee to consider the problem of communalism. Shri Nath Pai was a member of it. The Government of India had prepared a report for it in which major riots in the country during the past year and a half had been recounted and their reasons discussed. As many as 23 riots took place during this period and according to the Home Ministry's report 22 of them were started by members of what is called the minority community. This report has not yet been published, but it should be.

These 23 riots include riots in Calcutta, Nagpur, Aurangabad, Cuttack as well as some other parts of the country. I take it that the report of the Home Ministry is based upon reports received from the State governments. But the reports of the State Government should be based upon facts, and the facts proclaim loudly enough that these riots were started by some of our Muslim friends.

Who Wants Riots?

When I say some Muslim friends I am setting apart other Muslims. Not all Muslims want communal riots. There are also patriots and peace-loving people among Muslims. Those who toil and take care of their families do not want to play with fire and violence. But there is certainly a section of Muslims— and this needs to be said without mincing words—that wants to bring communalism into the country. Let us not make the mistake of covering up facts. There is certainly a class that kindles the fire of riots. This is not my personal opinion, this is what the report says.

After this report was ready there was a riot in Indore on June 2, when Master Chandgi Ram's procession of 300 people was sought to be stopped in a Muslim mohalla. This is also in the Home Minister's report.

Then there was a riot in Jagatdal, where processions of Durga and Mahavir were stoned from a mosque. Later there was a riot in Chaibasa, where a Ram Naomi procession was attacked with bombs.

Now I come to Bhiwandi. Bhiwandi is 35 miles away from Bombay. It has a Muslim majority. For many years one of our Muslim brethren has been the Chairman of the municipality there. There is nothing objectionable in it. There is frequently some tension in Bhiwandi on occasions like Ganesh festival and Shivaji Jayanti. Since the last couple of years, when Congress leaders of Maharashtra decided to participate in Shivaji Jayanti function with great enthusiasm our Muslim brethren of Bhiwandi also changed their attitude. Perhaps they thought Shivaji is a national hero, we should also participate in his Jayanti. The people of Bhiwandi welcomed this. But this time a few days before the function 30, 35, 37 leading Muslims of Bhiwandi tried to put some conditions on the procession.

Why? Were they the people who were to decide if the Shivaji Jayanti procession should be taken out or not? Were they the people to decide the route of the procession? Were they to decide what slogans were to be raised?

The Conditions of Bhiwandi

I am surprised—and also sorry—to see that Home Minister Shri Chavan—he is not present in the House, he is on sick bed—stated in the Rajya Sabha that those conditions were proper.

He should not have said so. Could any self-respecting society accept these conditions? And what were those conditions? One was that the procession would not carry a saffron flag. Was not the saffron flag the flag of Shivaji Maharaj? Was there no flag in this country before the tricolour? Can we think of Gandhiji without the tricolour? Pandit Jawaharlal Nehru's picture in the Central Hall has the tricolour in the background. If we cannot think of Gandhiji without the tricolour we can also not think of Shivaji Maharaj without the Bhagwa.

And why are Muslims against the Bhagwa? Does Islam say saffron is a bad colour? Does the Quran say the saffron colour should be opposed? Had the Constituent Assembly decided after independence that the Bhagwa should be India's flag would the Muslims have revolted? Still the condition was put in Bhiwandi that there should be no Bhagwa flag in the procession. And Shri Chavan, who claims to have inherited the heritage of Shivaji Maharaj, says the conditions were right. Sahyadri had come to the defence of the Himalayas, but how low it has fallen! The demand to separate Shivaji Maharaj's flag from the Shivaji Jayanti procession can never be accepted. And I am happy that the Marathis of Bhiwandi—small as they are in number—declined to accept this condition.

The second condition was that Gulal must not be sprinkled. Why? Gulal is the symbol of love. We sprinkle Gulal when we are happy. Gulal has no connection with religion. When I was in Ahmedabad there was a procession of one lakh people and they coloured me all red with Gulal. It was a political procession. Should anyone object if a little Gulal was used in a Shivaji Jayanti procession?

Another condition was—we shall decide the route of the procession. A meeting of the two parties was called, which the municipal Chairman did not attend. Those prominent Muslims who had put out a statement also did not come for the meeting. However, later it was said we are taking back our conditions. Now I feel this taking back of the conditions was a drama, a fraud which was meant to put the Hindus off their guard and confuse the Government of Maharashtra. And the purpose was served.

What Were the Slogans?

Now it is said that there was a disturbance in the procession because some people raised unauthorised slogans. What were those unauthorized slogans? How many people raised them? According to newspaper reports they were a handful. In a procession of 10-15 thousand people there could be some people who raised slogans that were apart from the slogans decided upon. I can also understand resentment about them. The few Muslims who participated in the procession could have left it. If they very much resented the slogans they could have expressed their resentment by holding a peaceful strike in Bhiwandi the next day. They could have approached the Maharashtra Government and demanded action against people raising such slogans. But they used the slogans as an excuse to attack the procession. When the procession went into the narrow street of the fish market . . . (*Interruption*)

Shri Sita Ram Kesri (Kastikar) : What were those slogans ?

Shri Vajpayee: I do not know. The Government should find out. I would like to know what they were. But an attack on a procession cannot be allowed simply because wrong slogans were raised. In Ahmedabad too wrong slogans were raised: "Jo Islam se takrayega woh choor choor ho jayega", but no one attacked that procession. No one can be allowed be take the law in his hands.

But the procession was attacked and fires were started in many places in the city of Bhiwandi. The attack and the arson took place at the same time . . . (*Interruption*) . . . Ismail Sahib asks, who started the fires? I would like to tell him that they were started in Hindu localities. I can give their names, but that is not necessary. It is clear that the attack on the procession was pre-planned and things had been collected. The plan was to burn down the mohalla when the people went to participate in the procession.

Bhiwandi Plunged in Darkness

There are other proofs of the advance plan. The rioters cut off the water connection, plunged Bhiwandi into darkness by cutting the power connection, and cut off telephone communication. Fire brigade engines that were to put out the fire were attacked with stones and bombs. When a fire engine came from Kalyan its driver was struck in the chest with a spear and it could not reach Bhiwandi. Can all these things be done without planning?

The weapons that were seized—they can be seen at the Bhiwandi police station—included newly-made spacers and Molotov cocktails which could set the whole city on fire.

Our friends in the Congress have not escaped the damage. Bhiwandi is a big centre of handlooms and powerlooms. The factories belonging to Congressmen have been reduced to ashes. One Dr. Acharya had a 12-bed hospital and 88 per cent of his patients were Muslims. That hospital too was reduced to ashes.

The question is, what did the Government of Maharashtra do about it?

Bhiwandi is 35 miles away from Bombay. Did the government of Maharashtra not know that there was tension in the town, some prominent citizens had put conditions on the Shivaji Jayanti procession, and that people had become agitated because of them? Could the government not have jailed those 35 or 37 citizens? Could it not have made arrangements for the procession? Home Minister Shri Chavan says 700 policemen were on duty there. Do you know they had no rifles? When policemen were later sent from Bombay they too were not given rifles. And yet they were ordered to open fire. Bullets made of what could they fire? The Government of Maharashtra will have to say why they were not given rifles. Firing was ordered, but there were no guns to fire.

Minister Asleep

Chief Minister Shri Vasantrao Naik himself took 24 hours to reach Bhiwandi. Opposition leaders tried to contact the Chief Minister on the phone but they could not succeed. Then a phone call was made to Shri Kalyanrao Patil, Minister of State in the Home Department. The reply was that the minister was asleep. Bhiwandi was burning but the Minister of Maharashtra was literally sleeping. Is this how communalism will be eradicated?

I want to know why the army was not sent into Bhiwandi. If it could be sent to Jalgaon, why not to Bhiwandi? If it had been sent, and if the homes reportedly storing arms had been searched, we would not have witnessed the terrible scene we saw in Bhiwandi. But the Government of Maharashtra was apathetic, it failed to do its duty, it took things casually, it is guilty of fatal apathy.

Along with Bhiwandi there was a riot in Jalgaon. It is said there was a gambling den in a Muslim mohalla, and it all started from there. In Pahar there was a riot because a saffron flag on a temple was removed. Those who removed it were goondas. It was not necessary to say to what community they belonged. The police were present and the flag was removed in their presence. After this there was trouble in Goregaon too. On the 5th a truck laden with people came there. They threatened and terrorized the people and said there would be a riot on Shivaji Jayanti day. The police took no action against them too.

The riots of Bhiwandi were pre-planned. One more proof of this is available in the daily *Loksatta*. It is a Marathi newspaper and not a paper of our party.

On May 11 its Bhiwandi correspondent filed a report according to which a shopkeeper told him—the letter is in Marathi, I am paraphrasing it in Hindi—he has a rationing shop—on May 6, members of a certain religion lifted rations in large quantities from his shop—enough for 8 days. So he suspected there would be some trouble on the 7th. Clearly those who lifted the rations knew something was going to happen on the 7th.

Home Minister's Tears

Our newspaper have also reported what arrangements the Government made after the riots started. Shri Chavan went to Bhiwandi. That was right. I praise him for that. But I did not appreciate the fact that Shri Chavan began to weep when there was a riot in Maharashtra but there were no tears in his eyes when there was a riot in Ahmedabad. I understand his sorrow. But the Home Minister of India should express his reaction as a national leader, not as a leader of Maharashtra. We went to Bhiwandi and was addressing a meeting when a man came running and said, run, run, 17-18 people are coming to kill me with spears, they have set fire to my restaurant, a restaurant was torched in the broad daylight just 20 feet away from where Shri Chavan was speaking. It is true Shri Chavan rushed, the police also rushed with him, but by then the restaurant had been reduced to ashes.

Sir, there is one more incident. The disturbance started on Friday night. Goondas collected. They had bombs and Molotov cocktails. When the people telephoned the police, five policemen arrived but when they saw 200 goondas had collected they took to their heels. People saw them running away, and when they were stopped the policemen said, we too have lives to lose, can we fight with sticks, we should have guns and there should be bullets in the guns. I doubt if the Maharashtra Government really wants to stop these communal riots from spreading.

Now the question is, why are these riots started? I agree our Muslim brethren lose more in the riots. There is greater loss of life and property among them. But it does not become the Home Minister to say so in the Rajya Sabha. Had he not said so I would not have referred to it. The Home Minister said Muslims of Bhiwandi have suffered the most. Children and women have died. Have only Muslims died? I say his statement is beyond the truth. On the night of the 7th more Hindus died. And even supposing the statement is true, shall we now start giving community-wise figures of those who died? Newspapers are not permitted to report how many Hindus died and how many Muslims. But the Home Minister lost his balance and made a statement that has evoked an intense reaction in Maharashtra. It has created a wave of resentment all over Maharashtra. Hindus are unhappy because he made a wrong statement, and the Muslims are unhappy because they suffered heavily. He should not have made such a statement.

Three Reasons of Riots

But the question is, why are riots started? I call upon the House to think about this. I have not yet reached any conclusion. Some Muslims start the riot knowing that they may lose life and property.

There could be three reasons of why they start riots—one reason may be that our Muslim brethren have concluded that now there is no place for them in India, no guardian for them, so it is better to die fighting than to live. This may be one reason.

Another reason may be that some Muslims are connected with Pakistan and indulge in rioting at Pakistan's behest. Pakistan wants to tarnish out image. Hindus are being driven out of Pakistan. If atrocities are committed on Muslims in India, Pakistan would get the opportunity of making propaganda against India.

The third and the most important reason seems to be some Muslim leaders do not want Muslims to merge with national mainstream. They do not want Muslims to join different political parties on the basis of ideology. They do not want Muslims to become Communists or Congressmen or Jan Sanghis. They want Muslims to remain aloof and under the leadership of fundamentalists Maulavis. So they are ready even to fling people

into the fire to establish their leadership . . . (*Interruption*) . . .
Sir, the issue is not whether Muslims riot or not. This is the
Home Ministry's report. Figures speak for themselves. They are
burning figures. You cannot connive at the truth. We will have
to think about these reasons.

A Riot: Action and Reaction

There is one more question. It is argued—even if Muslims
start riots—suppose the Jagannath temple in Ahmedabad was
attacked—why did people take revenge? Suppose the Ram
Naomi procession in Chaibasa was attacked with bomb, why
did the Hindus get angry? Suppose a couple of Muslims create
a disturbance, why are the innocent made to pay for it? I agree
innocent should not be punished. I agree the feeling of revenge is
not good. We cannot allow any individual to take the law in his
hands. But will the rule apply only to Hindus? Will it not apply
to Muslims? Is throwing a bomb on a Ram Naomi procession
a personal quarrel? Is attacking a Shivaji procession a personal
quarrel? And along with these clashes fires were set at various
places. We must understand two things. Whatever reason our
Muslim brethren are getting more and more communal, and as a
reaction Hindus are getting more and more aggressive. Nobody
made the Hindus aggressive . . . (*Interruption*) . . . If you want
to give the credit for this to us we are willing to take it. But, Sir,
Hindus will no more take a beating in this country. The tradition
of taking a beating went on for 700-800 years. Hindus will not
start. Hindus will not initiate. Hindus will not kindle the fire
with their own hands . . . (*Interruption*) . . . Yes, I am speaking
as an Indian. Sir, that is why I said in the beginning that my
submission to those who want to fight communalism is that you
cannot fight communalism by ignoring Muslim communalism.
If you promote Muslim communalism the other feeling will run
high. Communalism is like a double-edged sword, it acts both
ways . . . (*Interruption*) . . .

Dr. Maitree Basu (Darjeeling): Thank God I am not a Hindu.

Shri Vajpayee: Had you been a Hindu it would have been a matter of shame for the Hindu Society . . . (*Interruption*) . . .

Shri Randhir Singh (Rohtak): A Hindu does not talk like this. This is very wrong.

Shri Y.P. Mandal (Samastipur): Today you have shown your true form. You have used very low language . . . This is the language of communalism . . . (*Interruption*) . . .

Shri Kanwar Lal Gupta (Delhi Sadar): Sir, it would be better if you silence them. Otherwise not even the Prime Minister would be able to speak. We shall see how she speaks . . . (*Interruption*) . . .

Mr. Deputy Speaker: All the other hon. Members who are interrupting will have their chance to speak and they can refute the arguments of Mr. Vajpayee. They should listen to him now.

Shri Ramavtar Shashtri (Patna): One should not talk about women like this.

Smt. Indira Gandhi, the Prime Minister: I do not like to interrupt and I have always advised members on all side of the House to listen to whoever is speaking. If I have done so on this occasion it was to point out to Hon. member Shri Vajpayee that he was using this opportunity to say things which will deeply hurt all minorities . . . (*Interruption*) . . .

Shri Vajpayee: It is a matter of opinion.

Smt. Indira Gandhi: I am perfectly entitled to say this speech is going to create bad atmosphere in the country. I am certainly entitled to draw the hon. Member's attention to that. It is not only a question of Muslims. It is a questions of Sikhs, Buddhists, Jains, Christians and all other minorities . . . (*Interruption*) . . . as also of Harijans and backward communities.

Shri Vajpayee: I am not yielding; the hon. Prime minister did not raise any point of order.

An hon. Member: We do not accept that he speaks on behalf of all Hindus.

Shri Kanwarlal Gupta: The prime minister has no right to interfere in his . . . (*Interruption*) . . .

Shri Rabi Ray: In this House we are all Indians, neither Hindus, nor Muslims.

Shri N.K.P. Salve (Betul): Is it chivalrous to address the other Hon. lady member like that? Would you do it to your sister? The basic question is because we enjoy certain immunity are we completely free to cast off all decorum and are we free from the law of decency ? Is he entitled to call the lady what he said?

Shri Vajpayee: Sir, I am sorry . . .

Shri Dhireshwar Kalita (Gauhati): Sir, on a point of order.

Mr. Deputy Speaker: He is not yielding. Let him finish his speech. All right. What is your point of order?

Shri Dhireshwar Kalita: The point of order is this. This is a very serious question. It may incite riots in our country. So I want to say that that portion of his speech should be expunged.

Mr. Deputy Speaker: It is your opinion. Now only without being tense, can the debate continue? Mr. Vajpayee, please conclude.

Shri Vajpayee: Sir, I have not said anything. This is not the first time I stand in the House to speak. No member of this House can say I have made a speech that would incite passions . . . (*Interruption*) . . .

Shri R.S Yadav (Barabanki): I think Shri Vajpayee has been somewhat carried away, but he did not mean it. What he said about the Hon. member should be expunged.

Shri Vajpayee: Nothing should be expunged.

Shri S.A. Dange (Bombay Central South): I want all those words to remain. I do not want any expunction . . . (*Interruption*) . . .

Mr. Deputy Speaker: Order, order.

Shri Vajpayee: Sir, I do not think I have said something in my speech that would incite passions. If the lady feels I have said something insulting about her I am willing to take it back . . . (*Interruption*) . . . If someone says I am not a Hindu what is objectionable in my saying in reply 'it is good that you are not a Hindu'? . . . (*Interruption*) . . .

Shri Randhir Singh: We are all brothers, whether Hindu or Muslim. All are Indians.

Shri Vajpayee: Sir, as I was saying, communalism cannot be fought by promoting Muslim communalism . . .. (*Interruption*) . . . Keep quiet, madam, you did not feel ashamed to join hands with Muslim League . . . (*Interruption*) . . .

Shri Tarakeshwari Sinha: Smt. Indira Gandhi joined hands with the Muslim League in Kerala . . . (*Interruption*) . . .

Smt. Indira Gandhi: Now it is all the more clear that you are with the Jan Sangh.

Shri Tarakeshwari Sinha: You too joined hands with the Muslim League to form the Government . . . (*Interruption*) . . .

Shri Vajpayee: Sir, what will happen to me in a quarrel between two ladies? . . . (*Interruption*) . . .

Smt. Indira Gandhi: I am not speaking as a woman or as a lady; I am speaking with great indignation on behalf of the Indian nation . . . (*Interruption*) . . .

Shri Vajpayee: You are heading a minority Government. You resign and get out . . . (*Interruption*) . . . One who broke her own party is talking of the nation.

I would like to make it clear that what I said Hindus are becoming aggressive it was not my intention to justify that aggressiveness . . . (*Interruption*) . . . Listen to me, and understand. I went to Ahmedabad, where riots had taken pace, and asked people not to take the law in their own hands. My speeches are proof of this. In today's speech I have said I do not approve of the sentiment of revenge. But one cannot close one's eyes to the situation. The situation is that Muslims are becoming more and more communal and Hindus more and more aggressive . . . (*Interruption*) . . . We must understand both these dangers and take steps to remove them.

Wherever there is a riot the name of the Jan Sangh is dragged in . . . (*Interruption*) . . . The Raghuvar Dayal Commission's report has been received and it says the Jan Sangh has no hand in the riots in Ranchi . . . (*Interruption*) . . .

Mr. Deputy Speaker: We have allotted 3 hours. I am not shutting you out, but I am putting it into the House. We have taken about 40 minutes. I am just drawing your attention to it.

Shri Kanwar Lal Gupta: Tell the Prime Minister not to disturb.

Shri Vajpayee: Sir, communalism has been very much made a ploy for votes. I would like to warn political parties that now they would not even get votes by playing up Muslim communalism . . . (*Interruption*) . . . The Muslim League in Kerala . . . (*Interruption*) . . .

Shri Randhir Singh: All this drama for votes . . . (*Interruption*) . . .

Shri Vajpayee: In Kerala the Muslim League is addicted to power. My friend Shri Chandrajeet Yadav says the candidate from Muslim Majlis may get all Muslim votes . . . (*Interruption*) . . .

Shri Chandrajeet Yadav (Azamgarh): What you say is wrong. You present everything wrongly. You also present Indian culture and Indian civilisation wrongly . . . (*Interruption*) . . .

Shri Vajpayee: Now you are going back on your words. Is this your morality? Yesterday you had yourself said . . . (*Interruption*) . . .

How to Fight Communalism

The question is, how do want to fight communalism? The Bharatiya Jan Sangh believes in the ideal of a secular state . . . (*Interruption*) . . . This is not a laughing matter. Those who have entered into an alliance with the Muslim League should not have the temerity to make charges against us. Those who live in glass houses should not throw stones at others. Their government rests on the support of the Muslim League and they call us communalists. Those who choose candidates for elections on the basis of communalism are calling us communalists. Those who get India into the Rabat conference and humiliate it are calling us communalists . . . (*Interruption*) . . .

The Bharatiya Jan Sangh has never said there should be discrimination on the basis of communalism in the country. We want neither discrimination nor partiality. We have accepted equal citizenship laid down in the Constitution. The doors of the Bharatiya Jan Sangh are open to all Indian citizens. But if a Muslim enters Jan Sangh, posters appear in Delhi calling him a kafir. The language the Muslim League used against Maulana Azad and other nationalist Muslim is now being used against Muslims joining the Jan Sangh.

This is not the way to fight communalism ... (*Interruption*) ... I want to conclude.

The question is, what should be done to tackle communal disturbances? There are some long-term measures. We will have to take this question out of politics and solve it on a national level.

The Prime Minister had initiated the National Integration Council, but it was made a weapon of propaganda against the Bharatiya Jan Sangh. The Council should be expanded. It currently does not include the Organisation Congress, the Swatantra Party, the Samyukta Socialist Party . . . (*Interruption*) . . . The Prime Minister should create an atmosphere for all the nationalists parties to come together . . . (*Interruption*) . . . and adopt concrete steps to solve the problem of communalism.

Who Is, and Who Should Be, in the National Integration Council

It is also necessary that nationalist leaders like Shri M.C. Chagla, Shri Hamid Dalwai, Dr. Jeelany and Shri Anwar Dehlavi should be included in the National Integration Council. Whom the Prime Minister should include depends upon her. But is she prepared to say anything about Muslim communalists? It is known to all that in Bhiwandi the Tamir-e-Millat had vitiated the atmosphere. But did anyone name it? The Shiv Sena is being criticised and it should be . . . (*Interruption*) . . . We too are being dragged in. Not that we are bothered. We are not here at the Prime Minister's pleasure, we are here in spite of her. We too represent the people of the country . . . (*Interruption*) . . . But when there is question of some Muslim communal organisation

their lips are sealed. What is the Jamiat-ul-Ulema doing? What
did the Tamir-e-Millat do in Bhiwandi? But is there anyone to
speak about it? . . . (*Interruption*) . . .

It is also necessary to institute judicial inquiries where
communal riots take place. Passions would have cooled down if
the Maharashtra Government had promptly ordered a judiciary
inquiry. But they said they would make a magisterial inquiry and
so that the people had to agitate for judicial inquiry. Conduct a
judicial inquiry wherever a riot takes place and implement its
recommendations.

I complain that the Maharashtra Government did not
implement the recommendations of the Integration Council. The
intelligence department was not strengthened. The police were
not readied for preventing riots.

What is happening with the Raghuvar Dayal Commission's
recommendations? A commission was set up for Ahmedabad
and a commission has been set up in Bhiwandi. But will the
recommendations of all these commissions be thrown into
the wastepaper basket? Will every problem be tested on the
touchstone of politics? Since the partition of the Congress the
nexus between communalists and communists is on the increase
and they have the Prime Minister's blessings. This is the reason
why communalism is growing.

I have nothing to say to my communalist friends, but to
those who are patriots in the Congress and those whose voice
of conscience had awakened in the presidential election I put a
question: are you ready to look at the problem of communalism
in its reality? Are you ready to solve it as a national problem?

The situation is serious, the country stands at the brink of
destruction. We must rise above the politics of votes to look at
this problem. If we made a mistake, show it to us, we are ready
to correct it. If Jan Sangh workers were at fault in Bhiwandi we
are ready to take action against them. We shall correct them.
But what is the position with other parties? We will have to do
some introspection, we will have to search our souls, and we will

have to launch countrywide campaign to solve the problem of communalism on a national level.

The longer we delay the more this problem would worsen, and then there will neither be democracy in this country nor will your dreams of establishing socialism be fulfilled.

Smt. Indira Gandhi: Sir, I am not speaking just to score points. In the past I have never interrupted an Hon. member while he was speaking. I have done this time because in the first place I felt it deeply, and secondly, because I have the courage of conviction. In my opinion the Hon. member has done a great disservice to the country and its minorities. This is such a serious occasion and this subject is so delicate that taking up his axioms could prove still more dangerous. I have no intention of doing so. So far as the other points and figures are concerned Shri Shukla will reply later.

Shri Vajpayee has used this occasion mainly to attack Muslims and all minorities in general. He has proclaimed with his raised voice in the old Hitler style. I know what he said and what words he used, as I was present at the time.

Shri Kanwar Lal Gupta: You had taken training.

Smt. Indira Gandhi: What training I took is the business of the Indian people, not yours. I do not know the words Shri Vajpayee used, but he has challenged me for something. I would like to tell him that I have never shirked a challenge, and never will. We should face the Indian people.

Shri Vajpayee: The Prime Minister should not lose control over herself.

Smt. Indira Gandhi: I am not losing control over myself. I am only saying this with all emphasis. I am not given to losing my control over myself.

Shri Vajpayee: I am also ready to face any type of challenge.

Smt. Indira Gandhi: Please do not talk like that. I am used to Shri Vajpayee and his party attacking me. Even in public statements they demean me by levelling baseless charges. They charged the Home Minister because he spoke frankly and with great sorrow. Actually Shri Vajpayee tried to extract something else from all this. He even tried . . . (*Interruption*) . . . Shri Gupta, please understand that I am going to say what I want to say. What you said by way of interruption is irrelevant . . . you have to understand this right now . . .

What happened in Delhi and the riots elsewhere were all lumped together, which is very sad. And no one among us wants to escape the responsibility. I cannot say definitely, but we should face the facts. Shri Vajpayee asked why these riots start. Are these small incidents, where a stone was thrown and a riot started? A riot may flare up when somebody kills somebody else for the first time.

It can also be caused by the atmosphere created by speeches like the one we heard today. It is the atmosphere that starts the disturbance.

And this is not a new thing. It is also not the first thing that it has happened. It is perhaps a coincidence that when people connected with the RSS or Jan Sangh go somewhere riots erupt in the surrounding areas, after some time. I do not know if this is a coincidence, but for me and for people who think about it this is certainly a strange coincidence. I think the Hon. member has been rightly advised to examine the situation and find out why these things happen.

It is very easy to level a charge against somebody. But there can be better way to tackle the situation. I am not saying this is just impossible. I have not studied it, which is mainly why I am going there. Possibly something more could be done there. There is always scope for improvement. I do not know what advance information the Government had. But there is no doubt that since this particular party got some seats in this House and in the assemblies it is raising this poisonous topic still more openly. While Shri Vajpayee was speaking some Hon. members shouted that some of his comments should be expunged. I am happy they were not. I want them to remain on record so that future generations could see the real thinking of the Jan Sangh—not the forceful Hindi that Shri Vajpayee uses from time to time, but the truth behind the words. Today we saw naked Fascism behind those words.

A lot of time was given to Shivaji. There would be no one in the country, let alone in the House, who would not have respect for Shivaji. But using his name for fanning the flames of communalism is not doing justice to him.

Shri V. Krishnamurthy: It is an offensive act.

Smt. Indira Gandhi: Communalism is bad, whether of Hindus or Muslims or Sikhs. It is also not true that whenever it flared up we have not strongly condemned it. Whenever a Muslim organisation or individual used inflammatory words we criticised it. But this does not mean we cannot criticise the wrong things said by members of the majority community. As I have already said people of the majority community have a special responsibility in the areas where they live. They are not just people but people with a special responsibility. As Hindus are in much greater in numbers than Muslims, Christians and other minorities in this country they have special responsibilities. But it is also possible that at some places other people may be the majority . . . At some places it may be the Sikhs, they have a greater responsibility towards the minorities. They may be Hindus or Muslims or somebody else. Similarly in Kashmir Muslims are in the majority. They have a similar responsibility there—of seeing that Hindus live in peace and security. This emphasis only shows that Hindus are not ready for all this. The atmosphere in the country has become so poisonous. Now we know such thoughts are being instilled in the minds of people. It is true that not all people are good, but there are also good people whose responsibility it is to meet such adverse circumstances. In the event of such an unfortunate incident we must try to help those in difficulties. We must think of how we can prevent such things from happening again. But misusing such events to level charges against people is to strike a blow at minorities. And if they repeat the same behaviour at other places it would be all the more wrong.

We all know that such incidents begin with small things. Why do they think of them on such a big scale at all? Shri Vajpayee said in Ahmedabad that people should not take the law in their hands. But for me the rest of his speech looked as if he was emphasising one point—we shall not do all this. What does this mean? It means 'we shall take the law in our hands, we shall take action, we must take steps'. What else does it mean?

Shri Vajpayee: I had not said so.

Smt. Indira Gandhi: This is what I understood the speech to mean. If that was not the meaning I hope he would clarify what it means and tell people not to do so. His own people are not doing so.

Shri Vajpayee: But the Congress can do it. Members of the Congress party can do it.

Smt. Indira Gandhi: So far as I know, there was a lot of commotion there. I may be wrong, but so far as I can understand he was short of giving notice that he and his party were going to do some special things. If this reaction meant there should be riots and lives of minorities be endangered it is very bad. They are on this path. This is what I could understand from his speech.

Shri Manoharan: The whole trouble is that Shri Vajpayee is unmarried.

Smt. Indira Gandhi: Unfortunately married people in his party are no better. Actually they are very bad.

As I said Shri Vajpayee did not do justice to Shivaji's memory. He has also done injustice to our old philosophy. Tradition does not include depriving the minorities of their rights. Actually the smritis state that our country opened its doors to people of all other religions and other customs and given them protection. We do so even today.

So the Hon. member is presenting a very different concept of India before the world. This is a bad thing. This concept is not in accordance with tradition. Actually the Jan Sangh . . . *Interruption* . . . I hope Shri Vajpayee does not think I am giving him so much importance . . . *Interruption* . . .

Shri Vajpayee: Shri Manoharan may have that complaint.

An. Hon. Member: Indianisation . . .

Smt. Indira Gandhi: I have already referred to the underlying idea. It is connected with the atmosphere created in the House and in the country. Shri Vajpayee just declared the Muslims started the riots. He asked, why? And he himself gave the answer—because they feel they cannot live in India. So they are launching this deadly battle. This is the cause. That is what I could understand from his speech.

Shri Vajpayee: This is one reason . . . *Interruption* . . .

Smt. Indira Gandhi: All right, it is one of the reasons . . . *Interruption* . . .

Shri Vajpayee: I had said so. There is nothing wrong in it. It is being objected to . . . *Interruption* . . .

Smt. Indira Gandhi: No objection is being raised. I would like the Hon. member to read some of the speeches made by members of his party who have said exactly this that Muslims cannot live in India unless they are Indianised.

Shri Vajpayee: Now, it is my turn to challenge the Prime Minister. Let her produce a single speech, and I am prepared to take action against that Jan Sangh leader.

Shri Shashi Bhushan: Shri Golwalkar and Hon. Shri Balraj Madhok said so.

Smt. Indira Gandhi: Shri Golwalkar said . . . *Interruption* . . . They say that they are distinct from the RSS. We do not think that they are distinct. Certainly not I am told, I am not absolutely sure, that the members who joined certain Governments on behalf of the Jan Sangh have been members of the RSS. I think there are any number of speeches which can be produced on these lines.

Shri Vajpayee: Talk of the Jan Sangh, the Jan Sangh.

Smt. Indira Gandhi: Talk about whom?

Shri Vajpayee: I am talking about you, not about the Jamiat-ul-Ulema. Otherwise you will get into difficulties. You have seen what speeches the leaders of the Jamiat-ul-Ulema were making.

Smt. Indira Gandhi: We oppose all such speeches, whatever the community or organisation the people making them belong. There is no doubt in this, and we have never hesitated to say so.

As I said earlier, whenever such a thing has been brought to my notice I have always spoken about it in private and in public meetings and elsewhere. On no occasion have I mentioned only one party if another party was also doing similar things.

One small point. The hon. Members opposite call themselves the old Congress but on no occasion do they dissociate themselves from many of the things which were done when they were with us . . . *Interruption* . . . Sushila perhaps came late. She does not know what I have said. I have no intention of talking about a particular incident.

Dr. Sushila Nayar (Jhansi): What is it you mean by saying so?

Smt. Indira Gandhi: I do not want you to do it, but you do it. You know yourself. Why should I waste the time of the House? I merely wanted to draw their attention. I am sure they all know what I am talking about.

Dr. Sushila Nayar: Political speech.

Smt. Indira Gandhi: I am making this a speech, what has everybody else done? What did Mr. Vajpayee make? Was it not a political speech? (*Interruption*) . . .

I am talking about a situation. What I am saying goes much deeper than what happened merely in Bhiwandi or Jalgaon or Ahmedabad. All these things form part of an atmosphere that is created. This is what I am trying to say, and I think it is extremely important that all Members of Parliament, as indeed all Indian citizens, think about these things far more deeply. You will be given all the facts about this. Chavanji has given the facts as known on the first day, and Shuklaji will give you whatever has come to our knowledge since then. But it is time for us not to regard these happenings merely as isolated incidents that take place, incidents which we debate. It is time to realize that it is kind of communal thinking, these speeches and articles which come out in newspapers which are creating this atmosphere, and it is no use just getting up and saying, 'You prove that we did it.'

Shri R.S. Yadav: Please explain what you are going to do.

Smt. Indira Gandhi: Action required by the situation there will certainly be taken.

Shri R.S. Yadav: The House should know what you think.

Shri Piloo Mody: I appreciate what the Prime Minister is saying but she goes on saying the same thing. What I would like to know is what her contribution is to the positive aspects of a programme which will depress this communalism and put it underground.

Smt. Indira Gandhi: I think Mr. Piloo Mody has entirely missed the point of what I have said. We do not want to put this underground. On the contrary I welcome Mr. Vajpayee's speech because we feel that for the first time he has come overground as far as this question was concerned. We do not want to put it underground. We wanted it to be overground and we want to fight it with all the strength at our command. This is not something which can be solved with a speech . . . *Interruption* . . . Shri Mody knows nothing about the Indian people. I happen to know them much better than him. I do not wish to take the time of the House any more . . . *Interruption.* I am not yielding now to anybody. Shri Yadav asked what steps would be taken. There are no new steps in that sense. People have suffered and we have to see firstly what relief has to be given immediately and what we can do on a slightly long-term basis. There is already an enquiry going on and it will come to its conclusions but I admit that I do not know how much such enquiries help. Now, apart from the question of relief and so on, we must all get together and see how we can prevent this kind of atmosphere growing, and how we can go down to the people, village by village and mohalla by mohalla to create that type of neighbourly feeling which in the last analysis is the only protection. The police can help in a particular situation but ultimately it is only one's neighbours who can be of real help. It is only the atmosphere in the country that can prevent this kind of rioting and senseless attacks on people. It is not just a question of whether somebody threw a stone, why should not people get angry? That is where you judge the maturity of the people. If people had done something wrong, by all means catch the guilty. But you do not watch the guilty. In fact the guilty are the first to get away and it is only the innocent who are looted and murdered.

Bhiwandi a Warning and a Challenge

Shri Vajpayee: Sir, it would have been better if you had given me the opportunity to speak after the Home Minister. I admit that Rule 143 does not provide for a reply, but this discussion has gone on for a long time. Many things have been said that needs to be replied to. However, I accept your ruling.

The Chairman: You wrote for a personal explanation, so I am giving you a chance.

Shri Vajpayee: The Home Minister is still to reply. That day he was not in the House; he was ill. Perhaps I criticised him very harshly. But I would like to clarify one point in that connection. When I said that Shri Chavan wept at the time of riots in Maharashtra but was not similarly affected by the riots of Gujarat perhaps I wrongly created the impression that he considers himself more as the leader of Maharashtra and does not have the same feeling or affection for other parts of the country. I had submitted that we will have to rise above party considerations to look at the problem of communalism. That the Syndicate should be criticised for the riots in Ahmedabad because it is in power there and we should not feel about it while we should be more affected by all the riots in Maharashtra, where the Indicate is in power . . . (*Interruptions*)

Shri Nambiar (Tiruchirappalli): On a point of order, Sir, is it a second speech or personal explanation?

Shri Sheo Narain: Are you the Master of the House?

Shri Vajpayee: And that was the context in which I said my words should be misconstrued. Not only that, the Prime Minister had deliberately presented my speech in a distorted form.

Shri Shashi Bhushan: Sir, why is he getting this extra time?

Mr. Speaker: Will you please sit down?

Shri Vajpayee: Sir, the Prime Minister said . . .

Smt. Indira Gandhi: Have you received a written copy of his personal explanation in advance, Sir?

Shri Vajpayee: Sir, what objection does the Prime Minister have?

Smt. Indira Gandhi: No objection. I wanted to know.

Mr. Speaker: Mr. Vajpayee said that he wanted to make a personal explanation. It is not a speech. It is a personal explanation. I have allowed it. The Prime Minister wants to know whether I have received a written copy in advance. No.

Shri Vajpayee: Sir, you have given permission. I have the right to remove the misunderstanding that has been created about my speech. The Prime Minister said: 'Shri Vajpayee has used this occasion to launch an attack on the Muslims in particular and, I think, all minorities.'

There has been no reference to 'all minorities' in this discussion. Where did these minorities come from? Does my speech refer to minorities? Sir, I have not even held all Muslims responsible in my speech. Can this truth be falsified? I would like to draw your attention and the attention of the House to what I had said. Sir, look at portions of my speech. Has not the Prime Minister heard it? I said not all Muslims want riots, there are patriots among Muslims too, there are peace-loving people among Muslims too—people who toil and care for their families. They do not want to play the game of violence and arson. But the Prime Minister dragged in all Muslims—and not only all Muslims but also Jains, Buddhists, Sikhs, Harijans and the backward classes, and tried to create the impression that I am against all minorities, and she is the only champion of the minorities in this country.

The Prime Minister may have seen Shri Frank Moraes's article titled 'Exploiting the Minorities', in which he has appealed to her—for God's sake do not indulge in the exploitation of the minorities. Sir, I have been charged with inciting the passions of Hindus through my speeches. Is this the only place for me to do that? . . . (Interruption) . . .

Shri Shashi Bhushan: You fan the flames of communalism everywhere.

Shri Vajpayee: Can I not make speeches outside the house? By your grace thousands of people come to listen to me. I have recently visited the Home Minister's constituency—Satara, Sholapur, Karad, Ahmednagar—and let him make inquiries through the intelligence department and say if there was anything objectionable in the speeches I made there. I never said anything that would create tension. So quite a few members might have wondered why I spoke like this in the House that day. Sir, I spoke deliberately. I did not threaten. I wanted to warn. Heed the warning. If the Lok Sabha does not heed this warning, adverse effects in this country cannot be prevented. This is not a threat.

Some hon. Member: It is.

Shri Vajpayee: Sir, this is a warning. Can we prevent Hindu communalism from growing by compromising with Muslim communalism? We cannot. So if you decide to fight at all, decide to fight communalism of both types; we are with you. But that day the Prime Minister did not say a single word about the Tamir-e-Millat. She was silent on the Shiv Sena. We refused to make an alliance with the Shiv Sena in Bombay. We could have made it, and Shiv Sena leader Shri Bal Thackeray said it was a passing thought (*Interruption*s).

Shri Madhu Limaye (Monghyr): Sir, I have a point of order.

Shri Shashi Bhushan: Sir, this is not a personal explanation. I too would like to reply to him.

Mr. Speaker: You may give a personal explanation on specific matters, do not say anything beyond that.

Shri Kanwar Lal Gupta: Why is the Prime Minister impatient? Why does she not allow him to speak? Do not be impatient. Listen to him.

Shri Madhu Limaye: Sir, there would be controversy without any reason if nobody is prepared to voluntarily abide by the rules. You have permitted Shri Vajpayee to give a personal explanation, but I do not see any word of personal explanation in this. He is replying to a discussion. If you have the right to reply you may do so, I do not mind, but the procedure of personal explanation should not be misused. I know Shri Vajpayee always interrupts on such matters. I never speak, because I want to give members an opportunity to speak . . . (*Interruption*) . . . I am not taking revenge on Shri Vajpayee, I always like to give a chance, but after all there has to be a procedure. All this controversy would not have arisen if he had given his personal explanation in writing and business conducted according to procedure. I hold that rules should be observed.

Mr. Speaker: I quite agree. So long I saw . . .

Shri Vajpayee: Permit me to reply to the discussion. You did not do so.

Mr. Speaker: There is no question of a discussion here.

Shri Vajpayee: Why not?

Mr. Speaker: I gave you an opportunity for a personal explanation, but so far you have not made any statement.

Shri M.L. Sondhi (New Delhi): Sir, you may hear my point of order. Let me make a brief submission on this.

Mr. Speaker: Let me first reply to the first point of order.

Shri M.L. Sondhi: This is a connected matter.

Mr. Speaker: I shall listen to it later on.

Shri M.L. Sondhi: You do not give an opportunity whenever a point of order is raised to enable a few members to bring their points of view. And this has happened on many occasions when Shri Madhu Limaye is holding his point of order.

Mr. Speaker: You are the only gentleman who will go on like this. This is the last time I want to avoid this headache.

Shri M.L. Sondhi: You may please hear me before making this remark.

Mr. Speaker: First I want to reply to this point of order.

Shri M.L. Sondhi: I am only claiming my right.

Mr. Speaker: I say there is no right. Please sit down. Let me reply to the first point of order. What is all this wasting of time? The point of order raised by Shri Madhu Limaye is fully justified. I am sorry that I could not trace that request of his. Please confine yourself to the personal explanation and not enter into a regular debate.

Shri Vajpayee: I am not entering into a debate. I said I did not say this in my speech. The Prime Minister has put words in my mouth. I did not threaten, I wanted to warn. Is this not a personal explanation?

Mr. Speaker: There is a lot of difference. You entered into a debate.

Shri Vajpayee: There will be some debate and the Home Minister is still to reply.

Mr. Speaker: Give your statement in brief.

Smt. Indira Gandhi: I too want a reply.

Shri Vajpayee: I have invited the Prime Minister to a public debate with me on communalism on All India Radio. The people will decide.

Mr. Speaker: This cannot be a personal explanation.

Shri Vajpayee: But repeating things that I did not say, ignoring the facts I presented and raising a fright, trying to project oneself as the champion of the minorities—this is not the way to fight the problem. Bhiwandi is a warning, Bhiwandi is a challenge. People of this country will have to pay heed to this warning, they will have to accept this challenge. But the first condition for this is that we will have to take this problem out of party politics. Is the Prime Minister ready to do so? Her speech says she is not. She misrepresented my speech. Thank you.

23

The Rama Temple Movement[*]

L.K. Advani

Sri Rama is the unique symbol, the unequalled symbol of our oneness, of our integration, as well as of our aspiration to live the higher values. As Maryada Purushottam, Sri Rama has represented for thousands of years the ideal of conduct, just as Rama Rajya has always represented the ideal of governance. There is scarcely a language in our country into which the Ramayana has not been translated. There is scarcely a folk tradition which does not celebrate the life and legend of Sri Rama. And one saint of our land after another, one saintly tradition after another has immersed itself in devotion to Him: the sacred Sri Guru Granth Sahib celebrates and invokes Sri Rama about two thousand four hundred times. Gandhiji died with His name on his lips.

It is natural therefore that the place of His birth has been an object of the deepest devotion for Hindus through the millennia. The inscription which has been found at the site and which speaks of a magnificent temple with a pinnacle of gold, dedicated to Lord Vishnu Hari who had humbled King Bali and defeated the wicked Dashanana, that is, Ravana; the record of the unremitting struggle of the Hindus to regain the site; the

---

[*] Extracted from the BJP's White Paper on Ayodhya and The Rama Temple Movement, Bharatiya Janata Party, Delhi, 1993, pp. 1–4.

pathetic history of their worshipping the spot from a distance when they were denied access to it, of their circumambulating it all these bear testimony to their deep and abiding, and indeed stirring, devotion to Sri Rama.

On the other hand, the structure which Mir Baqi put up on the orders of Babur never had any special significance from a religious point of view. It was purely and simply a symbol not of devotion and of religion but of conquest. Correspondingly, quite apart from its being an obstacle, preventing Hindus from worshipping the birthplace of their idol, Sri Rama, it was for the country the symbol of its subjugation.

As I mentioned, the Hindus had been trying for centuries to reacquire access to the spot and to reconstruct the magnificent temple. That was one stream of the Ayodhya movement—a stream that has been unbroken through centuries, one that predates by centuries all the persons and organisations which are today associated with the Ramajanmabhoomi movement. The Sadhus and Sants who set up the Ramajanmabhoomi Nyas in 1986—when no political party or organisation was seized of the matter—represent that continuous stream in our times.

But another powerful current arose among the people, and the confluence of the two has given the power to the Sri Ramajanmabhoomi movement which we see today. The manner in which the State bent to fundamentalists and terrorists, the manner in which self-styled leaders of minorities sought to revive the politics of separatism which had led to the Partition of the country, and even more so the manner in which Prime Ministers and others genuflected to them; and the double standards which came more and more to mar public discourse in India to the point that the word 'Hindu' became something to be ashamed about, to the point that nationalism became a dirty word these ignited a great revulsion among the people. As all this was being done in the name of 'Secularism', it led people to feel that what was being practised was not Secularism but a perversion.

The people began to search for what true Secularism meant, they began to wonder how our country could at all survive if Nationalism was to be anathema. Reconstructing the temple for Sri Rama became the symbol of this rising consciousness—ridding the country of the perversities to which it was being subjected in the name of Secularism, forging a strong and united country. The object of the movement thus became not just to construct yet another temple, the object became to put our country back on its feet, to purify our public life, our public discourse. This is how in 1989 the Bharatiya Janata Party formally decided to lend its shoulder to the cause the Party was responding to the deepest urges of our people.

But even though this tug of the people was what had led the Party to take up the cause, even though I had myself spelt out this perspective as I commenced the Rathyatra, my colleagues and I were surprised at the way our people responded. We were overwhelmed. It is only then that we saw how deep was their devotion to Sri Rama, how deeply they felt that they were not being listened to in their own country, how outraged they were at the politics of vote-banks and double-talk, and the talking down to them, of the preceding fifteen years.

The rest is history. Our governments refused to pay heed to the intense longing of the people with regard to Ramajanmabhoomi. And I regret to say that the Courts heeded our people no more. The governments remained lost in calculations; our leaders continued to be obstructive, and to put their trust in being clever; our Courts allowed themselves to remain entangled in legalisms. The anger which had been welling up across the country, and which would have found a smooth and peaceful outlet if Kar Seva had been allowed on 2.77 acres of land adjoining the disputed structure, exploded on December 6. Disregarding the exhortations of the movement leaders, who had planned to shift the structure only after appropriate legislation, the Karsevaks pulled down the structure. For millions in the country, the construction of the temple had begun.

But the Karsevaks did more. They did not just erase a symbol of our subjugation. They did not just begin building a symbol of resurgence. They showed us as if in a flash how far we have to travel. For the country reacted in two diametrically opposite ways, as virtually two different peoples. For a handful those in government, in political parties, and in large sections of the English Press, for instance, what had happened was 'a national shame', it was 'madness', it was 'barbaric'. For the rest of the country it was a liberation sweeping away of cobwebs. The depth of devotion to Sri Rama, the depth of anger at the recent politics, had surprised me, as I said: the depth of the chasm between these two nations the microscopic minority at the top and the people did not.

But as the organs of communication, Parliament, the English Press, Doordarshan were in the hands of the very persons whose politics and double-talk the Karsevaks were tearing down, calumny was rained down upon the Karsevaks, on the Ramajanmabhoomi movement, on the BJP in particular.

The Government's White Paper is part of this campaign of calumny. It is full of evasions and half-truths. Even within Government, voices were raised to protest at its concealments— it was pointed out, for instance, that the White Paper did not contain a word about the negotiations which the Prime Minister had conducted with the Sadhus and Sants, and with several of us.

The calumny called for the antidote of truth: it was necessary to save the great and mighty movement so that it would continue to be the vehicle of national resurgence, it was necessary to set the record straight. The BJP thus decided to prepare a true White Paper on the Ayodhya movement. A group of scholars was put together to study the documents, to obtain records from within Government too—and to obtain the direct testimony of those with whom the Prime Ministers and their representatives had negotiated.

The result is in your hands. This is a unique narrative on at least two counts:

- It contains many hitherto unpublished, confidential documents, for instance, on pages 81-89, readers will find the internal confidential summary which the Prime Minister's own Special Cell had made of the case of the VHP and the AIBMAC, and they would be led to ask why the fact that the Special Cell had reached such conclusions was kept hidden from the country.
- It contains the first-person testimony of the most eminent and pious Sadhus and Sants, as well as of others as to what transpired in the discussions the Prime Minister and his emissaries had with them.

Based as it is on such a wealth of primary evidence and given the meticulous care with which the Paper has been prepared, this document brings to light many facts which most of us would not have known. Few of us for instance would remember that while Shri Narasimha Rao sought time now to study the problem, he had himself been the head of the Committee of Ministers which Shri Rajiv Gandhi had set up to examine the Ayodhya issue in 1987, a little nugget which the Government's White Paper does not mention at all. Few of us would remember that as long ago as 1955 the courts had bewailed the fact that the issue was being entangled in litigation and had directed the concerned court to conclude the matter expeditiously. Few of us would remember that the High Court had itself said that many of the issues cannot be settled by the judiciary. Few of us would know the contrast that marked the handling of the issue by three Prime Ministers. Few of us would know how every time a solution was at hand—from the Ordinance of Shri V.P. Singh to the formula which a Minister of Rao's Government canvassed with my colleagues and me—the step was reversed and disowned. Few will remember the devices by which the courts have been, and have allowed themselves to be, enmeshed.

All this and much more is documented to the dot here. This White Paper thus is a document of record. It puts together primary evidence to garner which even historians will be tuning to it years hence. The Ayodhya movement, in particular the erasure of Mir Baqi's insignia of conquest and the commencement of the Temple of Sri Rama, has already occasioned deep reflection and rethinking in our country on what a truly secular polity should be, on how a country can even survive if the deepest sentiments of 85 percent of its people are spurned, on how we should find better ways to attend to such issues so that the people are not driven to force solutions on all. In no section is this rethinking deeper and more evident than the Muslims.

I am certain that this White Paper will further this process of national reflection. It is thus more than a document of record. It is the interim report of a movement for national resurgence. I therefore commend it to all our countrymen wholeheartedly.

24

A Clash of Classes and Cultures[*]

Nirad C. Chaudhuri

A very important consequences of the new intellectual activities has to be noted in conclusion. It is already a factor in the political and social life of the country, and it might have much greater importance in the future. The intellectual movement has created a social class whose outlooks, ideas, behaviour, and social role are utterly different from those of the traditional and the numerically stronger part of the middle-class. That is to say, the new intellectual movement has added another minority to the many minorities already existing in Indian society. Instead of making for the cultural fusion of the people of the country it has strengthened the cultural stratification which had already gone far.

Besides, the alienation between the new intelligentsia and the traditional Hindu middle-class is virtually complete. The new middle-class knows very little about the old, and when reminded about its existence feels inclined to scoff at it. Perhaps if the need arose the new intelligentsia could, by dint of trying, arrive at an external understanding of the traditional Hindu middle-class, such as a European or American living in India might, but the new intelligentsia and its ideas were bound to

[*] Extracted from *The Intellectual in India*, Nirad C. Chaudhuri, Associated Publishing House, New Delhi, 1967, pp. 36–37.

remain unintelligible to the traditionalists. They can regard the Westernized type of Indian only as a renegade or usurper.

In such circumstances a resolution of the conflict could be brought about only by the complete subordination of the one to the other. At this moment, through the disappearance of British rule, political power has passed to the new intelligentsia, because they were the only men who could take over and run the modern administration of India. But through the adoption of universal suffrage and other democratic steps in regard to government, the traditionalists are becoming more and more powerful, and it is quite possible that they will become dominant in the life of the Indian people in the very near future.

What will happen to the new intelligentsia then is a question worth discussing. If one could assume the existence of the great fervour in convictions and strength of character in this class one might have expected a social and political clash, as a result of which the new order could yet dominate India as a minority imposing itself on a majority. But no such prediction can be made at this time. The downfall of the present rulers and of the new intelligentsia may both equally result. All that can be done now is to recognize the existence of the conflict, both actual and potential. The British rulers of India ignored or at all events underrated the power of the new class. Today this class is nearly always monopolizing the attention of foreign observers, and the traditionalists are being virtually ignored by them.[*]

---

[*] The results of the general election of 1967 are bound to attract world attraction to the Hindu traditionalists.

25

An Area of Awakening[*]

V.S. Naipaul in Conversation with Dileep Padgaonkar

It is with some trepidation that I went to meet V.S. Naipaul in his bright, spare and elegant flat in London. This was because of a comment of his I had read several years before.

Talking to Ms. Michiko Kakutani of *The New York Times* he had made no secret of his intolerance with those who fail to appreciate his work. 'I can't be interested in people who don't like what I write because if you don't like what I write, you're disliking me,' he told her. 'I can't see a Monkey— you can use a capital M, that's an affectionate word for the generality reading my work. No, my books aren't read in Trinidad now—drumbeating is a higher activity, a more satisfying activity.'

Now my own attitude to his work had been ambivalent. I had always admired—and this is putting it mildly—the quality of his prose. It has been praised so often and in such laudable terms that anything I say would be plainly superfluous. Suffice it to state that even his sternest critics regard him as one of the world's foremost living writers.

---

[*] Extracted from *Sunday Times of India*, 18 July 1993.

But then his works, when I first read them, evoked in me feelings of anger and even resentment. Naipaul's account of third world nations and peoples, though pitilessly lucid, lacked, in my youthful eyes, the understanding that empathy alone brings. Not only did Naipaul not display any such empathy but he appeared to be frankly hostile to the people he wrote about.

'I do not have the tenderness more secure people can have toward bush people,' he told Ms. Kakutani. 'I feel threatened by them. My attitude and the attitude of people like me is quite different from the people who live outside the bush or who just go camping in the bush on weekends.'

The very titles of his first two books on India, *An Area of Darkness* and *A Wounded Civilization*, made it clear that he regarded this country as yet another, indeed extravagant, example of decay and decomposition, inertia; violence, fear and generally of intellectual puerility and relentless moral turpitude. His was a stark vision: one which lacked the flimsiest hope of progress or redemption.

'Poise, a sense of proportion and that irony which Naipaul finds must be maintained if one wants to help. Otherwise, criticism is self-indulgence. It must attack, even denounce, but it must not deny human beings their humanity. In *An Area of Darkness* Naipaul comes dangerously close to doing that,' the poet Nissim Ezekiel had written.

I was 20 when this article first appeared and its contents had met with my thumping approval.

In later years, however, when the attraction I had felt for ideologies or world views which claimed to explain everything about everything began to fade, Naipaul's books seemed to ring true. In the meanwhile, he, too had changed. The opening sentence of his great novel, *A Bend in the River* (1979), read: 'The world is what it is; men who are nothing, who allow themselves to become nothing, have no place in it.' From this ominous note of dark despair to the celebration of a million mutinies in India ten years later Naipaul has indeed travelled quite a distance.

My trepidation vanished within minutes of my arrival at his flat. Naipaul is a small, elegantly dressed man who uses gestures sparingly, speaks with a mellifluous Oxbridge accent and treats his Indian visitor with exquisite courtesy. He had once described himself as an 'unrepentant snob' but during our conversation the flashes of the snobbery were few and far between.

I noticed one in particular: when he pointedly referred to the brand name and year of the bottle of champagne which he generously opened half-way through our conversation. The conversation turned out to be much like the champagne: 'Soft and deep, the steel of the backbone will be concealed in a luscious velvety glove', as the *Moet et Chaudon* is generally described.

Dileep Padgaonkar (DP): Many expatriate writers are either hostile to their new environment or else are subjugated by it. But you appear to have turned to your advantage your situation. You seem to belong neither here nor there but always elsewhere. And you seem to constantly redefine this 'elsewhere'. Each day of writing is a day for redefinition, for probing, for questioning . . .

V.S. Naipaul (VSN): Exactly, the reason is that you carry so many ideas in your head. Because of the spread of education and the collapse of empires there has been such a great extension of freedom, this is very new in the world. Education and freedom enable you to get away from concerns about roots and identities.

I can carry all my history in my head, all my travels, the fist music I heard (Hindi film music of the thirties and the forties), the first language I was exposed to (Bhojpuri Hindi). And I can do all this without any stress in my mind. Nobody really lives in a single culture. Even Africa has been subjected to many, many influences. To talk about a 'pure African' culture makes little sense.

Take Indian cooking: it has ingredients from so many cultures. Indeed how can you say 'I am an Indian'? India means the world, in a way.

People live in several worlds at the same time. But many do not want to admit this. They stick to foolish notions. For example I came across someone in New York who said: 'I drink Coca-Cola because I am an American.' But you don't drink coffee because you are an Arab, or tea because you are a Chinese or chocolate because you are a Mexican. I should be able to say: 'I drink Coca-Cola because I like Coca-Cola.'

DP: In India we have seen time and again that people have been either aggressive or apologetic about their cultural identity. In today's India it is difficult to get people to admit that there are several layers to a cultural identity: Hinduism in all its pluralistic splendour, the contribution made by Islam's long presence in the subcontinent, the exposure to the West.

VSN: The alternatives—traditionalism versus westernism— might be false. There is no either/or because the essence of literature, iniquity and philosophy is a constant examination of oneself and one's world and one's own culture. One hopes to leave the world with different ideas than those given to one when one entered the world.

The alternatives proposed in India could lead to brutal clashes. Remember that India was trampled over, fought over. It had destroyed itself by its wars. It was almost at a standstill. You had the invasions and you had the absence of a response to them. There was an absence even of the idea of a people, of a nation defending itself. So there is no reason really for people to be either aggressive or apologetic about all this.

DP: Unless of course the perception is that you have to contend with the 'other'. Some of this is reflected in *India: Million Mutinies Now*. For the past ten or 12 years the feeling in India has burgeoned that Hinduism faces a threat from the mushroom growth of Islamic fundamentalism. It began with the revolution in Iran. The Islamisation process of Pakistan under General

Zia exacerbated that feeling. The collapse of the Soviet Union and the subsequent rise of Islamic nations in Central Asia, the Salman Rushdie affair, similar harassment by fundamentalists of liberal Muslim intellectuals in India: all these factors taken together persuaded some forces to argue that a divided Hindu society cannot counteract Islamic fundamentalism.

VSN: I don't see it quite in that way. The things you mentioned are quite superficial. You cannot be a fundamentalist if you want to go and live in America. Ask any Iranian where he wants to go: it is to America. If that is your goal you cannot be a fundamentalist. I think fundamentalism is a passing phase even in Islam. It is a religion on the defensive.

What is happening in India is a new, historical awakening. Gandhi used religion in a way as to marshal people for the independence cause. People who entered the independence movement did it because they felt they would earn individual merit.

Today, it seems to me that Indians are becoming alive to their history. This has not happened before. Romila Thapar's book on Indian history is a Marxist attitude to history which in substance says: there is a higher truth behind the invasions, feudalism and all that. The correct truth is the way the invaders looked at their actions. They were conquering, they were subjugating. And they were in a country where people never understood this.

Only now are the people beginning to understand that there has been a great vandalising of India. Because of the nature of the conquest and the nature of Hindu society such understanding had eluded Indians before. In pre-industrial India people moved about in small areas unaware of the dimension of the country and without any notion of a community or a nation. People seemed to say: we are all right here. The West may be disastrous. But we are not affected.

Now, however, things seem to be changing. What is happening in India is a mighty creative process. Indian intellectuals, who want to be secure in their liberal beliefs, may not understand what is going on, especially if these intellectuals happen to be in the United States. But every other Indian knows precisely what is happening: deep down he knows that a larger response is emerging even if at times this response appears in his eyes to be threatening.

We have to be careful about something else happening in the world. It might be news to you. I recently received a document, the text of a lecture given by some sort of an expert on India who teaches at Trinity College, Cambridge. The lecture was on fundamentalism. In it we are told that Islam was brought to India by traders and merchants and that places of Hindu worship became absorbed into Mohammedan places of worship.

Well, all this is absurd and it is said by a serious scholar. This ties in with what one read in *The Independent* recently. Its correspondent in Delhi reported that the Indians removed the Hindus from Kashmir to give their armed forces a free hand. So the expulsion of the Hindus was self-done; it had nothing to do with attacks on them. I don't know how true this is.

However, we are aware of one of the more cynical forms of liberalism; it admits that one fundamentalism is all right in the world. This is the fundamentalism they are really frightened of: Islamic fundamentalism. Its source is Arab money. It is not intellectually to be taken seriously, etc.

I don't see the Hindu reaction purely in terms of one fundamentalism pitted against another. The reaction is a much larger response . . . Mohammedan fundamentalism is essentially negative, a protection against a world it desperately wishes to join. It is a last-ditch fight against the world.

But the sense of history that the Hindus are now developing is a new thing. Some Indians speak about a synthetic culture: this is what a defeated people always speak about. The synthesis may be culturally true. But to stress it could also be a form of response to intense persecution.

This is sometimes taken to absurd lengths by Nirad Chaudhuri, for instance, who in the midst of the massive vandalism speaks about Hindu aggressiveness. He talks about Al Baruni coming as though peacefully and Hindus reacting to them in an aggressive manner. This is nonsensical.

DP: This new sense of history as you call it is being used in India in very many different ways. Some use it for short-term political gain. But there are those who, well beyond the pale of Hindu political forces, are striving to come to terms with the past. It is revealing, is it not, that leftists in India now think it necessary to quote Vivekananda, the poets of the Bhakti movement. All the same, my worry is that somewhere down the line this search for sense of history might yet again turn into hostility towards something precious which came to us from the West: the notion of the individual . . .

VSN: This is where the intellectuals have a duty to perform. The duty is the use of the mind. It is not enough for intellectuals to chant their liberal views or to abuse what is happening. To use the mind is to reject the grosser aspects of this vast emotional upsurge.

We all live in a universal civilization. Some more than others. We have our individual particularities. But we are all inhabited by universal civilization. It is very hard to go back.

DP: Are you more pessimistic about Africa, which also figures prominently in your work, than other regions of the world?

VSN: I do not think in terms of pessimism and optimism. That is not the way I look at the world. Economists and political analysts are writing off Africa. But the cultural people are playing it up. Again the mind is not at work. When discussing Africa it is always: 'Let's go and feed them. We need black votes in America.' Or 'Let's write about African pots and African music'. It's never: 'Let's consider this carefully.'

After the bomb blast in Bombay I read a leader in one of the papers here in London. Lots of words. But the last lines were: 'There is an optimistic way of considering India. And there is a pessimistic way of considering India.' Now what do you make of this?

What needs to be done about Africa? I have not read anything about Africa by American black people or Caribbean black people of Brazilian black people. Analysis has not occurred. Why? That is the great gap about Africa. You have Africa studies departments all over. They invite African writers, give them seats. They get praise. But that is meaningless. They are not doing any work. Africa is going to hell. There is no one writing about its political failures. No one is analysing them. This pains me: this absence of the mind at work.

I met a Latin American writer once who had gone as a delegate to a North South conference in Mexico. And he said to me: 'Oh, Mexico, you cannot imagine the corruption out there.' I asked him: 'Did you talk about that?' He said, 'No.' Well, what is the point of going to a conference in Mexico and not talk about corruption? You know what corruption does to societies. If you don't talk about it in a conference what good does it serve to do so in a corner?

DP: When you take a look at Asia you find that self-analysis is notable for its absence. It is difficult to name a single, outstanding essayist in such advanced places as, say, Singapore. India may be somewhat different but not different.

VSN: You know that in India the reaction to my books on India has been tepid. The overall assumption is that I must not be critical of where I come from. This is a good liberal attitude. The advanced countries are expected to produce self-analysis, Critical literature. The retarded countries are expected to produce literature which praises the existing order. No one in Africa will write, for instance: 'All this dance and music is jolly good but what about the rest?'

The intellectuals and the liberals have divided the world into two. There is one advanced section where literature and thought endlessly recreate culture in the way Leonard Woolf talked at Cambridge in the 1890s about remaking culture all the time. And then there is another section where you have nothing but praises, praises and praises. I can't accept that.

When I began to write my first books in a gentle, comic vein I came in for much criticism. And I responded by saying: I don't think any English writer would ever say, 'Mr. Dickens writes with disregard for his country. He ridicules England, his background. He must create nice characters.' But they will say all this about my work.

DP: Do not forget that until very, very recently many intellectuals felt that it was their duty to uphold the nation-state against an onslaught from imperialism, cultural aggression and so on. This is one reason why they were not critical about their environment.

VSN: That is dangerous, is not it? I came back in 1966 from East Africa. This is five years before Idi Amin and quite a few years before the current obscenities that are going on in, say, Kenya. I talked to a weekly newspaper here in England and suggested that this should be written about. And they said: 'But how can you make such a suggestion? This would be giving comfort to South Africa.' But I said: 'This has nothing to do with South Africa. It had to do with people living in East Africa.' Look what has happened.

DP: Seventy years of the Soviet Union did precisely that. You could not criticize any aspect of the Soviet system because that would mean playing into the hands of the CIA. Entire generations of intellectuals have grown up convinced about this.

VSN: It's worse than that. With that kind of lying you create lesser people. I went to Czechoslovakia shortly after the Velvet Revolution. It was impossible to talk to these people who fought the revolution. They had been so censored, they had read so little, they had stopped exercising their mind, they had stopped looking at the world. I talked to East Germans too. They were also intellectually damaged. It will take two or three generations to make them decontaminated.

The achievement in India is that you had two sides of the independence movement as enshrined in Gandhi. One is the political struggle and the other the effort to get rid of the caste system, of reforming society, his South African training. You had two battles: one to cleanse the country of foreign rule and the other to cleanse oneself. One looked outward; the other inward. I see no reason why the two cannot be combined. If this is not done then ten years later people will say 'Why did not you tell us? Look at the mess we are in now?' Mind is mind. Truth is truth. A great deal of what you have written about Islamic fundamentalism, intellectual double standards and so forth has subsequently proved to be true.

Do not forget the Caribbean. I mention this because a Dutch edition of *The Middle Passage* has just come out after 32 years. It is very pleasing to know that the book is still considered relevant.

DP: How does it feel to learn that you have been prescient?

VSN: It convinces you that nothing matters more than to be truthful. Having your side, having to protect your side: that is so false. Such writing becomes redundant in five years. The other thing I have learnt is never to be taken in by passing events.

A passing event would be, for instance, the Rushdie affair, it is not going to bend affairs. Writing to me is to be truthful, to cast my mind five years hence. If you were to write about England now and you choose to write about Mr. John Major would you pause to think: who would be interested in this even two years from now?

DP: Why have you not written more about Western societies?

VSN: I have written quite a lot. Have you read *Enigma*?

DP: I have.

VSN: It is a serious look about England, about England's development in the 30 years. It is written in an oblique way; but the focus on England is there. I have written about the American south too. My interest, however, began with who I am. I have explored the strands in my upbringing. India, Caribbean, slave society in the background (historically), England.

DP: Where did the interest in Islamic societies come in all this?

VSN: There were Mohammedans among us in Trinidad. The Indian community there had strong bonds. Incidentally, they still do in Guyana. But in Trinidad you had the Negro movement, a racial movement, headed by Mr. Eric William. This was in 1956. It brought us closer to the Mohammedans. Please understand that my interest is not in Arab Islam. It is in Islam outside the Arab world, in countries conquered by the Arabs or influenced by the Arab religion. When my book on these countries was published they wanted an Arab to review it. But what does an Arab know about Malaysia or Pakistan or Iran?

I think that the sense of injustice, the tragic sense of the world which you find in the countries I have mentioned will transmute itself into something very creative.

DP: Did you feel the same way about Indian Muslims?

VSN: No. We talked of other things. Those people are considerably lost. This is something that their fathers and grandfathers had brought about. They had not thought their ideas through. When Iqbal spoke about the need for Islam to have its own society he had not worked out the consequences. He had not considered the possibility of Bosniaisation in the subcontinent.

Iqbal maintained that Islam was not a matter of private conscience. What was needed was an Islamic society, an Islamic nation. But how do you create a society of believers? How about those who were going to be left behind? It is amazing that this thought did not occur to him. I attribute it to the fear of thinking things through.

You find a similar fear about Somalia; send the food, lend the troops, get exciting film footage. That is childish thinking. Because the problem of Somalia is profounder than feeding them for five days or five weeks.

DP: I am led more and more to believe that governments act for the sake of television . . .

VSN: Oh yes! That explains why everything that they have to say is couched in one liners: 'We are going to feed you even if it kills you.'

DP: How did you react to the Ayodhya incident?

VSN: Not as badly as the other did, I am afraid. The people who say that there was no temple there are missing the point. Babar, you must understand, had contempt for the country he had conquered. And his building of that mosque was an act of contempt for the country.

In Turkey they turned the Church Of Santa Sophia into a mosque. In Nicosia churches were converted into mosques too. The Spaniards spent many centuries reconquering their land from Muslim invaders. So these things have happened before and elsewhere.

In Ayodhya the construction of a mosque on a spot regarded as sacred by the conquered population was meant as an insult. It was meant as an insult to an ancient idea, the idea of Ram which was two or three thousand years old.

DP: The people who climbed on top of these domes and broke them were not bearded people wearing saffron robes and with ash on their foreheads. They were young people clad in jeans and tee-shirts.

VSN: One needs to understand the passion that took them on top of the domes. The jeans and the tee-shirts are superficial. The passion alone is real. You can't dismiss it. You have to try to harness it.

Hitherto in India the thinking has come from the top. I spoke earlier about the state of the country: destitute, trampled upon, crushed. You then had the Bengali renaissance, the thinkers of the 19th century. But all this came from the top. What is happening now is different. The movement is now from below.

DP: My colleague, the cartoonist, Mr. R.K. Laxman, and I recently travelled thousands of miles in Maharashtra. In many places we found that noses and breasts had been chopped off from the statues of female deities. Quite evidently this was a sign of conquest. The Hindutva forces point to this too to stir up emotions. The problem is: how do you prevent these stirred-up emotions from spilling over and creating fresh tensions?

VSN: I understand. But it is not enough to abuse them or to use that fashionable word from Europe: fascism. There is a big, historical development going on in India. Wise men should understand it and ensure that it does not remain in the hands of fanatics. Rather they should use it for the intellectual transformation of India.

DP: This would imply a fairly radical revision of many of the basic assumptions we have made regarding the country: the nature of Indian society, the way it is to be governed, its place in the world.

VSN: What kind of assumptions?

DP: One basic assumptions flows from the Constitution. When it was adopted, its architect, Dr Ambedkar, made a speech in which he said in substance: today we have performed a revolutionary act. We have put not the village, the caste or the community at the centre of the scheme of things but the individual. Schematically speaking, this importance given to the individual is inspired by the American and French revolutions and by the enlightenment. The feeling now is that the individual will be subjugated if the basis of Indian nationhood is to be Hinduism alone. That is a potential danger.

VSN: There are too many people who think like you for that to be realized. Fortunately, this movement in favour of the individual has come as a result of education, of several generations of educated people. There are enough people who are educated, who feel like you, who read you and your papers to fight this. There is a self-regulator; thermostat which should take care of the problem.

DP: I hope you are right. But the possibility that the individual will be displaced frightens me no end. This is important for all people but especially for the Dalits and women. Women in particular. They are the ones who are in many respects in the forefront of progress. They should not be endangered. The Hindutva idea of a woman should not confine her in the 'Sita-Savitri' mould.

VSN: That is dreadful. And that needs to be fought for many reasons. One of the most important surely is the economic imperative. You can't keep the economy going with such notions. The economic liberalization should help to counter the trend. I hope liberalization is moving ahead . . .

DP: It is. The atmosphere has clearly changed. Attitudes are beginning to change. Indians are rediscovering the entrepreneurial spirit.

VSN: What about the modern, moderate elements in the BJP?

DP: Some fine people who belong to the modernist stream have recently joined the party. This is all to the good. However, I am afraid that there are not enough of such elements to contain the extremist trends. Time has frozen for them. They want to recreate the golden age which did not exist in the first place. All the same, that educated people—doctors and engineers for instance—are backing the BJP not because they necessarily subscribe to everything that goes under the name of Hindutva but because they are disillusioned with the Congress system or because they are genuinely worried about the rise of Islamic fundamentalism.

At any rate, whatever the reasons, Indians are now discussing, admittedly in a chaotic and confused manner, several issues concerning the country. I wonder however whether the debate can be conducted meaningfully if it is couched entirely in Western vocabulary.

VSN: Well, perhaps, you need to do what Ananda Coomaraswamy did for Indian aesthetics.

DP: Or Radhakrishnan for Indian philosophy.

VSN: Yes.

DP: I was in my last years of college when I read *An Area of Darkness*. And I was angry. Then came *A Wounded Civilization*. And I flew into a rage again. I told myself how can he bring himself to write about the country in a horrible way? Finally there is *A Million Mutinies Now*. This time I can only say: How much I have grown up!

VSN: *A Wounded Civilization* is what we have been talking about. It is about a conquered people. It is the refusal to accept this fact that explains the instinctive reaction to the book. This was a devastated people who felt smaller and smaller.

DP: I must not exaggerate this. But in retrospect your three books on India taken together read in many respects like an autobiography of many of those belonging to my generation.

VSN: What a wonderful thing to say.

DP: I was angry and hostile, mind you, but with the passage of years I have realized that on many important issues I may not have been lucid enough to admit to myself that things were wrong.

VSN: Lucidity was easier for me because I was from the outside. But let me also say this. Very few Asian countries have thrown up grand men as India has done . . . very, very grand men. Both in this century and in the last one.

DP: What have you been reading lately?

VSN: I read ten books at a time. But one which has gripped my attention is a book on travels in Africa written in 1795 by a young man who is about to die. It is a classical account.

The beginning is boring: descriptions of races, climate, crop productions and so on. Then he talks about his capture by a tribe, his attempts to survive. Three out of four Africans, he says, are slaves: slavery is so much a part of life that it is a measure of money. 'Give me two slaves worth of cotton'—that sort of thing. It should be read. It has marked Black Africa to this day maybe.

There are two issues about Black Africa I would like to go into. Why is there no Arab guilt about Black Africa? The Arabs were importing slaves all along. African eunuchs were employed to guard harems. Castration of Black Africans was common practice in Sudan and upper Egypt. And why is there no sense of guilt in Brazil where slaves were imported until 1888? It probably has to do with the intellectual traditions of these countries. A sense of guilt of shock is doubtless linked to analytical abilities . . .

DP: In India you do have a sense of guilt. But more than guilt you have a strong sense of atonement. Prayaschitta. You atone for what the caste system has done to the Dalits, what, in more recent times, has happened to the minorities and so on.

VSN: There, again, you have an original Indian response. I told you: there is truly historic and creative development taking place in India.

26

The Nehruvian Framework[*]

Girilal Jain

As discussed earlier, two processes have been on among Hindus since the early nineteenth century—modernization and self-renewal. Of the two processes modernization has in a sense been stronger. For one thing, behind modernization has stood the appeal and power of the dominant Western civilization, which has been all-encompassing as no other has ever been. For another, it has plainly been out of the question to organize the economy and polity on a non-Western basis. All attempts to conceptualize an alternative, beginning with Gandhiji and ending with Jayaprakash Narayan in the 1970s, have come a cropper. For our purpose, the power and appeal of modernization is best illustrated by the easy sway Pandit Nehru acquired in the wake of independence.

Nehru was Gandhiji's lieutenant and heir-designate during the freedom movement. But he stood for a very different India from the master's and, as independence approached, he left the latter in no doubt that he was determined to have his way. The letters exchanged between them on the eve of independence speak volumes. Nehru was dismissive of the Mahatma's approach as outlined in the *Hind Swaraj* (1908) and the Mahatma acquiesced

[*] Extracted from Girilal Jain, *The Hindu Phenomenon*, UBS Publishers, Delhi, 1994, pp. 89–112.

in it virtually without protest, though it may be recalled, Gandhiji had taken the initiative in raising the question of what kind of India was to be built on achievement of freedom, emphasising that he still stood by his old vision. Gandhiji did not reply to the issues raised by Nehru.

Perhaps he realised that he had played his role. Regardless, however, of whether he realised it or not, the time was truly up for him. This is not to deny either his heroic role in the struggle to contain passions unleashed by partition or the historic importance of his martyrdom. But, in the final analysis, that only facilitated Nehru's pre-eminence and the downgrading of his only potential rival, Sardar Patel, who incidentally was no Gandhian either.

The Sardar had better insight (not just administrative and organizational skill) into India's needs. But the atmosphere was not propitious for him precisely because the Hindu element in his personality was stronger than the modernist with its emphasis on socialism and secularism as articulated by not only Nehru but other leaders such as Jayaprakash Narayan and Ram Manohar Lohia who has come into prominence in the 1942 Quit India movement. Thus while Gandhism and Gandhians have been a marginal phenomenon in independent India, Nehru continues to dominate the thinking of the Indian intelligentsia three decades after its death. Modernizers are still in command.

Nehru's role in the modernization of India is still well known. There is, however, another face of Nehru which places him, even if indirectly, among the proponents of Hindu civilisation. This, of course, is not one of Nehru's prominent faces. He rarely allowed it to come to the fore. But unlike most of his followers, Nehru was deeply involved with the problem of the cultural-civilizational personality of India.

Nehru himself spoke and wrote extensively for well over four decades. Much of what he wrote as prime minister between 1947 and 1964 is still not available for scrutiny. As such, we have to rely primarily on S. Gopal's assessment of him as spelt out in his three-volume study of Nehru. So far, no one else has been allowed full access to the Nehru papers. There is, however, evidence to show that somewhere at the back of Nehru's mind lurked reservations regarding the path on which he had helped launch India. Though this evidence is available publicly in the collection of his speeches, it has been neglected.

This is particularly surprising because it is well known that Nehru struggled to discover the soul of India as no other Indian public figure did; Gandhiji's struggle was of an altogether different kind, though it was far more valiant. Nehru was handicapped in a variety of ways. He did not know Sanskrit or for that matter any Indian language well enough. He did not have direct access to Indian tradition even by way of folklore since Motilal Nehru had deliberately westernised himself and brought up Jawaharlal in a manner appropriate to an English gentleman. He was educated at Eton and Harrow. Nehru was essentially not a deep thinker. To the extent he was interested in ideas, he was familiar only with ideas current in Britain in his impressionable years; Fabian socialism, for instance.

Above all, he approached India's past, historical as well as spiritual, through British scholars who inevitably saw India through their culturally coloured prisms. Western scholarship was also in its infancy. Much more valuable work was done when Nehru was too deeply involved in public affairs to keep track of it. As it happened, the more valuable work was done by French and German Orientalists who were not accessible to him on account of the language barrier. Many of us still encounter this difficulty.

Nehru's intellectual background led him to take a synthetic (aggregationist) view of Indian culture, though on a more careful reflection, it should have been possible for him to recognize, on the other hand, its integral unity founded on yoga, of which the Veda itself is a fruit, and on the other, its capaciousness on the strength of the same boundless yogic foundation which placed no limit on the freedom of the human spirit. Inevitably this synthetic view of Indian culture led him—especially in view of the Persianized cultural background of his own forebears and of the Kashmiri Pandit community in the plains and, indeed, in the valley itself—to accept the theory of a Hindu-Muslim cultural synthesis. The fact of partition must have provoked some doubt in his mind. He was too sensitive and honest an individual not to be shaken by so traumatic a development.

But, by then, it was too late for him to review and restate his basic position, even if he were so inclined. No political leader in his position could afford to do so. And if it was too late before partition, it was certainly worse after independence when he was charged with the task of covering up the wounds inflicted by the Muslim League in the hope that the cover-up would allow the healing process to take over in course of time. All that makes it truly remarkable that he allowed himself to say as much as he did. Three of his speeches deserve attention in this regard. The first of these was his address to the convocation of The Aligarh Muslim University on 24 January 1948. In it he said:

> I am proud of India, not only because of her ancient, magnificent heritage, but also because of her remarkable capacity to add to it by keeping the doors and windows of her mind and spirit open to fresh and invigorating winds from distant lands. India's strength has been twofold: her own innate culture which flowered through the ages, and her capacity to draw from other sources and thus add to her own. She was far too strong to be submerged by outside streams, and she was too wise to isolate herself from them, and so there is a continuing synthesis in India's real history, and the many political changes which have taken place have had little effect on the growth of this variegated and yet essentially unified culture.
>
> I have said that I am proud of my inheritance and our ancestors who gave an intellectual and cultural pre-eminence

to India. How do you feel about this past? Do you feel that you are also sharers in it and inheritors of it and, therefore, proud of something that belongs to you as much as to me? Or do you feel alien to it and pass it by without understanding it or feeling that strange thrill which comes from realization that we are trustees and inheritors of this vast treasure . . . You are Muslims and I am a Hindu. We may adhere to different religious faiths or even to none; but that does not take away from that cultural inheritance that is yours as well as mine.

In view of his bitter experience of events leading to partition, it is inconceivable that Nehru could be so naive as to believe even vaguely that educated Muslims could possibly regard themselves as 'sharers and inheritors' of the cultural heritage he was speaking about. In fact, it would be reasonable to infer that he said what he did precisely because he knew that the opposite was true.

Nehru posed another question to his audience: 'Do we believe in a national State which includes people of all religions . . . and is essentially secular as a State, or do we believe in the religious, theocratic conception of a State which regards people of other faiths as somebody beyond the pale?' He, of course, did not remind them that only a few months earlier many of them had sympathised with, if not actively worked for, Pakistan. But he did speak of 'one national outlook' which would inform the working of the Indian state, though he did not spell out the source for the development of that 'one national outlook'.

In a different way and in a different context, though, Nehru expanded on this theme. In his address in the inauguration of the Indian Council for Cultural Relations in New Delhi on 9 April 1950, he said:

One can see each nation and each separate civilization developing its own culture that had its roots in generations hundreds and thousands of years ago. One sees these nations being intimately moulded by the impulse that initially starts a civilization going on its long path. That conception is effected by other conceptions and one sees action and interaction between these varying conceptions.

Culture, if it has to have any value, must have a certain depth. It must also have a certain dynamic character. If we leave out what might be called the basic mould that was given to it in the early stages of a people's growth, it is affected by geography, by climate and all kinds of other factors. The culture of Arabia is intimately governed by the geography and the deserts of Arabia because it grew up there. Obviously, the culture of India in the old days was affected greatly, as we see in our literature, by the Himalayas, the forests and the great rivers of India among other things. It was a natural growth from the soil. The individual human being or race or nation must necessarily have a certain depth and certain roots somewhere. They do not count for much unless they have roots in the past, which past is after all the accumulation of generations of experience and some type of wisdom. It is essential that you have that. Otherwise you become just pale copies of something which has no real meaning to you as an individual or as a group . . .

This emphasis on roots, depth, past, basic mould and soil must come as a surprise to all those who are not familiar with this little known face of Nehru. It must also raise the question why he did not develop this theme and indeed why he kept this face of his, by and large, so well covered. Many answers are possible.

The last of the three addresses I have in view was the Azad memorial lecture Nehru delivered on 22 February 1959. He said:

When Islam came to India in the form of political conquest it brought conflict; it encouraged the tendency of Hindu society to shrink still further within its shell. Hence the great problem that faced India during the medieval period was how these two closed systems, each with its strong roots, could develop a healthy relationship.

The philosophy and the world outlook of the old Hindus was amazingly tolerant. The Muslims had to face a new problem, namely, how to live with others as equals. They came into conflict with Christendom and through hundreds of years the problem was never solved. In India, slowly a synthesis was developed. But before this could be completed, other influences came into play.

Typically, Nehru skirts inconvenient issues. He does not tell us why the Christian-Muslim encounter did not lead to a synthesis despite the common Semitic origins of the two faiths, or how Hindus and Muslims could move towards one if both were truly closed systems, or why Hindus shrank into their shell before the onslaught of Islam since they had not faced a hostile civilization earlier. He also uses the wrong concept of tolerance in relation to Hindus and Hinduism in place of the proper one, which is 'comprehensive' or 'all-embracing' or 'total'. Hindus were 'amazingly tolerant' because their dharma (worldwide) provided for every possible expression of the human spirit and indeed they so remained in spite of their decline for centuries for the same reason.

We can, however, let all that pass. The statement is notable for us, on the one hand, for its admission that the Hindu-Muslim conflict had not been resolved when the British arrived on the scene to produce new complications, and, on the other, for its diagnosis of the cause of the Hindu decline and the cure. Nehru, as is well known, generally avoided the first and was preoccupied with the second problem. The same, incidentally, was true of the Mahatma, with the difference that while he saw a resolution of the problem in social reform, with heavy emphasis on removal of untouchability, Nehru regarded the development of science and technology through the mediation of a strong state and contact with the West, which for him included the Soviet Union, as the key to India's future.

Thus, it is possible to take the view that Nehru put aside the issue of the pre-eminence of Hindu civilization because he was convinced that Hindus needed first to overcome the weakness resulting from their lagging behind in the field of science and technology. It must be remembered that he grew up in Britain in the age of optimism before the First World War when the Western man entertained little doubt that limitless progress was possible, if not inevitable, and that science based on reason and technology were the instruments of that march into the future. Nehru, it may also be recalled, spoke frequently of the need to overcome 'superstition' and to cultivate the scientific temper. He did not identify Hindus as his target audience. But they were his target audience.

It is inconceivable that Nehru was not sensitive to Muslim resistance to modernization and secularization. Indeed, it can safely be assumed that he left them alone in respect of their Personal Law and did not seek to bring them into the orbit of a common civil code precisely because he was aware of the depth of their opposition, though that is clearly an essential part of a modern polity based on the principle of equal citizenship. Perhaps he expected that their attitude would change in course of time under the pressure of forces unleashed by the spread of education, economic development and the democratic political process. If he ever spelt out his views on how the Muslims would come out of their ghetto psychology after independence, it has still not been made public. Alternatively, it is possible that he was too busy managing the affairs of the state of India on a day-to-day basis to be able to pay attention to this problem. We just do not know Nehru's views on a long-term resolution of the Muslim question.

Nehru spoke often of the need for 'national integration'. But if he ever defined what that called for by way of change among

Muslims in practical terms, I am not aware of it. The addresses quoted earlier do not contain any action programme. He denounced communalism. He was particularly harsh on what he called 'Hindu communalism' on the ground (as he explained in a letter to Dr. K.N. Katju, at one stage his home minister) that it would be far more dangerous in view of the power of Hindus in independent India. In reality, his perspective provided for nothing nobler than co-existence between Hindus and Muslims. His was basically a programme which would help avoid riots, which understandably revolted him as they did other sensitive Indians. Indeed, the policy of secularism cannot realistically be interpreted otherwise, the grandiose theories notwithstanding. It certainly did not provide, even in theory, for a cultural synthesis. It sought to bypass the civilizational-cultural issue altogether.

It is beyond question that no issue occupied so much of Nehru's time and energy as Kashmir. This was clearly an obsession with him so much so that it would be no exaggeration to say that he allowed his whole foreign policy to be heavily influenced by it. The reasons for this are complex and need not detain us in the present exercise. Three points may, however, be made in respect of his handling of the problem. First, having placed himself in a vulnerable position by offering to hold a plebiscite, he allowed himself to be blackmailed by Sheikh Abdullah. The evidence is overwhelming. The near-independent status he conceded to Jammu and Kashmir violated his very concept of the kind of Indian state which could protect India's unity. It would be relevant to recall his opposition to Punjabi Suba in this connection. Similarly, the manner in which the Sheikh rigged the election to his Constituent Assembly could not but have caused the deepest hurt to Nehru. It negated his commitment to democracy.

Secondly, Nehru effectively used the Kashmir issue to silence his critics. It is truly remarkable that as India's position in the state became precarious, necessitating the overthrow and imprisonment of the Sheikh and maintenance, by New Delhi, in power in Srinagar of one corrupt regime after another, the more successful was Nehru in using the Kashmir card at home. Clearly, the Indian people acquiesced in this self-deception. The psychology behind this acquiescence needs to be explored. It has not been, to the best of my knowledge. It, however, seems to me that our presence in Kashmir served as a substitute for cultural self-assertion for Hindus, especially for the Western-educated elite engaged, albeit unconsciously, in a desperate search for an ersatz substitute. In plain terms, Nehru or no Nehru, we have not been ready for a genuine cultural self-affirmation.

Finally, once he had accepted, whether of his own volition or under coercion, a constitutional arrangement for Kashmir which would preserve the 'identity' of Kashmiri Muslims, above all a product of their relative isolation from the rest of the country on account of geographical factors, he had also acknowledged, even if only by implication that he could not use the Kashmir 'experiment' to promote a change in the attitude of Muslims in the rest of the Indian Union. This brings me to the point I made earlier regarding Nehru's lack of confidence in his ability to persuade Muslims to get out of the psychological and cultural ghetto of their own making and join the mainstream brought forth, in his view, by the process of modernization. It does not follow that Nehru's secularism was phony; but it does mean that it was lame. To borrow the Chinese phrase, it did not walk on two legs. It wobbled on one, though Muslims provided him a crutch in the shape of electoral support which facilitated his and the Congress party's stay in power.

The Nehru order, however, did not rest on the secular pillar alone. It would have collapsed long ago if it had. The Nehru structure has stood mainly on three pillars in conceptual terms— socialism, secularism and non-alignment—and these concepts have been interlinked. Nehru's was an integrated worldview. As such, it is only logical that if one of them becomes dysfunctional, the others must get into trouble. In my opinion, they have.

Socialism was clearly central to Nehru's worldview. For, it shaped his views on nationalism, democracy, secularism and non-alignment as well. Nehru, it may be recalled, was the first Congress leader to define nationalism in terms of anti-imperialism and link anti-imperialism to the Soviet leadership's effort to fight capitalism both at home and abroad. No significant non-Marxist Congress leader bought this proposition when Nehru began to propound it in the twenties because they were opposed to socialism at home. But they could not produce an alternative definition of nationalism for the simple reason that they could not explicitly link it with the country's cultural past for fear of offending the Muslims. So, finally, Nehru's formulations prevailed. The triumph became complete when he came to dominate both the ruling party (after Sardar Patel's death in 1950) and the government and gave an anti-Western tilt to the country's foreign policy in the name of non-alignment.

It is possible that Nehru, a man of moderation, would not have gone as far as he did if, for one thing, Krishna Menon, who had spent much of his adult life in London amidst socialists of different varieties, had not come to exercise enormous influence on him and if, for another, the West under Britain's inspiration had not tilted towards Pakistan on the Kashmir issue.

It follows that the concept of secular nationalism more or less divorced from the country's cultural heritage could not have been a viable proposition if it was not girded by the promise of a brave new socialist world of equality. As far as I know, Nehru never spoke of creating a new India. Mother India stuck to him as he said she stuck to every Indian whatever he may do or think. On account of the same restraint, he did not think in terms of dragooning India into the socialist Utopia as Stalin did in the Soviet Union and Mao Zedong in China. There was also another side to his personality which linked him to India's past. He was more than a deeply moral human being. He yearned for spiritual light. He was particularly drawn to Swami Vivekananda and the Ramakrishna Ashram. It is known that he sought solace from

Anandamai to whom Indira Gandhi also turned. Once he visited Sri Aurobindo Ashram as well and met The Mother. Dr. S. Radhakrishnan, President of the Indian Republic, disclosed that in the last years of his life, Nehru used to come to him frequently to listen to the Upanishads which, as *The Discovery of India* shows, always fascinated him. Even so, it cannot be denied that his programme was intended to produce a new Indian in the style of the new Soviet man or China man.

For Nehru, freedom was meaningful mainly if it paved the way for economic growth. He said so publicly again and again. Similarly, for him, democracy was meaningful if it facilitated movement towards economic and social equality. His was a commitment not so much to liberal democracy which prizes liberty more than equality as to democratic socialism which reverses the order of priorities. Nehru did not play havoc with the Constitution in his search for socialism. He was too imbued with the spirit of liberalism to do that. It could not occur to him that non-democratic means would be justified in the pursuit of socialism. But by emphasizing equality and, in the process, undermining the concept of the liberty of the individual, he created an atmosphere in which it became possible for his successors, Indira Gandhi foremost among them, to play with the Constitution and the constitutional arrangement. The Emergency would have been inconceivable if demagogues, sired by Nehru, however unwittingly, had not prepared the ground.

This, however, takes us too far afield. I am here interested in establishing that socialism, however vaguely defined and implemented, was the linchpin of the Nehru system and that the system cannot possibly survive the disappearance of this linchpin. The linchpin has clearly disappeared. The collapse of the Soviet system and state and the opening of the Chinese economy to multinationals would by themselves have settled the issue. As it happens, the threat of bankruptcy as a result of the mismanagement of the economy since the very start of planning in the early fifties and more particularly in recent years has forced the Government of India to make a volte-face. It has abandoned all the dogmas and shibboleths of the Nehru-Indira Gandhi era. And the irony of it is that a Congress (I) government is presiding over this great reversal.

I am not unaware of the fact that this is not the popular interpretation of Nehru. And I cannot possibly insist that this is more valid than the popular one. Indeed I could not have put it forward if I had not become sensitive to the concept of the power of the time spirit in recent months. This has led me to the conclusion that much more could not have been successfully attempted by way of reaffirmation of Hindu civilization in the period in question.

It is not particularly relevant to speculate on the 'ifs' and 'buts' of history. So, I would not wish to speculate on what turn India could have taken if Sardar Patel, or C. Rajagopalachari, or Rajendra Prasad had taken over as prime minister in place of Nehru, except to say that each of them would have been out of tune with the dominant sentiment in the Third World and among the Indian intelligentsia.

The real, as Hegel said, is rational. Things are what they are because in the given interplay of forces, they could not possibly have shaped differently. And it is the correlation of forces that shapes history not ideology. On the contrary, an ideology itself is a product of those forces. On this reckoning, our cultural-civilizational reaffirmation had to await the collapse of communism and its Third World expressions such as Arab nationalism, and the acquisition of a certain measure of scientific, technological, economic and military strength by us. Islamic revivalism-fundamentalism is, of course, not a direct offshoot of communism; it antedates the latter by centuries. But in the post-war era it has been as critically dependent on Soviet power as has been pan-Arabian.

Thus, it is possible to think of Hindu self-affirmation and self-renewal as a process to which Gandhiji and Nehru contributed considerably and to conclude that L.K. Advani, with his quiet but confident assertion of the primacy of Hindus and Hinduism in India, fits in this unfolding progression. Advani too can ask Muslims the same questions Nehru posed at Aligarh in 1948.

The fact that the Nehru order was under strain since the Chinese attack in 1962 and in visible decline in recent years is seldom recalled in the public discourse on the Ramjanmabhoomi issue. But that only shows how lopsided the discourse is.

The Chinese attack knocked down two myths: one, that communist states do not commit aggression which is supposed to be the peculiarity of imperialism, and two, that the policy of peaceful co-existence could help avoid the need for military preparedness. If it were not for the bitter dispute between the Soviet Union and China, which obliged Moscow to befriend New Delhi, it would have put paid to the policy of non-alignment as such. That, however, only postponed the demise. It materialized in 1989, when the Soviet Union itself disintegrated.

Nehruvian socialism has been in deep trouble for a quarter of a century. By 1967, it was obvious, except to Marxists and fellow-travellers, that all that it had done was to have spawned a regime of corruption, slowed down economic growth, degraded the country's public life and generated enormous tension in society.

The pursuit of these two policies has been a reflection of the partial nature of the Hindu recovery. A more confident Hindu psyche would never have spurned the US offer of cooperation [President Eisenhower's offer in 1954 of 'proportionate' military assistance, proportionate, that is, to India's size, importance and potentiality, in comparison to Pakistan, with which the US had then concluded a mutual security pact and embraced the illusion of friendship with China in the occupation of Tibet. China 'repaid' Nehru with (1) demands on Indian territory in disregard of the internationally recognized watershed—the highest mountain range principle; (2) friendship with Pakistan; and (3) an outright attack on India in 1962] and allowed Pakistan to seek military parity with, if not superiority over, this country. Similarly, such a psyche would never have reconciled itself to an economic philosophy which would stunt the growth of the agricultural as well as the business community.

This un-Hindu disregard for power, economic and military, and the illusory belief that social equity is possible in conditions of economic weakness is also the product of minds nurtured in the tradition of Chaitanya's Bhakti movement which Bankim Chandra Chatterjee criticized in *Anandamath*. It is not an accident either that this tradition among Hindus has weakened since independence, as Hindus have grappled with the problems of the state, as it weakened among the Sikhs when they battled the Mughals and the Afghans, or that it is invoked by all those who swear by a 'composite culture' and are alarmed at the reintroduction of the Kshatriya element in the urban Hindu's personality. In my view, the second phase of the freedom struggle, 'the struggle to regain its Hindu identity', will involve a reconstitution of the fragmented Hindu personality along lines different from the one pursued so far, so that the missing Kshatriya constituent of the old Hindu personality is restored. As for secularism, supposedly the third leg of the Nehruvian tripod, two points have to be made. The first is the usual one, which is that Hinduism is tolerant and, therefore, secular. This is valid and it is sheer dishonesty or naiveté to suggest, as is being widely suggested these days, that Hinduism can admit of theocracy. That is a Muslim privilege which no one else can appropriate.

Secondly, the dominant concern of Hindus over the last 200 years has been with achievements in the secular realm—education, trade, industry, equality with the British before independence and with the West since independence. The upsurge I have been speaking about, in fact, relates wholly to the secular realm. This does not mean that our spiritual-religious heritage has no place in this scheme. But it does mean that Hindus have recognized once again, as they did in the past, that the secular realm has to be secured if a culture and a civilization has to flourish. Swami Vivekananda emphasized the importance of secular achievements and so did Sri Aurobindo.

Society and culture, it need hardly be said, are interlinked. Social changes brought about by secular forces are duly reflected in culture in course of time. That has been happening in the case of Hinduism. It is not being Semitized and it cannot be Semitized as a result of a deliberate design on the part of some individuals or groups. But from being a confederation of ways of life, it has had to move towards being a federation. To put it differently, the small society has had to give way to larger ones as small economies and polities have had to give way to larger ones. Only a secular and modern intelligentsia could have presided over these changes. The task would have been beyond the reach of traditional elites. That is the true significance of secularism. It may be called the 'midwife of Hindu nationalism'.

The concept of secularism and the secularization process have, of course, not been a Hindu monopoly. Members of other religious groups have also pursued them but essentially as individuals. Muslims as a group have certainly shunned the concept as well as the process to the extent they can in a larger modernizing and, therefore, secularizing society. This is evident from the rapid expansion of traditional mosque-attached madrasahs (schools), opposition to one common civil code and adherence to the Shariat. Faith can never be a private affair for most Muslims. As such, political parties and leaders have to woo them as Muslims. This has inevitably produced a backlash of which the Ramjanmabhoomi issue has become one major expression.

I do not fault Muslims for their reluctance and even refusal to take to the secularization process. Nor can I applaud Hindus for their participation in this process. For while the spirit of liberalism and pluralism, which the West represents, is alien to Islam, as it has developed since the eleventh century when the orthodox ulema triumphed over philosophers, Sufis and other kinds of innovators, it is in conformity with Hinduism which revels in plurality. But this divergence creates a serious problem for both which the self-proclaimed secularists have refused steadfastly to face.

Finally, it is a pity that there does not exist the slightest awareness, either among Hindus or Muslims, that Muslims need the rise of Indian civilization as much as Hindus, if not more. Indeed, such is the grip of the misrepresentation of Hindutva in anti-Muslim terms that its proponents, including some leaders of the Bharatiya Janata Party, themselves, speak of it defensively.

History knows of any number of instances when a community has needed to be protected, or liberated, from, its own 'leaders': Germans under Hitler; Russians under Stalin; Chinese under Mao Zedong; and, more recently Iraqis under Saddam Hussain, for example. Hitler and Saddam Hussain first let loose a reign of terror at home and broke the spirit of their own peoples before they went to war with other countries. Indeed, the war at home is central to all dictators. Stalin got an opportunity to extend his tyrannical rule to eastern Europe only towards the end of the Second World War. Earlier he, like Mao later, had to be 'content' with mass massacres at home, and he was about to return to that 'sport' at the time of his death in 1953. To extend the argument further, while the West has doubtless celebrated the collapse of communist tyrannies in eastern Europe, the principal beneficiaries have been the peoples of those unhappy lands.

Indian Muslims, I am convinced, after many years of reflection, too, like Hindus, need self-renewal; unlike Hindus, they have proved incapable of engaging in such an exercise even under the stimulus provided by British rule, and only the triumph of Hindutva can help create a milieu which obliges them to try and overcome the inertia of tradition reinforced by the ulema.

I must confess that, like many others, I too have tended to think in terms of leaving Muslims to their ghetto mentality, and to oppose the demand, by BJP leaders, among others, for a uniform civil code. My argument has been that so large and obstinate a community cannot be pushed against its will, that any attempt to do so would aggravate existing tensions and that such a risk should best be avoided. I have also had no reason either to believe that 'modernizers in the community are anything but an utterly marginal phenomenon or to dispute that the ulema continue to represent it. That, incidentally, was also why I was not opposed to the scandalous piece of legislation known as the Muslim Women (Protection of Rights on Divorce) Act which, in fact, denies even utterly destitute Muslim divorcees in danger of becoming vagrants the right to alimony from their former husbands.

Incidentally, this attitude is also proof that our secularism has become a euphemism for callous indifference to the fate of Muslims. V.P. Singh and others may woo them in their search for power, but they cannot offer them a way out of the ghetto mentality. The BJP offers them such a way, though it too does not know the glorious implications for Muslims of the Hindutva platform and harps on the old demand for a common civil code.

A common civil code can be, indeed is, part of a nationalist platform which, on the one hand, demands that all citizens live under the same laws, and, on the other, entitles Parliament, or any other legally constituted body, to enact such laws for all citizens. But it cannot figure prominently in the Hindutva platform which must, by its very nature determined by the Hindu civilization's unlimited catholicity and broadmindedness, seek to influence by way of example and not engage in coercion. The Hindu temperament also militates against uniformity and coercion. Unlike Muslims, Hindus have never sought to fix a mould in which Hindu personality must be shaped. Indeed, in the case of Brahmins, the personality shaped by the tradition of memorizing texts is yielding place to a different one, better attuned to critical analysis. Pandit Nehru could recite no Sanskrit shloka. That apart, however, the proponents of 'secular nationalism' cannot sidetrack certain questions. Since they too cannot deny that Muslims, on the whole, have remained frozen in their attitudes, as illustrated by their passionate adherence to the Muslim Personal Law, they owe it to themselves to explain why this remains the case after more than four decades of life under a secular political order, and what they propose to do to end this stagnation. They should not beat about the bush and indulge in tirades against Hindu 'communalism', or fascism, or whatever new term of abuse they can borrow from the West; for they also cannot be so ridiculous as to argue that it in any way accounts for the prevalence of the ghetto mentality among Muslims.

It is common knowledge that, if anything, the revivalist, fundamentalist sentiment among Muslims has become stronger in the past decade or so when hundreds of millions of petrodollars have poured in from Saudi Arabia, Libya and other oil-rich countries, and that the terrorist menace we now face in Kashmir is one offshoot of this revivalist-fundamentalist upsurge. For, it cannot be disputed that the Jamaat-i-Islami played a key role in whipping up initially an anti-India hysteria in the valley and that hundreds of madrasahs under its control, generously financed by its patrons abroad, have provided the recruiting ground for Pakistan-backed terrorists and secessionists.

I understand from Muslim reformists, a rare species, that the position of poor Muslim women has deteriorated as a result of the Muslim Women (Protection of Rights on Divorce) Act, which Rajiv Gandhi pushed through Parliament in 1986 under pressure from the ulema, because it has taken away from them what little protection Section 125 of the Criminal Procedure Code had given them earlier. This may or may not be the case. The condition of poor Muslim women has been too bad to deteriorate much further. But it is indisputable that Hizb-i-Islamia, an underground outfit in Jammu and Kashmir, has forced even educated Muslim women to return to the burqa. No secularist Hindu is likely to lose his sleep on such an insignificant development! But they cannot deny that this constitutes a violation of the spirit of rights conferred by the Constitution as much on Muslim women as on anyone else.

It is sheer escapism and worse (dishonesty) to talk of bride burning or maltreatment of women among Hindus in this specific context. Apart from the undeniable fact that Hindu women are coming into their own in millions as a result of education and employment outside the home, laws exist and more stringent ones can be enacted to deal with such problems among Hindus. Muslim women cannot be given similar protection under the existing dispensation. Moreover, no one can possibly suggest that Hindus have insulated themselves from the winds of change. On the contrary, Hindu society is being, as it were, reconstituted and there is no organized resistance to it.

One of the greatest problems of Hindu society, and, by that logic, of Indian society, is the fragmentation of the Hindu social order into more and more castes. Inevitably, our fundamental struggle is to restore a kind of unity, without which, it makes little sense to talk of Hinduism. We have to produce a sense of coherence in an order which has become, over the centuries, increasingly fragmented and chaotic. All our social movements in the last 200 years and all our political movements in the last 100 years should be seen in that context. So viewed they would not look divisive and, therefore, unhealthy. I do not, for instance, regard Kanshi Ram and the Bahujan Samaj Party which he has launched as a disaster in spite of his spiteful attacks on Brahmins who have helped preserve our heritage under extremely trying circumstances. This is part of a larger struggle to reverse the process of fragmentation and restore the original chaturvarna (fourfold) order to the extent it is viable in the present context. The struggle is going to be long and painful. It requires large minds and large hearts to be able to accommodate so many currents which are addressed to a common purpose, the common purpose being a new sense of coherence, a new sense of unity without break in continuity.

It would be premature yet to sound an optimistic note, but I sense, even if still vaguely, the possibility of a profound change in Indian Muslims also. The issues involved in this formulation are clearly too many and too complex. So, I will limit myself to a few observations.

First, no worthwhile attempt has been made for decades to define Indian nationalism in Indian terms for the simple reason that no one has been able to accommodate the Muslim factor within the framework of Hindu civilization. Nehru talked of a Hindu-Muslim cultural synthesis but one has only to refer to his address to the Aligarh Muslim University in 1948 and to the Indian Council for Cultural Relations in 1950 (mentioned earlier) to know that he came to entertain serious reservations about it.

Secondly, the Indian intellectual-political elite sought to fill the void arising out of the absence of a conscious articulation of a nationalist ideology with the talk of secularism. This strategy worked for so long on two counts. First, there existed, in the Congress, an organization which could represent Hindu aspirations in the secular realm and treat Muslims as its clients in all but name. Second, the Hindu recovery of self-confidence and, therefore, need for self-affirmation in civilizational terms was of an order that it could be accommodated within the Congress framework.

Surely, these conditions no longer obtain. The Congress has grown weak over the years; with the arrival of the Janata Dal and its offshoots on the scene, Muslims have got another option and therefore want to be wooed rather than treated as clients; and, above all, Hindu recovery, going back to the eighteenth century, has finally acquired such power and momentum that it cannot be content to operate in disguise which is all that was possible under the Congress umbrella. So they have erected their own institutional arrangements with the Rashtriya Swayamsevak Sangh as the base and the BJP the VHP and other organizations as its arms.

Thirdly, a series of developments—the collapse of pan-Arabism, or Arab nationalism, symbolized currently by the defeat of Saddam Hussain's Iraq; return of Western powers to the Gulf; disappearance of a rival anti-US power centre in Moscow; renewed tensions between Sunni-dominated Baghdad and Shia Iran; failure of the Islamic revolution in Iran to justify itself in terms of results; and the power struggle in Tehran—must create for Indian Muslims a psychological situation the like of which they have not faced. Since the beginning of the decline of the Mughal Empire in the early eighteenth century, a critical point for Indian Islam, there has existed for them a centre of hope and reference. No such reference-hope centre exists now.

Leaving aside the implications of the rise of the RSS-BJP-VHP combine as a significant factor in Indian politics, it is about time we pay attention to the hitherto neglected question of the impact of Hindi on Muslim youth in north India. For all we know, a return, even if slow, to one-culture situation may have begun. The process cannot but be prolonged and painful and the pace may not be good enough for modernists. But obsession with speed is alien to Indian civilization which underwrites the Indian nation-state.

I for one see no alternative to it. This is my view of the place of Muslims in India—one strand in the multistrand Indian civilization interacting with others. This is also my interpretation of what Pandit Nehru meant by cultural synthesis. Only he did not attach to language the importance I do.

27

Hindutva: The Kinetic Effect of Hindu Dharma[*]

S. Gurumurthy

Introduction

Hindu Dharma is a relatively new name for what has been timelessly known as Sanatana Dharma. Hindu Dharma is geographically Indian, or Bharatiya, but it is universally valid because, unlike other schools of thought, it accepts all other and diverse thoughts without rejecting any. This all-inclusive school of thought was a nameless philosophy that did not need to distinguish itself from others, as there was no other thought system from which it needed to be distinguished. It was a thought that did not need an identity different from other thoughts as it accepted all other thoughts as valid. It is only when exclusive schools of thoughts emanated from the Abrahamic stable, which rejected the validity of all thoughts other than those of the concerned Abrahamic school, Sanatana Dharma needed to distinguish itself form the exclusive Abrahamic thoughts. It is not Hindu Dharma which rejected the Abrahamic thoughts,

[*] Extracted from S. Gurumurthy, 'Hindutva: The Kinetic Effect of Hindu Dharma', Centre for Policy Studies, http://cpsindia.org/index.php/art.132-articles-by-s-gurumurthy

but it is the Abrahamic thoughts which rejected the Hindu Dharma. With the result that the Sanatana Dharma had to acquire and accept a name to distinguish itself; not because it was an exclusive thought but because it was an inclusive thought and all other thoughts exclusive. This is how the word Hindu evolved to distinguish the exclusive Abrahamic thoughts from Hindu Dharma or Sanatana Dharma. The name was meant not so much to distinguish Hindu Dharma from others as it was to distinguish the newly emerged exclusive thoughts from the inclusive Hindu Dharma.

Secular India's Allergy to Ancient India

In secular India, where anything associated with ancient India is viewed with suspicion as communal and unfriendly to a secular way of life, the definitions of what constitutes Hindu, Dharma, Hindu Dharma and Hindutva are rendered contentious by the secular polity that is largely defined and directed by vote banks. Nevertheless, as politics penetrates every aspect of life including the impenetrable institution of family, any discussion on the socio-cultural life of a nation, particularly a nation like Bharatvarsh, which has an unbroken, though disturbed, tradition of thousands of years, is a complex and demanding one. More so because our nation has drifted away from public domain; it has been preserving its core lifestyle stealthily for hundreds of years under alien rule, and has continued its stealthy living for five decades even under the independent indigenous rule. The task is even more difficult, because any discussion on understanding the core values of our ancient life represented by Hindu Dharma has to be carried out in a situation that is confounded by such drift and stealthy living. What was and is even now original to the Hindu people has become a hidden virtue; the Hindus have lost the confidence to openly live with it because of secular India's explicit and institutionalised allergy to traditional India. Yet Hindu Dharma is the core of India's tradition.

Proper understanding of India's traditional values represented by the concept 'Dharma' requires a dispassionate discussion on the socio-cultural life of this ancient nation, uninhibited by the politics of the day. Traditional India is largely the product of Hindu Dharma. The concept of secularism evolved in the mono-religious Christendom. As a result of the misapplication of this Christian concept to the multi-religious Hindu Dharma, which does not distinguish between different faiths and accepts all faiths, the Hindu Dharma was itself equated to the exclusive Abrahamic faiths. This has made an understanding of the meaning of Hindu Dharma even more difficult.

Secularism is a concept evolved within Christianity; it was never designed to handle a multi-religious situation. Only the Hindu tradition, and certainly not Christian secularism, has accepted and handled a situation where multiple religions are accorded validity. This fact has not been internalised in the understanding of secularism in free India. We have refused to understand that outside the history and geography of India there is no multi-religious social, cultural and political matrix which can be presented as a benchmark for this ancient nation. We have tried, incorrectly and inappropriately, to make the secularism of Christendom as benchmark for this ancient nation's modern polity. Consequently, understanding of different elements of ancient India has been rendered difficult in modern conditions, conditions for which the rules have been laid by Christendom.

Dharma, Hindu, and Hindu Dharma

To understand Hindu Dharma one has to be clear about the meaning of the word Hindu and also the import of what Dharma means. Both words are difficult to define, but the word 'Dharma' is even more difficult to comprehend, particularly in English. This is a word that the ordinary people of this country understand and apply in their day-to-day life, but it is difficult for even scholars to properly define for scholarly discussion. For,

Dharma is based on experience, rather than explanation. For the intellectual, explanation is more important than experience; and, for the ordinary, experience is more important than explanation.

If the word 'Hindu' signifies the collective identity of the people of this ancient land, then their experience of the world and life enshrined in a continuously evolving belief system approximates to the idea of Hinduism. The Hindu experience, or Hinduism, is the longest known and living continuity in the world. And perhaps the most chequered one. The Hindu tryst with humans—why?—with all living creatures, and with nature and in fact the entire creation, has been a fascinating story of a civilisation that grappled with the complexities of humans and of the creation as whole on a practical plane.

This civilisation had the wisdom to let the accumulated human experience to handle current human problems, even as it firmly believed that the eternal values of creation would continue to guide the destiny of humans. The Hindu understanding of the world is conditioned by the Hindu experience of nature and the propensities of humans; and the immutable laws of nature as translated into continuously evolving rules of life in observable form were called 'Dharma'.

This in brief is the story of the endogenous evolution of the Hindu society. But the discussion cannot be limited to the endogenous evolution alone. We also have to deal with the exogenous factors that impacted and are continuing to impact on the body, mind and intellect of the Hindu society.

Hindu Dharma: A Non-combative Socio-cultural View Intertwined with Politics and Economics

Pandit Deendayal Upadhyaya, one of the well-known thinkers of independent India, repeatedly asserted, in his profound exposition of 'Integral Humanism', that human life is integral. No aspect of life is autonomous, or compartmental. This is true both at the micro and at the macro level. In fact, this integral nature is not limited only to the humans. It extends to the whole of the creation. Pandit Upadhyaya refers to the integration of the Vyashti, the individual, Samashti, the collective, and the Parameshti, the creator. There is integral relationship in the creative processes; and this applies particularly to the relationship between humans and nature. Given this integral relationship, and even limiting it to humans only, the politico-economic life of a nation cannot be divorced from its social and cultural life.

Socio-cultural behaviour of the people impacts and shapes the economic and political construct of a nation. Economic and political dimensions in turn have a vital bearing on the socio-cultural evolution of a society. The modern world moves on economic theories and econometrics. Every decision, concerning political, diplomatic or security aspects, is linked to economics. Yet even the die-hard West-centric economic and social thinkers feel that there is something like a '20% missing link' in economics. What is that missing link? That is culture. Culture is the uniqueness in the personality of a society. It is inextricably mixed with economics. And economics interfaces politics. Therefore there is an inseparable linkage between society, culture, economics and politics. Not only are they interdependent, they exert enormous mutual influence. It is admitted that economics influences culture. But culture influences economics more than economics influences culture. Therefore any analysis of socio-cultural life will have to factor in economic and political dimensions as well.

As a faith, Hinduism is inclusive, and inner-directed. It does not impose itself on its own adherents. So no question of its imposing itself on others arises. This principle of life has been observed and unfailingly put into practice by the inhabitants of this land since time immemorial. That was why they could receive invading Sakas and Hunas and assimilate them and integrate them into their society. That was why they could receive the Jews, Parsis, Shia Muslims and the early Christians— all of whom came as refugees, with their thoughts and beliefs orphaned in their own lands—and treat them as equal members of this ancient society. There was no modern constitution that guaranteed rights to minorities then; there were no secularists to protect them from the majority. It was the majority inhabitants, seeped in their Hindu Dharma, who protected them. The non-conflicting nature of Hindu Dharma is not just a matter of theory, but an observed practice that has been followed and adhered to for ages.

Hindutva: The Kinetic Form of Hindu Dharma

Hindu Dharma represents the potential energy of the Indian people. But without the manifestation of that potential energy in its active form, it was unable to gather together its adherents to face the challenges. Hindutva is the kinetic aspect of Hindu Dharma. Hindu Dharma or Hinduism was never organised. Nor was it organisable. Organisation and Hinduism were contradictory terms. A thought which accepted all other thoughts as valid, which found fault with none and demeaned and discredited none, can never be organised, because organisation is always motivated to build strength around a thought against another. If there is no 'other' thought and all thoughts are acceptable and valid then there is no need to organise. This was the strength of Hinduism or Hindu Dharma. It did not need an organisation, and it was incapable of being organised.

But when it was faced with the onslaught of the Abrahamic faiths which rejected other thoughts, considered their followers as kafirs and heathens, and denied them even the right to live, Hinduism slowly assumed a kinetic form. Hinduism had to acquire this form to secure its defence against the thoughts that used physical might against Hinduism. This is how Hinduism, which had internal kinetic dimensions that led to continuous evolution and to change with continuity, and which did not need any external kinetics, began to develop external kinetics as defence against the thoughts that sought to extinguish it.

That was how Chhatrapathi Shivaji thought of and was motivated to establish a Hindavi Swarajya; this was an unprecedented departure from the traditions of the Hindu nation. Never in the history of Hindus was there a kingdom which had a religious connotation or implication. In fact, the Hindu concept of Rajadharma protected the desachara of even the conquered people; it made it obligatory on a conquering king to respect the beliefs and lifestyle of the conquered people. Thus the victory or defeat of kings did not mean any impact on or change in the lifestyle or beliefs of the people. But, since the Abrahamic faiths were powered by the state and the army, to defend itself Hindu Dharma also had to manifest an external kinetic form that allowed it to take defensive counter-actions. Over the years such counter-action became the kinetic force of the Hindu society, and came to be known as Hindutva. Hindutva is the kinetic aspect of Hindu Dharma. For an unorganised thought like Hinduism, this kinetic aspect is necessary; without Hindutva, the kinetic force inherent in Hinduism, Hinduism was incapable of saving itself from the aggressive Abrahamic faiths. Those aggressive faiths would have long overrun Hindusim, if it were not protected by Hindutva.

The Transition of Hinduism to Its Kinetic Form Hindutva

An introductory background to the modern theoretical understanding of Hinduism or Hindutva is essential for any discussion on reinstating Hindutva in the socio-cultural life of Bharatvarsh. This takes us to a discussion on what constitutes Hindutva as it might be understood through the exposition of scholars and literature which the modern world and the modern Hindu are familiar with. As the modern Hindu and the world at large are the principal factors that need to be tackled—the ordinary Hindu is already in tune with the concept of Hindutva in his total lifestyle—this discussion is focussed on the more recent and modern understanding of Hindutva. It is focussed on Hindutva as it is defined outside the intellectual process of the Hindutva movements; but this definition is not very different from the understanding of Hindutva within the Hindu movements.

'Hindutva', 'Hinduness' and 'Hinduism' are not independent but interchangeable concepts. The statesman-philosopher, Dr S. Radhakrishnan, said in his lectures at the Oxford University that originally the word Hindu had geographical, not creedal, significance. It signified the geographic identity of Bharat, the identity of the people in a particular geographic area, that is, Bharatvarsh; the term did not signify any particular faith or method of worship. Hindu was the name of the people of Bharatvarsh, the national identity of Bharat. Even in the sense of a faith, Hinduism is unlike Semitic religions, particularly Islam and Christianity, which have a global agenda to Islamise or Christianise the world, which means converting the adherents of other faiths and beliefs and eliminating those faiths. The goal is not denied. It is only the means and the methods that are in dispute or debate. The Hindu view is in direct contrast to this Semitic mission.

The best definition for Hinduism is given not by any scholar on Hinduism, but the one contained in *Encyclopaedia Britannica*, a compilation that perceives the world from a Christian standpoint. On Hinduism, the encyclopaedia says:

> The Hindu is inclined to revere the divine in every manifestation, whatever it may be, and is doctrinally tolerant, leaving others—including both Hindus and non-Hindus—to whatever creed and worship practices suit them the best. A Hindu may embrace a non-Hindu religion without ceasing to be a Hindu, and since the Hindu is disposed to think synthetically and to regard other forms of worship, strange Gods, and divergent doctrines as inadequate rather than wrong or objectionable, he tends to believe that the highest divine powers complement each other for the well-being of the world and the mankind.

Quoting this from the encyclopaedia, a Constitution Bench of the Supreme Court held in 1977 that Hinduism is a non-conflicting religion. Later, when the political idiom of India began to be influenced by Hindu Dharma through the kinetics of Hindutva, the Supreme Court had to consider the meaning of Hindutva. After considering the meaning and content of Hinduism and Hindutva, the Court held in 1994 that Hindutva, the kinetic effect of Hinduism, too is a non-conflicting and secular idea. So conceptually and practically, Hindutva, which is the kinetic effect of Hindu Dharma, is a non-conflicting idea. And so it has been in history and in practice. The Hindavi Swaraj of Chhatrapathi Shivaji is the first state that adhered to Hindu Dharma. Otherwise it was the general rule of Rajadharma which was the governing rule of this land. The addition of the world Hindu as a prefix to the rule of Shivaji was in response to the Islamic theological rule which had devastated the Hindu land everywhere.

Strength as Weakness: Inability to Handle a Faith That Denies Validity to Other Faiths

That it is non-conflicting in precept and practice is the distinctness of Hindutva. It is its differentiating uniqueness, its strength, and also its weakness, particularly in its interface with Islam and Christianity. In the Christian view, Hindutva is a pagan idea. Paganism everywhere collapsed in the face of Christianity, because it did not know how to deal with a faith that denied the foundations of all faiths other than its own. Analysing why the Roman Empire and Roman paganism collapsed under the onslaught of Christianity, *Encyclopaedia Britannica* says:

> Christianity consistently practised an intolerant attitude to Judaism and paganism as well as heresy in its own ranks. By practising its intolerance vis-à-vis the Roman Emperor cult, it thereby forced the Roman Empire on its part into intolerance. Rome, however, was not adapted to the treatment of a religion

that negated its religious foundations, and this inadequacy later influenced the breakdown of paganism.

It is not just the fate of Roman paganism; all pagan religions collapsed the same way before the onslaught of Christianity. Pagan religions were unfamiliar with a religion like Christianity, which negated the foundations of all other religions. Till Christianity arose on the horizon, no religion negated the foundations of another religion. It is only Christianity which introduced the idea of a religion rejecting another religion and claiming to be the true religion. Even Judaism, even though it claimed to be the only religion, did not invalidate or negate other religions. . . .

Hinduism is similar to the pagan religions as it does not negate the foundations of other religions, and in fact accepts all other religions. Therefore, like the Roman pagan religions, Hinduism must also have been a candidate for collapse; but it did not collapse. Why Hinduism did not collapse has stunned the forces inimical to it. More than theological foundations, it is the socio-religious structure of Hinduism that protected it. Its defences were too complex for any armed or ideological aggression of the kind that felled the other pagan faiths. What these defences were, and continue to be, will be discussed at some length later in this article.

While Hindutva did not and will not collapse in the face of Christianity, it has been hurt and hurt grievously in many areas. It is being hurt and injured even now. The Hindu belief that all faiths are sacred human experiences is fundamentally incapable of handling a faith like Christianity, which completely denies validity and legitimacy to any faith other than itself. It is difficult even to make the Hindus imagine that there could be a faith that denied validity to another. This inability persists even today. This is one of the greatest challenges to Hinduism in Bharat.

The Islamic belief in exclusive validity is identical to that of Christianity. But the problems of Hindus in their interface with Islam are even greater. Islam came into Bharat mainly as an invading faith; it was imposed here through statecraft and military, both of which were driven by faith. The interface between Hindutva and Islam has been highly violent. Will Durant says that Islamic invasion of India is the bloodiest invasion in history. The Islamic impact on India led to huge transfer of populations and territories from the Hindus to Islam. First Afghanistan, then Pakistan and Bangladesh, ceased to be part of Bharat, after the people in those societies ceased to be part of the Hindu society. . . .

Even a greater problem is posed by the inability of the adherents of Hindutva to believe that a faith could deny and even claim, as a matter of faith, the right to eliminate other faiths. As a result, Hinduism is handicapped in facing the aggressive proselytising thrust of Christianity, which is founded on the premise that Christianity alone has the patented know-how for human salvation, and no other faith is valid. It is handicapped in understanding that the trigger for Islamic terrorism is the very belief that only Islam has the right to exist, and no other faith has such a right.

So the real problem of Hinduism lies in the theology of Islam and of Christianity. The problem is not the Muslims or Christians; not even the organised Church or the Mosque. The problem is their fundamental religious belief that negates other faiths the right to exist. This is where proselytising faiths differ fundamentally from those that do not proselytise. This is where even the Judaic faith, which is part of the Abrahamic family, differs from Christianity and Islam. The Jewish faith is a racial faith; it believes in domination, but not in elimination of other faiths by conversion.

The Challenge: The Notion among Hindus, Even Hindu Scholars and Leaders, That All Religions Are of the Same Nature or Have the Same Goals

The internalised experience of the Hindus over millennia that all religions are same has settled in the genetic code of the Hindus. This was blindly applied to the Semitic religions also when they arrived in India. This is evident from the intellectual and social responses to Judaism, early Islam and early Christianity when they reached the shores of India. This is also partially true of our response to the Parsi religion. But these faiths, when they arrived in India, were refugee faiths, having been driven out from their lands by their enemies or quarrelling cousins, like in the case of Shias who were driven out by their Sunni cousins.

The general truth about these faiths is that they never recognised or shared the Hindu idea of Dharma, which was the common denominator of the multitude of faiths within Hindutva. In fact this was and continues to be an area of unresolved theological conflict between these alien religions and Hindutva. This conflict was less pronounced in the cases of Judaism and Zoroastrianism, which were racial religions not open to other races, and which therefore did not insist upon Hindus converting to these faiths. They became like separate castes in Bharat. But this conflict became pronounced and even violent in the case of Islam and Christianity, which entered Bharat as refugee faiths and turned into invading faiths after the Islamic hordes and colonialists entered Bharat.

The violence arose because of the spirit of conversion that was not only inherent in them, but also was ordained as a compulsive trait of a believing Christian or Muslim. *Encyclopaedia Britannica* records that Columbus set out to sail to India because he believed that Satan, in the form of Hinduism, had taken refuge in India, and further believed that unless this hindrance called Hinduism were to be removed through Christian missions, the impending return of Christ, which was on hand, would be indefinitely delayed. Thus the colonial powers had as much a religious motive as an economic-commercial motive fuelling their urge for expansion. The less said about Islamic invasion of India the better. It was motivated as much by religious fervour as by the desire to loot.

These two proselytising religions are violent by nature, because of the idea and institution of conversion that is inalienable from the core of their faith. The faith in these religions is incomplete unless the faithful simultaneously invalidates and de-legitimises other faiths; hence their hostility to the Kafir and the Heathen; and hence their core institutions of Jihad and Crusade designed to deal with the non-believer in their exclusive faiths.

All this continues to be beyond the comprehension of the Hindu mind. So, even the scholarly Hindus, and Hindu religious leaders, continue to believe that Christianity and Islam are just like our own religions, except that these faiths tend to emphasise their point of view very strongly. The misbehaviour inherent in these religions is attributed to the zealots among them. . . . So long as religious conversions are inherent and compulsive to a faith, that faith shall be violent to other faiths. To hold the followers responsible for such violence and exonerate the fundamental religious doctrines which preach such violence is a miserable intellectual failure of the Hindus. The misreading of these two religions, of understanding them in the image of Hinduism, is the biggest intellectual and philosophic failure of Hinduism.

Removing this gross misconception from the minds of Hindu religious leaders, scholars, and others is the first and the greatest challenge facing Hindu society and Hindu religious leaders and scholars. Hindu leaders and scholars must study the Islamic and Christian scriptures thoroughly. They must undertake a massive effort to make the Hindus understand the theology of both. They must engage Islam and Christianity in an open debate so that modern audiences may listen and watch. They must openly question the Christian and Islamic belief that all other beliefs are illegitimate; question their classification of humans into Faithful and Pagan or Kafir; torment them on what they mean by Jihad and ask them whether Hindus are Kafirs and Heathens.

This alone will throw them on the defensive. Their aggressive pursuit of their religious and political goals can be checkmated only if they are thrown on the defensive. The only thing that will shame them is the public exposure of the narrowness and violence inherent in their faith and theology. . . .

Hindu religious and social leaders must also link up globally with the leaders of other non-proselytising faiths. They must strike alliances with Buddhists, with the remaining pagans in Europe, Africa and the Americas who are trying to revive their traditions, and also with the enlightened followers of Semitic religions all over the world, particularly among the Christians who do not agree with the mission of Christianising the world. We should also ally with enlightened sections of Islamic societies in Iraq, Iran and Egypt and with the tribal chiefs of Afghanistan.

The Evolution of Hindutva in Vote-bank–based Secular Polity

Hindu Dharma, which almost got eclipsed in the public domain and went underground in independent India under the Nehruvian spell, began to assert itself again in the public domain in the late 1980s and early 1990s through the Ayodhya movement.

The secular polity of independent India had gradually turned into a game of minority appeasement for votes; it had consequently become anti-Hindu. The Ayodhya movement evolved as a corrective to this distortion. The movement brought about massive political changes in the country; it put the pseudo-secular polity, parties and leaders on the defensive. The BJP, with its agenda of Hindutva, became the largest political party in less than a decade and captured power in 1998 as part of a coalition.

Today Hindutva is the mainline thought of the country. Pseudo-secular political parties and their leaders are in the process of giving up secularism to fight elections on the basis of good governance. Politics is in the process of being restored to political parties, which were only appeasing the minorities for votes just a decade ago. Expressing allergy to Hinduism and Hindus had become part of the political process and normal secular ideological expression. But today this style of politics is fetching negative returns.

Now one can disagree with Hindutva, but cannot disregard the Hindus or distance themselves from Hinduism any more. Imagine the government of Kerala extending the rights of minority institutions to Hindu educational institutions! This would have been unimaginable without the tectonic shift that is taking place in the national polity. Secular political parties are seeking to make a distinction between Hinduism and Hindutva, implying that Hinduism is good, but not Hindutva. But some reflection would show that Hindutva is only the kinetic manifestation of the dormant potential of Hinduism; it is the defensive force of the only non-conflicting and non-combative religious faith.

Hindutva is no more a marginal idea today. It is now the mainline thought. It is Hindutva that has been setting the agenda for national debate for the past decade and more. The emergence of Hindutva as the mainline thought places special responsibilities on those leading the Hindutva movement. Unlike the minority-led movements which can agitate and go on agitating as perpetual dissenters, unconcerned about governance and the running of the country, the Hindutva movement has the responsibility to ensure that national governance is not affected, whichever party is in power. It is the alienation of the Hindus from the establishment which turned the majority Hindus into dissenters in the decades following Independence. As a result of such alienation the majority of this country never felt that it was in power as Hindus. In fact the very idea of majority rule was defined as opposed to the idea of secularism.

The polity of independent India prior to the Ayodhya movement and rise of Hindutva had virtually no character. It was a polity that was driven by personalities rather than ideology. The cult of personalities as the centre of politics, without any ideology informing and driving the polity, has almost ended with the ascension of the BJP to power. Whether the ruling BJP asserts its Hindu character or not, whether it owns up to its basis in Hindutva or not, it is always seen as a Hindu force.

With Hindutva emerging as the central focus of the nation and pseudo-secularism getting marginalized, the earlier phase of the marginalisation of Hindutva and Hindus in politics is over. The Hindu movements now will have to reconsider their posture of perpetual dissent, and turn into mainline drives of the country. It is true that the Hindu agenda remains largely unfulfilled. But the Hindu movement has a difficult situation to handle. It cannot agitate and at the same time it cannot give up its ideological thrust. Any agitation today is seen as a rift within the Hindu movement. So the Hindu movement needs to handle the situation with extreme dexterity and skill.

The Need to Avoid Creating or Contributing to Create the Image of a Reactionary, Intolerant and Violent Hindutva, and of the Hindu Organisations as the Counterparts of Islamic Terrorist Outfits

Today, when communications have linked the whole world and anyone saying something or any event happening in a remote corner is soon broadcast all over the world, all debates have become global, and so has all opinion making. This is particularly so where the debates concern a nation like Bharat, which constitutes 1/6th of humanity, and which is perceived to be an emerging global player in the economic and strategic fields. It is even more so, when the debate concerns Hindutva in relation to Islam or Christianity, which are global faiths with powerful global lobbies supporting them.

The world suffers from utmost ignorance about Hinduism. The ordinary world sees it as another exclusive faith. Most people in the world do not believe that there can be a religion that grants the validity and legitimacy of other religions. The world is used only to religions that proclaim not only their exclusive validity, but also the falsity of all other religions. Such ignorance pervades those in the media and even many of the intellectuals. Their knowledge of religions is limited, and they treat all of them to be about the same. They tend to understand Hinduism and Hindutva only through their understanding of Islam or at best of Christianity.

The Christian West thinks that all religions other than Christianity are like Islam. They believe that Buddhism is like Islamic extremism, and they find evidence for this belief in the 'Aum Shirinyo' phenomenon of Japan. They think that the Hindutva movement in Bharat is the counterpart of Islamic fundamentalist movements in Pakistan or Indonesia or Malaysia. The difference between the Semitic faiths and the Hindu pantheon of faiths is largely unknown to the world, particularly the Western world. Even scholars are unaware of the difference between Hindutva and Islam for instance.

Today it is the media that is informing scholarship and not the other way round. The leaders of the Hindutva movement must understand that Hinduism and Hindutva are being judged on the analogy of Islam and Christianity. For, to the West, religion means only Islam and Christianity. They understand and judge other religions only on their understanding of these two Semitic faiths.

The profane media-generated opinion, which happens to be mostly incorrect, is a problem for Hindutva and the Hindu organisations. The latter are in danger of being bracketed with Islamic extremist and terrorist organisations. Why go out of India? Even within India the pseudo-secular and left elements always juxtapose Hindu organisations with the Islamic extremist organisations; they always tend to compare and club together a Hindu organisation like Bajrang Dal with the Islamic SIMI. This is a ready trap into which the Hindu organisations and their leaders keep falling repeatedly. In the process Hindutva is being regarded as a cousin of Islamic extremism and Hindu organisations as the mirror-image of Islamic terrorist and extremist organisations.

The leaders of the Hindutva movement must understand that Hindutva is the only thought that lacks global support. Equally it is a thought that it has as its adversaries two of the most powerful global thoughts, Islam and Christianity. It requires sound strategy and great skill and dexterity to navigate the Hindutva movement through this maze of global overseeing. The leaders of Hindu organisations need extensive training and deep thinking to undertake this highly demanding enterprise. They must choose words that cannot be faulted; employ language that cannot be questioned. They must project an image of being the victims of Islamic terror and extremism rather than as their equal or equivalent counterparts. The Hindu organisations must understand that it is only the state that can fight terror with fire. The society can only generate fierce public opinion against terror to enable the government to fight terror freely and without being constrained by the human rights industry, and by the liberals and other intellectual anarchists.

This is an area to which the Hindutva movement and the leaders of the movement need to devote adequate time and attention. They must devise proper strategy. They must develop proper leadership and appropriate tools and language for articulation. For, on them depends the opinion that the world shall form of the Hindutva movements and the view it shall take of Hindutva.

Since global opinion is very crucial to fight Islamic terror, which is a globally linked and globally directed phenomenon, it is necessary for the Hindu organisations to start correcting the distorted opinion created in the past by the omissions and commissions of the Hindutva movement and its leadership. This needs to be attended to immediately on an emergency footing. If need be diverse chosen leaders of the movement will have to travel to important countries in the world, meet opinion-makers within and outside of the national establishments and ensure that the obvious difference between the Islamic and Hindu movements are clearly explained to them, that these differences are clearly etched in their understanding. Now is the time when the world will be receptive to such viewpoints; it was not so two years back. The situation offers a challenge as well as an opportunity.

Hindu Dharma Is Inherently a Global Thought: Hence the Challenge of Factoring Global Influences

In the present context, with mass communication invading individuals, families, societies and nations, there is cross-country interface between different cultures, which also influences and impacts national cultures. Today there is an undeniable and unstoppable global influence over national cultures. All over the world there are debates taking place about the consequences of such cross-country influences, about the creeping westernisation of all cultures, about the homogenisation of all cultures into a single global construct. Even within the West there is growing resentment towards the Americanisation of the European culture. Particularly the French feel so. In fact there are debates that points towards emerging global conflicts over culture.

As early as 1994, long before Islamic terrorism struck at the US and the West as intensely as it began doing later, a leading strategic thinker in the US wrote about a possible clash among civilisations driven by Christian, Islamic, Buddhist and Hindu religions. This was written in the context of Islamic fundamentalism emerging as the greatest threat to the West. The author perceived a possible future scenario where the West might be ranged against all the Rest. He advised the West to come to terms with the Rest in order to avoid large-scale violent clashes.

While this particular scholar spoke of clashes among civilisations defined by religion, another thinker felt that the clashes would indeed arise along civilisational lines, but what defined civilisations was not religion, but technology. According to him there would be clashes among pre-modern, modern and post-modern civilisations, which are deeply differentiated from each other by technology. Thus cultural divide, whether the culture is defined by religion or technology, is increasingly perceived as an important element, perhaps the most important element, in forging and breaking global relationships and alliances.

It is necessary—indeed it is a challenge—to factor global perceptions and development in any socio-cultural or socio-economic study of India. For, India driven by Hindu Dharma is susceptible to global influences more than any other country. This is for a host of reasons, some of which have been suggested by Dr Abdul Kalam, the current President of India. Paraphrasing Dr Kalam, the reasons for the peculiar susceptibility of India to global influences are: First, India has been a land that was repeatedly invaded and totally colonised for centuries, and so the colonial hangover distorts its mind. Second, by faith and conviction it has an inclusive and global mind, it believes in vasudhaiva kutumbakam, and so, philosophically, it can never be insular. Third, it has no sense of retaliation and so it cannot reject even those who have in the past harmed it. Fourth, it has greater flexibility in accepting outsiders and so it makes very little distinction between those who are its own and those who are outsiders. [A most striking example of this phenomenon is Sonia Gandhi's acceptability to the Congress party.] Fifth, it has huge Indian diasporas; the number of Indians outside India is as large as 30 million, with every one of them relating to at least three persons in India as relatives and friends. Lastly, the Indian people account for 1/6th of global population and a country of that size and number cannot remain isolated from the rest of the world. For all these reasons, India is inevitably susceptible to global cultural influences.

India cannot be insulated; therefore, unless India influences the world, the world is bound to influence India. The only way India can neutralise global influence on India is to influence the world and bend it towards its way. This is a huge challenge. Today India's actual capacity to influence the world is unproven and its potential capacity is suspect. While the world, which means the West, ceaselessly and comprehensively influences

Hindu India, there is hardly a matching Indian influence on the world or the West. This is because the main vehicle of Western influences on India in the last century was not the West outside India, but the English-educated elite and the leftists within India. They do the work of the West in India. They influence India towards the Western views and ways. They make India believe that it has nothing worthwhile with which to influence the world and it has every reason to be influenced by the world. They continue to dominate the Indian debate even now. This great challenge too needs to be met.

The response to this challenge lies in establishing an acceptable language and style of communication to get across to the important, vulnerable and critical segment of Hindu society comprising the English-educated elite. The Hindu leadership must understand that the English-educated population in Bharat is more than the total population of England. It is this segment which controls and handles the levers of power and influence in the society. Their influence over the Indian establishment, including the government, business, finance, media, politics, academics and public discourse in general, is totally disproportionate to their numbers. Their understanding of the real Bharat, its history and traditions, its values and culture, is minimal, and often wrong. Some among them even detest all ideas and things Indian. Following the Western view of gender relationships and under the influence of feminism—which has nearly destroyed the institution of the family in the West—some of them are even apologetic about being women in the normal sense of the term.

These influences are gaining force, and even legitimacy, in the Indian discourse. This has accentuated the tussle between the modern and the tradition in India at various levels; it has influenced everything from discourses in the public domain to quarrels and disputes within families. So the Hindutva movement, that spans a large canvas extending from the traditional mathas to the modern, westernised and even Christianised versions of Hindu organisations like the new spiritual orders, must specially target this English-educated and the partially and fully westernised. This requires detailed planning and execution.

If the challenge of westernisation and cultural invasion—which is becoming an issue all over the world, and shall probably be the principal reason for the emerging clash between Islam and the West—can be handled, and even defied and defeated by any society, it is only the Hindu society. Hindutva has the philosophical flexibility and diversity of traditions that allows it to make tradition a part of the present, a part of the immediate context of the individual, without making traditional practices remote or distant. This has been achieved by the Hindu society and the exponents of Hindutva by locating Hindu traditions and beliefs deeply within the filial, local and social contexts.

How to handle the English-educated segment of the Hindus needs to be discussed in detail. But suffice it to say at this stage that this issue is a challenge. It needs to be handled deftly. But, let there be no doubt that it can indeed by handled; Hindutva has the civilisational and cultural resources to handle this challenge.

The Main Reason for the Diffused and Confused Hindu Identity among the English-educated: Even as We Became Free, We Allowed Our Minds to Remain Colonised

One of the principal reasons why India is porous to foreign, to be precise, Western, influences is that after Independence India never even attempted to de-colonise itself. Instead of illegitimatising the colonial rule and invasions and reinstalling the unconquered India, the Indian leadership perpetuated a defeated and colonised India. Far from distancing themselves from the colonial rule, personalities and influences, the rulers of independent India came to terms with and perpetuated colonial institutions and personalities. Independent India even adorned the last colonial ruler on the highest governmental position of the land.

The Nehruvian approach rationalised the colonial influences as necessary for national development. When Indian leaders set about rebuilding India after we attained freedom, the Nehruvian approach prevailed over the Gandhian in re-shaping the society, polity and economy of India. The conflict between the Nehruvian and the Gandhian approaches was clearly articulated by the two proponents themselves already in 1928. Pandit Nehru was clear that Western culture should dominate India and it could not be avoided. He even charged that Gandhi had virtually kept the nation obsessed with village and khadi. He asserted that Rama Rajya was no good even when Rama reigned. Nor did he want it back. The extent of hostility Nehru displayed had shocked Gandhiji. He found Nehru's views diametrically opposed to his own views about the future India, where native ways and views of life would dominate and the modern Western ways would be adopted extremely selectively only in unavoidable situations. Finally, it was the Nehruvian views that prevailed, and the Gandhian way was relegated to the margins.

One consequence of this dominance of the Nehruvian approach was that our Independence turned out to be a mere transfer of power, not freedom from the British; Independence came to represent merely a change of the rulers with almost no change in the character of the rule or the attitudes of the rulers to the people of India and to the ideas and things Indian. Anglo-Saxon values and norms continued to be the soul of the Indian state that came into being after Independence. There was little of indigenous ways in the polity of India following Independence. Whatever was native was made the subject matter of ridicule. Secular India virtually targeted the traditional and religious India. To make matters worse, we took to the socialist form of economy and so whatever tradition remained, that became a prey to the leftist and socialist onslaught.

Thus, the divide between the Indian establishment and the Indian people remained despite Independence, and even widened as independent rule took roots. Consequently the socio-cultural life of Bharat is today stretched and divided between the two extremes of Anglo-Saxon lifestyle, institutions and norms on the one hand and the native lifestyle, institutions and norms on the other. This divide is partly explicit and partly hidden. While this struggle has been going on in India since Independence, with the Nehru family directing the debate against the native ways of life, the initiative has been partly wrested by two socio-political mass movements in the late 1980s and early 1990s, namely the Mandal movement and the Ayodhya movement.

Conclusion

What follows from this discussion is that Hindutva is the kinetic form of Hindu Dharma. This form is an evolution dictated by the absence of organised strength in Hindu Dharma. Its evolution was necessitated by the fact that Hindu Dharma had no conflict with other religions and therefore it was non-combative in character. Since Hindu Dharma was non-conflicting and non-combative in nature, it lacked the aggression needed to face the aggressive Semitic faiths that had a global mission to convert the whole world to their faiths. Since Hindu Dharma accepted the validity of all faiths, it could not deny that validity and legitimacy to the Semitic faiths also, despite the fact that they denied not just validity to Hindu dharma, but also theologically denied it the right to exist as a religion.

With these structural weaknesses arising out of its inclusiveness, the adherents of Hindu Dharma evolved over centuries a facet of Hindu Dharma that responded to the onslaught of others; that is how the kinetic form of Hindu Dharma, namely Hindutva, was born. The entire freedom movement was in substance powered by the implicit kinetics of Hindutva.

But free and independent India, which was hijacked by those who believed in the secularism practised in Christendom, turned the secular Indian allergic to Hindu Dharma. This distortion confounded the mind and polity of India for over four decades.

The Ayodhya movement evolved as a corrective to this distortion and brought balance to the polity of India. Now the kinetic form of Hindu Dharma, Hindutva, is the mainline thought despite the fact that the political idiom of India remains secularist; but the secularism that was practised for the first four decades is not the secularism that is being practised now. What was once understood as 'dharmanirapekshata' or neutrality of the state towards religious faith, which approximated to the Christendom's view of secularism, is now recognised as 'sarvapantha samabhava' or equal protection to all religions, which is the very essence of Hindu Dharma. So the kinetic form of Hindu Dharma, that is Hindutva, has forced a reinterpretation of secularism to make it consistent with the Hindu Dharma.

Notes

Chapter 1: The Political Context

1. Sanjay Lodha, Suhas Palshikar and Sanjay Kumar (ed), *Electoral Politics in India: Resurgence of the Bharatiya Janata Party*, Routledge, Oxford, 2017, p. 5.
2. Pradeep Chibber and Rahul Verma, 'The BJP's 2014 Resurgence', in ibid., p.29.
3. Francis Barclay, Chinnaswamy Pichandy and Anusha Venkat, 'Indian Elections, 2014: Political Orientation of English Newspapers', *Asia Pacific Media Educator*, 24 (1), pp. 7—22, 2014.https://www. researchgate.net/profile/Francis_Barclay/publication/285557660_ Indian_Elections_2014_Political_Orientation_of_English_ Newspapers/links/56d5611e08ae9e9dea67dd24/Indian-Elections-2014-Political-Orientation-of-English-Newspapers. pdf?origin=publication_detail
4. Reuters report, 27 March 2014. https://www.indiatoday. in/elections/story/jayalalithaa-jaya-pm-candidate-aiadmk-narendra-modi-bjp-nda-modi-wave-lok-sabha-polls-2014-186433-2014-03-27
5. Paul Scott, *The Jewel in the Crown*, Random House e-books, 1966, p.171.
6. Walter Crocker, *Nehru: A Contemporary's Estimate*, Random House India, NOIDA, 2008, p. 153.
7. Ibid., p. 129.
8. Madhav Godbole, *The God Who Failed: An Assessment of Jawaharlal Nehru's Leadership*, Rupa, Delhi, 2014, pp. 266—67.
9. Nirad C. Chaudhuri, *The Intellectual in India*, Associated Publishing House, Delhi, 1967, p.36.

10. Swapan Dasgupta, 'With Foes Like These: India's Over-Important Left', *The Times of India*, 1 September 1993.

11. Interview with Yogendra Yadav, *Economic Times*, 10 February 2014, https://economictimes.indiatimes.com/opinion/interviews/narendra-modi-and-party-our-next-target-yogendra-yadav/articleshow/30153688.cms

12. 'If Modi is elected, it will bode ill for India's future', *The Guardian*, 10 April 2014, https://www.theguardian.com/commentisfree/2014/apr/10/if-modi-elected-india-future-gujarat

13. 'Can anyone stop Narendra Modi?', *The Economist*, 5 April 2014, https://www.economist.com/leaders/2014/04/05/can-anyone-stop-narendra-modi?fsrc=scn/tw/te/pe/ed/modi

14. 'It's a contest of two competing ideas of India', *The Hindu*, 26 April 2014, https://www.thehindu.com/elections/loksabha2014/its-a-contest-of-two-competing-ideas-of-india/article5941163.ece

15. Announcement: Idea of India Conclave, 4—5 July 2014, https://communalism.blogspot.com/2014/06/announcement-idea-of-india-conclave.html

16. http://www.catchnews.com/india-news/nearly-40-awards-returned-during-award-wapsi-says-govt-actual-list-has-40-more-1486392266.html

17. 'Bharatiya Jana Sangh 1952—1980, Policies and Manifestoes', Vol.1, Bharatiya Janata Party, New Delhi, 2005, p. xi.

18. Quoted in Christophe Jaffrelot, *The Hindu Nationalist Movement and India Politics, 1925 to the 1990s: Strategies of Identity-Building, Implantation and Mobilisation*, Viking, 1996, p.309.

19. Quoted in ibid., p. 314.

20. 'RSS ideologue blasts Vajpayee; PM is petty, says Dattopant Thengdi', Rediff on the Net, 16 February 1999, http://m.rediff.com/news/1999/feb/16bjp.htm

21. Bharatiya Jana Sangh 1952—1980, Policies and Manifestoes', Vol. 1, op. cit., p. x

22. *India Today*, 6 July 1998, https://www.indiatoday.in/magazine/nation/story/19980706-murli-manohar-joshi-now-a-perfect-minister-826508-1998-07-06

23. 'The Election Interview: Murli Manohar Joshi', rediff.com, 23 February 2002, http://m.rediff.com/election/2002/feb/23_upr_swam_int_1.htm

24. Mushirul Hasan, 'The BJP's Intellectual Agenda: Textbooks and Imagined History', in Wendy Doniger and Martha C. Nussbaum

(eds), *Pluralism and Democracy in India: Debating the Hindu Right*, Oxford University Press, New York, 2015, pp. 243—57.

25. *Washington Post*, 19 March 2005, p. A-21. http://www.washingtonpost.com/wp-dyn/articles/A48096-2005Mar18.html?tid=a_inl_manual

26. https://www.business-standard.com/article/economy-policy/it-s-stupid-if-you-are-not-in-gujarat-ratan-tata-107011301075_1.html

27. For the most informed account of Narendra Modi's record of governance in Gujarat, see Uday Mahurkar, *Centrestage: Inside the Narendra Modi Model of Governance*, Random House India, Gurgaon, 2014. Also see Bibek Debroy, *Gujarat: Governance for Growth and Development*, Academic Foundation, New Delhi, 2012.

28. S.L. Rao, 'Sophisticated Swadeshi: The Nationalist Argument against Foreign Investment Is Self-Serving', *The Telegraph*, 9 September 2002, https://www.telegraphindia.com/opinion/sophisticated-swadeshi-the-nationalist-argument-against-foreign-investment-is-self-serving/cid/1016003

29. Mahurkar, op. cit., p.150.

30. Bibek Debroy, 'Reducing Corruption—the Modi Government Agenda', in Bibek Debroy, Anirban Ganguly and Kishore Desai (eds), *Making of New India: Transformation under Modi Government*, Wisdom Tree, Delhi, 2019, pp. 69—76.

31. Swapan Dasgupta, 'Is this an Ideological Government?', in Bibek Debroy, Anirban Ganguly and Kishore Desai (eds), *Making of New India: Transformation under Modi Government*, Wisdom Tree, Delhi, 2019, pp. 3—9.

32. Radhika Ramaseshan, 'The Messages, Mathematics and Silences that formed the BJP's UP win', *Economic and Political Weekly*, Vol. 52, No. 11, 18 March 2017, https://www.epw.in/journal/2017/11/web-exclusives/messages-mathematics-and-silences-formed-bjps-win.html

Chapter 2: Motherland, Religion and Community

1. Sugata Bose, *The Nation as Mother and Other Visions of Nationhood*, Penguin Viking, Gurgaon, 2017, pp. 2—3

2. Sabyasachi Bhattacharya, *Vande Mataram: Biography of a Song*, Penguin Books, New Delhi, 2003, pp. 43—44.

3. Translated by Aurobindo Ghose in 1909, ibid., pp. 100—01.

4. Translated by Sugata Bose, op. cit., p. 16.
5. Ibid., p. 4.
6. Chetan Bhatt, *Hindu Nationalism: Origins, Ideologies and Modern Myths*, Berg, Oxford, 2001, p. 39.
7. There are many unofficial English translations of the RSS prayer in the public domain. I have chosen this one because, despite the archaic language, it best captures the overall meaning. http://ramakrishnagoverdhanam.blogspot.com/2012/02/namaste-sada-vatsale-rss-prayer.html
8. William Gould, *Hindu Nationalism and the Language of Politics in Late-Colonial India*, Cambridge University Press, Delhi, 2005, pp. 119–20.
9. Radhakumud Mookerji, *Nationalism in Hindu Culture*, Theosophical Publishing House, London, 1921, p. 50.
10. Ibid., pp. 29—30.
11. Quoted in Bhattacharya, op. cit., p. 12.
12. Ibid., pp. 11—12.
13. *Harijan*, 1 July 1939, quoted in ibid., pp. 40—41.
14. Ibid, pp. 31–45.
15. William Gould, op. cit., pp. 267—68. Also see Gyanendra Pandey, *The Ascendancy of the Congress in Uttar Pradesh 1926–34*, Oxford University Press, New Delhi, 1978, pp. 114—53.
16. Partha Chatterjee, 'Agrarian Relations and Communalism in Bengal, 1926-35', in Ranajit Guha (ed.), *Subaltern Studies I: Writings on South Asian History and Society*, Oxford University Press, Delhi, 1982, p. 31.
17. Gould, op. cit., pp. 77—81.
18. Amiya P. Sen (ed.), *Bankim's Hinduism: An Anthology of Writings by Bankim Chandra Chattopadhyay*, Permanent Black, Ranikhet, 2011, pp. 333—34.
19. Tapan Raychaudhuri, *Europe Reconsidered: Perceptions of the West in Nineteenth Century Bengal*, Oxford University Press, Delhi, 1988, p. 30.
20. Amiya P. Sen, *Hindu Revivalism in Bengal 1872-1905: Some Essays in Interpretation*, Oxford University Press, Delhi, 1993, p. 309.
21. The enumeration of caste in the decennial census operations was also accompanied by delineating caste hierarchies. The exercise was arbitrary, but it led to the formation of caste associations anxious to improve their ritual status and secure a higher place in the official hierarchy.

22. Gyan Pandey, 'Rallying Round the Cow: Sectarian Strife in the Bhojpuri Region, c. 1888–1917', in Ranajit Guha (ed.), *Subaltern Studies II: Writings on South Asian History and Society*, Oxford University Press, Delhi, 1983, pp. 60—129.

23. John R. McLane, *Indian Nationalism and the Early Congress*, Princeton University Press, Princeton, 1977, p. 288.

24. Christophe Jaffrelot, *The Hindu Nationalist Movement and Indian Politics, 1925 to the 1990s: Strategies of Identity-Building, Implantation and Mobilisation*, Viking, Delhi, 1996, pp. 207—10.

25. https://www.inc.in/en/in-focus/tryst-with-destiny-speech-made-by-pt-jawaharlal-nehru

26. https://www.firstpost.com/politics/1200-years-of-servitude-pm-modi-offers-food-for-thought-1567805.html

27. Letter of W. Hastie to *The Statesman*, 24 September 1882, quoted in Amiya P. Sen (ed.), op. cit., p. 253.

28. Jagdish Bhagwati, *A Stream of Windows: Unsettling Reflections on Trade, Immigration and Democracy*, MIT Press, Cambridge, Massachusetts, 1998, pp. 509—13. Also see R.C. Majumdar, *Historiography in Modern India*, Asia Publishing House, London, 1970, pp. 46—57; and Shankar Sharan, *Marxism and the Writing of Indian History*, India First Foundation, Delhi, 2007.

29. H.L. Erdman, *The Swatantra Party and Indian Conservatism*, Cambridge University Press, Cambridge, 1967, p. 10.

30. 'BJP the most anti-intellectual party: Ramachandra Guha', *Outlook*, 15 March 2016, https://www.outlookindia.com/newswire/story/bjp-the-most-anti-intellectual-party-ramchandra-guha/933618

31. Aatish Taseer, 'Does India's Right-wing Have Any Ideas?', *New York Times*, 29 November 2016, https://www.nytimes.com/2016/11/29/opinion/does-indias-right-wing-have-any-ideas.html

32. Pankaj Mishra, 'Modi's Idea of India', *New York Times*, 24 October 2014, https://www.nytimes.com/2014/10/25/opinion/pankaj-mishra-narendra-modis-idea-of-india.html

33. Pratap Bhanu Mehta, 'The Age of Cretinism: India's Reactionary Modernism', *Open*, Vol. 10, No. 33, 20 August 2018, p. 37.

34. Arthur Bryant, *The Spirit of Conservatism*, The Bonar Law College, Ashridge, 1932, p. viii.

35. Russel Kirk, *The Conservative Mind*, Stellar Classics e-book, 2014, loc. 481.

36. Roger Scruton, *The Meaning of Conservatism*, Palgrave, Basingstoke, 2001, p. 1.
37. Russel Kirk, op. cit., loc. 741.
38. Viscount Hailsham, *The Conservative Case*, Penguin, Harmondsworth, 1959, p. 29.
39. Ibid., p. 35.
40. Wolf Lopenies, *The Seduction of Culture in German History*, Princeton University Press, Princeton, New Jersey, 2006, p. 24.
41. Roger Scruton, op. cit., p. 24.
42. Russel Kirk, op. cit., loc. 455.
43. David Miller, *On Nationality*, Oxford University Press, Oxford, 1995, p. 36.
44. David Willets, *Modern Conservatism*, Penguin Books, Harmondsworth, 1992, p. 6.
45. Roger Scruton, 'Decencies for Skeptics', *City Journal*, Spring 1996, https://www.city-journal.org/html/decencies-skeptics-11811.html
46. Kenneth Minogue, 'Liberalism, Conservatism and Oakeshott in Cowling's account of Public Doctrine', in Robert Crowcroft, S.J.D. Green and Richard Whiting (eds), *The Philosophy, Politics and Religion of British Democracy: Maurice Cowling and Conservatism*, Tauris Academic Studies, London, 2010, p. 33.
47. Viscount Hailsham, op. cit., p. 19.
48. Quoted in Kenneth Minogue, op. cit., pp. 36—37.
49. David Miller, op. cit., p. 88.
50. Roger Scruton, *The Meaning of Conservatism*, p. 105.
51. David Miller, op. cit., p. 85.
52. Quoted in David Miller, op. cit., p. 125.
53. Frank Furedi, *Populism and the European Culture Wars: The Conflict of Values between Hungary and the EU*, Routledge, London, 2018, pp. 67—75.
54. Ibid., pp. 71—72.
55. David Miller, op. cit., p. 163.
56. Ibid., p. 173.
57. C.A. Bayly, *Recovering Liberties: Indian Thought in the Age of Liberalism and Empire*, Cambridge University Press, Delhi, 2012, p. 3.
58. I am grateful to Pratap Bhanu Mehta for these suggestions.
59. C.A. Bayly, *Origins of Nationality in South Asia: Patriotism and Ethical Government in the Making of Modern India*, Oxford University Press, Delhi, 2001, p. 10.
60. Ibid., p. 1.

61. Ibid., pp. 43—44.
62. Ibid., p. 78.
63. C.A. Bayly, *Recovering Liberties*, p. 94.
64. Asok Sen, *Iswar Chandra Vidyasagar and His Elusive Milestones*, Riddhi-India, Calcutta, 1977, pp. 54—55, p. 143.
65. Ibid., pp. 74—55.
66. C.A. Bayly, *Recovering Liberties*, pp. 144—45.
67. Asok Sen, op. cit., p. 55.
68. Ibid., pp. 89–90.
69. Amiya P. Sen, *Bankim Chandra Chattopadhyay: An Intellectual Biography*, Oxford University Press, Delhi, 2011, p. 22.
70. Michael S. Dodson, *Orientalism, Empire and National Culture: India 1770–1880*, Cambridge University Press, Delhi, 2011, p. 111.
71. Amiya P. Sen, *Bankim Chandra Chattopadhyay*, pp. 96—97.
72. Amiya P. Sen, *Hindu Revivalism in Bengal 1872-1905: Some Essays in Interpretation*, Oxford University Press, Delhi, 1993, p. 152.
73. C.A. Bayly, *Origins of Nationality*, op. cit., p. 24.
74. Ibid., p. 55.
75. Ibid., p. 54.
76. Tapan Raychaudhuri, *op. cit.*, pp. 9—10.
77. Ibid., p. 11.
78. C.A. Bayly, *Recovering Liberties*, p. 1.
79. Hulas Singh, *Rise of Reason: Intellectual History of 19th Century Maharashtra*, Routledge India, Delhi, 2016, p. 55.
80. Chetan Bhat, *Hindu Nationalism*, p. 52.
81. Ibid., p. 54.
82. Satadru Sen, 'The Conservative Animal: Bhudeb Mukhopadhyay and Colonial Bengal', *Journal of Asian Studies*, Vol. 76, No. 2, May 2017, pp. 363—81.
83. Tapan Raychaudhuri, op. cit., p. 40.
84. Ibid., p. 43.
85. C.A. Bayly, *Recovering Liberties*, p. 216.
86. Partha Chatterjee, 'Nationalist Thought and the Colonial World' (1985) in *The Partha Chatterjee Omnibus*, Oxford University Press, Delhi, 1999, p. 57.
87. Earl of Ronaldshay, *The Heart of Aryavarta: A Study of the Psychology of Indian Unrest*, Constable & Company, London, 1927, pp. 59—60.
88. Dipesh Chakravarty, *The Calling of History: Sir Jadunath Sarkar and His Empire of Truth*, University of Chicago Press, Chicago, 2015, p. 143.

89. Prachi Deshpande, *Creative Pasts: Historical Memory and Identity in Western India, 1700–1960*, Permanent Black, Ranikhet, 2013, p. 153.

90. Ibid.

91. Dipesh Chakravarty, op. cit. p. 212.

92. Ibid., p. 209.

93. Chetan Bhat, op. cit., p. 35.

94. Ibid., p. 36.

95. R.C. Majumdar, *Swami Vivekananda: A Historical Review*, Advaita Ashram, Kolkata, 2013, pp. 106—07.

96. Amiya P. Sen, *Hindu Revivalism*, p. 345.

97. Tapan Raychaudhuri, op. cit., p. 29.

98. Amiya P. Sen, *Bankim Chandra Chattopadhyay*, p. 15.

99. Tapan Raychaudhuri, op. cit., p. 150.

100. Amiya P. Sen, *Bankim Chandra Chattopadhyay*, p. 26.

101. Ibid., p. 94

102. Tapan Raychaudhuri, op. cit., p. 153.

103. Ibid., pp. 237—43.

104. Amiya P. Sen, *Hindu Revivalism in Bengal*, pp. 312—13.

105. R.C. Majumdar, *Swami Vivekananda*, p. 98.

106. Amiya P. Sen, *Hindu Revivalism in Bengal*, pp. 288—89.

107. Chetan Bhat, op. cit., pp. 17–18.

108. Ibid., p. 51.

109. Ibid., p. 63.

110. Ibid., p. 143.

111. Ibid., p. 145.

112. Ibid., pp. 155—56.

113. H.L. Erdman, op. cit., pp. 91—92.

114. Ibid., pp. 98–99.

Chapter 3: Politics and the Hindu Narrative

1. *The Times of India*, 12 January 2019, https://timesofindia. indiatimes.com/india/dont-let-2019-be-like-the-3rd-panipat-battle-amit-shah-to-party/articleshow/67495924.cms

2. Tapan Raychaudhuri, *Europe Reconsidered: Perceptions of the West in Nineteenth Century Bengal*, Oxford University Press, Delhi, 1988, p. 39.

3. H.L. Erdman, *The Swatantra Party and Indian Conservatism*, Cambridge University Press, Delhi, 1967, p. 10—11.

4.   Sabyasachi Bhattacharya (ed.), *The Mahatma and The Poet: Letters and Debates between Gandhi and Tagore 1915–1941*, National Book Trust, Delhi, 1997, p. 78.

5.   Faisal Devji, *The Impossible Indian: Gandhi and the Temptation of Violence*, Harvard University Press, Cambridge, Massachusetts, 2012, p. 53.

6.   Ibid., p. 52.

7.   R.C. Majumdar (ed.), *The History and Culture of the Indian People: Struggle for Freedom*, Bharatiya Vidya Bhavan, Bombay, 1988, p. 332.

8.   Ramachandra Guha, *Gandhi: The Years that Changed the World 1914–1948*, Allen Lane, Gurgaon, 2018, p. 138.

9.   R.C. Majumdar (ed.), op. cit., p. 336.

10.   Dhananjay Keer, *Veer Savarkar*, Popular Prakashan, Bombay, 1988, p. 228.

11.   V.D. Savarkar, *Hindu Rashtra Darpan*, Maharashtra Prantik Hindusabha, Poona, n.d, pp. 48—49.

12.   Chetan Bhat, *Hindu Nationalism: Origins, Ideologies and Modern Myths*, Berg, Oxford, 2001, p. 85—86.

13.   V.D. Savarkar, op. cit., pp 4—5.

14.   Ibid., p. 44.

15.   Chetan Bhat, op. cit., pp. 96—97.

16.   Ibid., p. 105.

17.   V.D. Savarkar, op. cit., p. 13.

18.   Ibid., p. 10.

19.   Chetan Bhat, op. cit., p. 128–29.

20.   Ibid., p. 129.

21.   Ibid., p. 130.

22.   'RSS officially disowns Golwalkar's book', *The Times of India*, 9 March 2006, https://timesofindia.indiatimes.com/india/RSS-officially-disowns-Golwalkars-book/articleshow/1443606.cms

23.   Rakesh Sinha, *Understanding RSS*, Har-Anand Publications, Delhi, 2019, p. 88.

24.   Swapan Dasgupta, 'Hedgewar's Legacy: Limitations of Elitist Hinduism', *The Statesman*, 1 April 1989.

25.   Jyotirmaya Sharma, *Terrifying Vision: M.S. Golwalkar, the RSS and India*, Viking/Penguin, Delhi, 2007, p. 22.

26.   Ibid., pp. 16–26.

27.   B.D. Graham, *Hindu Nationalism and Indian Politics: The Origin and Development of the Bharatiya Jana Sangh*, Cambridge University Press, Cambridge, 1990, p. 55.

28. Jyotirmaya Sharma, op. cit., pp. 21—22.
29. Rakesh Sinha, op. cit., p. 119.
30. 'Bharatiya Jana Sangh 1952–80: Policies and Manifestoes', Party Document, Vol. 1, Bharatiya Janata Party, New Delhi, 2005, pp. 268—69.
31. Chaturvedi Badrinath, *Dharma, India and the World Order: Twenty-one Essays*, Pahl-Rugenstein, Bonn, 1993, pp. 310—11.
32. Ibid., pp. 311—12.
33. Chetan Bhat, op. cit., p. 165.
34. Devendra Swarup (ed.), *Deendayal Upadhyaya's Integral Humanism: Documents, Interpretations, Comparisons*, Deendayal Research Institute, New Delhi, 1992, pp. 14—15.
35. Ibid., p. 15.
36. Ibid., p. 13.
37. T.N. Madan, *Modern Myths, Locked Minds*, Oxford University Press, Delhi, 1997, p. 245.
38. Gyanendra Pandey, *The Construction of Communalism in Colonial India*, Oxford University Press, Delhi, pp. 241—22.
39. Ibid., p. 245.
40. T.N. Madan, op. cit., pp. 235—37.
41. Ibid., p. 237.
42. Bhikhu Parekh, *Colonialism, Tradition and Reform: An Analysis of Gandhi's Political Discourse*, Sage Publications, Delhi, 1989, pp. 93—96.
43. Mukul Kesavan, *Secular Common Sense*, Penguin India, Delhi, 2001, pp. 28—29.
44. T.N. Madan, op. cit., p. 276.
45. Ashis Nandy, *The Romance of the State and The Fate of Dissent in the Tropics*, Oxford University Press, Delhi, 2003, p. 39.
46. Nirad C. Chaudhuri, *The Continent of Circe*, Chatto & Windus, London, 1967, p. 34.
47. Nirad C. Chaudhuri, *The Intellectual in India*, Associated Publishing House, Delhi, 1967, p. 36.
48. Girilal Jain, *The Hindu Phenomenon*, UBSPD, Delhi, 1994, p. 93.
49. L.K. Advani, *My Country My Life*, Rupa & Co, 2008, p. 347.
50. Ibid., pp. 347—49.
51. Ibid., p. 350.
52. S. Gopal, *Jawaharlal Nehru, Vol. 2, 1947–1956* (e-book) (Vintage, London, 1979), loc. 1686.
53. Mani Shankar Aiyar, *Confessions of a Secular Fundamentalist*, Penguin India, Delhi, 2004, p. 134.

54. S. Gopal, op. cit., loc. 151.

55. L.K. Advani, op. cit., p. 351.

56. Sarvepalli Gopal, *Imperialists, Nationalists, Democrats: The Collected Essays*, Permanent Black, Delhi, 2013, p. 346.

57. Christophe Jaffrelot, *The Hindu Nationalist Movement and Indian Politics 1925 to the 1990s: Strategies of Identity-Building, Implantation and Mobilisation*, Viking/Penguin, Delhi, 1996, p. 202.

58. Rajeev Bhargava, *The Promise of India's Secular Democracy*, Oxford University Press, Delhi, 2010, pp. 26—27.

59. 'Minorities must have first claim on resources: PM', https://economictimes.indiatimes.com/news/politics-and-nation/minorities-must-have-first-claim-on-resources-pm/articleshow/754218.cms

60. 'Sonia's new Riot Act', https://www.indiatoday.in/magazine/nation/story/20110718-congress-sonia-gandhi-nac-bill-godhra-riots-746808-2011-07-09

61. Christophe Jaffrelot, op. cit., p. 314.

62. Pradip Kumar Datta, 'VHP Ram: The Hindutva Movement in Ayodhya', in Gyanendra Pandey (ed.), *Hindus and Others*, Viking, Delhi, 1993, p. 46.

63. *Organiser*, 31 January 1993, p. 7.

64. Ibid., p. 99.

65. Ibid., p. 104.

66. Achin Vanaik, *Communalism Contested*, Vistaar Publications, New Delhi, 1997, p. 318.

67. Martha C. Nussbawm, *The Clash Within*, Harvard University Press, Cambridge, Massachusetts, 2007, p. 1.

68. Pankaj Mishra, 'Modi's Idea of India', *New York Times*, 24 October 2014, https://www.nytimes.com/2014/10/25/opinion/pankaj-mishra-narendra-modis-idea-of-india.html

69. Sarvepalli. Gopal, *Imperialists, Nationalists, Democrats*, p. 217.

70. Christophe Jaffrelot, op. cit., p. 309.

71. Ibid., p. 314.

72. Personal conversations with L.K. Advani.

73. 'Is Sarva Dharma Samabhava Back?' *Economic and Political Weekly*, 28 February 2015, p. 8.

Index